Employment and Labour Market in North-East India

This book examines the structural changes in the labour market in North-East India. Going beyond the conventional study of tea and agricultural sectors, it focuses on the nature, pattern and structure of work and employment in the region as well as documents emerging shifts in the labour force towards farm to non-farm dynamics. The chapters explore historical developments in employment patterns, labour market policies, issues of gender and social-religious dimensions, as well as point to growing forms of casual, informal and contractual labour across sectors.

Through large-scale data and detailed case studies on unfree labour in plantations and those employed in crafts, handloom and the manufacturing industry, the book provides insights into labour and employment in the region. It also delves into the temporal and spatial dimensions of non-farm employment and its relationship with rural income distribution and labour mobility. By bringing interdisciplinary perspectives from scholars working on North-East India, this work fills a major gap in the political economy of the labour market in the region.

The volume will be useful to scholars and researchers of development studies, North-East India studies, labour studies, economics, sociology and political science as well to those involved with governance and policymaking.

Virginius Xaxa is Professor of Eminence and Bharat Ratna Lokapriya Gopinath Bordoloi Chair at Tezpur University, Assam, India.

Debdulal Saha is Assistant Professor at the Centre for Labour Studies and Social Protection, Tata Institute of Social Sciences, Guwahati Off Campus, Assam, India.

Rajdeep Singha is Assistant Professor and Chairperson at the Centre for Labour Studies and Social Protection, Tata Institute of Social Sciences, Guwahati Off Campus, Assam, India.

Employment and Labour Market in North-East India

Interrogating Structural Changes

Edited by Virginius Xaxa,
Debdulal Saha and
Rajdeep Singha

Routledge
Taylor & Francis Group

LONDON AND NEW YORK

First published 2019
by Routledge

2 Park Square, Milton Park, Abingdon, Oxfordshire OX14 4RN
52 Vanderbilt Avenue, New York, NY 10017

Routledge is an imprint of the Taylor & Francis Group, an informa business

First issued in paperback 2019

British Library Cataloguing-in-Publication Data
A catalogue record for this book is available from the British Library

Library of Congress Cataloging-in-Publication Data
A catalog record has been requested for this book

ISBN: 978-1-138-55037-7 (hbk)
ISBN: 978-0-367-47941-1 (pbk)

Typeset in Sabon
by Apex CoVantage, LLC

Dedicated to late Professor Sharit K. Bhowmik

Contents

PART IV
Employment diversification   317

Figures

Tables

Contributors

Piyali Bhowmick is a PhD scholar at the Tata Institute of Social Sciences, Guwahati Off Campus, India. She obtained MA in sociology from Ambedkar University Delhi, New Delhi and MPhil in social sciences from TISS Guwahati campus. Her areas of research include labour process, family and kinship, migration, social networks and sociology of everyday lives.

Bornali Borah is currently a doctoral scholar at the Centre for the Study of Regional Development, Jawaharlal Nehru University, New Delhi, India. The title of her doctoral thesis is 'A Gendered Analysis of Work and Implications for Women's Well-Being: A Comparative Analysis of Assam and Meghalaya'. She has earlier worked as Assistant Professor at the University of Delhi.

Anjan Chakrabarti is Associate Professor, UGC Human Resource Development Centre, University of Burdwan, West Bengal, India. His research interests include development in North-East India, agrarian relations, agriculture in Bengal and policy research. He is author of *Economic Development and Employment in Sikkim* (2009) and editor of *Interrogating Development: Perspectives on the Economy, Environment, Ethnicity and Gender* (2017).

Anamika Das is currently pursuing her PhD in economics at the Centre for the Study of Regional Development, Jawaharlal Nehru University, New Delhi, India. Her areas of interest include rural non-farm employment and informal economy. She has worked as research fellow at the Centre for WTO Studies of Indian Institute of Foreign Trade, New Delhi.

Otojit Kshetrimayum is Associate Fellow and Coordinator of the Centre for North-East India at V.V. Giri National Labour

Institute, Noida, India. Earlier, he taught in the Department of Sociology, Sikkim University, and was a senior fellow in Women's Studies and Development Centre, University of Delhi. He has extensively worked on the issues on labour and employment in North-East India with special reference to social security, migration, child labour, skill and entrepreneurship.

Snehashish Mitra is currently pursuing PhD from the National Institute of Advanced Studies, Bengaluru, India. His research interests include migration, policy, urbanisation and resource management of North-East India, and informal labour network, and he has done extensive fieldwork throughout Western Assam and Eastern Mizoram. He was associated with the Calcutta Research Group, where he worked on India's 'Look and Act East Policy' and frontier urbanisation.

Ajaya Kumar Naik is Assistant Professor at Indian Institute of Dalit Studies, New Delhi, India. His areas of research are informal sector, employment, poverty and caste-based discrimination. He is co-author of *Caste, Discrimination and Exclusion in Modern India* (2015).

Bhagirathi Panda is Professor in the Department of Economics, North-Eastern Hill University, Shillong, India. Earlier, he was a faculty member at IIM Shillong and a visiting fellow in AIT, Bangkok. He has undertaken several research projects on topics such as rural non-farm employment, the National Rural Employment Guarantee Scheme and the Act East Policy.

Jajati Keshari Parida is Assistant Professor at the Department of Economic Studies, Central University of Punjab (CUP), India. He was earlier Deputy Director, National Institute of Labour Economics Research and Development, NITI Aayog, Government of India, and Assistant Professor, College of Vocational Studies, University of Delhi. He has several contributions in peer-reviewed journals including *World Development*, *Social Indicators Research*, *Economic and Political Weekly*, *Indian Journal of Labour Economics* and *Indian Economic Review*.

Rama Ramswamy is Assistant Professor in Mizoram University, Aizawl, India. She works in the area of entrepreneurship development and marketing, and her current areas of research interests are artisan and agriculture clusters. She has undertaken two projects on handloom clusters in North-East India funded by the University Grants Commission, Government of India.

Debdulal Saha is Assistant Professor at the Centre for Labour Studies and Social Protection, Tata Institute of Social Sciences, Guwahati Off Campus, Assam, India. Previously, he was post-doctoral fellow and guest lecturer at the International Center for Development and Decent Work, University of Kassel, Germany. He is the author of *Informal Markets, Livelihood and Politics: Street Vendors in Urban India* (2017), co-author of *Financial Inclusion of the Marginalised: Street Vendors in the Urban Economy* (2013) and co-editor of *Food Crisis and Its Implications for Labor* (2013) and *Work, Institutions and Sustainable Livelihood: Issues and Challenges of Transformation* (2017).

Padmini Sharma is an MPhil scholar at Tata Institute of Social Sciences, Guwahati Off Campus, India. She obtained MA in labour studies and social protection from the TISS, Guwahati Campus. Prior to joining MPhil, she was a research fellow at TISS, Guwahati. Her recent article on 'Services in Virtual World: Understanding Work in Delivery Service of E-Retailing' was published in the *Journal of Management and Labour Studies* (2017).

Rajdeep Singha is Assistant Professor and Chairperson at the Centre of Labour Studies and Social Protection, Tata Institute of Social Sciences, Guwahati Off Campus, Assam, India. Before joining TISS, he taught in the Department of Economics at St. Joseph's College (Autonomous), Bengaluru, and was Research Associate at the Indian Institute of Management Bangalore. He is the co-editor of *Work, Institutions and Sustainable Livelihood: Issues and Challenges of Transformation* (2017).

Nitin Tagade is currently Assistant Professor at the Department of Economics, Savitribai Phule Pune University, Pune, India. He has several articles in his credit published in journals and edited books related to food security, employment and land policy.

Virginius Xaxa is Professor of Eminence and Bharat Ratna Lokapriya Gopinath Bordoloi Chair at Tezpur University, Assam, India. Prior to joining Tezpur University, he was Professor and Deputy Director of the Tata Institute of Social Sciences, Guwahati Campus (2011–6). He taught sociology at the Delhi School of Economics, University of Delhi (1990–2011), and

North-Eastern Hill University, Shillong (1978–90). He is the author of *Economic Dualism and Structure of Class: A Study in Plantation and Peasant Settings in North Bengal* (1997) and *State, Society and Tribes: Issues in Post-Colonial India* (2008). He is also co-author of *Plantation Labour in India* (1996) and co-editor of *Social Exclusion and Adverse Inclusion: Adivasis in India* (2012) and *Work, Institutions and Sustainable Livelihood: Issues and Challenges of Transformation* (2017).

Preface

North-East India has emerged as a distinct politico-administrative category. The government of India's 'Look/Act East Policy' has made the North-East important and strategic in the context of industry and employment as well. Despite being endowed with its rich biodiversity, and having a distinct identity in terms of climatic conditions, language, religion, ethnicity, the North-Eastern Region remains under-developed in terms of infrastructure, industrial development and employment opportunities. The hills present a type of social formation different from that of those living in the plains. With a shrinking agricultural sector, non-farm employment in rural areas is the only option available to the workforce of the region to derive a livelihood. Not surprisingly, self-employment, among different categories of occupation, accounted for more than 60 percent of total employment. The expansion of self-employment is mainly due to lack of gainful wage employment both in rural and urban areas. While informality in farm and non-farm activities is growing, casual and temporary workers within the formal sector are also increasing significantly. Thus, the process of labour market development in the region is leading to a shift of labour force not only from the rural to the urban but also from farm to non-farm activities. Under the changing nature of political discourse, the labour market, employment structure and work arrangement in North-East India are being reshaped. The questions that we pose to interrogate are: how and what kind of structural changes are taking place in the North-East labour market, and how are these changes similar or different from the rest of India?

Statistical data and systematic studies on various aspects of labour markets and employment for the whole of the NER is hard to access. Various active labour market policies have been initiated both by the central and the respective state governments for employment and income generation in the region, but no systematic evaluation of these programmes has been made to understand their impact. This was realised while designing the core course on 'Labour in North-East India' for the master's programme in Labour Studies and Social Protection at the Tata Institute of Social Sciences (TISS), Guwahati. Thus, the objective was to come up with a comprehensive volume emphasising theoretical and empirical studies on the labour market and employment in North-East India, so that it can be used as reference as well as textbook. This volume tries to bring together scholars engaged in studying issues related to work, employment and labour markets in the region. Keeping this in mind, the Centre for Labour Studies and Social Protection of the Tata Institute of Social Sciences, Guwahati, had organised a two-day seminar on 'Labour Markets in Eastern Himalayas and North-East India: Changing Patterns and Emerging Issues' during 29–30 April 2016. The volume has emerged from the contributions at the seminar. In the volume, research questions have been presented through 13 chapters across four sections. Each section addresses a set of research questions. The first section discusses how the labour market in the North-East has evolved historically and the changes that are taking place across different social groups and gender in the current development trajectory. The type of work arrangement, the labour and employment relations pursued and the ways by which they have undergone changes in the major industries of the region have been discussed in the second section. The questions on why and how labour mobility is proceeding and what kind of labour market is being formed are deliberated in the third section. The fourth section explores why diverse employment opportunities are becoming prominent livelihood options in the region.

Without support, encouragement and generosity from various individuals and institutions, it would not have been possible to complete this volume. To begin with, we thank the International Center for Development and Decent Work (ICDD), University of Kassel, Germany, particularly Christoph Scherrer and Birgit Felmeden, for financial support to organise the seminar. We thank the faculty, staff and students of TISS Guwahati campus for their contribution and support to make the seminar possible. We express our sincere gratitude to all the contributing authors of this volume who had earlier presented their papers in the seminar and later agreed to work together with us. Without their support, we could not have brought this volume within the stipulated time. We thank Madhuparna Banerjee, who has efficiently produced the copy-edited version of this volume. We appreciate comments and suggestions that we received from anonymous referees. We would also like to thank the entire Routledge team, especially Shashank Shekhar Sinha (Publishing Director) and Antara Ray Chaudhury (Development Editor) for their support and cooperation at every stage, from ideation to execution of the volume.

Our special thanks to the late Professor Sharit K. Bhowmik, who actively participated in this seminar and encouraged us to convert it into an edited volume. To his memory, we dedicate this book.

Abbreviations

CAGR	Compound annual growth rate
CDS	Current daily status
CFC	Common Facilities Centre
CMCL	Cement Manufacturing Company Limited
CSO	Central Statistical Organisation
CSR	Corporate social responsibility
CSTs	Christian Scheduled Tribes
CTC	Crush, tear and curl
CV	Coefficient of variation
CWFW	Contributing women family workers
DoNER	Development of North-Eastern Region
ETP	Ethical Tea Partnership
GVM	Gramya Vikash Mancha
HHCs	Hindu High Castes
HOBCs	Hindu Other Backward Classes
HSTs	Hindu Scheduled Tribes
IHDS	India Human Development Surveys
ILO	International Labour Organisation
KVIC	Khadi and Village Industries Commission
LFPR	Labour force participation rate
MGNREGA	Mahatma Gandhi National Rural Employment Guarantee Act
MPCE	Monthly Per Capita Expenditure
NCEUS	National Commission for Enterprises in the Unorganised Sector
NCO	National Classification of Occupation
NDC	National Development Council
NEC	North-Eastern Council
NER	North-Eastern Region

NESCH	North-East Support Centre and Helpline
NFHS	National Family Health Survey
NIC	National Classification of Industries
NID	National Institute of Design
NIFT	National Institute of Fashion Technology
NRHM	National Rural Health Mission
NSSO	National Sample Survey Organisation
OBC	Other Backward Class
PCI	Per capita income
PMGSY	Pradhan Mantri Gram Sadak Yojana
PSUs	Public Sector Undertakings
RNF	Rural non-farm
RNFE	Rural non-farm employment
SC	Scheduled Caste
SDGs	Sustainable Development Goals
SDP	State Domestic Product
SHDC	State Handloom Development Corporation
SME	Small and Medium-sized Enterprise
ST	Scheduled Tribe
TRLM	Tripura Rural Livelihood Mission
TTAADC	Tripura Tribal Areas Autonomous District Council
ULFA	United Liberation Front of Assam
UPSS	Usual Principal and Subsidiary Status
WPR	Work participation rates

Introduction

Debdulal Saha, Virginius Xaxa
and Rajdeep Singha

North-East India continues to be peripheral and underdeveloped, though it has always been considered to be the gateway to South-East Asia. The development of this region is crucially linked with India's progress. While the region is historically linked to international markets, various national and international forums have stressed the region's trade potential, which may be realised by developing an industrial corridor. Development of the North-Eastern Region (NER) has been marred with insurgency, militancy, illegal immigration, conflict and strife. Conflicts over natural resources have been brewing in the region for decades. While the region has abundant resources, the challenges facing the management of natural resources are huge. A large part of the challenges can be attributed to natural calamities and disasters. Most parts of the region are susceptible to sudden changes due to floods and earthquakes. Such disasters, apart from ethnic and separatist strife, have been contributing to the swelling number of internally displaced persons, which in turn has led to diminishing livelihood opportunities. Often it becomes impossible to look at the issues individually. Border conflicts, security problems, the presence of refugees, internally displaced persons, ethnic conflicts, mass-scale displacement due to natural disasters and environmental degradation are all issues that get enmeshed with each other and have overwhelming bearing on the local labour markets.

The labour market in the region has remained unique. In the face of various geographical, political and economic instabilities and other common developmental challenges, the region has suffered from a low rate of industrialisation and limited growth of the modern service sector. With decreasing agricultural and allied activities, the share of employment in non-farm activities is continuously increasing, not only in the urban sector but also in the rural setting in recent times. The cultural ethos governing labour market participation is also different, which *inter alia* reflects on the distinctive composition of the labour force across gender and social groups. Post-reform-period labour mobility makes the labour market of North-East India volatile and complicated. In view of this structure of the labour market, the nature of work and employment across the region has been changing, especially over the last two decades. Workers in the region have also been facing the consequences of globalisation and restructuring of the global labour market in forms of subcontraction, casualisation and contractualisation, and the poor are taking recourse to informal sources of earning livelihoods including self-employment. Some of the issues of labour and employment have been partially addressed by agriculture and the plantation economy. All these suggest that a systematic and detailed understanding of the labour market and its various facets in the NER need to be explored. Given the limited available literature, one can say that the region has not paid due attention to labour research and policy. This may be due to the problem of inadequacy or non-availability of statistical data. Under the changing nature of political discourse, the labour market and employment are being reshaped. Thus, against this backdrop, it would be interesting to look into the various issues related to work, employment and the labour market in the current development trajectories of the region. Keeping this in mind, the Centre for Labour Studies and Social Protection (CLSSP) of the Tata Institute of Social Sciences (TISS), Guwahati campus, organised a two-day seminar (29–30 April 2016) on the issues of the labour market in the context of the North-East and eastern Himalayas in India. The seminar was funded by the International Center for Development and Decent Work (ICDD), University of Kassel, Germany. The key issue that emerged in the seminar concerned a single broad issue – structural changes underway in the labour market. This volume on the issues of labour, employment and labour market is an outcome of that concern. In this volume, we limited our lines of enquiry to the type of structural changes undertaken, how they are pursued in the sphere of employment and the labour market and what is the nature and pattern of these changes. In all, 13 papers out of 25 presented were considered for publication, as they focused on issues of structural changes. Contributions are based on both theoretical and empirical studies. The 13 chapters are presented across four sections – structure and patterns of employment in North-East India; labour and employment relations in industries; migration and labour mobility; and employment diversification.

Labour and employment in North-East India

Unlike other regions in India, the cultural ethos governing labour market participation is different in North-East India and reflects the distinctive composition of its labour force across gender and social groups. The first section of this volume places the labour and employment development discourse of North-East India against a historical backdrop, as well as that of ethnicity, religion, geopolitics and gender. Virginius Xaxa, in the first chapter, conceptualises labour in the context of the North-East and discusses the emergence of the labour market. He draws a distinction between 'labour' and 'labour market' in the context of the North-East. Xaxa's chapter is a historical exploration of the nature and type of employment dating from the precolonial to the colonial and then the postcolonial period. Xaxa tries to situate employment against the backdrop of the larger political economy of the region. Prior to the advent of British rule, people living in the hills differed from those in the plains with regard to the type of social formation. The plains of the region, being at a higher stage of social formation as compared to the hills, were marked by more elaborate division of labour. While division of labour in the hills was essentially based on age and sex, in the plains it went beyond that, including caste as well as the position occupied by individuals in the institutions of the state. British rule accelerated the process of diversification of labour and opened different avenues of work and employment, the most important being government service and wage labour in plantations and extraction industries such as oil, which had emerged under the British rule. In precolonial times, there was demand for labour. Labour was of course neither free in the legal sense nor in sense of freedom from ties with the land. Remuneration for labour was either in form of land or maintenance grants provided by the state rather than a form of wage or salary. Characteristics of the labour market underwent changes with time. Although legality pertaining to bonded labour had collapsed, ties of labour to land were generally kept intact. This is evident in the relatively small size of landlessness in the hills. As India embarked on the path of national reconstruction, there was a rise in the infrastructure development process, the expansion of government employment and the introduction of industry such as small and medium, as well as the growth of trade and commerce. Xaxa further shows that there was steady movement of people from outside into the region, which diversified employment along ethnic and religious lines, resulting in many forms of conflict in the region. The second chapter, written by Anjan Chakrabarti, delves into development trajectories and labour markets in the north-eastern states of India. The main objective of this chapter is to explore the pattern of growth and development in the north-eastern states in the last three decades. To do so, comparative estimates of growth rates were measured state-wise on the basis of per capita state domestic product (SDP), with respect to long-term acceleration/deceleration, as well as considering sectoral rates and shares and highlighting the pattern of employment both in formal and informal sectors. Further, the role of the 'Look East' policy in employment generation and economic development is examined in this chapter. While per capita income has been on the rise at a moderate rate, there is a reduction in income inequality and declining inter-states disparities. However, the concerning factor is that growth is only visible where the Indian state played the role of the principal economic agent. Chakrabarti argues that owing to absence of a credible manufacturing sector and with limited volume of trade and commerce, transport and communication, and banking and insurance, the labour market failed to respond positively. Declining income from the agricultural sector and the corresponding rise of population engaged in agriculture indicates marginalisation of the rural workforce. The north-eastern states have remained as net importers of food and non-food items; thereby, the economy of the region has failed to become self-sustaining and self-regenerating. A decentralised development model in the region has failed to keep the promise of bringing equitable development across the north-eastern states. Further, central development grants have been unable to create any positive trickle-down effect on the primary sector. The major hindrances – physical non-proximity, difficult hilly terrain and the lack of developed communication – are identified in order to realise development programmes. As a result, the size of the labour market has remained small, closed and bounded. The chapter critically examines the role of the 'Look East' policy in economic growth and development in north-eastern states. However, the policy is found to be ineffective in transforming the economy of the North-East. Chakrabarti suggests building a durable relationship with Bangladesh by addressing the issues of immigration, water disputes, roads, railways and the water transport system. This would particularly stabilise trade, employment and the labour market scenario in the region.

Chapter 3, written by Ajaya Kumar Naik and Nitin Tagade, discusses the changing patterns and growth of the workforce and unemployment rate in the NER and analyses the quality of workers by their activity status, education level and informalisation of employment across different population segments and socioreligious groups. The results show that the unemployment rate in this region is much higher than the national average. A closer look at the disaggregated level data across socio-religious groups in the NER shows that the unemployment rate is highest among Hindu High Castes (HHCs) (9.2 percent) and lowest among Muslims (4.4 percent). Notably, the high work participation rate (WPR) in the NER is associated with a high male unemployment rate. The male unemployment rate is substantially higher among the Scheduled Tribes (STs), which also registered a high WPR because of high female participation. Empirical data highlights that WPR is the highest among STs (57 percent) and lowest among HHCs (45.3 percent). While the female WPR among STs is the highest (36.6 percent), it is lowest (13.6 percent) among HHCs. A large number of workers in the NER are engaged in agriculture sectors, particularly in skilled agricultural occupations. The quality of employment varies from one group to another depending on the level of education among workers. The quality of employment among HHCs is relatively superior as compared to any other group that has been measured in terms of activity status, enterprise type and education level. It is to be noted that a large share of workers are engaged in government enterprises, and the share of informal workers and those engaged in the unorganised sector is also higher and increasing over the period. Naik and Tagade discuss some important features of the structure of employment besides the quality of employment of the region. Though the share of agriculture in the economy is declining, a large share of workers in the NER is engaged in skilled agriculture, with the highest proportion among STs (54 percent) and lowest among HHCs (22.2 percent). The share of workers belonging to HHCs is substantially high (53 percent) in the service sector. As far as the quality of employment is concerned, the share of workers receiving a regular salary is highest among HHCs (27 percent) and lowest among Muslims (7 percent); while the share in casual labour is highest (22 percent) among Hindu Other Backward Classes

(HOBCs), followed by scheduled caste (SCs). In the government sector, STs are in highest (77 percent) proportion and SCs the lowest (47 percent). This may be due to a better education level among STs in the region.

The participation of women in the workforce can be considered to be an indicator of development of any economy. However, in a country like India – where there is an increasing feminisation of the marginalised sections of labour – such participation cannot always be considered an improvement over non-participation. In Chapter 4, Bornali Borah presents an interesting picture. The women in NER enjoy a higher status than in the rest of India, as the northeastern states exhibit improved sex-ratios and better literacy rates, despite being considered backward. Based on the National Sample Survey reports and five quinquennial rounds of the NSS, after the 1990s (50th, 55th, 61st and 66th rounds as well as 68th rounds), this chapter shows that rural women tend to attain economic independence by processing forest produce, the majority of them being self-employed and engaged in the agricultural sector. Thus, despite the fact that the regional average of women's workforce participation exceeds the national average, in terms of employment prospects, the women workers of this region cannot be considered any better off than the rest of the states in India. This chapter highlights the dual burden of women's work. Women substitute paid labour with household chores and withdraw from the labour force as the income levels increase. Borah has discussed the distress-driven feminisation of labour at lower levels of income by showing the high rates of participation of women in the workforce and in large numbers as self-employed and the de-feminisation trend, wherein women withdraw from the labour force as income improves. The activity status distribution of women in the working age population, over the period 1993–4 to 2011–12, exhibits patterns of counter-cyclical movements from non-participation to participation by being self-employed. However, the feminisation of the rural workforce is not found, except in Manipur, as a result of the occupational shift of only male workers but also female labourers from the farm to the non-farm sector. Borah suggests that there is a need to improve the work scenario of women by creating appropriate employment opportunities for women, especially for the educated section; also, the shift of women workers from the farm to the non-farm sector should be encouraged and facilitated.

Employment and labour relations in industries

Industries in this region can be broadly classified into four types: agro-based (e.g., tea, food processing, etc.), forest-based (e.g., the plywood industry, sawmill industry, paper and paper pulp), resource extracting (e.g., oil, cement etc.) and home-based (e.g., the hand-loom sector, etc.). The issues of labour in industries remain largely unaddressed. Though various labour market policies have been initiated both by the central and state governments for employment and income generation in the region, there have been no systematic evaluation studies to understand the impact of these policies.

Assam is the largest tea-growing area, and it produces 50 percent of the country's tea. West Bengal comes next, with 17 percent of the tea produced. There are structural changes that are taking place in the plantation sector. While the casual labour force is seen in the industry, the growth of small tea growers is also burgeoning in the states. Besides tea plantation, similar trends are also seen in other plantation sectors in the region, such as in rubber, cardamom and cinchona. However, such changes are visible in other industries in the region. In view of this, the second section of the volume addresses the nature of structural changes in employment and labour relations in three important industries – tea plantation (agro-based), cement (resource-based) and handlooms (traditional and home-based). Chapter 5: 'Beyond Standard Outcomes: The State of Employment and Labour in Tea Industry of Assam', written by Debdulal Saha, Rajdeep Singha and Padmini Sharma, shows the failure of labour market institutions and the impact of structural changes that are taking place in the tea industry, with a special focus on Assam. Labourers in tea plantations who had migrated from different parts of the country had to succumb to practices of slavery owing to their deplorable socio-economic conditions during the colonial regime, and those who wanted to escape were forced to work through coercion. These labourers, for generations, have been tied to these enclave economies. The resultant belongingness is in reality a technique that binds the labourers and their families to estates without giving them any authority over such land, and leaving them economically, socially and politically excluded from the system. Along with the globalisation of the production network and increasing concern for ameliorating the conditions of its labourers, the concern for uplifting their economic and social status has taken a front seat. However, there seems to be no substantial improvement of conditions for labourers. In many instances, the labourers are deprived of basic facilities at work. The Plantation Labour Act 1951 came into existence to ensure decent working as well as living conditions for the workers, but these estates have fallen far short of ensuring such basic facilities. However, the limited focus of unions and other interested parties concerning an increase in wages and the quality of rations needs a drift towards enhancement of welfare mechanisms at the estates that in turn can ensure social upgradation of the workers. This chapter further assesses the welfare mechanism of four tea estates of Assam and analyses its potential towards the social upgradation of workers. Along with economic upgradation in the value chain of these industries, the estates need to focus on strengthening both quantitative and qualitative aspects of social upgrading rather than focusing solely on economic aspects. This is so because, unlike other work, plantation economies depend heavily on workers, who serve as an integral part within the economy. As increase in wages takes time; to address the deplorable working and living conditions, estates can work on improving welfare mechanisms. Though these plantations are covered through a number of legal instruments in the form of the Plantation Labour Act of 1951, the Minimum Wages Act of 1948 and so on and so forth, there seems to be lack of compliance of the same, and thereby a failure of labour market institutions.

In innumerable ways, the cement industry not only provides a boost to the economy, but, in an era of globalisation, it also facilitates development and rapid urbanisation. Not only in the tea industry (as evident from the previous chapter) are issues of vulnerability, exploitation and control over mechanisms common but also in other important industries, like cement, in Assam. Chapter 6 is another case study of labour relations in a manufacturing industry in Assam. Piyali Bhowmick's empirical study, using both qualitative and quantitative methods, focuses on the work mechanism and labour process of resource-extracted industry. This chapter shows the various layers of the organisational structure of the cement industry and the labour process. The authority of the industry does not depend only on the management but also on contractors and supervisors, who act as employers in terms of providing jobs to the workers. Along with technical force, technical tools are utilised in designing the flow of work in the control mechanism process. Harry Braverman's control mechanism has been taken into account in the analytical framework of this study. With semi-skilled and unskilled workers, the control mechanism is practiced at every possible level, relaxing its control to some extent for the skilled ones. Though structural changes in terms of informalisation and casualisation take place, the unskilled labour force is completely outsourced, while different divisions such as mechanical, electronics and instrumentation and process are hired based on contract. The most striking disparity between the regular and casual workers lies in the average daily earnings of a casual worker, which stands at Rs 240 (after deduction of provident fund (PF) and food cost, etc.) and that of a skilled permanent employee, who receives above Rs 10,000 per month in 2015. The increasing 'informalisation' of employment has gradually eroded the strength of trade unions. With the management's implementation of strategies to control labour, de-unionising has posed a challenge. Unlike the tea plantation industry, this industry is male-centric, and workers are highly deprived of some basic workplace requirements like holidays and wages. Bhowmick concludes that by not paying heed to the worker's voice and due to multiple controls exercised at different levels by the management, work gets degraded.

Often considered as the vestiges of the traditional sector, the handloom sector not only represents the rich heritage of India but is also the second largest employment provider after agriculture and has shown great resilience in surviving and sustaining over the ages. Traditionally, village enterprises in India were structured in the form of clusters where specialised products were manufactured, with raw material and labour inputs available in the village. The dynamism and economic success of numerous small and medium-sized enterprise (SME) clusters in the 1990s kindled the interest of researchers and policy makers in India, and clustering was revisited as a tool of development of SMEs in India. Chapter 7 presents a case study on Mizoram, where Rama Ramswamy maps the Thenzawl cluster, which has developed as a centre of weaving. The chapter shows that cluster processes, where a paradigm shift has occurred in the work pattern of weaving as an occupation, from a domestic chore to a commercial activity, have played a positive role in endogenous entrepreneurial growth in the cluster, creating a spin-off of enterprises leading to the formation of a spatial concentration of firms in Thenzawl. The cluster and the firms interviewed have shown remarkable growth in terms of growth of enterprises, total production and sales turnover. Ramswamy suggests that appropriate cluster intervention policies need to develop to synthesise endogenous synergies of the region (labour, gendered skill and social embeddedness of weaving) and translate them into developmental goals for the region. The appropriate interventions such as upgradation of technology, product and market development, building strong brands and creating networks and banking facilities will enable the cluster to sustain and grow.

Otojit Kshetrimayum in Chapter 8 examines the transition of the handloom industry in Manipur from a traditional craft to a commercial enterprise. The chapter interrogates the social, cultural and political dynamics of sex segregation in the handloom sector in Manipur. Weaving as an occupation has characteristics which are highly consistent with typical female stereotypes in society at large, and Otojit Kshetrimayum examines the extent weaving undergoes feudalisation. The study has observed that women's entrepreneurship in the handloom industry in Manipur is associated with the changing social and political structures and the expansion of the market on the supply side and the attributes of the culture of weaving on the demand side, bringing about some positive changes in the social, economic and political status of the women.

Migration and labour mobility

Migration into the region has always remained a contentious issue. However, in the last decade, there has been a huge outflow of labour migration from the region to other parts of India for different employment opportunities, especially in the informal economy sector. Another important aspect is labour mobility, which has made the labour market volatile and complicated (both in- and out-migration), especially in the post-reform period. Out-migration into casual labour (mainly in cases of the construction sector, other services sector such as the hotel and restaurant sector, saloon and beauty sector, security guards, business process outsourcing (BPOs) and so on) to other parts of the country, largely into major urban centres of the country – earlier Delhi, and presently Hyderabad, Chennai and Bengaluru – is common. Poverty, lack of employment opportunities, and deteriorating employment conditions in the tea industry, among others, lead to increasing out-migration. Lack of knowledge and information, especially among women, leads them to fall into traps of labour contractors/intermediaries. Demarcation between migration and trafficking seems to get blurred at this level. Another recent trend seen in the context of the NER is reverse migration. Migration in the NER has to be seen in the larger context of local conditions related to the sectoral labour absorption capacities, political insurgencies, infrastructural bottlenecks and the like.

Chapter 9, written by Jajati Keshari Parida, is an empirical exploration of the employment potential of migrant workers in Meghalaya. This chapter particularly focuses on recent trends and changing patterns of migration and migrants' employment patterns in Meghalaya, using the national-level migration data. It shows that the volume of both in-migration and out-migration are increasing in Meghalaya. A changing pattern of out-migration is taking place, with increasing urban-to-urban migration, a declining share of women, an increasing share of the younger age population and relatively high-skilled workers in the migration stream. Unavailability of a higher education benefit on the one hand and inadequate job opportunities on the other stimulate interstate youth migration from Meghalaya. Most of the out-migrants from Meghalaya are engaged in informal employment as casual labourers or are self-employed. To control out-migrants, the author suggests that the government could focus on both skill development and employment generation (in manufacturing and service sectors) within Meghalaya. This would not only check distress out-migration from Meghalaya but also would increase labour productivity and sustain the growth process in Meghalaya. Generating skills at various dimensions through an appropriate policy initiative could have a long-term socio-economic implication for the state as a whole. Though service sectors are generating quite a significant share of employment, which absorbs a large share of migrants, the stagnant manufacturing sectors in Meghalaya need to focus on generating employment, which in turn would drive economic growth on a sustainable basis.

While the previous chapter shows the macro-scenario of out-migration, taking Meghalaya as a case study, Chapter 10, written by Snehashish Mitra, discusses out-migration from various narratives, particularly drawn from fieldwork that has been conducted in the districts of Baksa and Nalbari in Western Assam. This chapter analyses different aspects of labour out-migration from North-East India into other parts of the country and to a wider global network by taking into account the political economy of livelihood, environmental changes and the conflict situation. The chapter delves into the ethno-specific cultures of labour to derive an anthropological understanding of migration from the region. While in-migration into the region, especially that from Bangladesh, has been an issue under both academic and political scrutiny, out-migration is yet to be studied extensively. Mitra stresses participatory policy formulation by taking into account the opinions of the local communities, who have been sustaining themselves by extracting natural resources long before the existence of the Indian state. The chapter suggests that a series of activities would usher in a new regime of labour participation by reconfiguring labour skills and mobility. However, Mitra raises questions about whether the changed scenario positively changes the fate of labourers in Baksa and Nalbari or whether it gives rise to a new series of contentions over ethnicity, indigenous rights and citizenship in India's northeastern frontier.

Emerging non-farm employment

This section intends to discuss trends and patterns of non-farm sector employment in the NER, which has grown over two decades, both in terms of generating additional employment opportunities for the rural workforce and also in its share as a part of rural net domestic product (NDP). With the decline of agricultural contribution to GDP and high dependency on employment, the rural non-farm sector has the potential to elevate the rural economy by providing opportunities for generating income as well as alternative livelihoods. The fourth section of the volume addresses the nature and structure of non-farm employment and employment diversification across the region.

Chapter 11, by Bhagirathi Panda, discusses employment diversification, which happens to be an important dimension of the process of structural transformation of an economy, particularly in the labour market. Based on various rounds of NSSO (50th, 55th, 61st, 66th and 68th), this chapter undertakes a temporal and spatial analysis of rural non-farm employment (RNFE) situation in North-East India. This comprehensive analysis shows some appealing findings. The share of the RNFE in the region during the period 1993–4 to 2011–12 has undergone a gradual but significant increase, from 21.6 percent to 40 percent. Within the region, the RNFE space exhibits significant regional unevenness. In 2011–12, the share of RNFE varied from as high as 69 percent in Tripura to as low as 22 percent in Arunachal Pradesh. The gender gap in the non-farm employment space in the NER shows significant closing compared to the country as a whole. On the sectoral composition front of RNFE, the services sector has experienced a significant fall, and it is the construction sector which has emerged as the leading sector both in terms of percentage share and growth rate. Process analysis of the factors responsible for the growth of the RNFE in NER shows the critical role of both distress (poverty) as well as developmental (agricultural growth, urbanisation and access to credit) factors. However, Panda suggests that both rural farm and non-farm simultaneously need to be protected. While the non-farm sector requires immediate regional, state and central-level action plans, agricultural productivity can be strengthened through crop diversification, commercialisation and market expansion, and surplus labour can be transferred to selected potential high productive non-farm sectors.

Chapter 12, by Anamika Das, is based on both secondary as well as primary data and focuses on the trends, composition and determinants of rural non-farm employment in Assam. The chapter has addressed the question of what drives the expansion of rural non-farm employment in Assam. Assam has witnessed an increasing trend in the share of RNFE over the period from 1993–4 to 2011–12. The state has witnessed an increase in rural employment in all the industrial categories of the non-farm sector except mining and electricity. The construction sector accounts for the highest percentage change in the share of rural employment in the state, followed by trade, hotel and restaurant. The quality of jobs generated in the rural non-farm sector has also deteriorated, as is evident in the dominant share of self-employed workers and increase in the share of casual workers in the non-farm sector, with a continuous fall in the share of salaried workers. A disaggregation of RNFE in terms of sex shows that male RNFE has witnessed highest positive percentage change in the construction sector, followed by the manufacturing sector. As regards female participation in RNFE, the positive percentage change in female participation in RNFE is highest in the construction sector over the period from 1993–4 to 2011–12, but the percentage change in women's participation in the manufacturing sector has been negative over the same period. On the whole, the manufacturing sector in Assam accounts for only 5.49 percent of rural workers in 2011–12. The study of determinants of RNFE at the individual level signifies that both push and pull factors are in operation when it comes to participating in the non-farm sector. As the level of education of rural workers improves, they are more likely to join the non-farm sector for higher returns. A U-shaped relationship between land cultivated and non-farm participation indicates that rural workers with little or no cultivable land are being pushed out of agriculture, and those with higher cultivable land may be lured to the non-farm sector by the possibility of higher potential returns of their investment of surplus generated in the agriculture sector. As regards the distributional aspect of RNFE, the primary survey of two villages indicates unequal distribution of rural non-farm income; i.e., non-farm income is concentrated among the households with a large size of land compared to the households with smaller land size. By Gini Decomposition, Das shows that income from non-farm sector raises the overall income inequality while farm income reduces inequality. The result may suggest that rural non-farm workers with better access to resources and skills are benefited more relative to their poorer counterparts, who face entry barriers in remunerative non-farm jobs.

The last chapter, by Rajdeep Singha, discusses the nature and types of employment diversification in Tripura. This chapter discusses the changes in the labour market and magnitude of occupation segregation in the state. Based on India Human Development Survey (IHDS) data, this chapter clearly shows that structural change is in progress and importance of farm sector is declining. Despite the significant growth of Tripura's GDP (8.63 percent between 2005 and 2014 at constant price), labour market expansion is limited. There is a significant change in terms of composition of the labour market. Households are moving out from the farm sector, and their dependency on agriculture for employment is diminishing. But the problem is that low-end jobs like daily wage jobs, particularly in the construction sectors, are in greater demand. The formal salaried sector has seen no growth. Hence, the movement of labour from one sector to another sector is not resulting in the improvement of the workers' socio-economic condition. There is virtually no upward mobility except specific work for women, for example, for professional, technical and clerical jobs. The rural and urban gap has also decreased due to increasing urbanisation and also by the increasing new types of jobs in rural Tripura. The Occupation Segregation index is significantly higher than the rest of India. The situation of marginalised groups like STs and SCs have improved during 2004–05 and 2011–12, but the degree of segregation is still high. The chapter shows that the main problem in Tripura is not about job creation but the quality of job. The earning gap between males and females is high in Tripura, which is a matter of grave concern.

North-east labour market in transition: challenges ahead

A lack of gainful employment opportunities is a characteristic feature of North-East India. While statistical data on various aspects of labour markets for the NER is hard to come by, labour force participation rates reflect low levels of development. It is evident from the chapters in this volume that there has been a declining trend of employment growth in almost all the states of NER during the last two decades. Agriculture and allied activities have the major share in employment, while non-farm activities constitute about one-third of total employment. Among non-farm activities, the manufacturing sector is relatively insignificant. Among different types of employment, self-employment activities accounts for more than 60 percent of total employment in this region. With the shrinking agricultural sector, non-farm employment in rural areas is the recourse for the workforce to derive livelihood, which is mainly informal in nature. It is evident that the process of labour market development in the region is leading to a shift of labour force, not only from rural to urban but also from farm to non-farm activities. The expansion of self-employment is mainly due to lack of gainful wage employment both in rural and urban areas. While informality in both farm and non-farm activities is growing, casual and temporary workers within formal sector have also been increasing significantly. These types of fragmented labour market lead to various labour market vulnerabilities and challenges in framing the policy discourse. These issues have been addressed in the book by taking into consideration both macro- and micro-level studies. The current development trajectory is tuned towards development of skills through vocational education and training. The NER is a veritable hub of indigenous knowledge in regard to weaving, textile craft, oral tradition, medicinal plants, etc. Vocational education and training in the NER have to be interlinked with local needs, particularly agriculture and indigenous industries, which will also have a larger bearing on youth (educated and uneducated) unemployment of the region. Besides tea plantation, other crops such as jute, rubber, bamboo, cane, ginger, turmeric etc. are grown in various states. They are still to reach their potential as far as market reach is concerned. These sectors along with food-processing industry, microprocessing units and tourism are avenues of revenue generation in the region which needs to be looked at.

Part I

Structure and patterns of employment in North-East India

Chapter 1

Labour and the labour market in North-East India

A historical exploration

Virginius Xaxa

What is known as North-East India is not a single politico-administrative entity. Rather, it is an agglomeration of a number of distinct politico-administrative units in which people and territory have been organised at different phases of history. For a long time, it comprised the seven states and union territories of Assam, Manipur, Tripura, Nagaland, Meghalaya, Arunachal Pradesh and Mizoram and was popularly known as the seven sisters. However, since 2002 the state of Sikkim has been added into the political entity. North-East India, unlike other geographical references such as Southern, Western, Northern or Eastern India, is more than a mere geographical position. Rather, it has developed into a distinct politico-administrative entity in the form of institutions such as the North-East Council and the Department of North-East Region (DoNER) in the Union Ministry. Yet the North-East is far from being a single distinct and homogenous region. An enormous diversity – geographical, economic, social and cultural – marks the region. The differences had and still have far-reaching implications on the nature of work, employment and the labour market in the region. This chapter attempts exploring the region through the lens of labour, employment and the labour market, keeping in mind the historical, ecological and administrative settings within which the people of the region had/have been located.

North-East India constitutes 8 percent of India's geographical area and a little less than 4 percent of the total population of the country (Rao 1983: 1). The entry of Sikkim into the North-Eastern Region in 2002 added 7,096 square kilometres to its territory, which makes up 3 percent of the total geographical area of the region (NEC 2015: xxviii). Geographically, the area of the region comprises hills and plains. Except Assam, other states of the region are predominantly hilly. Even the Manipur plain/valley comprises just over 10 percent of the total geographical area of the state (Ziipao 2016: 3). The difference between hills and valleys overlaps with ethnic and cultural differences. The hills are almost exclusively inhabited by tribes and the plains by non-tribes, though not exclusively. And yet both hills and valleys are enormously diverse with regard to ethnicity, language and culture. The scenario is the same even now.

Much of the area falling under the region called the North-East was part of the province of Assam under colonial rule. Manipur, Tripura and in a sense Arunachal Pradesh (NEFA) were exceptions. The existing politico-administrative form is an outcome of the reorganisation that the region had to go through following demands raised by the people of the hills for independent states, including cessation from India. Following reorganisation, Mizoram, Meghalaya, Nagaland and Arunachal Pradesh have emerged as tribal states. In the rest of the states, the tribal population forms a minority. They represent over 31 percent in Tripura, over 35 percent in Manipur and just over 12 percent in Assam (NEC 2015: 5–7). Prior to British rule, the bulk of this region constituted separate autonomous territories under kings, chieftainships and village headmen. They were annexed into the British territory at different phases of British rule, beginning from the early nineteenth century. Yet the region remained, by and large, isolated from the rest of the country all through British rule owing to lack of communication and the exclusive colonial administration designed for the tribal areas. Things have, however, greatly changed under India's agenda of rapid economic development and social change after independence.

Pre-colonial social formation

In the pre-colonial period, hills and valleys depicted different levels of economic and social formation. For example, valleys such as the Brahmaputra valley and the Imphal valley comprised kingdoms, having a well-established politico-administrative structure. Its foundation was laid on a higher stage of economic and social development, than the past as evident in the mode of livelihood and the accompanied technology and social division of labour and organisation. In the hills, on the contrary, there was no such development. Rather, the economic and social practices there varied widely. Those located in the fringe of hills and plains too had developed into kingdoms though their economic and social practices were not of the same level as prevalent in the Ahom and Metei kingdoms. The Jaintia and the Dimasa kingdoms may be taken as cases in reference.

Plains/valleys

The emergence of kingdoms had given rise to a system of hierarchical stratification. In the Ahom kingdom, for instance, below the king there were ministers named as *burhagohain, borgohain* and *borpatrogohain* who were consulted while appointing officials called *phukans, rajkhowas, baruas* and *hazarikas*. These officials in turn had the privilege of appointing other officials such as *boras* and *saikias*. Under the system, every commoner, that is, all anyone not belonging to the nobility, priestly class or to any other higher castes and who fell between 15 and 50 years old, was a *paik*. The paiks were organised into four-member groups called *gots*. Each got sent one member by rotation for public works like building roads, boats, etc., while the others took care of his land during his absence (Barbora 1998; Barua 1974). The duty of a paik was to render service to the Ahom state, for which in return he was not paid a wage but was granted 2 *puras* (approximately 3 acres of land) of hereditary cultivable land. The royal services that the paiks usually offered were in the fields of defence, civil construction (embankments, roads, bridges, tanks, etc.), military production (boats, arrows, muskets), etc. The Ahom kingdom did not have a standing army till the beginning of the nineteenth century, and its militia consisted of paiks (ibid.). There were two major classes of paiks – a*kanri paik* (archer), who rendered his service as a soldier or as a labourer, and a*chamua paik*, who rendered non-manual service and had a higher social standing. Most of the lower paik officers – *bora, saikia, hazarika, tamuli*, and *pachani* – belonged to the chamua class. With growing divisions of labour, in the course of time, paiks were organised in a *khel*. Khels were a kind of occupational guild which aimed at protecting the interests of paiks. The paiks in a khel were organised according to a gradation of officials. Hence, a bora commanded over 20 paiks, a saikia had 100 paiks, and a hazarika had 1000 paiks. The more important khels were commanded by a phukan (6000), a rajkhowa (or a governor of a territory), or a barua (meaning here a superintending officer) each of whom could command between 3000 and 12,000 paiks (Barbora 1998: 17; Barua 1974: 48–78).

Under the Meitei kingdom, there was a system of labour service similar to the hierarchy of the paiks of the Ahoms. This was known as *lallup*. It is believed to have been introduced during the reign of Pakhangba and was in force until the British took over the kingdom in the 1890s. The whole Meithei population was divided into four divisions which performed lallup for 10 days by rotation. The British abolished the system and introduced the land revenue system, dividing the kingdom into four *pannas* or divisions. Lallup entailed that every male between the ages of 17 and 60 had to place his services at the disposal of the state, without remuneration, for a certain number of days each year. The number of days thus placed was generally 10 in every 40. This 10-day service was so arranged that a man worked for 10 days and enjoyed an interval of 30 all the year round. When an individual is ready to perform lallup, he was entitled to cultivate for his support one *par* (approximately 1 hectare) of land, subject to the payment of tax to the *raja* in kind. If an individual wished to skip his turn of duty, he had to either provide a substitute or pay a certain sum, which would go to pay for a substitute if required, or the other members of the lallup were to agree to do the extra duty on receiving the money. An officer called the *lakpa* presided over every lallup or class of labourer, and he was responsible for the performance of the prescribed duties. Women were excluded from the lallup system (Singh 2017, 1984; Xaxa 1992).

The gradation of offices and system of paik and lallup were products of the demands of the evolving state. From this system, it can be inferred that the demand for labour was essentially for two kinds of work – military and administrative, skilled and unskilled work.

Hills

Administratively, the hilly regions lagged behind the plains. They did not have an elaborate hierarchical system as was in the plains. Nor did they have a uniform political system, though there were uniform modes of making a living. Broadly, there were three types of political systems in the hills. One was represented by tribes, who did not have a system of chieftainship. The village elders jointly took decision over village matters. The second kind was represented by tribes organised under a chief, who invariably took decisions in consultation with the elders of the village. Third were tribes controlled by a chief, and decisions on village matters rested solely on him.

In the hilly regions, people practiced the system of shifting culti-vation. The system is popularly known as *jhum*. It involves clearing of hilly slopes or forest areas, burning of the fallen trees and bushes and dibbling or broadcasting the seed in the ash-covered soil. When the fertility of the soil is lost, cultivators shift to other slopes/areas. They continue with this process until they return to the original slope or area. In this way, the cycle is maintained by rotation. In the past, the jhum cycle had been as long as 30 years. But this is no longer the case today. The increase in population and lack of alter-nate source of rural livelihood have been the key factors that have caused acute pressure on existing jhum land and led to shortening of the jhum cycle.

After the selection of plots, individual households carry out agri-cultural operations. Both male and female members participate in it; some work is generally done by males, whereas other is done by females. There are still other jobs in which both participate. The male members are largely involved during the initial phase of field preparation such as clearing forests, burning the debris, etc. Women and children begin participation in agriculture work from the sow-ing stage. Indeed, women play a dominant role in the later sphere of economic activity. Sowing of the paddy by broadcast is gener-ally done by them. They also engage themselves in sowing by dig-ging, weeding and harvesting, in which male family members also participate.

Some households seek assistance from outside the family to undertake such tasks as clearing of the forest, weeding, harvesting for individual households, and so on. Kin and neighbours combine to form a reciprocal labour group and work in each other's fields by turns. On the day work is being done in one's field, the owner of that field is required to serve a day's meal to all. Households obtaining such labour have to pay back by working for the number of days others have worked. A system of reciprocal labour thus constituted an important aspect of agriculture in the hills. Such an arrangement was more pronounced among the poorer sections of the agricultural population.

There were other modes of agricultural organisation, too. Those having control over land got it cultivated in a somewhat differ-ent way. There were chiefs to whom servants and bondsmen were attached. This gave them access to greater manpower, which in turn ensured a larger share of plots in shifting cultivation. Among the Mizos, the chief held land which was hereditary. The chiefs were entitled to allot sites and land to village households for shifting cultivation. For cultivating the land of the chief, the villages had to pay six tins (a container with carrying capacity of approximately 20 kg) of paddy per household per annum. The chief also enjoyed the privilege of having slaves (Datta 1986). Hence, he could get his land cultivated through them. The *Sema Naga* chief, too, parcelled out his land to the commoners, and in return the latter had to work in the chief's fields and even fight against his adversaries as and when called for without any payment. The chief was also entitled to a certain number of days' work from each villager annually (Zimik 1987: 41). The organisation of production in shifting agriculture did not correspond with any definite mode of utilisation of labour power. Indeed, use of slave labour was fairly widespread among many hill tribes of the region. The Akas and Nishis of Arunachal Pradesh, for example, freely entertained the idea of slavery. Slaves came mostly from the Khoa and Sulung tribes. They had to till the soil and look after the field, cattle and household of their masters. Their work included cutting forests and clearing of jhum fields as well as harvesting crops. In return for their services, they were provided with food, shelter and clothing (Misra 1979: 2). This system has changed since the prohibition of slavery. Nonetheless, the rich men either purchased slaves or procured a number of wives for themselves. Often wives among them were nothing but labourers in the field and servants in the domestic circle (ibid.). Earlier, slaves were recruited or captured during raids; later, they were purchased and procured on advancement of loan. The payment of rent in kind or labour in the chief's field or both taken together was also in vogue among some tribal groups engaged in shifting agriculture. Hence, in the pre-colonial period, in the North-East, a system of labour exchange existed. In return for labour, men were either granted land for their sustenance or provided with food. Labour was tied to the king and to the land.

Entry of colonial rule

The British took over control of the territory known later as the North-East from the Burmese after the Yandaboo Treaty of 1826. The Burmese had been making repeated incursion in the North-East since the second decade of the nineteenth century and had gradually established their rule over the region. The Burmese rule, marked by anarchy, had caused enormous devastation in the region. The

British declared war against the Burmese and expelled them from the region. They signed a treaty whereby the Burmese were not to meddle in the affairs of the region. A little later, the British annexed the Brahmaputra valley including the Sadiya Frontier Tract into their territory. Other areas, mainly the hills, were added to British territory at a later period during different phases (Rao 1983). The expansion of their rule required their administration, which required manpower with different knowledge, skills and competence. There was thus a demand for labour.

Colonial administration

The entry of the British in Assam and later to other parts of the region led to an enormous expansion of the colonial state, which led to a large demand of personnel for manning the state. The manning of the state was contingent on different kinds and levels of knowledge and skills, critical among them being initiation into modern English education. In fact, state employment became one of the most sought-after features of the labour market not only in early part of colonial India but throughout the period. The nature and kind of such employment had been there under the Ahom kingdom, but the scale was unprecedented. Further, unlike the precolonial period, where officials were rewarded for their work in terms of grants of land and control of labour, officials were remunerated for service in the form of salary and wages. Such a development was more pronounced in the regions of the North-East, which was not only under direct rule of the British but which also formed part of the tract that came under general regulation. This meant that there was greater prevalence of such phenomena in the Brahmaputra and Surma valleys. The other parts of the region were either not under direct administration of the British, such as the princely states of Manipur and Tripura, or were outside of the tract of general administration and named as frontier or excluded areas. The British interfered little with regard to administration in these regions. Rather, they allowed the traditional system of governance, with some changes to mark the authority of their rule.

The expansion of administration and the recruitment of people to man the administration led to the emergence of administrative centres. A territory under control was in general divided into districts, which eventually gave rise to district administrative centres. Since there were fewer districts, there were fewer towns in the region.

During the colonial period, a district was further divided into subdivisions and further into blocks/police outposts, which in turn led to the emergence of townships and the growth of trade and commerce. Though initially it was small, as the administration grew and diversified into different departments, like the executive and judiciary, the volume of labour in administrative service expanded manifold. This led to the unprecedented rise in the size of non-manual labour force in the region, or what is generally referred to as the new middle class. This was manifest in the form of civil officials with different positions and ranks, teachers, lawyers, judges and journalists. Besides non-manual labour, government offices also needed manual manpower, though their number was tiny in comparison to white-collar non-manual workers.

The developments in the regions other than Assam were different. The British rule in Manipur and Tripura was indirect. The old system rule in the form of the king, his ministers and his officials prevailed but under the overall supervision of the resident representative of the British. In other parts of the region, especially the hills, the British, like in Assam, had direct rule but interfered little with the traditional system of administration. The regions were initially administered under the Bengal Eastern Frontier and Regulation Act of 1873. The act prescribed the Inner Line System, which prohibited any subject living outside the area from living and moving therein (Misra 2012). Later the area was brought into the scheduled district under the Scheduled District Act of 1874. The term was used for remote and backward tracts of British India. Much later, new nomenclature was introduced in the form of excluded and partially excluded areas. In view of such a policy, there was little scope for the growth and expansion of the British administrative structure in the region. The new employment opportunities in the government sector, whatever little emerged, invariably came to be occupied by the migrant Bengalis and the Assamese, as the inhabitants of the hilly terrain had no tradition of reading and writing. It was only at a later stage that a few managed to enter into this new form of labour that had come to evolve in the region. This was largely due to the role of Christian missionaries who introduced modern education among the hill people. The reasonably educated few found new employment in the British administration or institutions run by the Christian missionary institutions. They generally held lower-level positions in the British administrative institutions.

In the missionary institutions, they were employed as teachers and catechists. The British administration, from time to time, faced the need of human labour for carrying out certain activities at the local level. In such situations, the administration forced people to provide labour without remuneration, somewhat similar to a system of compulsory labour exacted under the Ahom/Meithei kingdom. There was still another form of labour market that emerged in the hills of the North-Eastern Region under the colonial period. This was the interim time of the First World War and Second World War, when quite a number of people from the hills were recruited for varying jobs related to war operations.

Emergence of the tea industry

India under British rule saw the introduction of new economic enterprises which required labour on a large scale. This led to the widespread movement of population to the areas of such enterprises. Movement was restricted within the confines of a given geographical area and at times went beyond. There was even movement of population beyond the country. Of regions that witnessed large-scale movement of population into the region, Assam had been one of the most striking. In fact, while the population in India grew at 52 percent in the period 1901–51, it grew at 138 percent in Assam during the same period (Davis 1951; Rao 1983). With regard to the movements of population in Assam from other regions, two have been referred most widely. One is the movement of the population to tea plantation estates, which the colonial capital introduced in the region from the second half of the nineteenth century. The other is the movement of Bengali Muslim peasants from erstwhile eastern Bengal, now Bangladesh, who came more as a force to reclaim forest and swampy land for cultivation and settled there as cultivators.

Soon after Assam came under the British, there had been much experimentation to explore if tea could be grown. It is to be noted here that tea, by this time, was an item of consumption in Europe and had become an important item of trade in the European market. The major source of supply of this trade was China. However, due to the estranged political relations between England and China, the British had to look for alternate sources of supply, and this was how Assam and later northern parts of Bengal became fertile grounds for growth and expansion of the tea plantation industry in India. From the beginning, the tea industry faced an acute shortage of labour. The population in the region was not only small but also unwilling to work. There were two reasons for this. One is that the area to be brought under tea plantation was covered with dense forest, and it needed to be cleared. Two was the low wage, which did not provide the incentives they needed. In fact, the wage in the plantation industry was lower than what was in vogue in neighbouring non-plantation areas. According to the subdivisional officer of Karimganj, the wages of labourers as per the Emigration Act in 1883 was just 3 rupees per month, whereas the Bengalese in the adjoining areas earned without difficulty 7 rupees per month (Bhowmik 1986: 8). However, even if labour would have been available, it would not have been adequate, given the pace at which the tea industry had begun to grow and expand.

Failing to procure labour locally, import of labour from outside the region became a major concern of planters. An attempt was made to import Chinese labour, but they proved expensive and troublesome. The planters hence focussed on sources within India but located miles away from Assam. They evolved an organised system of recruitment which continued to operate till independence. Workers either returned home or settled as peasant cultivators in the vicinity of tea estates after completion of the contract. After having settled as peasant cultivators, they provided seasonal labour force in the tea estates (Xaxa 1985). Kingsley Davis estimated that there were about 5 lakh (a *lakh* is 100,000) such immigrants living outside tea estates around 1921. Including the 8.4 lakh immigrants and their descendants still working in the tea estate, the total population of this class of immigrants was estimated to be approximately 13 lakh, which accounted for 16.6 percent of Assam's population (Davis 1951). In 1980, this class of immigrants was estimated to be around 45 lakh (ibid).

The organised system of recruitment in operation was broadly of two types – contractor and the *sardari* system. The contractor system was the principal mode in the early phase of recruitment. It ceased to operate from 1915 under the Assam Labour and Emigration Act 1915 (Guha 2016: 85). The system was so bad that the government was forced to appoint a commission of inquiry as early as 1861. Following this, the contractors, steamers and boats carrying labourers were licensed. Labourers were also produced before the judicial and civil authorities and made to sign a contract. In effect, the new system worked the same as did the old one. Recruitment through abduction, enticement, fraud and raising hopes of earning high wages and attaining better living conditions were the normal means to lure and deceive the labourers. Much later, around the 1880s, alongside the contractor system, the sardari system evolved, which eventually replaced the contractor system of recruitment. A *sardar* was a tea garden labourer sent to his native place for recruitment of more labour for the tea garden (Xaxa 1985).

Since there was high demand for labour, ideally there should have been a high wage structure in the tea industry. The tea industry was, however, not prepared for it. The tea plantation enterprise, rather than paying wages based on supply and demand, sought to resort to forced labour (Bhowmik 1986: 9). This, however, could not be slave labour, as it was abolished not only in the west but also in India. As a way out, therefore, they resorted to what is known as indentured labour. Indentured labour ensured planters that the workers were bound to work on the plantation irrespective of the wages that they received. Indenture was a given a legal recognition under the Workman's Breach of Contract Act 1859. The act obliged the worker to work for a minimum period of five years once he has been recruited. Under the act, the worker was liable for prosecution for any breach of contract, but it gave him no protection against the employers and laid down no conditions with regard to arrangement of his transit to his native place on completion of his contract (Bhowmik 2011: 239).

Labourers who moved to work in tea gardens came from different geographical regions. Initially, labour came mainly from Bengal, Bihar and UP. However, later, the labour force came mainly from tribal-inhabited regions of Bengal and the Madras Presidency and the Central province. In other words, they came mainly from the tribal regions of Orissa, Andhra Pradesh, Jharkhand and Chhattisgarh. Immigrant labour for the plantation sector thus came from different cultural, linguistic and ethnic backgrounds. The population, as noted earlier, came in different phases. Many returned after completing their work in tea estates, and many stayed back in Assam. A large chunk also settled down in the vicinity of the tea estates and merged with the agricultural population. Thus, what is today known as tea garden population is of two kinds. One comprises those who still work in tea gardens, and the other consists of those who moved out of tea gardens and settled themselves as agriculturalists in the region. The two kinds of population are broadly referred to as the tea garden and ex-tea garden labour population (Pathak 1984).

Mineral and forest extractives

Besides tea, coal, oil/gas and timber have been the other important enterprises that had their genesis in the colonial period. They, as Saikia (2011) says, played a key role in the British imperial economy. After independence, the oil and gas industry became the subject of intense competition for control between the central and state government. This resulted later in Assam's economic blockade, which aimed at restricting oil flows outwards from Assam. Needless to say, these new enterprises required manpower, technical and non-technical, for their operations and thereby created a market for labour. In Digboi, about 22 percent of the labour force was obtained from Assam. The rest of the workforce was recruited mainly from eastern Bengal, the United Province (Gorakhpur) and from Punjab. As in the tea industry, much of the labour in the oil/gas industry, too, came from outside the region through recruitment by contractors and sardars. However, by 1924, the Labour Bureau was established, applications were registered and work was offered by rotation. Labour came mainly from eastern Bengal, Nepal, Uttar Pradesh and Punjab. Local labour came mainly from the districts of Goalpara and Sibsagar. Labour in the oil/gas industry was organised almost in the same manner as in tea plantation enterprises. The management was under the British, while administration at the supervisory level was under the British and Indians, notably the Assamese (Barua 2014: 164–184). The notable difference between the tea and oil industries is that there was space for occupational mobility in the oil/gas industry, and the wages were high. Linguistic and regional differences were maintained at the place of residence. This was evident in separate barracks, called lines, corresponding to the respective communities, as has also been the case in tea estates.

The timber industry was the other among the extractive industries that opened up new opportunities for employment. Timber was in demand for laying out railway lines as well as for building offices and residences for its officers. It was also in demand for the tea industry, where it was used not only for building planters' bungalows but was important for packing tea for transportation to centres of auction.

Transport and communication

During the colonial period, there was also growth and expansion of means of communication. Railways, however inadequate they may have been, added value to the region. So did the inland waterways. These means of communication did give boost to the local economy, especially tea, timber and oil, and opened up new avenues for employment.

Modern education

Colonial rule and administration opened up new avenues of employment: state functionaries and officials with varying hierarchical positions were needed to run the state machinery. Colonial rule in the region also saw the emergence of new kinds of economic activities in the form of industrial enterprises such as tea, timber and oil, as well as trade and commerce. These new activities required different kinds of knowledge, skills and training. This resulted in the growth and expansion of modern education which went beyond school education, extending to the foundation of institutions of higher education such as colleges. Of course, their numbers were small, but they offered new prospects of employment as teachers, lawyers, journalists, managers etc.

Post-independence scenario

The state had been the key engine of growth and development in post-independent India. Hence, there had been massive expansion of state administration and state-led development. Indeed, the role of private players in development, be it infrastructure such as roads, railways, power, irrigation, agriculture, industry, education and health, has been negligible.

At the time India gained independence, what marked North-East India was economic and social backwardness. Among the states and union territories in the North-Eastern Region, Assam is the most industrialised and urbanised and has a much better infrastructure than other states in the region. Nonetheless, it lags far behind other states of India. This being the feature of the region, the rapid development of infrastructure and socio-economic development has become the Indian states' main plank in North-East India. It is to serve this end that the government of India created a new institutional structure in the form of the North-Eastern Council (NEC) in 1972. This initiative has pushed the infrastructure development of the region at the forefront.

Infrastructure development

Quite a number of infrastructure development projects with regard to roads, railways and other means of communication had been initiated in the region since the late 1970s and 1980s. These paved the way for the emergence of a number of industries, cement and paper being the key among them. The building of infrastructure and the emergence of industries later needed manpower. Yet there was marked absence of participation of labour from the region in these projects. Of course, there were some exceptions, which came mainly from certain communities living in the plains of Assam. The marked absence of labour from the region was either due to the role of contractors who preferred to recruit labour from certain regions or due to the disinclination of local people from the hills to move out of their place or work as labourers. This may partly have to do with the agrarian social structure of the region. The absence of a skewed distribution of land generally marked the region. The region had therefore a low percentage of agricultural labourers. Landlessness was generally unheard of. The migrant labour brought in by contractors filled in this demand for labour and was involved primarily in earth cutting, earth removing and construction projects. The migrant labourers, whether employed in government or private projects, came mainly from Bihar, Jharkhand and Odisha. Wages paid to them were generally lower than the ones obtained by the local labourers. The contractor collected and distributed the wages among the labourers. He paid less than what was due to them. Medical facilities, as well as living place and sanitation amenities, were negligible (Xaxa 1989).

Durable employment opportunities emerged following the completion of projects, which were generally filled from among the educated in the region. They were not necessarily the local people. The presence of people from the hills even in regular employment has generally been weak. They have not been able to take advantage of these opportunities due to a combination of factors – one of them is disinclination to move out of their district or state. Further, they did not have information of employment opportunities in the new enterprises. Also, they lacked skills or qualifications.

Expansion of state administration

Post-independence, India saw further expansion of institutions introduced under colonial rule. This included state administration, modern education, industrialisation, transport and communication, etc. There has been a phenomenal change in the labour market situation in the hill states of the region following the formation of new states/union territories. The formation of separate states such as Nagaland, Meghalaya, Mizoram and Arunachal Pradesh, as well as autonomous institutions such as an autonomous district council, territorial council, etc., opened up opportunities for employment at various levels in the state bureaucratic structure. With further decentralisation of the administrative structure, there has been greater reinforcement of state employment in recent years. The creation of new districts and administrative set-ups in the region from time to time has contributed to the growth of new townships. At the same time, the push of the market, arising since the economic reform of 1991, has led to a spurt of new economic activities and a shift of the population from rural to urban. Since 2001, however, there has been a phenomenal increase in the tribal urban population, especially in the hills. In fact, the share of tribal population to total urban population ranges from over 70 percent in Meghalaya and Nagaland to over 90 percent in Mizoram as per 2011 census. The same is merely 6 percent in Manipur and 5 percent in Assam. This has led to a visible change in the nature of occupation. The number of people engaged in the secondary and especially tertiary sector has seen steadily rising. However, only a small section of those engaged in the secondary and tertiary sector work in the organised sector, the majority being part of the unorganised one. The expansion of modern education at the primary, secondary and higher education level post-independence gave a huge boost to the employment market. The diversification and specialisation of education at higher educational levels gave further impetus to employment opportunities in the educational sector.

Mineral extraction

The mineral and extractive industries have seen vast expansion in post-independent India. North-East India has not been an exception. Oil and natural gas extraction expanded. Refineries were installed at a number of places within and even outside states. The expansion did open new opportunities for employment of different positions and skills. Coal, limestone, timber and similar other extractive industries have spread in the region. These have been dependent more on migrant than on local labour. Further, there has been rampant use of child labour in extractive industries such as coal. For example, in rat-hole mining, the means and method of extraction demanded use of child labour. The state of Meghalaya may be taken as a point of reference. The use of child labour in coal extraction was so high that the National Commission for the Protection of Child Rights had to intervene in the matter and even conduct raids. Transport and communication in the North-East, like in other parts of India, have gone through a huge expansion in the post-independence, though it is still far from adequate. These have opened various avenues of employment, both short- and long-term.

Migration from North-East India

The foundation of the tea industry in Assam was facilitated by immigration of labour from northern, eastern, central and even southern India, which went on uninterrupted from the 1840s to the 1950s. Today, the tea industry is in the process of movement in the reverse direction. The growth of the tea industry had slackened after the great depression of 1929. This had a bearing on the scale of the recruitment of labour. There was a steady decline, and after a decade after independence, it had almost come to a halt. Indeed, there was already enough labour for carrying out the work in the plantation estates. By the 1970s, there was not much demand for fresh labour, and labour that was already existing had become surplus. This led to a decline in permanent employment and the rise of temporary and casual employment. The transition from formal labour to informal labour had begun, resulting in insecurity of employment and a decline in wages, living conditions and welfare measures. By the 1980s, tea estates had begun to experience acute problems of unemployment, and people had begun to move out for work elsewhere, either on a long-term or short-term basis. The problem was no different among those who had settled as agriculturists in the villages, as land held by them was far from adequate to support the expanding family. As early as the 1980s, a large number of girls had begun to move to Shillong, Meghalaya, to work as domestic workers, and by the 1990s they had added Delhi as one of their destinations. The volume of such migration has increased manifold since its genesis in the 1980s. Further, the out-migration is now no longer confined to girls. Young boys too have been increasingly moving out for work in towns and cities.

State employment in North-East India, like elsewhere in India, has been shrinking. This has much to do with the new economic policy of 1991 that has emphasised downsizing state employment as a part of the structural adjustment programme. However, no alternate systems of employment opportunities are emerging in the region. At the same time, there has been steady rise in levels of education, including higher education, among the people from the region, especially the hills. This has resulted in an unprecedented rise in educated unemployment, leading to movement of the people from the region to other parts of India in search of employment. Such was not the case until the early 1990s. In fact, after completing higher education in universities likes Jawaharlal Nehru University, Delhi, and similar other institutions in other parts the country, students invariably used to go back to their states. This is no longer the case today. Furthermore, even students at a lower level of training and skill have been moving out of the hills to seek employment, especially to South India. To the well-educated, the policy of reservation has acted as an aid. The North-Easterners are today visible in central government offices and central institutions of higher learning such as Delhi University, Jawaharlal Nehru University, Ambedkar University, the University of Hyderabad and similar other establishments. Others who have not been as fortunate have been working at call centres, hotels, restaurants, hospitals, beauty parlour, airlines and commercial establishments as sales men and women, as well as guards and housekeepers. Besides students who stay back, there are others who are located or studying in the region itself but are unable to find employment in the region. They too have been moving out of the region to other parts of India in search of employment. Some of these have even joined the domestic work sector.

The Statistical Profile of Scheduled Tribes in India prepared by the Ministry of Tribal Affairs, Government of India, points to the presence of domestic workers among Scheduled Tribes (STs) in North-East India. The data shows the presence of domestic workers in almost all states except Manipur, though the distribution among the states is far from even. Of the north-eastern states, the percentage of women domestic workers (aged between 15 and 59 years) to total female non-agricultural workers in 2011–12 was

8.5 in Arunachal Pradesh, 12.8 in Assam, 0.6 in Meghalaya, 0.2 in Mizoram, 0.3 in Nagaland, 1.2 in Sikkim and 5.1 in Tripura (ILO 2016). According to the NSSO 68th Round, the compound annual growth rate (CAGR) of domestic work in Arunachal Pradesh is 35.8 percent, Assam 3.1 percent, Meghalaya 5.7 percent, Sikkim 15.3 percent and Tripura 16.5 percent, while corresponding figures for Manipur, Mizoram and Nagaland are not available (ILO 2016). The phenomena are more notable in Assam and Arunachal Pradesh as compared to other states. The NSSO data point to a steady increase in the number of domestic workers, with Arunachal Pradesh leading. The hill tribal women getting into the domestic work sector is a new phenomenon among the tribal communities of the region. In Manipur, for example, the Manipur Domestic Workers Movement (MDWM), based in Imphal, has registered 1,500 domestic workers since its inception in 2007. It is the only organisation in Manipur which works for the rights of domestic workers and closely monitors their welfare, rights and dignity (The Peoples Chronicle 2017).

Conclusion

The existence of a labour market in the form of demand for labour precedes the advent of colonial rule in North-East India. This was evident in the demand for forced labour in precolonial times in the kingdoms that existed in the valleys and the practice of a sort of slave labour in the hills of the North-East. Those providing labour, of course, were neither free in the legal sense nor in terms of their ties with land. Remuneration for labour was provided by the state in the form of land/maintenance grants rather than a wage or salary. Under colonial rule, payment for labour did take the form of wages rather than land grants, but labour was far from free, both in the legal and non-legal sense. This was most evident in the tea industry until the second decade of the twentieth century. Since then there has been much change in the character of the labour market. Legal ties in the sense of bonded labour have been broken, but ties of labour to land have generally been intact. This is evident in the relatively small percentage of landlessness, especially in the hills. However, the land held is far from adequate, resulting in the increasing movement for salaried jobs/wage labour within the region and outside.

References

Barbora, Sanjay. 1998. 'Plantation Systems and Labour Movements in North East India', M.Phil. Dissertation, Department of Sociology, Delhi University.

Barua, Arun Kumar. 1974. 'The Administrative System of the Ahom', Ph.D. Thesis, University of Gauhati.

Barua, Ditee Moni. 2014. 'Polity and Petroleum. Making of an Oil Industry in Assam 1825–1980', Ph.D. Thesis, IIT, Guwahati, April 2014, pp. 163–176.

Bhowmik, Sharit. 1986. 'Recruitment Policy of Tea Plantations', North-East Quarterly.

Bhowmik, Sharit. 2011. 'Ethnicity and Isolation: Marginalization of Tea Plantation Workers', Race/Ethnicity, 4(2): 238–253.

Datta, Partha Sarthi. 1986. 'Some Reflections on the Changing Agrarian Relations in Mizoram 1885–1986', Paper presented at Seminar on Changing Agrarian Relations in North-East since Independence, Shillong.

Davis, Kingsley. 1951. The Population in India and Pakistan, Princeton: Princeton University Press.

The Peoples Chronicle. 2017. 'Decent Work for Domestic Workers: A Dream or Reality?'. Retrieved from http://thepeopleschronicle.in/?p=9924. Accessed on 22 March 2017.

Guha, Amalendu. 2016. Planter Raj to Swaraj: Freedom Struggle and Electoral Politics in Assam, Guwahati: Anwesha Edition.

ILO. 2016. Indigenous Women and Domestic Work: A Study of Assam and Manipur (An ILO Research Initiative), New Delhi: ILO.

Misra, Bani Prasanna. 1979. 'Kirata Karyokiness: Modes of Production in Tribal Societies in North-East India', in A. Das and V. Nilkant (eds), Agrarian Relations in India, p. 75, Delhi: Manohar.

Misra, Bani Prasanna. 2012. Keynote Address. National Seminar on Governance, Socio-Economic Disparity and Unrest in the Scheduled Areas of India. Tata Institute of Social Sciences, Guwahati Campus.

North Eastern Council (NEC). 2015. Basis Statistics of North Eastern Region, Shillong: North Eastern Council Secretariat.

Pathak, Lalit P. 1984. 'The Enticed Immigrants: Imported Tribal Tea Labour in Assam, 1841–1960', The North-Eastern Hill University Journal of Social Sciences and Humanities, II(4): 15–28.

Rao, Venkata. 1983. A Century of Government and Politics in North East India, Vil.1 (Assam) (1874–1980), New Delhi: S. Chand Company Ltd.

Saikia, Arupjyoti. 2011. 'Imperialism, Geology and Petroleum: History of Oil in Colonial Assam', Economic and Political Weekly, 46(12): 48–55.

Singh, Pandit N. Khelchandra. 2017. The Historical, Archaeological, Religious & Cultural Significance of 'Kangla': The Ancient Citadel of Manipur. E-PaoBooks. Accessed 22 March.

Singh, M. Jitendra. 1984. 'Slavery in Pre-British Manipur: a Historical Survey', *Proceedings of North-East India History Association*, Fifth Session, pp. 79–84.

Xaxa, Virginius. 1985. 'Tribal Migration to Plantation Estates in North-East India', *Demography India*, 14(1).

Xaxa, Virginius. 1989. 'Some Observation on Migrant Labour in Assam', *Migrant Labour in India – Report of a Workshop*. Centre for Social Sciences, Surat.

Xaxa, Virginius. 1992. 'The Changing Agrarian Social Structure in Manipur', *Science and People*, September, pp. 1–9.

Ziipao, Raile Rocky. 2016. 'Infrastructure Development in Manipur: A Study in Social Dynamics', Ph.D. Dissertation, Tata Institute of Social Sciences (TISS), Mumbai.

Zimik, Chonchon. 1987. 'Naga Land Tenure Systems', M.Phil. Dissertation, Department of Sociology, Delhi University.

Chapter 2

Changing trajectories of economic growth and employment in North-East India

An empirical assessment

Anjan Chakrabarti

Connected with mainland India via a narrow corridor called the 'chicken's neck', squeezed between Nepal and Bangladesh, most of North-East India is bounded by India's international neighbours – China in the north, Bangladesh in the south-west, Bhutan in the north-west and Myanmar in the east. This has made the region strategically important for the country (NEDFi Databank).

According to the Census of India, 2011, the population of the North-Eastern Region (NER) of India, comprising eight states, namely, Arunachal Pradesh, Assam, Manipur, Meghalaya, Mizoram, Nagaland, Sikkim[1] and Tripura, stands at 45.48 million and these states accounts for 7.9 percent of the total land space of the country (ibid.). Among these eight states, the population of four of them, – Mizoram, Nagaland, Meghalaya and Arunachal Pradesh – has a tribal majority.[2] However, many scholars find it difficult to consider the region as a compact unit and have termed it as the North-East (Misra 2000; Hussain 2004).

Since colonial rule had followed a policy of 'separatism'/ 'distinct and isolated administrative areas' to govern the north-eastern areas, it became a daunting task for the Nehru-led government to frame a suitable policy of governance for these secluded north-eastern states, which were completely separated from mainstream British India. The North-East Region[3] (Mackenzie 1884 (2001); Guha 1977: 73) is inhabited by people having diverse ethnic, cultural, linguistic, religious and geographical affiliations. As observed by Verghese, the North-East Region is 'another India, the most diverse part of a most diverse country, very different, relatively little known and certainly not too well understood, once a coy but now turbulent and in transition within the Indian transition' (2004: 208). In addition, the near absence of cultural and political assimilation of the tribes of the North-East with mainland India and the limited impact of the Indian freedom struggle on the tribal-dominated north-eastern states had made the situation more complicated (Chandra et al. 2008: 142). The separation of Burma from the Indian subcontinent in 1937 and the partition of India in 1947 had accentuated the geo-political and economic isolation of this region. In fact, due to partition of India, the region lost its water, road and railway connectivity through erstwhile East Pakistan. The Chinese occupancy of Tibet and closure of the border with Burma further crippled the economic and political well-being of the region (Verghese 2001).

All the north-eastern states are treated as 'special category states'[4] which receive substantial financial and non-financial support from the central government. The special category status is decided by the National Development Council (NDC) on the recommendation of the Planning Commission. The Planning Commission has laid down certain criteria[5] for receiving a status of special category state, and the attributes are: (a) hilly and difficult terrain; (b) low population density and/or sizeable share of tribal population; (c) strategic location along borders with neighbouring countries; (d) economic and infrastructural backwardness; and (e)non-viable nature of state finances (Bhattacharjee 2014: 48). It has further been assumed by the Planning Commission that special category states have a low resource base and are not in a position to mobilise resources for their developmental needs, irrespective of their percapita income.

Currently, all the north-eastern states receive 90 percent of their plan assistance as grants and the remaining 10 percent as loans;[6] for the non-special category, it is 30:70. From the total central assistance available for state plans, funds are earmarked for externally aided projects and special area programmes and constitutional provisions within the state boundaries (Chakrabarti and Chakraborty 2010: 547–59).

In addition, for the economic and social development of north-eastern states, the North-Eastern Council was formed by the Act of Parliament of India in 1971. The North-Eastern Development Finance Corporation Ltd. was established in 1995, and in 2001, the union government set up the Department of Development of North-Eastern Region which, in 2004, was upgraded and named as DoNER or the Ministry of Development of North-Eastern Region (www.mdoner.gov.in/). This ministry looks after the development requirements of the region and advocates its special needs to other ministries of the government of India, as well as to policymakers.

At least 10 autonomous councils under the Sixth Schedule[7] of the Indian Constitution were created to strengthen the process of independent regional self-governance and socio-economic development. The inner-line permit[8] (introduced by the British government during the colonial era) has been continuing so that tribal-dominated regions remain insulated from the in-migration of people from outside the region. The policies of industrial licensing, concessional finance and investment subsidy for growth centres, as well as freight equalisation of some major industrial inputs, have also been used to promote economic development. The National Committee on the Development of Backward Areas commissioned by the Planning Commission in 1981 has identified three types of fundamental backwardness in the region: areas of tribal concentration, hill areas and chronically flood-affected areas. The whole of the North-East has been categorised as an industrially backward zone.

In spite of this, consecutively, for the last two decades, the northeastern states, barring Manipur, Nagaland and part of Assam, have achieved a double-digit growth rate, higher than the national average (Chakrabarti 2010: 103–7); however, the demands for separate statehood movements or various kinds of territorial/regional autonomy movements based on identity, ethnicity and cultural specificity also coexist. On many occasions, such movements tend to be violent. Economic reforms initiated in 1991 and thereafter have been making inroads, albeit, slowly. Keeping the nature of special category states in mind, it is true that at the policy level and in terms of major economic activities, the presence of the government remains strong, though the market has also made its presence felt in many north-eastern states.

With the presence of the liberal Indian state, it was expected that the north-eastern region of India would be placed on a high economic growth path, which would be self-sustaining and self-regenerating in nature; industrial activities would expand; central funding would make the investment-multiplier operative; income and employment opportunities would expand; and quality of life would improve. For strengthening and expanding LPG-led (liberalisation, privatisation and globalisation) economic linkages of the region with the rest of India and the world, the North-East has been identified as the focal point of the 'Look East' policy[9] pursued by the government of India. In the process, it was hoped that the north-eastern region would get economically, politically, culturally and socially integrated with mainland India and beyond. This chapter attempts to highlight the major development-related issues of the North-East. The principal part of the study explores the pattern of growth and development that the north-eastern states have experienced in the last three decades. Comparative estimates of growth rates measured state-wise have been analysed on the basis of per-capita state domestic product (SDP), with respect to long-term acceleration/deceleration, as well as considering sectoral rates and shares. Subsequently, an attempt has been made to observe the pattern of employment as experienced by the region over decades and to find out whether employment opportunities in the organised sector have increased or dwindled with the increase or decrease in growth rates. Further, the chapter attempts to gauge the degree of informality in the bounded labour market of the North-Eastern Region, along with the question of whether the 'Look East' Policy can change the present employment and economic scenario of the north-eastern states. The fiscal condition of the North-Eastern Region has also been scrutinised. The chapter further strives to understand the validity of the causal relationship between economic condition and the rise in social conflicts based on identity, ethnicity and cultural specificity in the north-eastern states of India. In the last section, an attempt has been made to provide certain alternative measures to overhaul the development of the North-East.

Growth scenario of the north-eastern states

The literatures on development economics have identified 'real economic growth' and 'growth of percapita income' as two major indicators for ascertaining the pattern of economic development in different regions. However, in the last few decades, the narrowness of this concept has frequently been challenged. Several scholars have pointed out that higher percapita income is correlated with indicators of the quality of life (Dasgupta 1993; Mauro 1995; Barro 1996). It can safely be said that development is not all about income, but it has a significant role to play in achieving different socio-political and ecological and environmental attributes, too.

Comparative analysis of growth rates
of north-eastern states of India

The compound annual growth rate (CAGR) of gross state domestic product (GSDP) and percapita GSDP have been calculated for the north-eastern states. Table 2.1 provides the growth trend of GSDP

Table 2.1 Compound growth rates (in percent) of GSDP at constant prices over three decades in north-eastern states of India

States	Decadal CAGR of GSDP			Decadal CAGR of percapita SDP		
	1980–90	1990–2000	2000–9	1980–90	1990–2000	2000–9
Arunachal Pradesh	8	17	13	5	15	12
Assam	4	18	15	2	16	13
Manipur	5	20	13	2	17	11
Meghalaya	5	23	13	2	8	12
Mizoram	18	17	10	14	14	7
Nagaland	8	24	16	4	18	10
Sikkim	11	16	14	8	13	13
Tripura	6	21	17	2	19	16
India	5.6	6.03	7	3.4	4	6
Mean	8.1	19.5	13.9	4.9	15.0	11.8
S.D	4.6	3.0	2.2	4.3	3.5	2.6
CV	56.4	15.3	15.6	87.3	23.1	22.2

Source: Calculated from GSDP figures at constant prices, Central Statistical Organisation, Ministry of Statistics and Programme Implementation, Government of India; www.mospi.gov.in (accessed on 10 October, 2009)

from 1980–1 to 2008–9. It is to be mentioned that 1980–1 was the base year for GSDP at constant prices for the period between 1980–1 and 1993–4, while for 1993–4 to 1998–9, 1993–4 was used as the base year; for 1999–2004, the base year was 1999. Finally, for 2004–5 and the period onwards, 2004–5 was taken as the base year. The overall GSDP growth rates have shown a fair degree of variation. While some states have witnessed rapid and phenomenal growth, the rest lagged behind the all-India growth rate. The notable feature is that between 1980 and 1990, Arunachal Pradesh, Mizoram, Nagaland, Sikkim and Tripura achieved a growth rate higher than the national average, while Assam, Manipur and Meghalaya have achieved a growth rate less than the national average. However, from 1990 to date, all the north-eastern states have achieved double-digit growth, and the growth rate continues to be higher than the national average. What are the underlying forces behind this double-digit growth for all the north-eastern states? First, most of the north-eastern states had low initial values of GSDP and, as a result, a minor increase in absolute figures generates a high value of GSDP growth in percentage term. Second, central investments in power, electricity, oil and gas, and other infrastructure development are also contributing indirectly to pull up the growth rate. Third, unlike the rest of India, government employment has not shrunk in the north-eastern states (both in absolute and percentage terms), which possibly contributes to the growth of the tertiary sector as well as the overall growth rates. These arguments may further be substantiated when sectoral contributions towards the GSDP are considered. It is to be noted that the standard deviation is continuously decreasing (from 4.6 in the 1980s to 3 in the 1990s and falling again to 2.3 in the 2000s) over the decades, and this implies that the growth rates of north-eastern states as well as of India have been converging along the trend, which is indeed a healthy signal.

Per-capita SDP growth rates of north-eastern states of India

The growth rate of percapita SDP (notwithstanding the narrowness of these indicators) and descriptive statistics like coefficient of variation (or CV) of the CAGR of percapita SDP have been used to validate the positive or negative impact of economic growth on the well-being of the population. The growth of percapita SDP for eight states along with India is presented in Table 2.1. In the 1980s, Assam, Manipur, Meghalaya and Tripura record the lowest percapita SDP growth, at 2 percent; as against these, the all-India growth rate was 3.4 percent. The performance of Nagaland is particularly noteworthy, as the growth rate has jumped from a moderate 4 percent in the 1980s to 18 percent in the 1990s. In the last decade, the disparity range (as indicated by the fall in coefficient of variations of growth of percapita SDP) has been reduced for individual states, but the overall growth of percapita income has started declining from the 1990s. However, the national average has increased to 6 percent in 2000–9, compared to 4 percent in the 1990s.

While in most states the standard of living (in terms of rise in percapita income) improved faster in the 1990s in comparison to the 1980s, the trend reversed in the last decade, except in Meghalaya. The main reason for this could be the comparatively higher growth of population in these states.[10] In Assam, the percapita growth rate declined in spite of a high SDP growth in 2000–9. The standard of living in the north-eastern states increased faster in the 1990s due to a combination of slackening of population growth and acceleration of SDP growth.

Disparities in percapita income

The general trend that emerges for India is such that convergent growth rates have not translated into equalising income across states (Ahluwalia 2011; Bakshi et al. 2015). The north-eastern states revealed reversal of the all-India trend. In fact, the coefficient of variation of percapita net state domestic product (NSDP) had been declining consistently during 1990–2000 and 2000–9. Table 2.2, and Figure 2.1 plot the growth rate of the north-eastern states for the period 2000–9 against the log of per-capita income (log PCI) in 2000. The downward slope suggests that there is a convergence in income levels. This implies that states with higher initial percapita NSDP, on average, grew slower, suggesting that the inequality across states was actually decreasing.

Acceleration and deceleration of growth of GSDP

To measure acceleration or deceleration in the growth rates over time log-quadratic form is convenient. It can be written in the following form:

$$\ln Y_t = a + bt + ct^2 + u_t$$
$\ln Y_t$ = Log value of GSDP
t = time
a = Constant term
t = time (in years)
$u_t = \ln v_t$
= error term such that $\ln v_t \sim IND\ (0, \sigma^2)$

Table 2.2 Model summary and parameter estimates

Dependent variable: growth of NSDP (at constant price) between 2000–9
Independent variable is PCI in 2000 (log scale)

Equation	Model summary					Parameter estimates	
	R square	F	df1	df2	Sig.	Constant	b1
Linear	.037	.231	1	6	.648	28.283	−3.913

Source: Results calculated by author through regression process

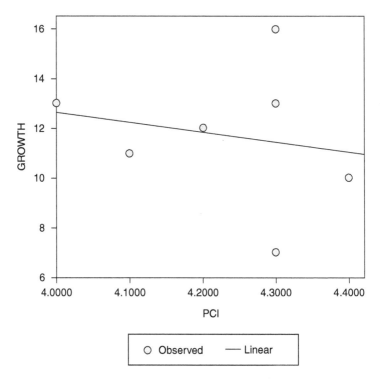

Figure 2.1 Relation between growth of NSDP (2000–9) at constant price and per capita income of 2000 (log scale)

Source: Drawn by author by using data used for Table 2.2

If the estimated value of c (depicted as instability coefficient) assumes significant (t-ratio is used as test statistics) positive value, then growth rate would accelerate, and in case of significant negative value, then growth would decelerate (Reddy 1978: 806–12). The incorporation time squared on the right-hand side of this equation, may give rise to a problem of multi-collinearity. This is avoided by the normalisation of time in mean deviation form, that is, by setting $t = 0$ at the midpoint of the series, and this allows the time (t) and its square (t^2) to become orthogonal (Boyce 1987: 262, 278). As it is further pointed out by Boyce, the normalisation of time affects only the estimate of b (coefficient of t), the estimate of c (coefficient of t^2) remains unaffected with respect to the normalisation (ibid.: 278).

The resulting log-quadratic estimates, along with change in exponential growth rates of SDP for the north-eastern states, during the '80s, '90s and post-'90s are presented in Table 2.3.

From Table 2.3, it is clear that Mizoram experienced the highest growth rate in the first decade, Meghalaya remained at the top during the 1990s and Tripura achieved the highest growth in the last decade (2000–9). For all the north-eastern states, growth rates have increased in the decade of the '90s (1990–2000) in comparison to the decade of '80s (1980–90). A marginal decline has been observed for a few states.

A comparison of the position of states in terms of exponential rate of growth of aggregate SDP (in constant prices) in the three periods – 1980–90, 1990–2000 and 2000–9 – shows a perceptible change in the rankings of the states over time (Table 2.3). States like Mizoram and Sikkim, which were ranked highest for the period 1980–90, reached the bottom of the ranking table in the period 2000–9. Tripura and Assam witnessed a remarkable transformation since the 1980s. They ranked sixth and eighth position in 1980–90 and made huge improvements and ranked first and third in the last decade (2000–9).

Long-term acceleration or deceleration measured by the estimated value of coefficient c shows that Arunachal Pradesh, Assam, Nagaland and Tripura are experiencing long-term acceleration in growth rates, and these growth rates are statistically significant at the 1 percent level. In contrast, Meghalaya and Sikkim are experiencing long-term deceleration. However, for Manipur and Mizoram, acceleration of growth is not significant. It should be noted that in the decade of the 1980s and '90s, Mizoram experienced the highest percapita SDP growth among all the north-eastern states, but growth rates of SDP consistently declined.

Sectoral growth rates and sectoral shares

We may now look at the growth of sub-sectors in order to gain more understanding of the sectoral performance (Table 2.4). Sectoral growth rates are compared with SDP growth rates to identify the sectors which are propelling growth in each decade. Simultaneously, lagging and leading sub-sectors within the sectors (primary, secondary and tertiary) have been identified to measure the intrasectoral variations in growth. It may be seen that except for a few states, the share of the primary sector has continuously been falling

Table 2.3 Ranking based on exponential growth rates[11] and acceleration/deceleration of growth rates in north-eastern states of India

States	Exp. growth 1980–90	Rank	Exp. growth 1990–2000	Rank	Exp. growth 2000–9	Rank	Instability coefficient (c)	Long-term growth pattern (1980–1 to 2008–9)
Arunachal Pradesh	8.2	3	15.7	7	15.9	4	0.002 (4.82)*	Acceleration
Assam	3.5	8	16.3	6	16.3	3	0.004 (6.22)*	Acceleration
Manipur	5.1	5	21.2	3	15.8	5	0.008 (1.0)	Acceleration
Nagaland	7.6	4	27.8	1	16.5	2	0.003 (4.18)*	Acceleration
Meghalaya	4.9	7	25.6	2	15.2	7	−0.002 (−8.95)*	Deceleration
Mizoram	20.8	1	16.8	5	9.8	8	0.003 (0.7)	Acceleration
Tripura	5.4	6	14.2	8	18.3	1	0.005 (7.6)*	Acceleration
Sikkim	11.8	2	17.9	4	15.6	6	−0.005 (−0.89)	Deceleration

Source: Calculated from GSDP figures at constant prices, Central Statistical Organisation, Ministry of Statistics and Programme Implementation, Government of India; www.mospi.gov.in

Note: T stats of instability coefficients are shown in parenthesis

*Significant at 1% level

Table 2.4 Sectoral distribution and sectoral compound annual growth
rates of SDP (1980–2009) in the north-eastern states of India

States	Origin of industry	Sectoral shares(average)			Sectoral growth (CAGR)		
	Sectors	1980– 90	1990– 2000	2000–9	1980– 90	1990– 2000	2000–9
Arunachal	Primary	48.7	38.1	31.4	8	15	16
Pradesh	Secondary	19.5	24.2	27.4	8	16	22
	Tertiary	31.7	37.6	41.2	8	22	18
Assam	Primary	50.1	47.2	38.1	3	19	9
	Secondary	15.3	16.2	16.3	4	20	14
	Tertiary	34.6	36.6	45.6	5	18	18
Mizoram	Primary	31.9	30.8	19.7	20	13	2
	Secondary	17.7	16.1	15.8	18	14	19
	Tertiary	50.5	53.1	64.5	18	20	11
Manipur	Primary	43.4	35.7	27.7	2	17	13
	Secondary	12.9	15.3	25.7	7	26	20
	Tertiary	43.7	49	46.6	8	19	14
Nagaland	Primary	30.5	28.2	31	7	25	14
	Secondary	14.6	14	14.6	13	12	16
	Tertiary	54.9	57.8	54.3	7	29	16
Meghalaya	Primary	33.8	30.3	29.8	3	23	14
	Secondary	19.3	17	18.1	3	21	22
	Tertiary	47	52.7	52.2	7	22	19
Tripura	Primary	47.9	40.7	25.3	3	17	19
	Secondary	10.6	10.1	21.7	4	25	15
	Tertiary	41.5	49.2	53	9	22	17
Sikkim	Primary	47.4	37.8	20.1	10	8	11
	Secondary	19.6	17.5	30.1	12	17	16
	Tertiary	33	44.7	49.9	12	21	15
India	Primary	24	20	16	4	3	
	Secondary	16	16	16	6	7	
	Tertiary	60	64	68	6.5	7.6	

Source: GSDP data at current price (as on 26.11.99), Central Statistical Organisation, Ministry of Statistics and Programme Implementation, Government of
India; www.mospi.gov.in

Note: For India, sectoral data at current price are available up to 2004–5; therefore, for the last decade, 2000–9, sectoral shares are taken up to 2004–5

from about one-half in the early 1980s to one-third or one-fourth
in 2000–9. In states, such as Sikkim and Tripura, the share of the
primary sector in SDP has come down to around 25 or 20 percent
by the end of 2009. The drastic reduction in the contribution of

the primary sector in these states (by 20–25 percentage points) during this period is partly compensated by the rise in income from the secondary sector and partly by the increase in income from the tertiary sector. In Assam, where the primary sector has also performed quite well, the share of the primary sector in SDP declined more moderately, by about 12 percent. In the states of Manipur, Arunachal Pradesh, Mizoram, Tripura and Sikkim, the share of the primary sector has declined significantly in the last two decades. In Arunachal Pradesh, for instance, the share of the primary sector, which was nearly 50 percent in SDP in the early 1980s, has come down to about 30 percent late in the decade from 2000–9. Even though the primary sector for all the north-eastern states has registered a double-digit growth since the 1990s, a falling share is worrisome because more than 60 percent of the people are deriving their livelihood from agriculture. This implies a drop in per-capita income from agriculture and allied activities. This is also hinting towards marginalisation and casualisation of agricultural workers. This phenomenon is true not only for the north-eastern states but is also happening in the rest of the Indian states. In Nagaland, an agriculturally backward state, the share of the primary sector has increased marginally due to a slower growth of the non-agricultural sector. In Table 2.4, it can be seen that share of the secondary sector in Nagaland has remained static consecutively in three decades, starting from the 1980s. A similar scenario also has been observed for Meghalaya.

Coming to the secondary sector, for the period as a whole (1980–2009), the sector recorded a slightly higher rate of growth in the 1990s in comparison to the '80s, but the average growth rate of the secondary sector remained lower than the tertiary sector. In the most recent decade (2000–9), the growth rate of the secondary sector not only declined sharply but even became much lower than the growth rate of the tertiary sector. Thus, in the '90s, the economy of the North-East Region was driven by the high growth of the secondary sector, while in the twenty-first century it was pulled down by the low growth rate of the secondary sector. This was the general pattern of development, especially in East Asia. In China, for instance, the secondary sector now contributes almost 50 percent of GDP. However, in India, at the aggregate level and at the regional level and sub-regional level, the tertiary sector became the largest contributor even before the secondary sector predominated the economy (Bhattacharya and Mitra 1990: 2445–50). If the share of manufacturing declines and services increase at the initial phase of development, then economic growth may be of the growth-retarding type (Barua and Bandyopadhyay 2005: 239–74).

Manipur and Sikkim are the only exceptions, where the secondary sector has increased and occupied more than a 10 percent share in SDP in 1990–2009. In no other state has the share of the secondary sector increased above 10 percent. In Nagaland and Meghalaya, the share of the secondary sector has remained stable around 20 percent for the last two decades. In the two other industrial states, Assam and Arunachal Pradesh, the share has risen marginally in the last two decades. Surprisingly, the secondary sector in Tripura, one of the backward states in the North-East, grew quite rapidly between 1990 and 2009. As a result, the share of the secondary sector in Tripura increased from 13 percent in 1990–1 to about 24 percent in 2000–9.

From 1980 to 2009, the tertiary sector recorded a high rate of growth. In the '80s, the pattern of the growth rate of the tertiary sector for the individual states remained similar to the secondary sector. However, the secondary sector failed to maintain the growth rate achieved in the '90s and became sluggish from 2000–9. Unlike the primary and secondary sectors, the tertiary sector maintained high growth rates in all three decades (except for states like Manipur and Nagaland) and propelled the overall growth of the economy. However, this needs to be confirmed by examining the sub-sectoral growth rates as well.

It has also been noted that the tertiary sector, rather than industry, has become the engine of growth in the last two decades. The tertiary sector has recorded the fastest growth in most of the north-eastern states, both before and after the reforms. In most states, the share of the tertiary sector now exceeds 50 percent of SDP. During the last two decades, the tertiary sector has grown notably for Manipur, Meghalaya, Nagaland, Tripura and Sikkim. With the exception of Nagaland and Meghalaya, the tertiary sector now accounts for almost 60 percent of SDP, and thus the tertiary rather than the secondary sector has become the engine of growth in most states.

From the foregoing analysis, the general impression that emerges is that the north-eastern states are experiencing a high rate of growth, and since the 1990s, the growth was initially propelled by the secondary sector and later by the tertiary sector; therefore, the economy of this region is on a steady growth path. However, this over-optimism disappears when we look at the major contributors of the primary,[12] secondary[13] and tertiary sectors.[14]From Table 2.5 it is evident that for all the north-eastern states, agriculture is adding most of the income to the primary sector. In the secondary sector, where most of the states have shown high growth rate and high contribution to the GSDP at current prices, except Assam, much of the contribution to the GSDP is coming from construction alone (more than 60 percent), where the role of government is felt strongly (see Table 2.6). In contrast, the share of manufacturing, the backbone of the secondary sector and indicator for industrialisation, is hovering around 2–5 percent. Only Assam is the exception, because Assam has a certain degree of a manufacturing base, and oil and natural gas do generate income for the secondary sector. Unlike other north-eastern states, a fair degree of expansion of the private sector has also taken place in Assam. This shows the absence of the private sector in secondary activities and a limited expansion of industrial activities among the north-eastern states. Similarly, for the tertiary sector, 50–60 percent of the contribution is coming from public administration, which broadly covers the services of the state government administration and other services (see Table 2.7). Again, other services include activities pertaining to educational, medical

Table 2.5 Major sectoral shares of state domestic product under the primary sector at current price (base year 1980–1, 1993–4, 1999–2000) in north-eastern states of India

States	Agricultural shares			Primary shares		
	1980–90	*1990– 2000*	*2000–9*	*1980–90*	*1990– 2000*	*2000–9*
Arunachal Pradesh	34.2	28.6	24.8	48.7	38.1	31.4
Assam	34.0	35.7	27.4	50.1	47.2	38.1
Manipur	39.8	30.6	23.6	43.4	35.7	27.7
Meghalaya	28.9	22.5	20.3	33.8	33.3	29.8
Mizoram	23.0	25.9	17.5	31.9	30.8	19.7
Nagaland	23.6	23.9	27.0	30.5	28.2	31.0
Sikkim	46.5	36.3	18.6	47.4	37.8	20.1
Tripura	38.6	33.5	21.2	47.9	40.7	25.3

Source: Calculated from the GSDP data at current prices; Central Statistical Organisation, Ministry of Statistics and Programme Implementation, Government of India; www.mospi.gov.in

Table 2.6 Major sectoral shares of state domestic product under the secondary sector at current prices in north-eastern states of India

States	Manufacturing			Construction			Secondary		
	1980–90	1990–2000	2000–9	1980–90	1990–2000	2000–9	1980–90	1990–2000	2000–9
Arunachal Pradesh	5.7	4	2.7	13.9	18.1	19.3	19.5	24.2	27.2
Assam	9.5	9	9.8	4.6	5.5	4.9	15.3	16.2	16.3
Manipur	5.7	3.9	6.7	6.3	8.3	16	12.9	15.3	25.7
Meghalaya	3.6	3.6	3.8	12.1	10.2	11.3	19.3	17	18.1
Mizoram	3.8	4.5	1.5	14.8	11.2	11.6	17.7	16.1	15.8
Nagaland	2.4	3.1	1.6	12.6	9.6	11.8	14.6	14	14.6
Sikkim	6	3.7	3.1	13.3	12.4	21.9	19.6	17.5	30.1
Tripura	5.6	3.2	3	4.9	6.8	16.2	10.6	10.1	21.7

Source: Calculated from the GSDP data at current prices; Central Statistical Organisation, Ministry of Statistics and Programme Implementation, Government of India; www.mospi.gov.in

Table 2.7 Major sectoral shares of state domestic product under the tertiary sector at current price (base year 1980–1, 1993–4, 1999–2000) in north-eastern states of India

States	Public administration			Other services			Tertiary sector		
	1980–90	1990–2000	2000–9	1980–90	1990–2000	2000–9	1980–90	1990–2000	2000–9
Arunachal Pradesh	9.8	11.4	15.7	8.5	13.8	11.6	31.7	37.6	41.3
Assam	3.9	6.2	6.5	8	8.9	11.6	34.7	36.6	45.5
Manipur	12.1	13.9	14.7	11.1	11.8	12.2	43.8	49	46.6
Meghalaya	14.4	14.3	13.5	8.4	9.3	8.2	47	52.7	52.2
Mizoram	16	16.4	19.8	11.3	11.8	12	15.5	53.1	64.4
Nagaland	19.1	17.7	13.2	12.6	12.7	8.1	54.9	57.8	54.3
Sikkim	9.8	13.5	16.7	7.6	12.2	14.9	33	44.7	49.9
Tripura	10.7	14.5	14	10.1	17	14.9	41.5	49.2	53

Source: Calculated from the GSDP data at current prices; Central Statistical Organisation, Ministry of Statistics and Programme Implementation, Government of India; www.mospi.gov.in

and veterinary, research and scientific, sanitary, recreational, the rest of the services, international and extra-territorial bodies, and lottery services. Therefore, the bulk of the income generated under 'other services' is primarily coming from government and quasi-government employment. This implies that the high share of tertiary sector to GSDP is also arising out of government employment and, more precisely, where the government is playing a direct role. In addition, barring Assam, tax-revenue collection as a percentage of GSDP is abysmally low for the north-eastern states. Therefore, the development process is solely depending on central assistance as grant-in-aid. Any reduction (though it is most unlikely) in central assistance will make the economy of this region more vulnerable. The private sector has not grown yet, as a result of which all these states have failed to create an economy outside agriculture, and most of them are still dependent on primitive agricultural methods.

Employment and unemployment scenario and labour market

Growth scenario and sectoral contributions to GSDP clearly indicate that one-third of the income is generated from the agricultural sector, and in the secondary and tertiary sectors, most of the income is generated where government is playing a direct role. The absence of the private sector, including manufacturing, is prominent, and this clearly indicates the smallness and closed nature of the market as well as the economy. Work participation rates (WPR) for most states of the North-East remain higher than the Indian average. In comparison to census year 2001, WPR has increased for Assam, Manipur, Nagaland, Sikkim and Tripura in census year 2011; however, Arunachal Pradesh, Meghalaya and Mizoram have experienced a decline in WPR during the same period. It has also been observed that the percentage of marginal workers has also increased for Assam, Manipur, Nagaland and Tripura (see Figure 2.2). Arunachal Pradesh, Manipur, Meghalaya and Mizoram have experienced a rise in the percentage of non-workers in 2011 compared to 2001. It is a moot point to analyse whether marginalisation is increasing across the states or declining. Compound annual growth rates for total workers, main workers and marginal workers would give a clearer picture. Barring Manipur, Mizoram and Meghalaya, growth rates of main workers remain less than the growth rates of total workers, and growth rates of marginal

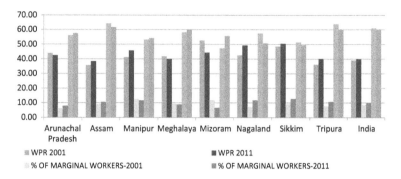

Figure 2.2 Change in work participation rate and the percentage of marginal workers and non-workers between 2001 and 2011 in north-eastern states

Source: Calculated from Census 2001 and Census 2011, Government of India

workers remain much higher than that of total workers as well as main workers (see Figure 2.3). Therefore, there is a high possibility that marginalisation may impact the agrarian sector and allow the informal sector to expand.

In an ideal situation, high economic growth allows employment to increase in the manufacturing sector and services like transport and communication, trade and commerce, banking and real estate, etc. However, this is most uncommon for the north-eastern states, as evident from the sectoral composition of GSDP. This has been corroborated by the fact that between 2001 and 2011, except Arunachal Pradesh and Manipur, the rest of the states of the North-East have observed substantial rise in the percentage of agricultural labourers and concomitant decline in the percentage of cultivators. Employment in household industries remained below 5 percent for all the north-eastern states except Manipur (see Table 2.8). However, for the majority of the states of the North-Eastern Region, the percentage of employment in household industries remained below the all-India average, and a decline in percentage has been observed in 2011 in comparison to 2001 for most of the states in India's North-East (see Table 2.8). This clearly attests to the non-industrial nature of the North-Eastern Region.

Therefore, increased marginalisation in the agrarian sector and non-industrial nature of the region will leave a vast majority of

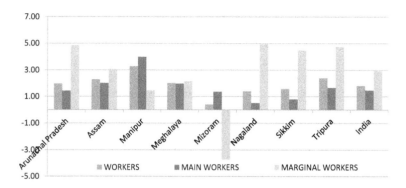

Figure 2.3 Compound annual rate of growth (in percentage) of workers, main workers and marginal workers between 2001 and 2011 in north-eastern states

Source: Calculated from Census 2001 and Census 2011, Government of India

Table 2.8 Changing employment pattern (in percentage) in north-eastern states during 2001–11

States/year	Cultivator		Agricultural labourers		Household industry		Other workers	
	2001	2011	2001	2011	2001	2011	2001	2011
Arunachal Pradesh	57.8	51.5	3.9	6.2	1.3	1.4	37.0	40.9
Assam	39.1	33.9	13.2	15.4	3.6	4.1	44.0	46.5
Manipur	40.2	44.0	12.0	8.8	10.3	7.0	37.6	40.2
Meghalaya	48.1	41.7	17.7	16.7	2.2	1.7	32.0	39.8
Mizoram	54.9	47.2	5.7	8.6	1.5	1.6	37.9	42.6
Nagaland	64.7	55.2	3.6	6.5	2.6	2.3	29.0	36.0
Sikkim	49.9	38.1	6.5	8.4	1.6	1.7	42.0	51.8
Tripura	27.0	20.1	23.8	24.1	3.0	2.8	46.1	53.0
India	31.7	24.7	26.5	30.0	4.2	3.8	37.6	41.6

Source: Calculated from Census 2001 and Census 2011, Government of India

people either to remain unemployed or to join the informal sector. Little penetration by the private sector and the small size of the market will leave smaller space in the informal sector. Alternatively, in the category of other workers, average employment is more than 40 percent in the North-Eastern Region, which is higher than the all-India average (see Table 2.8). However, the nature of employment in the north-eastern states is characteristically different from the rest of India. In fact, the 'other workers' category includes jobs in construction and the electricity, gas and water supply of the secondary sector and transport, storage and communication, trade, hotels and restaurant, banking and insurance, real estate, ownership of dwellings and business services, public administration, and other services – or, precisely, the entire tertiary sector of the economy.

A close look at the share of the various sectors in GSDP gives a clear indication that for the north-eastern states, the bulk of the income is generated from construction in the secondary sector and public administrative services and other services in the tertiary sector. Income from the electricity, gas and water supply of the secondary sector and transport, storage and communication, trade, hotels and restaurant, banking and insurance, real estate, and ownership of dwellings and business services in the tertiary sector remained quite low. Large public service employment shares a large component of income in the tertiary sector. In contrast, for the rest of the Indian states, public service employment is either declining or becoming static, and with the expansion of neo-liberal policy, employment opportunities have become market driven.

Growth and employment relationship

The general discourse is that increase in economic will entails rise in employment. This argument has been invalidated for various countries over time, and in many cases 'jobless growth' and expansion of informal employment have become more pronounced. In Table 2.9, it can be seen that Arunachal Pradesh, Assam, Tripura and Nagaland have experienced an increase in growth in the last decade. Barring Arunachal Pradesh, WPR has increased for the rest of the three states. However, this rise has been achieved through the rise in the percentage of marginal workers. For Arunachal Pradesh, the percentage of non-workers and marginal workers both have increased. This scenario clearly reflects that the rise in growth rates failed to bring commensurate increase in employment in the formal sectors. On the contrary, growth has declined for Meghalaya, Mizoram and Sikkim, and these three states experienced a decline in WPR percentage and a decline in marginal workers. The drop in WPR has matched the rise of non-workers in these three states, and this clearly reflects that unemployment has increased in these states.

Table 2.9 Growth–employment relationship in north-eastern states

State	Growth pattern	WPR (in percentage)	Marginal workers (in percentage)	Non-workers (in percentage)
Arunachal Pradesh	Acceleration	Decreased	Increased	Increased
Assam	Acceleration	Increased	Increased	Decreased
Tripura	Acceleration	Increased	Increased	Decreased
Nagaland	Acceleration	Increased	Increased	Decreased
Manipur	Static	Increased	Decreased	Increased
Meghalaya	Deceleration	Decreased	Decreased	Increased
Mizoram	Deceleration	Decreased	Decreased	Increased
Sikkim	Deceleration	Increased	Decreased	Decreased

Source: Generated from growth and employment tables cited in the chapter by the author

A close look at sector-wise (primary, secondary and tertiary) employment elasticity (see Table 2.10) reveals some interesting features. Employment elasticity for primary, secondary and tertiary sectors is higher than the national average. In fact, sector-wise employment elasticity is found to be highly elastic for the primary sector in Sikkim, for the secondary sector in Assam, Manipur and Nagaland, and for the North-Eastern Region as a whole. In the tertiary sector, except Tripura, employment elasticity remained much higher than the all-India average. The sectoral comparison has adequately shown that except Assam, the rest of the states' economies are non-industrial in nature, and the absence of the manufacturing sector is a long-term reality. Similarly, in the tertiary sector, the private sector's contribution to SDP is quite low. Therefore, it can be reiterated that a relatively higher value of sector-wise employment elasticity is the outcome of the contribution of sectors where the government is playing a direct role.

The economic structure and resultant employment structure is not only the outcome of postcolonial policies of the government of India, but also the colonial era and changes in political boundaries of India during independence did have considerable impact on the changing structure of the labour market and economy of north-eastern states.

However, its impact was negligible, and the reasons were: (a) the 'tea plantation was developed into enclave production without

Table 2.10 State-wise and sector-wise employment elasticity of the North-Eastern Region between 1993–4 and 2011–12

	Arunachal Pradesh	Assam	Manipur	Meghalaya	Nagaland	Sikkim	Tripura	NER	India
Primary	0.37	0.22	0.13	0.05	0.63	1.08	0.02	0.2	-.05
Secondary	0.2	1.46	1.07	0.71	1.19	0.38	0.93	1.11	0.66
Tertiary	0.58	0.56	0.43	0.75	0.69	0.36	-0.07	0.47	0.36
Total	0.28	0.4	0.45	0.26	0.73	0.42	0.35	0.37	0.22

Source: NSSO Unit Level data, 50th and 68th round on employment, GSDP figures at constant prices, Central Statistical Organisation, Ministry of Statistics and Programme Implementation, Government of India; www.mospi.gov.in

having any linkage with the hinterland' (Barua and Das 2007); (b) the wage policy pursued by the planters backed by the colonial authority was such that the wage rates in the tea gardens were much lower than what could be earned when employed by the railways and public works department or in agriculture (Dasgupta 1986: PE – 2); (c) the appropriation of land by the agents of the company without any compensation being paid to the owners of land; (d) the railway network passing through jungles connecting the tea plantation to the river/sea port and, thereby, leaving the entire hinterland in the outskirts, which prevented internal market formation; (e) the lack of technological changes in agriculture (Barua and Das 2007). With India's freedom and partition of the country, the traditional transportation routes, such as rail, road and river, linking the Chittagong and Calcutta ports became unavailable, and alternative routes of communication had become more expensive. For example, the road distance between Calcutta and Agartala had turned out to be about 2000 km as an effect of partition. In the pre-partition period, the bulk of the commodities could be transferred from Calcutta by ship along the coast to Chittagong port (the distance is around 582 km) and the shipment time was 24 hours; from there a 100 km journey could bring the commodities to Agartala (Banerjee et al. 1999: 2551).

However, policies followed in the post-independence period added macroeconomic imbalances to the region. Most available funds are being taken for payment of salaries to the burgeoning number of government employees; there is little available for investment in development. Absence of manufacturing and large-scale trading activities has made the multiplier inoperative, and India's North-East continues to be a net importer of goods and services. Outflow of funds also takes place through the low credit–deposit ratios of bank branches (Nathan 2005: 2488). Poor intra-state, inter-state and intra-country connectivity has further crippled the mobility of labour, goods and services and allowed the size of economy to remain small. This has direct bearing on the labour market and employment. In addition, continuance of the 'Inner Line Permit' has restricted the movement of labour to the North-East and, as a result, a bounded labour market became a reality over time.

During the liberalisation era (post-1990s), India shunned the policy of 'import substitution' and adopted a policy of export-led growth to overcome India's sluggish growth performances under protectionist and all-pervasive government policy regimes. This gave birth to India's 'Look East' policy, which is an admixture of foreign and free trade policy. Internal security concerns in the north-eastern states, which have strong international linkages, also played a catalytic role in formulating the 'Look East' policy. To counter the growing economic, political and military influences of China, India tries to develop cohesive relationships with East Asian and South-East Asian countries including Myanmar and improve trade balance with these countries. The North-East has been identified as the ideal buffer zone bridging South-East Asia, both for internal security purposes and to ensure development in that region. This new development paradigm in a way was the result of the failure of the 'old development paradigm', where the major thrust of development policy as articulated by various packages of development under the aegis of successive prime ministers since Deve Gowda was to pump in as much money as possible for the development of this region (Barua and Das 2007). However, the idea that the 'Look East' policy will become the engine of growth and transform the economy of the North-East remains elusive in nature and seems devoid of economic rationale. As pointed out by Barua and Das (2007), in comparison to the goods and services traded between India and the East and South-East Asian countries, goods and services produced in north-eastern states have hardly had any significant share in that trade basket. Transportation cost will abnormally escalate if goods are to be traded from India through the north-east to South-East Asia because of the distance and uneven topography, making this route economically unviable. As a result, India's entire trade with this region is still carried by maritime transport. Undoubtedly, the gateway can never be an efficient entry point for the exporters located in the hinterland.

Alternatively, by forging a durable relationship with Bangladesh and bringing time-honoured solutions to immigration problems and water disputes, the road, railways and water transport system through Bangladesh can become much more cost-effective and beneficial for the development of the economy and to create employment opportunities for north-eastern states vis-à-vis Bangladesh. As a matter of fact, the bulk of the goods and services can be traded from Calcutta along the coast to Chittagong port in Bangladesh and thereafter, through the Bangladesh railroad, the goods can be brought to Akhaura (around 100 km), adjacent to Agartola, and can be transported to various parts of the north-eastern states. This should substantially reduce the cost of intra-country trade with the

North-Eastern Region of India. Revival of riverine traffic between Calcutta and Assam through Sundarban and Bangladesh may be another feasible solution to facilitate trade in the North-East Region. This will help the entire subregion to grow. Oranges and pineapples from Meghalaya and ginger, tea, paat and mugaa silk from Assam may be exported to Bangladesh and from there to West Asia and Europe (Banerjee et al. 1999: 2551).

Fiscal condition of the north-eastern states

While discussing the finances of the north-eastern states, it has to be kept in mind that many of these states were created only to fulfil the ethnic, political and cultural aspirations of the people. During the reorganisation of the north-eastern states, a pertinent criterion was ignored that the territory in question must have revenue resources to fulfil its administrative as well as non-developmental expenditure. It was thought that with their existing potential in agricultural areas, hydro-electrical power and natural oil resources, these states would be able to achieve financial viability after getting help and protection from the central government in the initial years. From Tables 2.11 and 2.12, it is evident that, except Assam, most of the revenues for north-eastern states are coming as central assistance, which they receive by virtue of being special category states. However, this monetary assistance has failed to generate a multiplier effect because own-tax revenue as a percentage of total revenue receipts for all the north-eastern states (except Assam) has remained abysmally low.

Decades have passed since independence, but the economies of these regions are still suffering, and neither the central planners nor the state governments have any idea when these states will be viable financially. After receiving huge assistance from the union government, state governments have failed to raise internal resources to meet their non-developmental expenditure. There has been a tendency to multiply administrative units and employees beyond reasonable requirements, and their main task is to find ways to utilise the central funds. Fiscal stress has seriously constrained the states' ability to discharge the primary responsibility of developing social and economic infrastructure. According to a Reserve Bank of India analysis, many factors are responsible for the wide fiscal gap of these states including a growing interest burden, increasing pension liabilities, large administrative expenditures, losses incurred by

Table 2.11 Own tax revenue as percentage of total revenue receipts of the north-eastern states of India

States/Year	2000–1	2001–2	2002–3	2003–4	2004–5	2005–6	2006–7	2007–8	2008–9	2009–10
Arunachal Pradesh	2.15	2.85	6.40	2.77	3.34	3.29	3.13	3.41	3.66	4.15
Assam	25.37	26.45	6.01	25.27	27.36	26.83	25.48	21.92	22.96	36.24
Manipur	4.70	4.33	4.91	4.81	4.67	3.95	4.25	4.20	4.39	5.04
Meghalaya	15.12	11.75	11.24	12.70	13.44	14.46	14.23	13.07	13.14	12.89
Mizoram	1.74	2.20	2.73	2.47	2.64	3.33	3.43	3.53	3.57	3.63
Nagaland	3.69	4.14	4.60	2.90	4.26	4.65	4.29	4.38	4.08	4.35
Sikkim	7.58	10.15	5.09	8.05	6.18	7.50	8.18	7.33	7.46	6.87
Tripura	7.67	8.49	9.74	10.22	9.30	9.79	10.47	10.02	10.85	11.97

Source: Calculated from data of state budget (various years), CAG State Audit Reports, Reserve Bank of India; www.rbi.org.in, DOI: 10.01.2016

Table 2.12 Grants-in-aid from centre as percentage of total revenue receipts of the north-eastern states of India

States/Year	2000–1	2001–2	2002–3	2003–4	2004–5	2005–6	2006–7	2007–8	2008–9	2009–10
Arunachal Pradesh	79.20	82.24	78.78	79.39	72.55	69.64	74.69	62.85	66.70	75.00
Assam	34.85	35.51	86.19	36.81	35.91	35.67	32.38	32.06	35.76	4.94
Manipur	75.66	81.15	76.67	74.75	74.86	78.72	74.19	75.42	74.07	72.94
Meghalaya	52.90	65.89	67.90	61.99	60.53	57.11	56.29	55.66	57.66	61.37
Mizoram	82.82	87.51	82.71	83.79	82.01	75.75	75.16	72.00	76.00	78.79
Nagaland	85.49	90.26	88.72	83.62	82.80	80.11	80.99	78.28	80.16	82.16
Sikkim	50.56	64.89	27.97	43.51	35.70	32.83	30.03	27.51	33.79	39.93
Tripura	72.14	73.83	71.73	67.26	68.97	74.73	72.97	69.26	68.65	69.13

Source: Calculated from data of state budget (various years), CAG State Audit Reports, Reserve Bank of India; www.rbi.org.in, DOI: 10.1.2016

Public Sector Undertakings (PSUs), etc. The situation of the North-East Region appears complicated when they are compared to the rest of India and additional factors such as little scope for internal mobilisation of resources and large public service employment have made the situation worse.

Economy – society interface

It is quite evident from the foregoing analysis that the North-Eastern Region has been showing improvement on the economic front. Economic growth is getting better, and inequality has been reduced. Economic development thus achieved in the last three decades has failed to reduce the ethnic, cultural, social and political cleavages among the north-eastern states as well as between the north-eastern states and rest of India. There may not be any straight empirical results either to corroborate or to refute the existence of these cleavages. In fact, we failed to correlate qualitative variables like ethnicity and identity with purely economic variables, especially economic growth. As a result, there have been constraints to building up a working model of economics based on identity, ethnicity, culture or language. The market tries to play a homogenising role because everyone should receive wages according to their marginal productivity; therefore, ideally, caste, creed, religion, identity and ethnicity should be diluted once every one shall become part of market and everyone shall become a wage earner. However, the market also increases income inequality across communities, ethnic groups, and linguistic or cultural groups. The presence or absence of the market may have an implicit or explicit role to fuel or abate such types of movements, which require a thorough probe. In the case of the north-eastern states, the size and presence of market are small and labour force has little space in the small-sized market.

Alternatively, the major economic space has been occupied by the government, but it failed to accommodate a large section of the labour force. In addition, it has also been anticipated that funds disbursed by the central government, in many cases, have given birth to a group of elite parasites consisting of bureaucrats, politicians, contractors and insurgent groups. They are assumed to work in connivance and create shadow deterrent for proper use of funds for the all-round development of every section of the society. The brewing frustration of the common masses is often being diverted into intra-tribes, inter-language, inter-religion, and intra/inter-regional conflicts.

In many cases, the state buys or earns a short-run peace in lieu of providing constitutional safeguards for a particular group or gives more funds to that particular region from the state (e.g. arranging special provisions for Scheduled Tribes and Scheduled Castes, attributing special category status to north-eastern states, Kashmir, Uttarakhand, job reservations by the states of the North-East for the people belonged to those states, etc.). In most cases, neither the funds percolate down within that particular group nor are they empowered economically, politically or socially to hit the street in search of a separate identity or ethnicity. Economic backwardness or achieving high economic growth hardly justifies these movements because economic affluence may accentuate identity or ethnicity-based movement.

Where do we go from where?

The findings of the study unravel a few glaring inconsistencies that the north-eastern states have experienced over the last three decades. If we look at the growth scenario of the north-eastern states, the picture is not so gloomy, contrary to the general claim that the region is neglected, insulated and marginalised. Per-capita income grew at a moderate rate and income inequality declined. However, the concerning factor is that growth is only visible where the Indian state played the role of principal economic agent. The total absence of manufacturing industries run by the private sector and the absence of credible alternatives to economy outside agriculture have been the signals indicating that the centre's funds as different forms of development assistances have ultimately failed to create multiplier effect in the economy, and the corresponding resilience issue of the economy has been called into question. Declining income from the agricultural sector and the corresponding rise of population engaged in agriculture is indicative of the marginalisation of the rural workforce. The employment scenario has worsened in the last decade.

Another revelation is that most of the north-eastern states have remained the net importer of food and non-food items. As a result, the economy of the region has failed to become self-sustaining and self-regenerating in nature. Economic integration sought under a decentralised development model has failed to keep the promise of bringing equitable development across the north-eastern states. The issues of equitable justice, the right of self-determination, autonomy, cultural and linguistic identities, and other such issues have acted as the harbinger of ethnic and subregional assertions, dissents and militancy, which occasionally surfaced out at different times in different sub-spaces of the North-Eastern Region. The central development grants do not have any positive trickle-down effect at the grass roots and at the primary sector of the economy. Important inherent limitations such as physical non-proximity, difficult hilly terrain and lack of developed communication have been the major hindrances to realise the development programmes. Along with such hindrances, the long protracted insurgency issues in most of the north-eastern states have become the major bottleneck to forge economic, social and cultural development. Resultantly, the size of the labour market remained small, closed and bounded.

In fact, the 'Look East' policy has failed to move beyond academic exercises and has failed to bring about any credible ground level changes in the north-eastern states. Finally, the occasional use of coercive forces, doling out of funds and providing autonomy without accountability are the adhoc measures often used by the state to settle the unsettled socio-cultural and politico-economic issues rooted in the Indian soil, cemented on the notion of abortive post-colonial Indian nationhood. This chapter reaffirms the fact that the Indian state has failed to fulfil the economic expectations of the North-East. Resultantly, the grand Indian nation-state would certainly suffer from hyper-paranoia if a thorough overhauling of the policy on the North-East is not addressed properly.

Notes

1 Sikkim became an Indian state in 1975 and was classified as a 'special category state'. Prior to that, Sikkim was under monarchic rule. In 2003, the state of Sikkim became a part of the North-East Council.
2 According to the Census 2011, the percentage of Scheduled Tribe population stands at 64.2 percent for Arunachal Pradesh, 85.2 percent for Meghalaya, 94.5 percent for Mizoram, 89.1 percent for Nagaland, 32.3 percent for Manipur, 31.1 percent for Tripura, 20.6 percent for Sikkim and 12.4 percent for Assam, respectively. The all-India percentage stands at 8.2 percent.
3 During British rule, Alexander Mackenzie, in his book *History of the Government with the Hill Tribes of the North-East Frontier of Bengal*, in 1884, was possibly the first one to use the term 'North-East Frontier'

to identify Assam including the adjoining hill areas and princely states of Manipur and Tripura. Between late 1890 and the beginning of 1900, a proposal was mooted by the British rulers to merge Assam with East Bengal and conceive of the region as the 'North Eastern Province'. During colonial rule, Assam was referred as the North Eastern Frontier of Bengal.

4 Assam and Nagaland were accorded special category status in 1969; Manipur, Meghalaya and Tripura in 1972, when they were created; Sikkim in 1975; and Arunachal Pradesh and Mizoram in 1987.

5 Note submitted by the adviser, Financial Resource Division, Planning Commission, dated 16 November 2006 to the member (AS) and Deputy Chairman of the Commission. Also stated in Rajya Sabha in response to unstarred Question No. 1614 dated 3 December 2009.

6 Central assistance was provided to special category states as 90 percent grant and 10 percent loan from the beginning of the Fourth Five-Year Plan, except Assam and Jammu and Kashmir, which were covered under the pattern of central assistance of 30 percent grant and 70 percent loan, as in the case of non-special category states; the 90 percent and 10 percent formula was applied only in respect to the hilly areas of Assam and Ladakh regions of Jammu and Kashmir. This was extended to the entire area of these two states by a decision of the National Development Council only in October 1990 (Bhattacharjee 2014: 56).

7 The Sixth Schedule of the Indian Constitution makes special provisions for the administration of what were then 'The Tribal Areas of Assam'. In the colonial period, those areas were mostly protected enclaves, where tribal peoples could supposedly pursue their 'Customary Practices' including kinship and clan-based rules of land allocation. They were called 'backward tracts', later replaced by the term 'Excluded Areas' because they were excluded from the operation of laws applicable in the rest of British-controlled India. The Sixth Schedule provides for autonomous regions within those districts with elected councils, with powers to regulate customary law, to administer justice in limited cases and to determine the occupation or use of land and the regulation of shifting cultivation.

8 The lieutenant governor of Assam was empowered to introduce the Inner Line Regulation in 1873. According to this, no British subject could or go beyond a certain frontier that was drawn along the foothills of the north-eastern and south-western border of the Brahmaputra valley. The areas beyond the inner line were inhabited by the hill tribes, where the government did not want to apply complicated civil rules. The regulation enabled the hills tribes a special status. Most notably, the Inner Line Regulation did not define the actual boundary of the British possession, nor did it indicate the territorial frontiers. Its sole purpose was to prohibit the people from the plains from entering into the tribal-infested hill areas without the permission of the government and to provide a simpler administration for the hill people. The Inner Line Regulation of 1873 allowed the lieutenant governor of Assam to distinguish the areas between the 'Inner Line' and the 'outer line' (see Acharyya 1984; Sangkima 2004).

9 During the liberalisation era (post-1990s), India shunned the policy of 'import substitution' and adopted a policy of export-led growth to overcome India's sluggish growth performances under protectionist and all-pervasive government policy regimes. This gave birth to India's 'Look East' policy, which is an admixture of foreign and free-trade policy. Internal security concerns in north-eastern states, which have strong international linkages, also played a catalytic role in formulating the 'Look East' policy. To counter the growing economic political and military influences of China, India on the one hand tries to develop cohesive relationships with East Asian and South-East Asian countries, including Myanmar, and on the other tries to improve trade balance with these countries. The North-East has been identified as the ideal buffer zone bridging South-East Asia both for internal security purpose and to ensure development in that region. This new development paradigm in a way was the result of the failure of the 'old development paradigm', where the major thrust of development policy – as articulated by various packages of development under the aegis of successive prime ministers since Deve Gowda – was to pump in as much money as possible into the development of this region.

10 Between 1980–1 and 1990–1, the population of the north-eastern states together grew at an average rate of more than 2 percent per annum. Immigration from Bangladesh and Myanmar is partly responsible for the high population growth in this region.

11 Exponential form of growth curve can be written as

$$Y_t = ae^{bt}v_t$$

This can be transformed linearly as follows

$$\ln Y_t = a + bt + u_t$$

Where Y_t = Output
  a = Constant term
  t = time (in years)
  $u_t = \ln v_t$
    = error term such that $\ln v_t \sim IND\ (0, \sigma^2)$

By deducting 1 from the antilog of the estimates of the coefficient of b and multiplying it by 100, we calculate growth rate.
  Or, Growth rate = (antilog of estimated b-1) * 100

12 Primary sector consists of agriculture, forestry and logging, fishing and mining, and quarrying.

13 The secondary sector consists of manufacturing (registered and unregistered together), construction, and electricity, gas and water supply.

14 Transport (railways and transport by other means), storage and communication, trade, hotels and restaurant, banking and insurance, public administration, and other services together constitute the tertiary sector.

References

Acharyya, N.N. 1984. 'Modernization of Mizoram', Proceedings, NEIHA, 5th Session.

Ahluwalia, Montek Singh. 2011. 'Regional Balance in Indian Planning', http://planningcommission.gov.in/aboutus/history/spe_regional1206.pdf (DOI: 28.09.2015)

Bakshi, Sanchita, Arunish Chawala and Mihir Shah. 2015. 'Regional Disparities in India: A Moving Frontier', *Economic and Political Weekly*, 50(1): January.

Banerjee, Paula, Sanjoy Hazarika, Monirul Hussain, and Ranabir Samaddar. 1999. 'Indo-Bangladesh Cross-Border Migration and Trade', *Economic and Political Weekly*, 34(36): 2549–2551.

Barro, J. Robert. 1996. 'Democracy and Growth', *Journal of Economic Growth*, 1: 1–27.

Barua, Alokesh and Arindam Bandyopadhyay. 2005. 'Structural Change, Economic Growth and Regional Disparity in the North-East: Regional and National Perspectives', in Alokesh Barua (ed.), *India's North-East Developmental Issues in a Historical Perspective*, New Delhi: Manohar Publishers and Distributors.

Barua, A. and S.K. Das. 2007. 'The Look East Policy and the Northeast: New Challenges for Development', Paper presented at the conference on 'India's Look East Policy – Challenges for Sub-Regional Cooperation', Indian Council for Research on International Economic Relation and Omeo Kumar Das Institute of Social Change and Development, Guwahati, 7–9 October.

Bhattacharjee, Govind. 2014. 'The Reality of Special Category States', *Economic and Political Weekly*, 49(40): 48–56.

Bhattacharya, B.B. and Arup Mitra. 1990. 'Excess Growth of Tertiary Sector in Indian Economy: Issues and Implications', *Economic and Political Weekly*, 25(44).

Boyce, James K. 1987. *Agrarian Impasse in Bengal, Institutional Constraints to Technological Change*, New Delhi: Oxford University Press.

Census of India. 2011. http://censusindia.gov.in/2011-prov results/data_files/india/pov_popu_total_presentation_2011.pdf (DOI: 12.10.2014)

Chakrabarti, Anjan. 2010. 'Paradox of Growth: India's North-East in Context', *The India Economy Review*, 7.

Chakrabarti, Anjan and A.S. Chakraborty. 2010. 'Emergent Development Approach: A Critique of "Money-bags" Centre Directed Dole Development in North-East India', *Indian Journal of Political Science*, 71(2).

Chandra, Bipan, Mridula Mukherjee and Aditya Mukherjee. 2008. *India since Independence*, India: Penguin Books.

Dasgupta, Partha. 1993. *An Inquiry into Well-Being and Destitution*, Oxford: Clarendon Press.

Dasgupta, Ranajit. 1986. 'From Peasants and Tribesmen to Plantation Workers Colonial Capitalism, Reproduction of Labour Power and Proletarianisation in North East India, 1850s to 1947', *Economic and Political Weekly*, 21(4): PE-2.

Guha, Amalendu. 1977. *Planter-Raj to Swaraj: Freedom Struggle and Electoral Politics in Assam 1826–1947*, New Delhi: People's Publishing House.

Hussain, Wasbir. 2004. 'India's North-East: The Problem'. Paper presented as part of the 'Interaction on the North-East' Observer Research Foundation, New Delhi, 18 November.

Mackenzie, Alexander. (1884 first published) 2001. *North East Frontier of India*, New Delhi: Mittal Publication (first published as *History of the Government with the Hill Tribes of the North-East Frontier of Bengal*).

Mauro, Paolo. 1995. 'Corruption and Growth', *The Quarterly Journal of Economics*, 110(3): 681–712.

Misra, Udayon. 2000. *The Periphery Strikes Back: Challenges to the Nation-State in Assam and Nagaland*, Shimla: Indian Institute of Advanced Studies.

Nathan, Dev. 2005. 'Hill Economies of the North-Eastern Region: Emerging Challenges and Opportunities', *Economic and Political Weekly*, 40(24), 18–24 January: 2486–2488.

NEDFi Databank. http://databank.nedfi.com. Accessed 12 January 2014.

Reddy, V.N. 1978. 'Growth Rates', *Economic and Political Weekly*, 13(19).

Sangkima. 2004. *A Modern History of Mizoram*, Lushai: Spectrum Publication.

Verghese, Boobli George. 2001. 'Unfinished Business in the Northeast: Priorities towards Restructuring, Reform, Reconciliation and Resurgence'. Paper presented at Seventh Kamal Kumari Lecture.

Verghese, Boobli George. 2004. *India's Northeast Resurgent: Ethnicity, Insurgency, Governance, Development*, New Delhi: Konark Publishers.

Chapter 3

Structure and quality of employment in North-East India

A socio-religious analysis

Ajaya Kumar Naik and Nitin Tagade

The post-reform Indian economy, in many ways, is different from the pre-reform period of 1991. During the post-reform period, the Indian economy witnessed three major changes – high economic growth, poverty reduction and employment growth. The pace of improved income and poverty reduction depend on employment generation and its quality. Employment growth is a subject of intense public debate which has essentially revolved around two issues – the unencouraging employment situation since the 1990s at the aggregate and state level (Sundaram 2001, 2007; Bhattacharya and Sakthivel 2004; Bhaumik 2007; Ramaswamy 2007; Rangarajan et al. 2007, 2008; Abraham 2009) and the impact of employment growth on different economic and social segments of society (Srivastava and Srivastava 2010; Chowdhury 2011; Kannan and Raveendran 2012; Neetha 2014; Thorat et al. 2016).

However, in this entire debate, the issue of employment and its quality in the North-Eastern Region (NER) gets evaded because this region has small states. In fact, state-level analysis of the employment scenario has remained limited to the major states of India; only Assam has been analysed in detail, making it a standard for the whole of the NER. This is partly due to the problem of inadequacy or non-availability of statistically authentic data and partly because Assam by itself represents about 69 percent of the total population in the NER. However, the population of this region is not homogeneous in nature in terms of social and ethnic identity. Creating productive employment opportunities is an important issue in the NER because these states are agrarian in nature; have a poor industrial base; lack infrastructure; depend on public sector employment; have undergone large-scale migration for livelihood, political insurgency and violence; and have experienced gross negligence from the centre and their respective state governments towards their overall development. In spite of having vast natural resources, the states lag behind the rest of the country in terms of various developmental outcomes. As per the National Sample Survey Organisation (NSSO) 2011–12, the poverty and unemployment ratio of all the north-eastern states, except Meghalaya and Sikkim, are higher or close to the national level. To address the developmental concerns of the region, the Department of Development of North Eastern Region was created in 2001, which was later converted into a union ministry in 2004 called the Ministry of Development of North Eastern Region. Since then, a large number of development projects have been undertaken by the ministry.

In this context, this chapter aims to analyse the structure and growth of employment among the states in the NER of India. The specific objectives of the study are to analyse the changing patterns and growth of the workforce and unemployment rate and to discuss the quality of workers by their activity status, education level and informalisation of employment in different population segments and socio-religious groups. The analysis has been carried out largely on the basis of the employment and unemployment survey for 2011–12 conducted by the National Sample Survey Organisation, Ministry of Statistics and Programme Implementation, Government of India. To examine past experiences, we have also estimated the growth rate of employment depending on the availability of comparative information from 1983 to 2011–12. In the analysis, NER includes eight north-eastern states, namely, Arunachal Pradesh, Assam, Manipur, Meghalaya, Mizoram, Nagaland, Sikkim and Tripura. This chapter is grouped into six sections. The first section provides details of the data and elaborates on some of the key concepts used in this chapter. The second section provides a demographic profile according to socio-religious groups in the states of the North-East. The third section details a comparative overview of workers based on activity status in the NER and India. The fourth section discusses the employment and unemployment situation in the NER. The fifth section provides a discussion on the structure of employment, and finally, the sixth section constitutes the concluding remarks.

Data source and methodology

As mentioned earlier, this chapter is based on NSSO survey data on employment and unemployment in 1983, 1993–4, 2004–5 and

2011–12. The size, structure and quality of employment are estimated by using the usual principal and subsidiary status (UPSS). The unemployment rates are estimated by using the current daily status (CDS). The quality of workforce in the NER is analysed by looking into the distribution of workforce by activity status, education level, enterprise type and informality of the workforce. The informal sector workers[1] and informal workers[2] are estimated by using the definition proposed by the National Commission for Enterprises in the Unorganised Sector (NCEUS) for 2004–5 and 2011–12 only. Though geographically similar, the region is extraordinarily diverse ethnically, culturally and economically. It is not possible to accommodate all the diverse groups in a single study. Therefore, the study has been analysed from the perspective of different socio-religious groups only. In the case of the NER, it is often claimed that the Christian Scheduled Tribes (CSTs) are in an advantageous position in terms of employability owing to their education in missionary institutions. Therefore, we have divided STs along religious lines into Hindu Scheduled Tribes (HSTs) and Christian Scheduled Tribes (CSTs). Other socio-religious groups will be named as All SCs, Hindu Other Backward Classes (HOBCs), Hindu High Castes (HHCs), Muslims, and the rest. In the 1993–4 NSSO survey, the information on OBCs was not collected. Therefore, we have analysed the data only for 2004–5 and 2011–12.

Demographic profile

The NER consists of eight states with a population of about 46.1 million, accounting for 3.7 percent of India's total population. The rural population is 4.4 percent of India's total rural population, and the urban population of the region is only 2.2 percent of India's urban population (see Table 3.1). Of the total population in this region, 81.3 percent live in rural areas. The percentage of STs is the highest, making up 29 percent of the total population of the region, followed by 22.6 percent Muslims. The religious distribution of the ST population shows that 11.3 percent are HSTs and 15.1 percent are CSTs. The share of HOBCs and HHCs is 22.6 percent and 15.6 percent, respectively. In this study, SCs account around 10 percent.

The caste composition, in ethnic terms, in different states of this region, is presented in Table 3.2. Of the total population in the NER, 68.6 percent are Assamese, making up the highest component

Table 3.1 Size of population by socio-religious group in different sectors (in millions): 2011–12

Socio-religious group	Rural		Urban		Total	
	Number	Percent	Number	Percent	Number	Percent
HST	4.82	12.9	0.39	4.5	5.21	11.3
CST	5.29	14.1	1.69	19.5	6.98	15.1
OST	1.01	2.7	0.20	2.3	1.20	2.6
All ST	11.12	29.7	2.28	26.4	13.39	29.0
All SC	3.53	9.4	1.21	14.0	4.73	10.3
HOBC	7.67	20.5	1.67	19.3	9.34	20.2
HHC	4.81	12.8	2.37	27.4	7.18	15.6
Muslim	9.42	25.1	1.02	11.8	10.44	22.6
Rest	0.93	2.5	0.10	1.2	1.03	2.2
Total	37.48	100	8.64	100	46.12	100
% to All India		4.4		2.2		3.7

Source: Estimated from NSSO Employment Unemployment Survey, 2011–12

Note: The abbreviations used are HST- Hindu Scheduled Tribes, CST- Christian Scheduled Tribes, OST- Other Scheduled Tribes (OSTs are those who are neither Hindus nor Christians), SC- Scheduled Castes, HOBC- Hindu Other Backward Castes, and HHC- Hindu High Castes

in the demographic profile; among other states, Sikkim, at 1.4 percent, forms the lowest, and Tripura, at 8.1 percent, makes up the second-highest component. The distribution of population as per socio-religious groups across the states in the NER shows that the share of CSTs is the highest in Meghalaya (36.1 percent) followed by Nagaland (27.5 percent), Mizoram (14.1 percent) and Manipur (11.4 percent), together accounting for about 90 percent of the total population of CSTs in the NER. Whereas HSTs are mainly concentrated in Assam (77 percent) and Tripura (18.7 percent), accounting for about 96 percent, the share of SCs is highest in Assam (79.6 percent) and Tripura (16 percent). The proportion of the Muslim population is the highest in Assam (92.8 percent), followed by Manipur (10.4 percent). Assam has the highest percentage (79.1 percent) of Hindu OBCs followed by Manipur (10.9 percent) and Tripura (6.7 percent). The HHCs are largely concentrated in Assam (80.2 percent), Sikkim (17.7 percent) and Tripura (10.6 percent). However, the ranking of the distribution of population by socio-religious groups in each state differs.

A few states have a predominance of CSTs, while in some states HOBCs are more prevalent, and in some states more than two

Table 3.2 Distribution of population by socio-religious groups in different states of the NER (in %): 2011–12

State		HST	CST	OST	ST	SC	HOBC	HHC	Muslim	Rest	Total
Sikkim	Row%	7.1	1.2	26.4	34.7	5.7	41.9	7.3	2.2	8.2	100
	Col%	0.9	0.1	13.6	1.6	0.7	2.8	0.6	0.1	5.0	1.4
Arunachal Pradesh	Row%	1.9	22.6	45.9	70.4	1.0	2.7	17.7	1.5	6.8	100
	Col%	0.5	4.6	53.8	7.4	0.3	0.4	3.5	0.2	9.3	3.1
Nagaland	Row%	0.5	96.7	0.2	97.3	1.6	0.0	0.6	0.4	0.1	100
	Col%	0.2	27.5	0.3	14.4	0.7	0.0	0.2	0.1	0.1	4.3
Manipur	Row%	0.4	30.6	0.3	31.3	4.4	38.8	8.5	10.4	6.5	100
	Col%	0.2	11.4	0.7	6.1	2.4	10.9	3.1	2.6	16.5	5.7
Mizoram	Row%	0.6	88.4	6.6	95.5	0.2	0.3	3.1	0.1	3.4	100
	Col%	0.1	14.1	6.1	8.0	0.0	0.0	0.5	0.0	3.7	2.4
Tripura	Row%	26.1	5.5	1.2	32.8	20.4	16.9	20.4	9.5	0.1	100
	Col%	18.7	2.9	3.6	9.1	16.0	6.7	10.6	3.4	0.2	8.1
Meghalaya	Row%	4.2	83.1	3.5	90.7	0.4	0.3	4.1	2.7	1.8	100
	Col%	2.4	36.1	8.7	20.5	0.3	0.1	1.7	0.8	5.2	6.6
Assam	Row%	12.7	0.7	0.5	13.9	11.9	23.4	18.2	30.6	2.0	100
	Col%	77.0	3.3	13.2	32.9	79.6	79.1	80.2	92.8	60.0	68.6
Total	Row%	11.3	15.1	2.6	29.0	10.3	20.3	15.6	22.6	2.2	100
	Col%	100	100	100	100	100	100	100	100	100	100

Source: Estimated from NSSO Employment Unemployment Survey, 2011–12

groups are dominant. States like Meghalaya, Mizoram and Nagaland are dominated by CST population (83.1 percent, 88.4 percent
and 96.7 percent, respectively), while in Sikkim, the HOBCs are
dominant, accounting for 41.9 percent of the state population.
There are some other states like Manipur, which have the dominance of CSTs and HOBCs (30.6 percent and 38.8 percent, respectively). Arunachal Pradesh has a predominance of HHCs along
with OSTs (around 53.8 percent of the ST in Arunachal Pradesh
have not opted for any religion and are part of OSTs in Table 3.2)
and CSTs, while Tripura has a mixed population comprising HSTs,
SCs, HOBCs and HHCs.

Size of population and workers

The NSS unit level data provides information on employment
status. This includes the usual principal subsidiary status (UPSS),
usual principal status (UPS) and subsidiary status (SS) depending
on the duration of work. The UPSS includes both the UPS and the
SS, where the UPS refers to the activity in which the workers were
engaged most of the time during the reference period of the last 365
days preceding the date of the survey; the SS refers to those workers who are engaged in an economic activity for a smaller duration
in the reference period. The conceptual alignment is similar to that
of the census definition of total worker, main worker and marginal
workers, respectively. In this section, an attempt has been made to
provide the comparative overview of employment in the NER and
India.

In the NER, the total workers are 15.4 million, accounting for
about 52 percent of the total population in 2011–12 (Table 3.3).
The share of total workers and main workers to the population
at the national level is higher in India as compared to the NER.
The main workers in 2011–12 were 48.2 percent in the NER and
51.6 percent in India. All the same, the share of marginal workers
to total workers is relatively low in the NER. The share of marginal workers to total workers is 6.5 percent in the NER, as compared to 8.1 percent in India. In fact, the size of the workforce
increased sharply in the NER, close to the population growth over
the last three decades. The growth in total workers during 1983
to 2011–12 is relatively higher in the NER as compared to India.
A further enquiry into the work participation rate (WPR) by UPSS
status shows that at 51.6 percent, it is relatively lower than in India

Table 3.3 Size of population and workers in the NER (in millions)

Year	Male				Female				Total			
	Population	UPSS	UPS	SS	Population	UPSS	UPS	SS	Population	UPSS	UPS	SS
North-East Region												
1983	7.7	6.4	6.3	0.1	7.0	1.7	1.2	0.5	14.8	8.1	7.4	0.7
1993–4	10.5	8.5	8.2	0.3	9.9	2.9	2.0	0.9	20.4	11.3	10.2	1.2
2004–5	13.1	10.9	10.7	0.2	12.4	4.4	3.0	1.4	25.5	15.3	13.7	1.6
2011–12	14.9	11.9	11.8	0.1	15.0	3.6	2.7	0.9	29.9	15.4	14.4	1.0
GR (%) (1983–2012)	2.3	2.1	2.2	–1.0	2.6	2.6	2.9	1.7	2.5	2.2	2.3	1.3
All India												
1983	196.8	172.9	169.1	3.7	187.4	87.6	65.2	22.5	384.3	260.5	234.3	26.2
1993–4	263.1	225.6	221.5	4.1	249.3	108.5	78.0	30.5	512.4	334.2	299.5	34.7
2004–5	332.7	282.2	277.6	4.6	312.9	134.9	101.1	33.8	645.6	417.1	378.7	38.4
2011–12	387.5	312.9	309.1	3.8	373.6	118.3	87.1	31.2	761.1	431.2	396.2	35.0
GR (%) (1983–2012)	2.4	2.1	2.1	0.1	2.4	1.0	1.0	1.1	2.4	1.8	1.8	1.0

Source: NSSO Employment Unemployment Survey (various years)

Note: 1. Population and workers are in the 15–59 age group
2. The UPSS indicates the total worker while UPS and SS denotes main and marginal workers

as a whole, where it is 56.7 percent (Table 3.4). This shows that a substantial proportion of workers in the 15–59 age group have opted not to work and probably has undertaken education, unless they are not trapped into unemployment, particularly after 2004–5. This is probably true, as the WPR has declined sharply in the NER from 2004–5 to 2011–12 after a steady increase (from 1983) in comparison to the national WPR, which declined over the period between 1983 and 2011–12.

The positive side of workforce in the NER is the relatively higher share of main workers to the total workers as compared to the whole of India. Despite this positive feature, low female participation in economic activities is of crucial importance. The share of male and female workers to their population size in the NER is 79.6 percent and 23.7 percent, respectively, in 2011–12. These figures for the national average are 80.7 percent and 31.7 percent, respectively. This means that a large share of improved employment opportunities in the NER is going into the hands of the male counterparts.

Table 3.4 Share of total, main and marginal workers in the NER and India (in %): 2011–12

Year	Male			Female			Total		
	WPR (UPSS)	WPR (UPS)	% of SS to UPSS	WPR (UPSS)	WPR (UPS)	% of SS to UPSS	WPR (UPSS)	WPR (UPS)	% of SS to UPSS
	North-East Region								
1983	83.0	81.3	2.1	24.2	16.4	32.1	55.0	50.4	8.4
1993–4	80.5	78.0	3.1	29.1	19.9	31.5	55.6	49.9	10.3
2004–5	83.3	81.5	2.2	35.7	24.5	31.4	60.1	53.7	10.6
2011–12	79.6	78.9	0.9	23.7	17.7	25.3	51.6	48.2	6.5
GR	−0.1	−0.1	−3.0	−0.1	0.3	−0.8	−0.2	−0.2	−0.9
	All India								
1983	87.8	85.9	2.2	46.8	34.8	25.6	67.8	61.0	10.0
1993–4	85.8	84.2	1.8	43.5	31.3	28.1	65.2	58.5	10.4
2004–5	84.8	83.4	1.6	43.1	32.3	25.0	64.6	58.7	9.2
2011–12	80.7	79.8	1.2	31.7	23.3	26.4	56.7	52.1	8.1
GR	−0.3	−0.3	−2.0	−1.3	−1.4	0.1	−0.6	−0.5	−0.7

Source: NSSO Employment Unemployment Survey (various years)

Status of employment – unemployment scenario

The status of employment and unemployment scenario in the NER is discussed in the following subsections. In the first subsection, we will discuss workforce participation rate, followed by unemployment rate in the second subsection and the structure of workforce by industry group and occupation in the third subsection.

Workforce participation rate

The workforce/work participation rate (WPR) is the ratio of workers to the total population in the working age of 15–59 years, which depicts the demand side of the labour market. The NSSO estimate of WPR for the 15–59 age group in 2011–12 for India is 56.7 percent, which is slightly higher than 51.6 percent in the NER at aggregate level (Table 3.5). A substantial variation exists in WPR across socio-religious groups in the region. The highest WPR is witnessed among STs (56.8 percent), followed by HOBCs (53.1 percent), SCs (49.0 percent) and Muslims (48.3 percent), and the lowest is among HHCs (45.3 percent). Among STs, a wide variation in WPR exists across religious groups; at 61.3 percent, WPR is highest with OSTs percent, followed by 58.2 percent among CSTs

Table 3.5 WPR in the 15–59 age group across socio-religious groups (in %): 2011–12

Socio-religious group	Rural			Urban			Rural + Urban		
	Male	Female	Total	Male	Female	Total	Male	Female	Total
HST	82.8	26.5	54.9	65.5	14.1	41.4	81.4	25.6	53.8
CST	76.1	48.0	62.2	64.6	28.8	46.7	73.2	43.1	58.2
OST	78.5	51.1	65.0	61.7	25.6	43.9	75.6	46.7	61.3
All ST	79.2	38.9	59.2	64.5	26.1	45.6	76.6	36.6	56.8
SC	80.3	19.8	49.0	83.9	14.7	48.9	81.3	18.4	49.0
HOBC	81.9	27.3	54.1	79.7	15.6	48.5	81.5	25.2	53.1
HHC	77.6	11.9	45.1	76.9	16.9	45.6	77.4	13.6	45.3
Muslim	84.4	14.4	49.0	75.0	6.9	42.0	83.4	13.6	48.3
Rest	76.7	40.8	59.4	52.7	41.6	47.9	74.4	40.9	58.4
Total	80.8	25.2	52.8	74.6	17.9	46.2	79.6	23.7	51.6
All India	82.0	37.0	59.7	78.4	20.9	50.5	80.7	31.7	56.7

Source: Estimated from NSSO Employment Unemployment Survey, 2011–12

and 53.8 percent among HSTs. In India, female WPR is low compared to male WPR because of the cultural norms which decide the overall WPR. The total WPR across socio-religious groups is the highest among females belonging to STs, followed by HOBCs, SCs and Muslims.

Between the 2001 and 2011 population census, the WPR increased in India from 38.1 to 39.8 percent; however, the reason for this has been largely attributed to the increase in the WPR of marginal workers (Venkatanarayana and Naik 2013). The NSSO employment-unemployment survey also shows little increase in workers both in the NER and all India between 2004–5 and 2011–12. But the absolute number of female workers declined from 4.4 million to 3.6 million in the NER, and it declined to 118.3 million in 2011–12 from 134.9 million in 2004–5 in India (Table 3.3). There was a heated discussion on the reasons for this declining female employment and overall WPR of all segments of the population. It declined due to various reasons such as declining female participation in the workforce, an increase in participation in higher education and a decline in employment opportunity for female workers in certain selected industry groups (Chowdhury 2011; Kannan and Raveendran 2012; Srivastava and Srivastava 2010). We estimated the average annual growth in the WPR across socio-religious groups during 2004–5 to 2011–12. The decline in the WPR is universal across socio-religious

Table 3.6 Annual growth in WPR (in %): 2004–5 and 2011–12

Socio-religious group	Rural			Urban			Rural + Urban		
	Male	Female	Total	Male	Female	Total	Male	Female	Total
HST	−0.7	−5.1	−1.9	0.0	−3.4	−1.8	−0.6	−5.2	−1.9
CST	−1.1	−4.8	−2.7	−0.6	−5.6	−2.4	−1.2	−5.2	−2.8
OST	−0.4	−3.6	−1.8	−0.6	−1.0	−0.5	−0.6	−3.8	−1.9
All ST	−0.9	−4.5	−2.2	−0.5	−4.9	−2.0	−0.9	−4.8	−2.3
SC	−1.1	−4.5	−2.3	0.1	−6.7	−2.0	−0.8	−5.2	−2.3
HOBC	−0.2	−6.9	−2.4	1.1	−3.3	0.1	0.0	−6.5	−2.0
HHC	−0.8	−11.8	−3.2	−0.5	0.8	−1.4	−0.7	−8.4	−2.7
Muslim	−0.6	−5.4	−1.6	−1.5	−8.9	−3.0	−0.7	−5.8	−1.8
Rest	−1.4	−4.3	−2.4	−6.5	3.5	−3.3	−1.8	−3.7	−2.4
Total	−0.7	−5.8	−2.2	−0.3	−3.5	−1.5	−0.7	−5.6	−2.2
All India	−0.9	−4.5	−2.1	−0.3	−2.1	−1.0	−0.7	−4.3	−1.9

Source: Estimated from NSSO Employment Unemployment Survey, 2004–5 and 2011–12

groups, varying between the highest, namely, the HHCs, at the rate of 2.7 percent, to the lowest, i.e., Muslims, at 1.8 percent. The CSTs have witnessed the highest decline, at the rate of 2.8 percent within STs. It is to be noted that the decline is observed among both the male and female population across socio-religious groups. It is less than 1 percent among males, though much more among females – 8.4 percent in the case of HHCs, followed by HOBCs at the rate of 6.5 percent, STs at the rate of 4.8 percent, and SCs at the rate of 5.2 percent per annum.

Unemployment rate

The unemployment rate is estimated by using the current daily status (CDS) method that depicts the supply side of the labour market. In the NER, the unemployment rate is 7.4 percent, which is relatively higher compared to that of 5.6 percent in India in 2011–12 (see Table 3.7). Female unemployment rates are higher than male in both the NER and India. In fact, the rate in the NER is almost double that of India.

The unemployment rate differs substantially according to socioreligious groups in the NER. The highest unemployment rate is observed among HHCs followed by STs and SCs, while the lowest is among Muslims. Within STs, the CSTs face a high unemployment

Table 3.7 Unemployment rate by current daily status across socioreligious groups (in %): 2011–12

Socio-religious group	Rural			Urban			Rural + Urban		
	Male	Female	Total	Male	Female	Total	Male	Female	Total
HST	6.0	13.7	7.3	13.9	31.1	17.2	6.5	15.0	8.1
CST	7.9	10.3	8.7	10.5	17.1	12.5	8.5	11.7	9.6
All ST	6.5	10.0	7.5	10.7	17.8	12.7	7.2	11.3	8.3
SC	6.2	10.8	7.0	8.9	22.1	11.1	7.0	14.1	8.1
HOBC	6.2	11.8	7.5	4.4	25.0	8.2	5.9	13.8	7.6
HHC	6.1	22.1	8.1	7.7	24.1	11.3	6.6	23.0	9.2
Muslim	4.2	3.4	4.1	5.2	22.9	6.6	4.3	5.0	4.4
Rest	4.8	0.4	3.5	4.5	6.2	5.1	4.7	0.8	3.6
Total	5.8	10.4	6.7	7.6	21.4	10.5	6.1	12.6	7.4
All India	5.4	5.9	5.5	5.0	8.5	5.6	5.3	6.6	5.6

Source: Estimated from NSSO Employment Unemployment Survey, 2011–12

rate (9.6 percent), and the lowest is among Muslims, with 4.4 percent. The unemployment among males is lower than among females. The pattern of the male unemployment rate is almost same as the aggregate. A large share of high unemployment among HHCs is because of the higher unemployment rate (23 percent) among its female counterparts. Similarly, HSTs females have also registered high unemployment (15 percent), followed by SC females (14.1 percent), the lowest being among Muslims (5 percent).

Employment opportunities in India improved from 2004–5 to 2011–12, while they got worst in the NER. The unemployment rate during this period in India declined marginally, at 5.3 percent per annum, while in the NER, it increased at the rate of 1.6 percent per annum (see Table 3.8). In the region, the STs have registered an 11.8 percent unemployment rate, while it declined sharply among Muslims to 6.6 percent. Within STs, the unemployment rate increased by 24.3 percent among CSTs and 3.1 percent among HSTs.

Structure of employment

In the following section, the structure of employment is discussed based on occupational and industrial groups by socio-religious

Table 3.8 Growth rate in unemployment rate across socio-religious groups (in %): 2004–5 and 2011–12

	Rural			Urban			Rural + Urban		
	Male	Female	Total	Male	Female	Total	Male	Female	Total
HST	1.1	7.6	2.7	8.0	−1.5	5.2	2.0	6.9	3.1
CST	22.9	34.8	27.2	13.3	20.7	15.9	20.5	30.9	24.3
All ST	8.5	17.7	11.4	10.6	12.5	11.1	9.2	17.2	11.8
SC	−6.7	−1.1	−5.6	−3.2	6.1	−0.9	−5.4	2.1	−3.8
HOBC	2.3	14.2	5.4	−8.3	−2.6	−6.0	0.1	7.4	2.3
HHC	−2.6	2.6	−1.9	−0.4	3.4	2.3	−1.8	3.1	−0.3
Muslim	−4.7	−16.8	−6.6	−8.9	1.4	−7.2	−5.2	−12.6	−6.6
Rest	−6.8	−33.9	−10.1	−4.5	0.5	−2.8	−6.5	−25.6	−9.5
Total	−0.1	6.0	1.4	−0.7	4.1	1.2	−0.1	6.3	1.6
All India	−5.2	−5.8	−5.4	−5.5	−4.4	−5.2	−5.3	−5.0	−5.3

Source: Estimated from NSSO Employment Unemployment Survey, 2004–5 and 2011–12

groups in the NER. The NSSO provides occupational groups, as used in the National Classification of Occupation (NCO). Prior to the 2011–12 round of the NSSO survey, the 1968 NCO was used, while the 2004 NCO was used in 2011–12. There is a significant difference between these two NCOs, and it is not possible to use the concordance at the three-digit level to make two NCOs, as given in the NSSO employment-unemployment survey, comparable. In the 1968 NCO, the main criterion of occupation classification is 'type of work performed', irrespective of the industrial classification of the establishment where workers are engaged; however, in the 2004 NCO, skill level and skill specialisation are considered for classification of occupation. The new 2008 National Classification of Industries (NIC) is used in the 2011–12 NSSO Employment-Unemployment survey, which is also not strictly comparable with the earlier 2004 NIC. In the 2008 NIC, new industry groups are added to accommodate new professions that are emerging in the economy due to technological advancement.

Distribution of employment by occupation

The occupational distribution of workers in NER shows that 62.4 percent of the workers in the 15–59 age group are engaged in two major occupation groups, namely, skilled agricultural workers and elementary occupations (see Table 3.9). The share of these two occupation groups in India is about 57.3 percent. Following these two occupational groups, 7 percent of the workers are engaged in craft and related trades. In the region, the share of professionals is about 6.5 percent as compared to that of 3.8 percent in India.

The share of occupational groups by socio-religious groups shows that a high share of workers, ranging between 22 percent and 54 percent of workers belonging to the HHC and STs, respectively, are engaged in skilled agriculture work. Within STs, the highest proportion, comprising 56 percent of HSTs, are engaged in this particular occupation group. In elementary occupations, the share of workers belonging to SCs, HOBCs and HSTs is substantially high as compared to the average share in the region. The share of legislators, senior officials and managers among Christians and the Hindu high caste is higher than in other socio-religious groups. In most of the white collar jobs in the region, jobs are dominated by CSTs, SCs, HOBCs and HHCs.

Table 3.9 Distribution of workers of age 15–59 years by occupation group across socio-religious groups (in %): 2011–12

Occupation groups	HST	CST	ST	SC	HOBC	HHC	Muslim	Rest	Total	India
Legislators, senior officials and managers	1.1	7.8	4.9	1.4	0.9	3.4	1.6	2.5	2.8	7.1
Professionals	3.8	3.0	3.3	8.5	7.7	12.4	5.5	0.7	6.5	3.8
Technicians and associate	2.2	7.5	5.4	2.9	3.7	6.9	2.1	2.6	4.3	3.5
Clerks	0.9	2.4	1.7	1.3	1.8	4.3	0.8	0.5	1.8	2.1
Service workers	8.5	8.2	8.1	10.0	10.8	17.3	10.1	3.7	10.4	7.8
Skilled agricultural workers	56.5	50.9	54.3	36.7	35.0	21.9	49.1	39.5	42.3	29.7
Craft and related trades workers	4.8	5.0	4.7	11.4	8.1	5.8	8.4	7.6	7.0	13.3
Plant and machine operators	1.0	2.7	2.0	2.7	2.1	4.5	2.7	3.0	2.6	5.0
Elementary occupations	19.5	12.3	14.9	21.3	28.8	20.3	16.0	38.7	20.1	27.6
Workers not classified	1.5	0.2	0.8	3.8	1.0	3.2	3.9	1.3	2.1	0.1
Total	100	100	100	100	100	100	100	100	100	100

Source: Estimated from NSSO Employment Unemployment Survey, 2011–12

Distribution of workers by industry group

The distribution of workers by industry groups is presented in Table 3.10. It shows that in the NER, more than half the workers are engaged in the agriculture sector, 16.8 percent in manufacturing and 32.4 percent in the service sector. The share of workers in the manufacturing sector in the NER (16.8 percent) is substantially lower than the all-India share of 25.2 percent. This shows the low industrialisation status of the region. The distribution of workers is substantially high in the agricultural sector in each socio-religious group, varying from the highest, 60.0 percent among STs, to the lowest, 27.9 percent among HHCs, followed by 39.0 percent among SCs. Within STs, the highest share of workers engaged in the agricultural sector is 68.6 percent among OSTs, followed by 64.1 percent among HSTs and 55.6 percent among CSTs. In the manufacturing sector, SCs constitute the highest share of workers, at 21.8 percent followed by HHC and Muslims, with 19.4 and 16.8 percent each; the lowest is 10.8 percent among OSTs. In the service sector, the share of workers belonging to HHC is substantially high, at 52.7 percent, followed by 39.2 percent among SCs and 21.3 percent among HSTs. Thus, the share of workers belonging to STs is largely engaged in the agricultural sector, while more than half of the workers belonging to HHCs are engaged in the service sector.

Table 3.10 Distribution of workers of age 15–59 years across major industry group by socio-religious group (in %): 2011–12

Socio-religious groups	Agriculture	Industry	Services	Total
HST	64.1	14.6	21.3	100
CST	55.6	13.6	30.8	100
Other ST	68.6	10.8	20.6	100
All ST	60.0	13.7	26.3	100
SC	39.0	21.8	39.2	100
HOBC	52.6	16.7	30.7	100
HHC	27.9	19.4	52.7	100
Muslim	54.9	16.8	28.2	100
Rest	66.2	21.0	12.7	100
Total	50.9	16.8	32.4	100
All India	46.1	25.2	28.7	100

Source: Estimated from NSSO Employment Unemployment Survey, 2011–12

The industry and service sectors have provided higher rates of opportunities employment between 2004–5 and 2011–12. The share of workers in the industry and service sectors has increased at the rate of 10.1 percent and 2.1 percent, respectively, during this period, while the agriculture sector declined at the rate of 3.1 percent (see Figure 3.1). The share of workers engaged in the industry sector in the NER is relatively higher than all India. In the industry sector, the share of workers has increased across all the socio-religious groups. However, it is the lowest among Muslims (6.0 percent) and highest among the STs (13.7 percent) and HHCs (12.0 percent). In the service sector, the share of workers has increased among all the socio-religious groups, except in the case of SCs, and Muslims whose employment share has declined by less than 1 percent. The highest growth in the share of employment is among the STs, at 4.4 percent per annum, while the lowest is among SCs at −0.4 percent.

The growth in the employment in service sectors has increased at a substantially high annual rate of more than 10.1 percent during 2004–5 to 2011–12. Further enquiry into identifying the industries with a high concentration of workers across socio-religious groups within the service sector shows that the highest (40 percent) percentage of workers are engaged in trade, followed by education (13.4 percent), public administration (12.7 percent) and transport (11.2 percent) (see Table 3.11). In trade, Muslims form the highest percentage (52.8 percent), followed by HHCs (44.6 percent).

Quality of employment

The quality of employment is more important than just providing employment opportunity of any sort for sustainable growth of the economy. In fact, the sustainable development goals (SDGs) also signify the importance of quality of employment in its specific target of achieving full and productive employment, decent work for all women and men, including young people and persons with disabilities, and equal pay for work of equal value by 2030, under Goal 8: 'Promote inclusive and sustainable economic growth, employment and decent work for all'. In this chapter, the quality of employment is measured in terms of the workers' activity status, nature of employment, education level of workers and informality of employment.

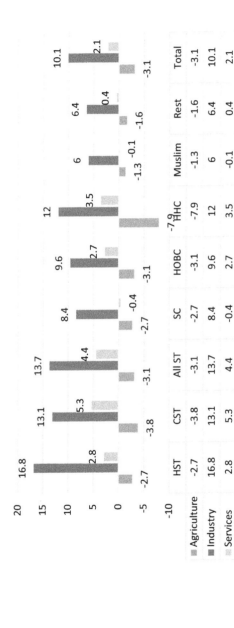

	HST	CST	All ST	SC	HOBC	HHC	Muslim	Rest	Total
Agriculture	-2.7	-3.8	-3.1	-2.7	-3.1	-7.9	-1.3	-1.6	-3.1
Industry	16.8	13.1	13.7	8.4	9.6	12	6	6.4	10.1
Services	2.8	5.3	4.4	-0.4	2.7	3.5	-0.1	0.4	2.1

■ Agriculture ■ Industry ■ Services

Figure.3.1 Annual growth in share of workers by industry group (in %) – 2004–5 and 2011–12

Source: Estimated from NSSO Employment Unemployment Survey, 2004–5 and 2011–12

Table 3.11 Distribution of workers of age 15–59 years by industry groups in service sector across socio-religious groups (in %): 2011–12

Industry groups	HST	CST	ST	SC	HOBC	HHC	Muslim	Rest	Total
Trade	44.6	31.9	35.0	39.3	38.5	40.1	52.8	24.0	40.4
Transport	8.1	9.5	9.0	11.3	9.7	8.8	19.4	16.7	11.2
Accommodation	6.9	4.7	5.4	4.1	5.1	2.2	0.8	7.4	3.7
Finance	1.0	0.7	0.8	0.6	1.8	3.9	0.2	0.7	1.6
Professional	0.2	0.2	0.4	2.0	0.4	2.2	0.2	0.9	1.0
Administrative	1.9	1.2	1.5	0.9	1.1	1.5	0.4	2.0	1.2
Public administration	10.7	28.5	23.0	8.1	9.9	12.7	3.5	13.6	12.7
Education	12.3	17.8	16.4	7.6	14.7	14.8	9.4	18.3	13.4
Health	2.0	2.5	2.6	0.7	1.8	1.8	1.5	4.4	1.8
Repair & service activities	3.5	1.4	2.0	8.2	8.8	5.1	4.3	5.7	5.3
Employers of domestic personnel	8.6	0.3	2.9	13.4	7.4	4.7	7.0	4.7	6.2
Rest	0.1	1.2	1.0	3.9	0.8	2.1	0.4	1.7	1.5
Total	100.0	100.0	100.0	100.0	100.0	100.0	100.0	100.0	100.0

Source: Estimated from NSSO Employment Unemployment Survey, 2011–12

Employment by activity status

The activity status of workers could be grouped in three major categories, namely, self-employment, regular salaried or wage earner, and casual labour. Self-employment refers to those who are self-employed, employers and unpaid family members. Casual labour workers are further classified into those who work in public work and other work. About 64.7 percent of the total workers in the NER are engaged in self-employment, followed by 18.3 percent in casual work, and about 17 percent are regular wage earners (Table 3.12). The share of self-employed workers is substantially high across socio-religious groups. The share of workers in the self-employed category is highest among Muslims (75.1 percent), followed by STs (70.7 percent) and SCs (64.2 percent), and lowest among HHCs (53.8 percent). Within STs, the HSTs constitute a higher percentage (74.6), followed by CSTs (67.2 percent). In the case of casual labour in public works, where workers were paid good remuneration and which is considered better than other casual work, the share of workers is higher among CSTs (4.1 percent), followed by SCs (3.6 percent) and all STs (3.5 percent), Muslims being at the lowest (1.6 percent). The workers belonging to HHCs and HOBCs have higher share in the other casual labour. The share of workers engaged in regular salaried work is highest (26.9 percent) among HHCs and lowest (6.3 percent) among Muslims.

Table 3.12 Distribution of workers of age 15–59 years by activity status (in %): 2011–12

Socio-religious group	Self-employed	Regular worker	Casual labour		Total
			Public work	Others	
HST	74.6	8.0	2.6	14.7	100
CST	67.2	19.4	4.1	9.4	100
All ST	70.7	14.8	3.5	11.0	100
SC	64.2	16.4	3.6	15.8	100
HOBC	55.5	22.3	2.5	19.6	100
HHC	53.8	26.9	3.0	16.3	100
Muslim	75.1	6.3	1.6	17.1	100
Rest	51.1	27.7	2.4	18.7	100
Total	64.7	17.0	2.8	15.5	100
India	50.7	19.7	1.4	28.2	100

Source: Estimated from NSSO Employment Unemployment Survey, 2011–12

Figure 3.2 shows that there is a positive growth rate of workers in the regular salaried and casual work activity status during 2004–5 and 2011–12, but the share of workers in self-employment has declined at –0.7 percent during the same period. The growth rate of workers in regular salaried work is highest at 1.8 percent among all activity status. Across socio-religious groups it is shown that CSTs have the highest growth rate in regular worker and lowest among Muslims at –3.2 percent. The growth rate of CST workers in all activity status is highest among all socio-religious groups.

Employment by enterprise type

The NSSO employment-unemployment survey collected information regarding the type of enterprise for non-farm workers. In the analysis, we have distributed the non-farm regular workers by enterprise type. In the NER, the share of workers by enterprise type shows that a substantially higher proportion of workers are engaged in public enterprises. By contrast, in India, more than 70 percent of the workers are engaged in private enterprises, and the remaining 30 percent are in government enterprises (see Figure 3.3). The share of workers by socio-religious groups shows that a high proportion of non-farm regular workers belonging to CSTs (79.3 percent), followed by all STs (76.8 percent) and HSTs (69.6 percent), are in public enterprises. The representation of SCs (46.9 percent) and Muslims (53.6 percent) in government enterprises is substantially low compared to other socio-religious groups in the NER. From 2004–5 to 2011–12, the share of workers in government enterprise declined at the rate of less than 1 percent. The highest decline is registered among SCs, HOBCs and Muslims, while in private sectors, the share of STs declined substantially (see Figure 3.4).

Employment by level of education

The educational level of workers is also an important indicator for measuring the quality of workers. In this analysis, we have classified the level of education into three layers, namely, low, medium and high. Low educational level stretches up to the primary level including illiterates; the medium level consists of middle and secondary education; and the high level consists of higher secondary, diploma, graduation and above. In the NER, 15.1 percent of the workers have high educational levels, as compared to 18.4 percent

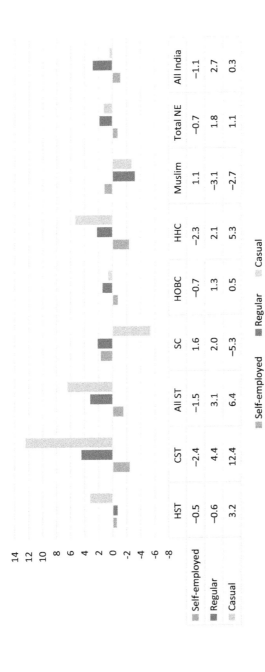

	HST	CST	All ST	SC	HOBC	HHC	Muslim	Total NE	All India
Self-employed	-0.5	-2.4	-1.5	1.6	-0.7	-2.3	1.1	-0.7	-1.1
Regular	-0.6	4.4	3.1	2.0	1.3	2.1	-3.1	1.8	2.7
Casual	3.2	12.4	6.4	-5.3	0.5	5.3	-2.7	1.1	0.3

■ Self-employed ■ Regular ■ Casual

Figure 3.2 Annual growth rate in share of workers by activity status (in %) – 2004–5 and 2011–12

Source: Estimated from NSSO Employment Unemployment Survey, 2004–5 and 2011–12

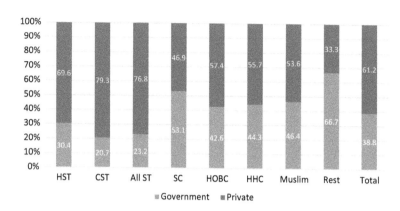

Figure 3.3 Distribution of regular wage-earning workers in the non-farm sector by enterprise type (in %) – 2011–12

Source: Estimated from NSSO Employment Unemployment Survey, 2011–12

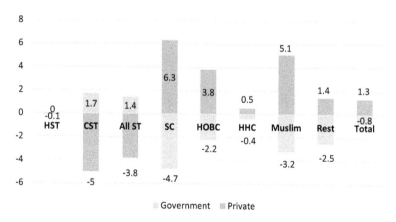

Figure 3.4 Annual growth in the share of workers in government and public sector enterprises by socio-religious groups (in %) – 2004–5 to 2011–12

Source: Estimated from NSSO Employment Unemployment Survey, 2011–12

in India in 2011–12 (see Table 3.13). The highest share of workers having high education levels belongs to HHCs (29.3 percent), followed by CSTs (19.4 percent), SCs (10.8 percent) and Muslims at the lowest (7.5 percent). The medium-level education in this region

Table 3.13 Distribution of workers of age 15–59 years by level of education in different socio-religious groups (in %): 2011–12

Socio-religious groups	No education	Low education	Medium education	High education	Total
HST	13.4	43.9	35.4	7.3	100
CST	6.9	31.5	42.2	19.4	100
All ST	10.7	36.6	38.2	14.4	100
SC	13.5	39.1	36.6	10.8	100
HOBC	14.8	29.2	39.4	16.6	100
HHC	8.4	23.0	39.3	29.3	100
Muslim	17.6	42.1	32.8	7.5	100
Rest	25.7	38.8	28.3	7.2	100
Total	13.3	34.5	37.1	15.1	100
India	28.2	23.9	29.6	18.4	100

Source: Estimated from NSSO Employment Unemployment Survey, 2011–12

is relatively high as compared to that in India. The share of workers having medium-level education is more or less equally distributed across socio-religious groups, with the lowest share among Muslims. In comparison to high- and medium-level education, the share of low-level education is substantially high among Muslims (42.1 percent). In the no education category, the share of Muslims is highest (17.6 percent), followed by HOBCs (14.8 percent) and SCs (13.5 percent), while the share of workers with low education is substantially low among CSTs (6.9 percent).

Informality of employment

The informal sector worker and informal worker are gaining attention in recent times. In India, there has not been any single definition of the informal sector. Different agencies of the government of India like NSS, DGET, etc., use varying definitions of the informal sector, depending on the specific requirement of each organisation. Keeping in view the absence of a uniform definition of the informal/unorganised sector in India, the National Commission for Enterprises in the Unorganised Sector (NCEUS) formulated a harmonised definition of informal/unorganised sector employment and informal/unorganised employment in India (Naik 2009). In this study, to analyse the informality of employment, we estimated the informal sector worker and informal worker by using the definition of NCEUS.

Table 3.14 provides information on the distribution of workers by nature of workplace, grouping into the informal and formal sector on the one hand and by the nature of work in which they are engaged on the other. Hence, they are divided into informal and formal workers. In the NER, the share of workers in the informal sector in the NER is 78.1 percent, while the all-India share is 82.1 percent. However, the share of informal workers is 89.9 percent, which is much closer to that in India (91.9 percent). The share of workers engaged in the informal sector is substantially low among HHCs (67.3 percent) and HOBCs (68.1 percent), while the share of other socio-religious groups varies from 81 percent to 90 percent. The share of informal workers amongst Muslims and HSTs is very high – 96.7 percent Muslims and 94.7 percent HSTs are informal workers, whereas only 80.5 percent HHCs and 84.5 percent CSTs are informal workers.

The issue of informalisation in India is a growing problem. Informalisation of workers occurs in both informal and formal sectors, although it is substantially higher in the former sector. However, the formal sector, which is considered to be stable and secure, also employs a large percentage share of informal workers. They are engaged in the formal sector with no social security and job security. The share of informal workers in the organised sector in NER is 55.2 percent, (see Table 3.15), which is relatively lower than India

Table 3.14 Distribution of workers by informal and formal sector and workers across socio-religious groups (in %): 2011–12

Socio-religious groups	Sector			Worker		
	Informal	Formal	Total	Informal	Formal	Total
HST	88.2	11.8	100	94.7	5.3	100
CST	76.5	23.5	100	84.5	15.5	100
All ST	81.2	18.8	100	88.6	11.4	100
SC	83.9	16.1	100	92.5	7.5	100
HOBC	68.1	31.9	100	90.3	9.7	100
HHC	67.3	32.7	100	80.5	19.5	100
Muslim	90.7	9.3	100	96.7	3.3	100
Rest	62.3	37.7	100	93.0	7.0	100
Total	78.1	21.9	100	89.9	10.1	100
India	82.1	17.9	100	91.9	8.1	100

Source: Estimated from NSSO Employment Unemployment Survey, 2011–12

Table 3.15 Distribution of informal and formal workers in the informal
and formal sectors (in %): 2011-12

Socio-religious group	Informal sector			Formal sector		
	Informal worker	Formal worker	Total	Informal worker	Formal worker	Total
HST	99.8	0.2	100	56.3	43.7	100
CST	99.7	0.3	100	35.0	65.0	100
All ST	99.7	0.3	100	40.5	59.5	100
SC	99.6	0.4	100	55.2	44.8	100
HOBC	99.9	0.1	100	69.8	30.2	100
HHC	98.6	1.4	100	43.2	56.8	100
Muslim	99.8	0.2	100	65.6	34.4	100
Rest	100	0.0	100	81.5	18.5	100
Total	99.6	0.4	100	55.2	44.8	100
India	99.6	0.4	100	56.4	43.6	100

Source: Estimated from NSSO Employment Unemployment Survey, 2004-5 and 2011-12

as a whole. The share of informal workers in the formal sector by socio-religious group shows that the share is high among HOBCs (69.8 percent), followed by Muslims (65.6 percent), while the lowest is among STs and HHCs in the NER. The share of formal workers in the informal sector is low, at only 0.4 percent.

The growth rate of workers in different sectors and types of work for the NER and India shows both good and bad news (see Table 3.16). The good part is that the share of workers in unorganised sectors has declined at the rate of 0.9 percent on one hand, and on the other hand, the share of workers in the organised sector has increased at the rate of 4.9 percent in the NER during 2004-5 and 2011-12. The other side of the story is a bit dismal, as the share of informal workers in the organised sector has increased at a high rate of 11.5 percent in comparison to the all-India level of 6.8 percent. At the all-India level, when the growth rate of formal workers in the organised sector is 0.9 percent, the same is declining at 2.2 percent per year in the NER. The highest declining growth rate of formal workers in the organised sector is recorded for HOBC (-7.2 percent), followed by Muslims (-7 percent) and SCs (-3.6 percent), whereas there is a minor improvement recorded in the growth rate for STs and HHCs. This shows that a high degree of informalisation of the formal sector is occurring in the NER.

Table 3.16 Annual growth in share of workers by nature of sector (in %): from 2004–5 to 2011–12

Socio-religious group	Informal sector			Formal sector			All sector		
	Informal worker	Formal worker	Total	Informal worker	Formal worker	Total	Informal worker	Formal worker	Total
HST	-0.5	-4.7	-0.6	19.8	-3.1	5.2	0.2	-3.1	0.0
CST	-1.5	13.2	-1.5	17.1	3.3	6.7	-0.5	3.4	0.0
All ST	-1.1	5.5	-1.1	16.5	1.9	6.1	-0.2	2.0	0.0
SC	0.1	15.6	0.1	2.9	-3.6	-0.5	0.3	-3.2	0.0
HOBC	-0.7	-13.3	-0.7	9.2	-7.2	1.7	1.1	-7.3	0.0
HHC	-2.1	22.5	-2.0	14.0	1.2	5.4	-0.4	1.7	0.0
Muslim	-0.2	-8.6	-0.2	11.3	-7.0	1.8	0.3	-7.1	0.0
Rest	1.2	-40.8	1.1	4.4	-13.7	-1.6	2.2	-13.9	0.0
Total	-0.9	4.9	-0.9	11.5	-2.2	3.6	0.2	-2.0	0.0
All India	-0.7	-1.4	-0.7	6.8	0.9	3.9	-0.1	0.8	0.0

Source: Estimated from NSSO Employment Unemployment Survey, 2004–5 and 2011–12

Conclusion

This chapter aims to understand the structure and growth of employment in the NER based on the NSSO survey on Employment and Unemployment for the years 2004–5 and 2011–12. The size, structure and quality of employment are estimated for different socio-religious groups. The total workforce in the NER is 15.4 million, accounting for 51.6 percent of the total 46.1 million population in the working age group of 15–59 years old in 2011–12.

A few of the aggregate features arise from the workforce in the NER. One, both the population and workforce have increased at a higher rate of growth annually in the NER as compared to all-India from 1983 to 2011–12. The annual growth in population and the total workforce is 2.5 percent and 2.2 percent per annum, respectively, in the NER, while it is 2.4 percent and 1.8 percent, respectively, in India. Two, the WPR is relatively low in the NER (51.6 percent) as compared to India (56.7 percent). The share of marginal workers to total workers, in fact, is low in the NER as compared to India. From 1983 to 2011–12, the WPR declined at the rate of less than 1 percent in both the NER and India, but the former registered relatively low decline. Three, the male and female differentials in WPR are wide in both the NER and India, although the former registered a substantially low female WPR. Four, the share of female main workers to total workers is substantially lower than that of India, and the share of female marginal workers to total female workers in the NER is close to India's, which registered a sharp decline after 2004–5.

The disaggregated level across socio-religious groups in the NER shows diverse features. One, the WPR is the highest among STs (57 percent) and lowest among HHCs (45.3 percent). The high WPR in the NER is largely because of large female participation. The group with low WPR is associated with low female participation. The female WPR among STs is the highest (36.6 percent) and lowest (13.6 percent) among HHCs. Two, rural areas have higher WPR in most socio-religious groups, along with the female WPR, but it is lower among HHCs. Three, the unemployment rate is highest among HHCs and lowest among Muslims (9.2 percent and 4.4 percent, respectively). However, the high WPR in the NER is associated with a high male unemployment rate. Therefore, male unemployment rates are substantially higher among STs, which also registered a high WPR because of high female participation.

The structure of employment brings out some important features. One, a large share of workers in the NER are engaged in skilled agriculture, with the highest proportion among STs (54 percent) and lowest among HHCs (22.2 percent). This is followed by elementary occupations, the highest among HOBCs (29 percent) and lowest among STs (15 percent). Two, a majority of the workers are engaged in the agricultural sector, followed by services and industry, in the NER. However, the share of STs and Muslims in agriculture is high, and the share of HHCs and SCs is low. The share of workers belonging to HHCs is substantially high (53 percent) in the service sector.

The quality of employment is measured in terms of activity status, enterprise type and education level. There emerge a few features. One, the share of workers receiving a regular salary is highest among HHCs (27 percent) and lowest among Muslims (7 percent), while the share in casual labour is highest (22 percent) among HOBCs, followed by SCs. Two, a large share of workers belonging to CST are engaged in the government sector. In the government sector, STs are in the highest (77 percent) proportion and SCs the lowest (47 percent). Three, the share of workers with a high education level is relatively low in the NER as compared to India as a whole, and the share is substantially high (29 percent) among HHCs and lowest (7.5 percent) among Muslims.

Finally, this chapter analyses how informalisation is becoming prominent in the NER. It is to be noted that informalisation may occur either at the level of sectors or workers. In the NER, the share of workers engaged in the unorganised sector is low as compared to informal workers. The share of workers in the unorganised sector is 78 percent, while the share of informal workers is 90 percent. The share of workers in the unorganised sector and that of informal workers are lower in the case of HHCs, but it is higher in case of other socio-religious groups. The share of formal workers in the unorganised sectors and that of informal workers among HHCs are 1.4 percent and 56.8 percent, respectively.

Notes

1 The informal sector workers are those engaged in the informal sector, which consists of all unincorporated private enterprises owned by individuals or households engaged in the sale and production of goods and services operated on a proprietary or partnership basis, with less than 10 total workers.
2 Informal workers consists of those working in the informal sector or households, excluding regular workers with social security benefits provided by the employers and the workers in the formal sector without any employment and social security benefits provided by the employers.

References

Abraham, Vinoj. 2009. 'Employment Growth in Rural India: Distress-Driven?', *Economic and Political Weekly*, 54(16): 97–104.

Bhattacharya, Badri Baran and S. Sakthivel. 2004. 'Regional Growth and Disparity in India: Comparison of Pre- and Post-reform Decades', *Economic and Political Weekly*, 39(10): 1071–1077.

Bhaumik, Sankar Kumar. 2007. 'Growth and Composition of Rural Non-farm Employment in India in the Era of Economic Reforms', *The Indian Economic Journal*, 53(3): 40–65.

Chowdhury, Subhanil. 2011. 'Employment in India: What Does the Latest Data Show?', *Economic and Political Weekly*, 46(32): 23–26.

Kannan, K. P. and G. Raveendran. 2012. 'Counting and Profiling the Missing Labour Force', *Economic and Political Weekly*, 47(6): 77–80.

Naik, Ajaya Kumar. 2009. 'Informal Sector and Informal Workers in India'. Paper presented at IARIW-SAIM Conference on 'Measuring the Informal Economy in Developing Countries', Kathmandu, Nepal, 23–26 September.

Neetha, N. 2014. 'Crisis in Female Employment: Analysis across Social Groups', *Economic and Political Weekly*, 49(47): 50–59.

Ramaswamy, K. V. 2007. 'Regional Dimension of Growth and Employment', *Economic and Political Weekly*, 42(49): 47–56.

Rangarajan, C., Padma Iyer Kaul and Seema. 2007. 'Revisiting Employment and Growth', *ICRA Bulletin (Money & Finance)*, 3(2): 57–68.

Rangarajan, C., Padma Iyer Kaul and Seema. 2008. 'Employment Performance of the States', *ICRA Bulletin (Money & Finance)*, November, 1–16.

Srivastava, Nisha and Ravi Srivastava. 2010. 'Women, Work, and Employment Outcome', *Economic and Political Weekly*, 45(28): 49–63.

Sundaram, K. 2001. 'Employment – Unemployment Situation in the Nineties: Some Results From NSS 55th Round Survey', *Economic and Political Weekly*, 36(11): 931–940.

Sundaram, K. 2007. 'Employment and Poverty in India, 2000–2005', *Economic and Political Weekly*, 42(30): 3121–3131.

Thorat Sukhadeo, Nitin Tagade and Ajaya Kumar Naik. 2016. 'How and Why? Prejudice against Reservation Policies', *Economic and Political Weekly*, 51(8): 61–69.

Venkatanarayana, M. and S.V. Naik. 2013. 'Growth and Structure of Workforce in India: An Analysis of Census 2011 Data', Retrieved from https://mpra.ub.uni-muenchen.de/48003/1/MPRA_paper_48003.pdf. Accessed in May 2018.

Chapter 4

Women's employment in North-East India

Trends and patterns[1]

Bornali Borah

The employment performance of India in the high-growth post-reform period has been the subject of intense debate and controversy, especially with regard to the appallingly low female workforce participation. Calculating women's work in labour force, however, suffers from a lot of biases – including conceptual and measurement-related issues implicit in the identification of women workers within the labour force or cultural biases. The conceptual and definitional problems that have conveniently narrowed down the spectrum of accounted work and labour in a way to overlook the significance as well as the extent of involvement of women have attracted the attention of many researchers. In India, these defining and operational difficulties in accounting women's work may be considered as one of the significant reasons for the appallingly low rates of participation of women in the labour force. Most of the work/labour burden borne by the women in India unfortunately does not fall under the conventional international standards of measurement for the 'economically active population' adopted by most statistical agencies. However, one cannot deny the fact that equating work with economic activities as accounted by the System of National Accounting (SNA) and encouraging visibility of women in such activities work towards their economic independence and empowerment.

The North-Eastern Region (NER) presents an interesting picture, as the states of this region display a greater participation in the labour force/workforce despite definitional limitations of capturing women's work by conventional labour surveys. However, there also exists the perception that women in the NER enjoy a higher status than the rest of India given that the north-eastern states exhibit improved sex ratios and better literacy rates, despite their backwardness in other developmental outcomes. This calls for an in-depth examination of the employment situation of women in this region. Since the region is characterised by the dominance of subsistence agrarian economies, coupled with a lack of infrastructure and poor industrial base, an increased participation may not be reflective of better living conditions or working conditions for the population, especially women. Thus, a detailed analysis of the region is important to understand the employment situation of females in this region. This leads one to probe into the quality and extent of employment of women workers and their involvement in other activities, as well.

Setting aside details of conceptual and definitional deficiencies that lead to the under-valuation and under-counting of women, this chapter attempts to understand the trends of women's participation and non-participation and the extent and pattern of their participation in the workforce of this region. The analysis is based on the quinquennial NSS surveys data which are supposed to provide comprehensive, detailed and also comparable sources of data on nationwide and state-wise employment/unemployment figures. Also, the NSS is preferred because of their conceptual precision and depth of information on various aspects of the work status of individuals, especially women. These results will be further juxtaposed with a comparison of gender disparities found in the employment scenario of the region. The chapter also sheds light on the workforce participation rates of women belonging to different educational levels. Labour force participation and the domestication trends of women in each of the north-eastern states are further examined as per their income levels, proxied by the monthly per capita expenditure.

The chapter has been divided into seven sections. In the first section, the labour force participation and workforce participation rates (WPR) of men and women in the eight north-eastern states, along with the regional and national average data, is discussed for the last five quinquennial rounds of the NSS covering the period from 1993–4 to 2011–12. The second section deals with the employment scenario of men and women, comparing and analysing gender differentials within the region. Agriculture being the prime avenue of employment, absorbing the maximum number of workers, the share of employment by males and females as well as agriculture's share of the net state domestic product (NSDP) has been also studied in this section. The third section discusses the unemployment problem in the NER, especially for those who are educated and unemployed. The fourth section further deals with the distribution of women from the working age group (i.e., 15–59 years of age) in various activities, including work as well as non-work (invisible) activities, etc. The participation of women in the workforce as per their education level is studied in the fifth section. Participation of women from different income levels in the labour force and domestic activities is studied in the sixth and seventh sections.

Labour force and workforce participation rates

The labour force refers to the population which supplies or offers to supply labour for pursuing economic activities for the production of goods and services and hence includes both 'employed' and 'unemployed' persons. The labour force participation rate (LFPR) is defined as the proportion of persons/person-days in the labour force to the total persons. The workforce, according to the usual status (principal status + subsidiary status), includes (a) persons who worked for a relatively long part of the 365 days preceding the date of survey and (b) those from among the remaining population who had worked at least for 30 days. The trends discussed in this chapter pertaining to the working age population, i.e., those 15–59 years of age, and their employment status are taken according to the usual status (ps+ss), i.e., by considering the usual principal status and subsidiary status economic activity together (see Table 4.1). These ratios are given per 1000 persons.

Table 4.1 Labour force participation rate (per 1000) for persons according to the usual status (ps+ss), 1993–4 to 2011–12

States	Year	Rural		Urban	
		Male	Female	Male	Female
Arunachal Pradesh	1993–4	506	410	525	109
	1999–2000	425	310	406	110
	2004–5	505	485	466	151
	2009–10	507	295	454	153
	2011–12	492	282	475	139
Assam	1993–4	541	172	559	124
	1999–2000	546	161	565	138
	2004–5	564	216	591	120

States	Year	Rural		Urban	
		Male	Female	Male	Female
	2009–10	573	168	550	107
	2011–12	564	129	573	97
Manipur	1993–4	483	311	456	230
	1999–2000	506	257	478	225
	2004–5	531	354	482	236
	2009–10	519	221	497	152
	2011–12	523	270	483	204
Meghalaya	1993–4	622	493	505	196
	1999–2000	559	419	407	211
	2004–5	572	480	470	314
	2009–10	582	373	483	235
	2011–12	529	392	515	210
Mizoram	1993–4	537	318	486	266
	1999–2000	563	441	487	265
	2004–5	597	441	491	288
	2009–10	606	410	534	298
	2011–12	599	405	507	267
Nagaland	1993–4	448	216	406	105
	1999–2000	532	451	433	217
	2004–5	561	511	471	277
	2009–10	555	362	465	164
	2011–12	590	371	509	224
Sikkim	1993–4	566	194	588	148
	1999–2000	519	245	557	225
	2004–5	570	323	564	177
	2009–10	584	320	602	150
	2011–12	586	492	628	274
Tripura	1993–4	530	136	529	150
	1999–2000	507	76	522	227
	2004–5	607	125	605	230
	2009–10	615	235	612	186
	2011–12	599	287	594	260
North-Eastern Region	1993–4	529	281	507	166
	1999–2000	520	295	482	202
	2004–5	563	367	518	224
	2009–10	568	298	525	181
	2011–12	560	329	536	209
All-India	1993–4	561	330	543	165
	1999–2000	540	302	542	147
	2004–5	555	333	570	178
	2009–10	556	265	559	146
	2011–12	553	253	563	155

Source: NSS Reports on Employment and Unemployment Situation in India

The data on women's participation in the labour force and work-force indicates a regional average, which is consistently ahead of the national average in both rural and urban areas. The high rates of women's participation in states like Arunachal Pradesh, Meghalaya, Mizoram and Nagaland contribute to the elevation of the regional average in rural areas, despite the sadly dismal rates in Assam and Tripura. It can also be evinced that Meghalaya and Mizoram contribute significantly to the urban average of women's participation in the labour force in the NER, the total of which exceeds the all-India average.

Workforce participation rates do not exactly follow the same trend as LFPRs (see Table 4.2). The workforce participation aver-age for males of this region is found to be below national average over the years for both rural and urban areas except for the 61st round of NSS (2004–5), where the rural male participation in the workforce exceeds the national average. This could be in response to distress conditions during that period. This upsurge in WPRs is also noted amongst women at the national as well as regional level for this round of NSS. Given that the women's workforce is mostly considered as the reserve army of labour to be pushed into the labour force in times of recession in the developing economies, this calls for a closer look at the type and pattern of employment the women are involved in, before considering the increased partici-pation of women in the workforce of this region as an improvement over non-participation.

The regional average for women's participation in the workforce reveals an increasing participation in the first three rounds followed

Table 4.2 Worker population ratio (per 1000) for persons according to the usual status (ps+ss) for the north-eastern states

States	Year	Rural		Urban	
		Male	Female	Male	Female
Arunachal Pradesh	1993–4	497	409	515	101
	1999–2000	422	310	399	100
	2004–5	500	410	461	148
	2009–10	499	293	438	148
	2011–12	483	278	457	127
Assam	1993–4	516	161	528	93
	1999–2000	529	151	522	112

States	Year	Rural		Urban	
		Male	Female	Male	Female
	2004–5	551	209	551	109
	2009–10	553	158	528	93
	2011–12	540	122	542	90
Manipur	1993–4	476	307	438	222
	1999–2000	495	253	445	211
	2004–5	524	351	456	221
	2009–10	499	212	472	146
	2011–12	510	262	456	182
Meghalaya	1993–4	621	493	499	189
	1999–2000	557	418	393	197
	2004–5	572	478	454	303
	2009–10	580	371	468	214
	2011–12	527	391	503	202
Mizoram	1993–4	528	319	483	264
	1999–2000	555	440	471	259
	2004–5	594	441	484	281
	2009–10	598	404	521	288
	2011–12	591	394	487	249
Nagaland	1993–4	436	230	377	98
	1999–2000	518	441	393	199
	2004–5	549	504	457	257
	2009–10	500	319	436	132
	2011–12	504	312	412	144
Sikkim	1993–4	562	195	580	135
	1999–2000	502	241	519	200
	2004–5	554	318	545	168
	2009–10	556	309	601	150
	2011–12	580	487	609	273
Tripura	1993–4	523	130	498	123
	1999–2000	504	73	494	75
	2004–5	549	85	504	100
	2009–10	583	188	556	191
	2011–12	562	228	525	113
North-Eastern Region	1993–4	520	281	490	153
	1999–2000	510	291	455	169
	2004–5	549	350	489	198
	2009–10	546	282	503	170
	2011–12	537	309	499	173
All-India	1993–4	553	328	520	154
	1999–2000	531	299	518	139
	2004–5	546	327	549	166
	2009–10	547	261	543	138
	2011–12	543	248	546	147

Source: NSS Reports on Employment and Unemployment Situation in India

by a decline in the 66th round (2009–10), but this decline is not sustained in the 68th round (2011–12); instead, larger numbers of women participate in almost all the north-eastern states. To start with, the participation in the 50th round (1993–4) was lower than the national average; however, owing to exceptionally higher WPRs exhibited by states like Arunachal Pradesh, Meghalaya, Mizoram and Nagaland, this region has succeeded in exhibiting a greater participation of women than the national average.

A large measure of literature puts forward that female participation in the labour market is higher in agricultural societies. When one keeps this trend in mind, the higher participation rates of women in this region is expected in the case of the NER, since these states are largely agrarian-based. Therefore, an increased participation in the workforce, in this case, does not necessarily reflect better living or working conditions for the population, especially women, who more often than not are unpaid, especially in these areas.

Nation-wide studies claim that tribal women are economically more active not only because of their economic condition but also because of the high status and relatively lower levels of restrictions laid on them by tribal laws. Thus, there exists the perception that women in the NER enjoy a higher social status than the rest of India given the higher sex ratios and literacy rates that exceed the national average. Another explanation of such high participation among tribal women could be the dependence of tribal population on forests for their livelihood, wherein women mostly engage themselves in processing forest produce.

Male vs female workforce participation

Though the overall participation of women of this region in the workforce is better than the rest of the country, a comparative look at the male versus female participation rates still display a large amount of gender disparity within the region. As in all the other states at the national level, male participation is evidently greater than female participation. Thus, it is clear that equal opportunities for women in the workforce and labour force do not exist despite improved sex ratios and female literacy rates, which are generally considered indicators of better status for women in any region.

The ratio of female to male workers in the rural and urban areas across the north-eastern states show that states like Assam and Tripura exhibit larger gender differentials in work participation than the national scenario. Also, while this gap is narrowed down in the case of rural areas, in urban areas it is more pronounced. The states showing less of this gender gap in participation are Arunachal Pradesh, Meghalaya, Mizoram and Nagaland; however, even these states conform to the urban norms of wider gender gaps. These details are provided in Table 4.3.

However, most rural women who contribute to the increased numbers of this region are involved only in the agricultural sector, which still employs traditional methods of cultivation. The agricultural practices in the region are of two broad distinct types, namely, (a) settled farming practised in the plains, valleys, foothills and terraced slopes and (b) shifting cultivation (*jhum*) practiced on the hill slopes.[2] This could be because of the feminisation[3] of the farm sector, given that the NER is primarily agrarian-based.

Women's work scenarios in a particular region cannot (and must not) be viewed as independent from the employment situation of men. Reddy (1975: 197–212) adopted the ratio of rural female cultivators to male cultivators as one of the explanatory factors in his study exploring the inter-state variations in the female labour force participation among rural women. He also mentions how areas of highly productive agriculture tend to have lower female work participation due to the 'discouraged worker effect' (Blundell et al. 1998). Reddy found that there exists an inverse relationship between density of rural population and female activity; this is because, with higher available employment opportunities, men are likely to be preferred over women for the same. He argues that the higher the density of population in an area, the greater will be the pressure on available employment opportunities. When there would be higher pressure on land, the rural workforce being mostly concentrated on the farm sector, men are likely to be preferred to women, thus leaving fewer opportunities for women to be employed, leading to the 'discouraged worker effect'. However, areas with low agricultural productivity exhibit higher female participation in agriculture, which is actually distress-driven. Along similar lines, Srivastava and Srivastava (2010), in their detailed sector-wise analysis of women's employment, acknowledged the 'creeping feminisation' of agriculture as a result of higher non-farm diversification of the male workforce in the rural sector. More and more men entered diversified occupations in non-agriculture, whereas women largely tended to fill the voids and remain in agriculture, which has been largely stagnant. Women who primarily behave as secondary workers in

Table 4.3 Ratio of female workers to male workers according to the usual status (ps+ss) across the north-eastern region over the last five quinquennial NSS rounds

States	1993–4		1999–2000		2004–5		2009–10		2011–12	
	R	U	R	U	R	U	R	U	R	U
Arunachal	0.823	0.196	0.735	0.251	0.820	0.321	0.587	0.338	0.576	0.278
Assam	0.312	0.176	0.285	0.215	0.379	0.198	0.286	0.176	0.226	0.166
Manipur	0.645	0.507	0.511	0.474	0.670	0.485	0.425	0.309	0.514	0.399
Meghalaya	0.794	0.379	0.750	0.501	0.836	0.667	0.640	0.457	0.742	0.402
Mizoram	0.604	0.547	0.793	0.550	0.742	0.581	0.676	0.553	0.667	0.511
Nagaland	0.528	0.260	0.851	0.506	0.918	0.562	0.638	0.303	0.619	0.350
Sikkim	0.347	0.233	0.480	0.385	0.574	0.308	0.556	0.250	0.840	0.448
Tripura	0.249	0.247	0.145	0.152	0.155	0.198	0.322	0.344	0.406	0.215
NER	0.540	0.313	0.570	0.372	0.636	0.406	0.516	0.339	0.576	0.346
All-India	0.593	0.296	0.563	0.268	0.599	0.302	0.477	0.254	0.457	0.269

Source: Estimated using the Workforce Participation Rates States in the NSS Reports on Employment and Unemployment Situation in India

households tend to show higher participation in times of distress (referred to as added worker effect) (Lundberg 1985). Also, the shift of the male workforce to the non-farm sector often leads to women workers filling up the void, which has been referred to as the feminisation of agriculture. Thus, it becomes essential to look at the links between male and female employment patterns for this region, precisely with respect to agriculture.

A comparison between the female and male agricultural workforce would reveal if there is a shift of the male workforce away from farming, making way for increased participation of women in agriculture. Table 4.4 displays the percentage share of agriculture and allied sectors in the states' NSDP and rural employment in the north-eastern states.

The contribution of agriculture to NSDP (as is evident from the percentage shares) indicates that there has been a decline in the share of agriculture, which in some states like Assam, Manipur and Meghalaya is more consistent when compared to the rest of the north-eastern states, except for Arunachal Pradesh. However, in the case of employment shares of the agricultural sector, there is a shift of workers of both sexes from farm to non-farm sectors at the all-India level, with some fluctuations. In the rural areas of the NER, except for Manipur and Tripura, all the other states of this region show significantly higher rates of women's participation in the agricultural sector compared to men. In the case of Manipur and Tripura, both men and women are seen to have shifted from farming to non-farm sectors. Though the drop of female participation in the farm sector is observed in both rural and urban areas of these states, the shift from farm to non-farm is more pronounced in the urban areas. This leads us to believe that there is a dearth of non-farm employment in the rural areas.

States like Arunachal Pradesh and Nagaland, on the other hand, have as high as 90 percent of the rural women's population engaged in agriculture, while Assam and Sikkim also display rates exceeding the national average of rural participation rates of women in agriculture. Meghalaya, however, is the only state that shows a consistent decline in participation rates in the agricultural sector for both the sexes over the entire period. The percentage share of the agricultural sector in NSDP and rural employment for the year 2011–12, in most of the states in this region, ranges from a percentage share of 9 percent to 26 percent, Arunachal Pradesh being an exception, which stands at 43 percent. The employment shares for women

Table 4.4 Percentage shares of agriculture and the allied sector in NSDP and employment in the rural areas

States	1993–4			1999–2000			2004–5			2011–12		
	NSDP	%M	%F	NSDP	%M	%F	NSDP	%M	%F	NSDP	%M	%F
ARU	45.71	79.20	96.20	39.37	75.60	95.10	29.79	74.00	92.70	42.89	71.11	90.37
ASS	42.07	78.20	83.20	42.26	64.70	79.40	33.51	69.60	88.30	26.77	58.60	79.04
MANI	37.87	66.00	60.30	31.94	78.00	69.60	28.98	69.40	69.10	20.48	55.94	24.12
MEGH	28.62	82.50	90.50	24.17	86.00	87.30	24.35	79.20	84.80	15.97	60.80	73.62
MIZO	33.11	86.60	93.40	23.25	84.00	87.50	24.55	84.90	91.10	19.75	76.49	74.69
NAGA	25.85	68.50	89.30	30.64	70.50	91.90	35.83	69.60	90.40	28.24	68.72	90.17
SIK	37.25	56.70	65.70	24.50	56.90	70.10	22.19	54.70	71.90	9.25	62.34	85.64
TRI	37.40	45.50	56.60	33.62	45.30	49.10	26.08	42.40	48.60	23.49	35.15	19.20

Source: Estimated using the tables on sectoral composition of NSDP in the CSO website and the industrial classification of workers provided in the NSS Reports on Employment and Unemployment Situation in India

ranges from 73 percent to 90 percent, except for Manipur and Tripura, which are 24.12 percent and 19.20 percent, respectively. Thus, it can be said that agriculture, despite its shrinking contribution to the states' NSDP, continues to employ a major portion of the region's workforce, particularly women. The fact that Manipur has consistently maintained its share of agriculture while the employment share in agriculture has declined indicates that there might be overcrowding in the agricultural sector for the rest of the north-eastern states and that there is a need to develop the rural non-farm sector in order to absorb the excess labour. Sikkim, where the percentage share of agriculture when compared to NSDP stands at a low of 9.25 percent, displays the percentage of women workers employed to be as high as 85.64 percent. This definitely highlights the poor employment conditions prevalent in rural areas and underscores the concentration of women workers in the agricultural sector.

Another point to note here is that the percentage share of male and female employment in the agricultural sector of this region does not reflect the clustering of the women workforce as a result of non-farm diversification of the male workforce. The occupational shift from the farm to non-farm sector is not limited only to the male workforce of this region.

Unemployment rates

When one observes the unemployment rates of the north-eastern states, the regional average for both sexes exceeds the national average. However, a closer inspection of state-wise values reveal that it is the phenomenally high unemployment rates of Assam, Tripura and Nagaland in the recent rounds that seem to have inflated the regional measure of unemployment among women (urban women in particular), causing it to be above the national average. Employment in the agricultural sector being mostly seasonal in nature, the usual status of unemployment fails to capture the extent of unemployment, particularly in this sector. However, unemployment rates among the educated section do reflect employment prospects for the educated section in the region, and a comparison of the unemployment rates of the educated (for both sexes) might yield important insights regarding the gender disparity in the employment situation for the educated sections.

Table 4.5 reveals that the unemployment rates among educated males and females of this region exceeds the national average in

Table 4.5 Usual status (ps+ss) unemployment rates for the educated persons of age 15 years and above for the north-eastern states

States	Year	Rural		Urban	
		Male	Female	Male	Female
Arunachal	1993–4	358	118	6	171
Pradesh	1999–2000	3	49	5	164
	2004–5	33	29	9	48
	2009–10	12	43	49	56
Assam	1993–4	226	390	97	449
	1999–2000	112	366	110	285
	2004–5	106	225	99	140
	2009–10	91	293	48	155
Manipur	1993–4	46	47	89	86
	1999–2000	51	90	106	123
	2004–5	43	47	84	119
	2009–10	63	132	61	67
Meghalaya	1993–4	17	0	10	73
	1999–2000	14	68	50	108
	2004–5	9	70	40	40
	2009–10	19	47	51	162
Mizoram	1993–4	102	58	10	12
	1999–2000	62	0	65	54
	2004–5	20	8	20	60
	2009–10	62	142	61	105
Nagaland	1993–4	30	6	100	89
	1999–2000	49	99	140	150
	2004–5	61	64	76	120
	2009–10	228	367	85	298
Sikkim	1993–4	18	87	33	125
	1999–2000	128	99	89	172
	2004–5	61	83	64	62
	2009–10	110	58	1	0
Tripura	1993–4	97	337	108	31
	1999–2000	28	78	70	117
	2004–5	362	776	205	696
	2009–10	147	541	166	523
North-Eastern Region	1993–4	112	130	57	130
	1999–2000	56	106	79	147
	2004–5	87	163	75	161
	2009–10	92	203	65	171
All-India	1993–4	65	160	60	182
	1999–2000	56	146	62	143
	2004–5	44	152	51	156
	2009–10	35	118	36	122

Source: NSS Reports on Employment and Unemployment Situation in India

both the urban and rural sectors. The educated are taken to be those who have received a secondary level education, including those who have completed diploma/certificate courses. Normally, one attains this level of education at the age of 15 years and above. The high unemployment rates among both the educated men and women of the NER indicate the lack of adequate job opportunities in the region. These numbers indicate that educated males are more likely to be employed than the women of this region. For the educated female population of this region, the unemployment rate is lower than the all-India average from the earlier two rounds, but the trend is reversed in the latter rounds, and this is true for both urban and rural areas. In the 50th round (1993–4), the unemployment rate amongst educated women was lower compared to educated males in the rural areas of Mizoram, Meghalaya and Nagaland and also in the urban areas of Manipur, Tripura and Nagaland.

A decline in the unemployment rates among the educated population of both sexes in the 68th round (2011–12) may be observed in the all-India estimates. In contrast to this, however, in the NER, the unemployment rates among the educated section seem to have increased – with the exception of urban educated men. These numbers could be attributed to the fact that perhaps the pull factors like highly paid jobs with social security are inadequate to absorb the educated women (as well as educated rural men) into the workforce of this region.

Women's participation in workforce and other activities

A total activity distribution of women in the working age population would reveal the nature and extent of women's involvement in *visible* as well as *invisible* work. The composition of women workers can be studied by scrutinising the employment status of the women, which helps showcase the type of their employment. The literature states that women workers often make a shift from non-participation to self-employed status to come to the rescue of their families in times of distress. Another noted phenomenon is the casualisation of women, wherein because of loss of access to resources like land, etc., coupled with low earnings of the family, women are drawn towards the workforce and forced to take up casual jobs with low wages. Thus, a glance into the status of the employment of women workers can fairly give us an idea about the work conditions of the female population in the NER.

This section also accounts for the percentage of women belonging to the working age population who engage in the grey area of invisible work (i.e., women participating in domestic activities, including the allied activities specified in NSS activity codes 92 and 93) along with women workers under different employment statuses. The role women play in what has come to be known as the 'care economy' falls outside the definitional boundaries of work. In India, especially women's indispensable role in the domestic sphere – which goes largely unnoticed – tends to reduce their participation rates to a large degree in the labour market.

At the national level, the greatest participation of women is seen under the self-employment status, especially in the case of rural women. This is attributed to the blurred distinction between work and non-work activities in the rural scenario. Also, women workers often make a shift from non-participation to self-employed status to come to the rescue of their families in times of distress. The NER is no exception to this.

The problem here, however, is that in this relatively large self-employed sector, it is difficult to distinguish and draw a line of demarcation between the primary and secondary workers, who are also included in the surveys. These secondary workers, more often than not, tend to be unpaid family labourers who step in during times of distress – a recurring example of the push factors affecting women's presence in the labour force. As Bhalotra and Umana-Aponte (2010) note, in developing countries like Asia and Latin America, women tend to move from outside the labour force to being self-employed in times of distress. Abraham (2009) also observed the same (usually) distress-driven nature of employment, where employment growth is due to the entrance of the (previously) non-working population – women in particular – to supplement the household income when the family's income falls below minimum sustenance levels; they tend to withdraw from the workforce when household incomes improve.

The four quinquennial rounds for the status distribution of female activity from the post-reform period show a decline of self-employed women from both rural and urban areas; a marginal increase in regular employed women workers; a decline in the casually employed; and a marked increase in those pursuing higher education. Most of the north-eastern states display a decline in the case of self-employed women (with Sikkim being the only exception to this trend, showing a significant increase of 37.06 percent in 2004–05 to 62.7 percent in 2011–12 in the rural areas and 9.36 percent to 18.2 percent in the urban areas). The figures also showcase the fact that urban women are more likely to be confined to domestic duties as opposed to their rural counterparts, who show higher rates of self-employment owing to their involvement in the agricultural field (albeit as unpaid family labour). This distress-driven nature of the so-called self-employment of rural women in the NER is evident from Table 4.6.

As of 2004–5, a sudden spurt in the self-employed rural women's section and decline in the percentage of women involved in domestic activities is apparent, but the subsequent round registers a decline in the percentage of working age women in the self-employed sector, indicating the role of women in acting as an *insurance mechanism* for the rural households in times of distress. This trend of increased female participation in the workforce was also observed at the national level and was referred to by the studies as distress-driven in nature. The 68th round (2011–12) also registers an increase of those north-eastern women who are casually employed and pursuing education and continues to see a decline of those engaged in the domestic sector, as was observed in the 61st round (2004–5).

The all-India trend registers an increasing presence of women from the working age population in education and quite a few north-eastern states display this same trend. However, in the recent 68th round, we notice that in the North-East, there is a decline of participants in education from this age group. Among them, Manipur and Mizoram in particular display this decline in both rural and urban areas, while Sikkim shows this decline only in urban areas.

Rural women in general also display higher participation in domestic and allied activities, as manifested by code 93 in the NSS reports, in comparison to their urban counterparts who exhibit higher participation in domestic activities, only captured by the NSS code 92. This can be explained by the fact that the majority of the rural women derive their livelihood and economic dependence by processing forest produce. Most of these activities, for example, collection of fuel wood, water, etc., are accounted by the NSS activity status code 93. Urban women, on the other hand, engage in the care economy or in the 'status production' activities that keep them outside the purview of the labour force.

Table 4.6 Total activity status distribution according to the usual status (ps+ss) for females belonging to the working age population, i.e., 15–59 years old

Arunachal Pradesh

Activity status	Rural				Urban			
	1993–4	1999–00	2004–5	2011–12	1993–4	1999–00	2004–5	2011–12
Self-employed	60.97	43.03	59.42	37.86	5.13	6.77	9.67	9.63
Regular	3.52	0.80	2.02	2.46	8.65	7.07	8.90	7.64
Casual	0.94	3.49	3.05	2.06	2.68	0.73	2.56	2.28
Unemployed	0.23	0.07	0.40	0.74	0.96	1.85	0.55	1.94
Education	10.59	7.01	11.14	18.80	23.34	20.3	21.35	20.82
Dom. only	13.82	13.22	15.89	16.12	41.60	46.1	54.42	47.33
Dom+ allied	8.89	14.58	6.36	21.27	11.72	15.82	1.80	8.58

Assam

Activity status	Rural				Urban			
	1993–4	1999–00	2004–5	2011–12	1993–4	1999–00	2004–5	2011–12
Self-employed	12.19	13.73	23.01	11.37	3.80	4.05	4.46	5.90
Regular	4.78	5.32	2.90	3.22	6.17	8.35	8.97	5.72
Casual	8.33	6.37	7.13	3.22	2.60	2.89	3.14	0.57
Unemployed	2.37	1.71	1.02	1.06	4.87	3.22	1.72	0.96
Education	9.37	9.07	7.53	9.10	17.42	16.13	14.45	14.72
Dom. only	31.70	33.15	31.04	22.19	49.59	47.76	31.40	49.23
Dom+ allied	29.69	28.27	26.15	48.28	13.72	14.14	34.48	22.28

Manipur

	Rural				Urban			
	1993–4	1999–00	2004–5	2011–12	1993–4	1999–00	2004–5	2011–12
Self-employed	45.43	33.62	43.98	18.27	26.38	24.49	22.09	21.00
Regular	2.34	1.51	2.21	1.96	5.47	6.75	8.34	4.04
Casual	1.59	2.50	1.97	18.49	0.60	1.07	1.13	0.35
Unemployed	0.30	0.41	0.35	1.29	0.90	2.3	2.37	3.51
Education	17.80	17.05	16.98	14.89	27.15	24.06	18.15	14.75
Dom. only	20.08	23.27	20.09	28.97	32.64	29.47	39.64	40.17
Dom+ allied	11.19	20.11	12.90	14.81	5.64	10.69	7.40	14.97

Meghalaya

	Rural				Urban			
	1993–4	1999–00	2004–5	2011–12	1993–4	1999–00	2004–5	2011–12
Self-employed	64.14	59.77	66.19	46.22	12.76	8.11	5.86	12.86
Regular	2.07	2.21	2.25	5.74	14.55	16.98	36.91	14.27
Casual	8.88	10.11	7.97	10.00	3.64	3.05	2.02	2.54
Unemployed	0.00	0.29	0.43	0.23	1.08	2.15	1.72	1.16
Education	5.45	9.57	10.28	17.80	16.21	24.15	19.56	31.40
Dom. only	13.52	10.88	11.14	10.84	46.36	41.45	26.75	31.55
Dom+ allied	5.45	6.41	1.25	8.25	3.07	1.9	1.69	4.17

(Continued)

Table 4.6 (Continued)

Mizoram

	Rural				Urban			
	1993–4	1999–00	2004–5	2011–12	1993–4	1999–00	2004–5	2011–12
Self-employed	47.45	60.48	61.23	48.86	32.95	23.66	29.83	25.65
Regular	1.16	4.04	1.70	2.74	6.99	9.86	8.89	9.77
Casual	0.16	0.64	0.60	9.07	0.86	6.07	1.22	0.61
Unemployed	0.35	60.48	0.05	1.74	0.30	1.28	1.06	2.78
Education	11.51	7.96	11.00	8.62	18.78	20	21.97	19.02
Dom. only	18.87	10.08	14.48	15.70	19.52	20.75	28.38	29.51
Dom+ allied	19.07	16.43	10.78	13.03	19.02	17.62	7.59	11.61

Nagaland

	Rural				Urban			
	1993–4	1999–00	2004–5	2011–12	1993–4	1999–00	2004–5	2011–12
Self-employed	29.94	60.82	70.97	37.56	4.68	11.56	27.56	12.17
Regular	2.79	4.84	2.73	1.25	10.90	19.05	7.98	6.92
Casual	0.88	0.40	0.40	0.92	0.41	1.1	2.04	0.00
Unemployed	0.01	1.19	1.13	8.18	1.11	3.19	3.02	10.97
Education	22.16	14.42	11.19	22.01	20.84	25.42	22.91	24.50
Dom. only	4.47	11.30	9.49	9.04	15.31	31.41	31.86	26.90
Dom+ allied	39.32	4.68	3.58	23.44	46.15	7.48	3.69	18.19

Sikkim

	Rural				Urban			
	1993–4	1999–00	2004–5	2011–12	1993–4	1999–00	2004–5	2011–12
Self-employed	18.36	26.18	37.06	62.70	4.64	3.95	9.36	18.20
Regular	6.03	8.78	7.83	4.95	14.08	18.45	13.23	20.79
Casual	3.88	3.29	2.20	2.21	0.56	3.92	0.15	0.00
Unemployed	0.99	0.80	0.79	0.72	1.77	3.98	1.37	0.10
Education	13.83	13.94	15.83	16.22	16.48	12.58	15.62	9.24
Dom. only	32.91	33.34	21.06	8.34	55.38	55.78	57.93	46.95
Dom+ allied	23.94	11.28	13.79	3.07	2.38	0.04	1.48	4.72

Tripura

	Rural				Urban			
	1993–4	1999–00	2004–5	2011–12	1993–4	1999–00	2004–5	2011–12
Self-employed	11.18	3.62	5.85	8.80	4.45	1.19	3.12	3.22
Regular	1.77	2.47	1.51	2.74	10.45	7.9	8.78	10.51
Casual	6.59	4.21	5.20	20.14	3.62	1.17	1.55	2.11
Unemployed	1.60	0.37	0.26	8.52	4.52	0.96	1.07	20.89
Education	10.57	8.28	9.67	9.26	13.51	12.55	7.75	10.38
Dom. only	62.84	77.29	64.73	35.65	60.16	72.31	55.99	46.78
Dom+ allied	3.03	0.75	4.51	14.12	0.38	0.17	0.53	4.27

(Continued)

Table 4.6 (Continued)

North-Eastern Region

	Rural				Urban			
	1993–4	1999–00	2004–5	2011–12	1993–4	1999–00	2004–5	2011–12
Self-employed	36.21	37.66	45.96	33.96	11.85	10.47	13.99	13.58
Regular	3.06	3.75	2.89	3.13	9.66	11.80	12.75	9.96
Casual	3.91	3.88	3.57	8.27	1.87	2.50	1.73	1.06
Unemployed	0.73	8.17	0.55	2.81	1.94	2.37	1.61	5.29
Education	12.66	10.91	11.70	14.59	19.22	19.40	17.72	18.10
Dom. only	24.77	26.56	23.49	18.36	40.07	43.13	40.80	39.80
Dom+ allied	17.57	12.81	9.92	18.28	12.76	8.48	7.33	11.10

All-India

	Rural				Urban			
	1993–4	1999–00	2004–5	2011–12	1993–4	1999–00	2004–5	2011–12
Self-employed	29.81	27.08	32.40	21.88	10.24	9.29	11.28	8.83
Regular	1.45	1.57	2.00	2.21	7.01	7.30	8.94	9.25
Casual	20.27	19.23	17.07	13.07	6.10	4.41	4.06	2.90
Unemployed	0.56	0.54	1.00	0.66	1.78	1.36	1.90	1.22
Education	3.35	4.63	5.57	9.66	10.55	11.25	11.25	13.74
Dom. only	23.18	27.25	22.07	23.52	49.22	54.59	46.95	47.17
Dom+ allied	19.98	17.86	18.43	27.64	13.29	9.50	13.94	15.25

Source: Estimated using the NSS unit level records on employment and unemployment situation in India

Another point worth noting is that there seems to exist an inverse relationship between women's participation in the labour force and domestic activities. States like Assam and Tripura in the NER, which display lower (regional) rates of women's participation in the labour force when compared to the national average, are also the ones with a higher percentage of women from the working age population involved in domestic duties of the household. These states also show a relatively larger proportion of Hindu population and lower concentration of STs. This could be because of the socio-cultural barriers, which are less marked in the tribal societies.

Education and participation of women in the workforce

While rising education and declining fertility both generate conditions that theoretically imply an increase in the female labour supply, in practice, data often fail to confirm these expectations. In fact, several studies suggest that *ceteris paribus*, labour force participation of women declines with education (Kingdon and Unni 1997; Das and Desai 2003; Klasen and Pieters 2012) and rises only with high levels of education. This section explores how the female WPR behaves with respect to education categories between the periods covering 1993–4 to 2011–12 (using four quinquennial NSS rounds) for each north-eastern state. The workforce participation of women in the working age group is studied here with respect to their education levels. The women workers are divided into seven education categories, namely: illiterates, below primary education, primary, middle, secondary, higher secondary education and the highest level, comprising graduates and above.

From the figures (see Figures 4.1 and 4.2) showing the trends of work participation of women belonging to different education categories cited later, there exists a U-shaped relationship between workforce participation of women and education in both urban and rural areas of India. There seems to be a decline in workforce participation as education levels increase, falling to a minimum level and climbing again with higher education levels. While this participation hits its minimum at the higher secondary level for rural areas, in urban areas, this minimum level/point occurs at the level of secondary education, followed by an upward trend in workforce participation. This seems to imply a greater likelihood of women with no or lower levels of education being more economically active than the educated women in India.

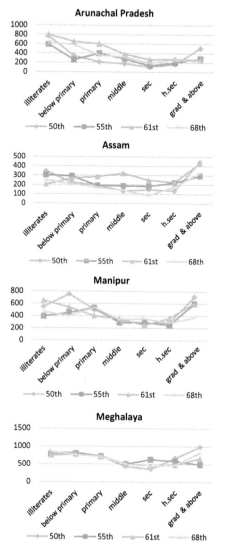

Figure 4.1 Rural female workforce participation by education categories in the north-eastern states, 1993–4 to 2011–12

Source: The trends are plotted using estimates from the unit level records of
NSS Reports on Employment and Unemployment Situation in India

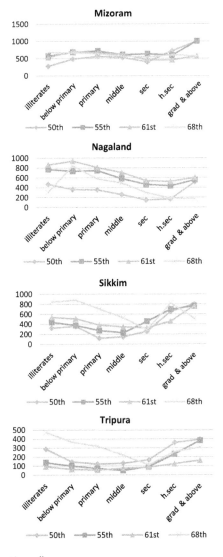

Figure 4.1 (Continued)

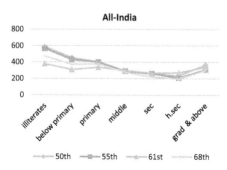

Figure 4.1 (Continued)

In *Sikkim*, the earlier rounds take a somewhat U-shape in rural areas, but the 68th round (2011–12) reveals that there is a minimum low at the secondary education level, following which the participation shoots up for the higher secondary level only to fall in the case of women graduates and above. This is indicative of either one of two things: that the educated women choose to remain unemployed because of a lack of proper employment opportunities or that they opt out of the workforce in order to enhance their social status. In the urban areas, participation in the workforce and education levels do not take the U-shape; however, an unambiguous rise follows the trough at the higher secondary level. This could indicate that urban areas have attractive avenues that draw the highly educated.

Arunachal Pradesh does not stick to this U-shaped relationship between women's workforce participation and education. While the 50th round (1993–4) does portray a bit of the U-curve in rural areas, reaching its lowest at the secondary education level, participation of women in subsequent rounds with high levels of education is not impressive. This could be due to lack of proper opportunities for the educated section and could well be an indicator of the discouraged worker effect. In the urban areas also, the participation of highly educated women has fallen over the years in this state. Given the high rates of unemployment among educated women, this definitely points towards the lack of adequate job opportunities for the educated section.

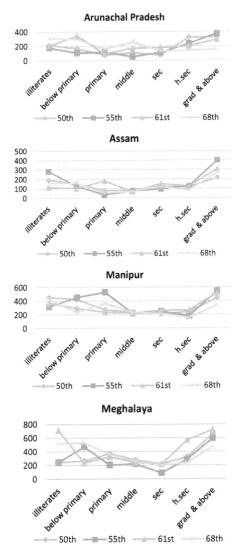

Figure 4.2 Urban female workforce participation by education categories in the north-eastern states, 1993–4 to 2011–12

Source: The trends are plotted using estimates from the unit level records of NSS
Reports on Employment and Unemployment Situation in India

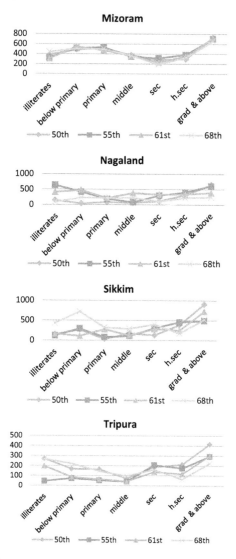

Figure 4.2 (Continued)

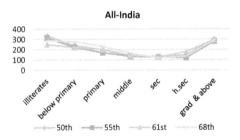

All-India

400
300
200
100
0

illiterates · below primary · primary · middle · sec · h.sec · grad & above

50th   55th   61st   68th

Figure 4.2 (Continued)

Nagaland displays higher work participation among the illiterates, while participation declines to a minimum at the higher education levels in rural areas. Urban areas show some participation from the educated section, but this has also fallen in the recent rounds. This state also shows high rates of unemployment among the educated women both in rural and urban areas.

Manipur somewhat sticks to the U-shaped curve in both rural and urban areas; the trough occurs at the secondary level for rural areas, and for urban areas it is at the higher secondary level. Women participating in the workforce again show a decline for those belonging to higher education groups over the years. The figures here indicate high unemployment rates among educated women in both urban and rural sectors.

In *Mizoram*, participation rates do not display different patterns for different educational categories in the rural areas; however, the urban scenario indicates a greater participation of illiterates and low education groups, which then declines to a minimum at the secondary education level, after which there is an uptick in participation.

With *Tripura*, rural workforce participation with respect to different education categories takes a V-shape in the 68th round (2011–12), showing a steep decline while education levels increase until secondary education, followed by a steep rise for the higher secondary and graduation and above group. The steep increase in participation in urban areas is observed for those who belong to education levels of higher secondary and above.

Meghalaya displays the same pattern for both rural and urban areas except that the minimum level of work participation rates is observed at the higher secondary level in the case of rural women and secondary education for urban women.

The rural women's workforce participation in *Assam* for different education levels shows that the minimum level was for women belonging to the higher secondary level of education during the early rounds, while at the 68th round, it was at the secondary level education. The workforce participation trend of the urban women of this state, however, indicates a clear rise for women belonging to the higher secondary level and graduation and higher levels of education.

Illiterate women are drawn into the workforce by various push factors in operation and, in many cases, they cannot afford to remain unemployed, which necessitates their participation in the workforce. The educated women, however, tend to have certain expectations and prefer not to take up menial and low-paid jobs, which lead to lower participation rates for this category of women. Also, these educated women more often than not belong to families of higher statuses, which encourage female seclusion of women. Some studies have even argued that women's withdrawal from the labour force is not just a sign of a family's high status but that this action in itself contributes to increased status (Papanek and Schwede 1988; Standing 1991). This action of withdrawal of a woman from the labour force despite high education is assumed to elevate the family's honour and status in society. This is in keeping with what Papanek (1979) says about women often substituting paid labour with 'status production activities' such as bearing, rearing and nurturing children and household maintenance. For those who belong to the highly educated group, however, there exist incentives that their 'own income' effect overpowers the negative 'income effect' from their spouses[4] as well as the substitution effect resulting in greater workforce participation. Though Figures 4.1 and 4.2 confirm that pull factors at the highest education levels draw women into the workforce, it also suggests that the participation rate for highly educated women has fallen in recent years, indicating lack of incentives in the labour market for this group, particularly in the north-eastern states. No such marked trend of decline has been observed for the illiterate section and lower education groups.

Thus, it can be said that the nature of employment even in the NER is seemingly distress-driven, and at the higher education end, the lack of proper job opportunities leads women to opt out of participating in the workforce. Improvement in educational levels, as may be safely concluded, does not seem to have resulted in better opportunities in the labour market for women of this region.

Income levels and women's labour force participation

Now assuming women's participation is driven by push factors, i.e., if it is distress-driven, it should follow that with improved household incomes, women (who mainly fall into the secondary workforce category) should ideally retreat from the labour force. Given this, the female participation in the labour force should be inversely related to income levels. The U-shaped curve of the female labour participation rate, as theorised and empirically tested (Schultz 1990; Mathur 1994; Goldin 1995; Mammen and Paxson 2000), puts forward that female labour participation rates follow a certain pattern which is apparently higher in traditional agricultural societies, mostly as unpaid family labour.

To study this relationship further, households have been divided into various decile classes as per their household monthly per capita expenditure (MPCE) to study female labour force participation. The MPCE deciles are calculated for each of the north-eastern states separately and not as per the national MPCE or regional MPCE estimates. This means that though not on absolute terms of the MPCE deciles, the proportion of population belonging to each nth decile for each of the eight states would be comparable.

Among the rural households of India, this inverse relationship between female labour force participation and income levels (MPCE taken as a proxy) is apparent only in the 50th (1993–4) and 55th rounds (see Figure 4.3); in the latest rounds, there seems to be increasing participation as the income of the household increases (except for the state of Meghalaya).

From Figure 4.3, it may be noticed that *Sikkim* displays a somewhat declining trend in participation among rural women for higher MPCE deciles in the latest round of NSS, and an increased participation of rural women in labour force in recent years is observed when compared to earlier rounds. Labour force participation of rural women when plotted against household monthly per capita expenditure (HHMPCE) deciles in the state of *Arunachal Pradesh*

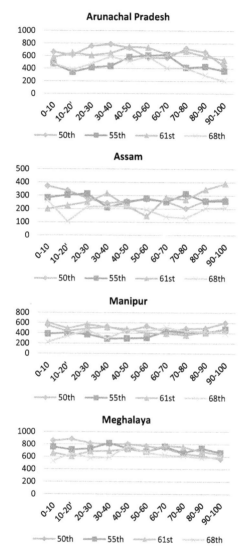

Figure 4.3 Rural female labour force participation rate across state-specific MPCE deciles from the 15–59 age group (1993–4 to 2011–12)

Source: The trends are plotted using estimates from the unit level records of NSS Reports on Employment and Unemployment Situation in India

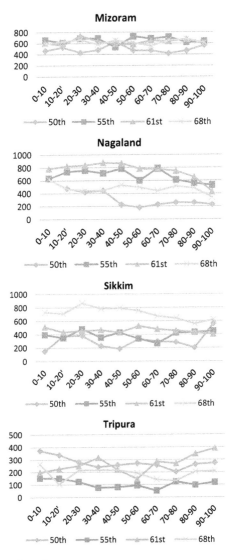

Figure 4.3 (Continued)

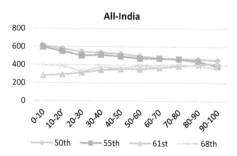

Figure 4.3 (Continued)

takes the shape of an inverted U showing larger participation of women belonging to the middle income groups and a decline in participation from women belonging to the highest deciles. However, the decline in participation is more marked in the recent NSS round.

Labour force participation of rural women of *Nagaland* do not display any consistent pattern over the rounds; however, the recent rounds register greater participation of women belonging to all deciles; the lowest participation comes from the deciles at the upper extremes. *Manipur* displays a lot of variation over the rounds and across the deciles and does not follow a particular pattern. The 68th round shows a lower participation in the lower deciles compared to the earlier rounds and again registers a decline in participation for the upper deciles, unlike the earlier rounds. Thus, the highest participation in labour force is registered by the seventh decile in the 68th round, but for the earlier rounds the highest is at the upper extremes. In *Mizoram*, the participation of rural women in the labour force shows a lot of fluctuation across the deciles, but despite the decline registered for women belonging to the highest deciles, it is not the lowest across all deciles. For *Tripura*, the rural women's participation in the labour force shows a steep rise for the highest deciles in all the rounds except for the 55th round. Rural women of *Meghalaya* belonging to the different deciles do not show extreme fluctuations, and the numbers remain quite high across the deciles and over the NSS rounds. However, the decline in participation rates is observed in the highest decile, which again is consistent over the rounds. *Assam*, on the other hand, shows an increased labour participation rate among rural women belonging to the highest deciles.

The all-India trend of labour force participation of urban women across the MPCE deciles reveals a smooth decline as incomes improve, indicating a de-feminisation trend but also a slight rise of deciles at the upper extreme (see Figure 4.4). In the north-eastern states, there are no such symptoms of a consistent decline in labour force participation of urban women as their income levels improve, and the rising participation of women belonging to the highest deciles is consistent only in the states of Sikkim and Mizoram and over the time period under observation. Arunachal Pradesh also conforms to these trends in the earlier rounds, but in the 68th round, there is a fall in labour force participation of urban women belonging to the highest deciles. Another pattern followed by the north-eastern states is greater participation of women belonging to the highest MPCE deciles, as evident in the 50th and 55th round, and then a decline in participation observed across the same deciles for the 61st and 66th round.

Income levels and domestication of women

The division of domestic work based on gender stereotypes in India often leads to the withdrawal of women from the labour force when they have performed their roles in the capacity of the reserve army (of labour). In India, the recent withdrawal of women from the workforce, hence, the fall in participation rates, has been referred to as the 'de-feminisation' of the workforce. (Srivastava and Srivastava 2010; Himanshu 2011; Abraham 2013). There seems to be a strong relationship between household incomes and women's participation in domestic activity (or outside it). The domestication trends of women in the states of the NER and the all-India trends are, therefore, imperative in this study of the region.

The definitions of the domestic activities used here include the NSS code 92 as well as 93. At the all-India level, there seems to be a positive relationship between the levels of income and participation rates of women in domestic activities, as manifested in Figures 4.5 and 4.6. However, for urban women, there is a declining tendency of participation in domestic activities in the high-income groups.

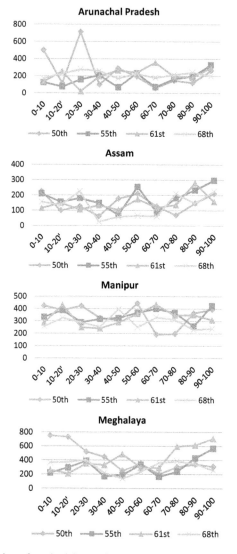

Figure 4.4 Urban female labour force participation rate across state-specific MPCE deciles from the 15–59 age group (1993–4 to 2011–12)

Source: The trends are plotted using estimates from the unit level records of NSS Reports on Employment and Unemployment Situation in India

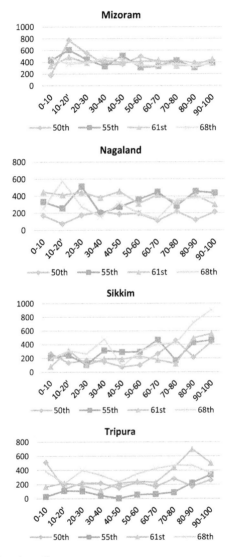

Figure 4.4 (Continued)

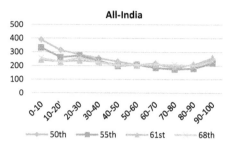

Figure 4.4 (Continued)

As is evident from Figures 4.5 and 4.6, most of the north-eastern states not only display fluctuating patterns of rural women participating in domestic activities (including the allied activities specified in NSSO activity codes 92 and 93)[5] across the MPCE deciles but also register a decreased participation among the highest deciles. Arunachal Pradesh and Nagaland, on the other hand, across all the four rounds of NSS, display a greater participation in domestic activities among women belonging to higher income rural households. For Mizoram and Nagaland, while the earlier rounds register less participation from the highest deciles, the trend has reversed in the latest round. Tripura also follows the trend of decreased participation for the highest income groups in the latest rounds.

Among the *urban* women, the decline of participation in domestic activities belonging to higher income level groups is observed in all the north-eastern states. This implies that the tendency of women to remain confined within four walls is the least for women in higher income groups. The initial drop in participation observed with the rise in income levels could be explained by the process of 'Sanskritisation'.[6] Working outside the home is deemed a low-status activity for married women; hence, the moment they surpass the dire necessities, these women tend to withdraw from the labour force. In this way, even improved education levels among women serve, ironically, not as a means to enhance their autonomy but their efficiency in status elevation (Eswaran et al. 2013). However, at very high levels of income where western culture is imitated, participation of women in the labour force is acceptable and is encouraged as long as family status is not compromised.

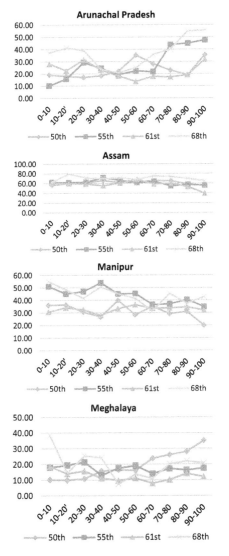

Figure 4.5 Rural female participation rate in all domestic activities (%) across state-specific MPCE deciles from the 15–59 age group (1993–4 to 2011–12)

Source: The trends are plotted using estimates from the unit level records of NSS Reports on Employment and Unemployment Situation in India

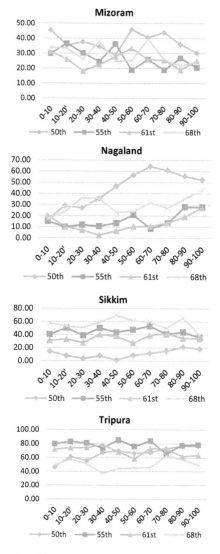

Figure 4.5 (Continued)

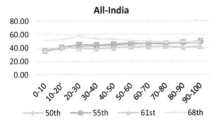

Figure 4.5 (Continued)

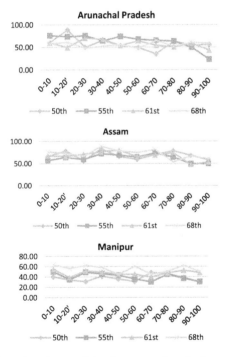

Figure 4.6 Urban female participation rate in all domestic activities across state-specific MPCE deciles from the 15–59 age group (1993–4 to 2011–12)

Source: The trends are plotted using estimates from the unit level records of NSS Reports on Employment and Unemployment Situation in India

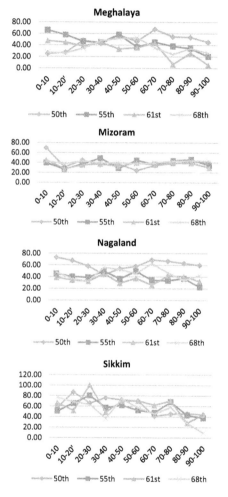

Figure 4.6 (Continued)

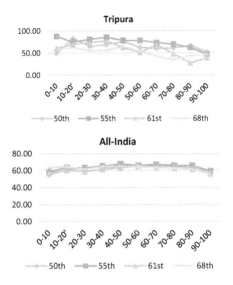

Figure 4.6 (Continued)

Conclusion

This analysis of the employment trends in the NER reveal higher rates of labour force participation and workforce participation among women, even exceeding the national average. The rural-urban differential in WPRs is visible in the region. This can be explained by the blurred demarcation of work and non-work activities. Also, rural women tend to attain economic independence by processing forest produce, the region being richly endowed with forest resources. The majority of women workers are found to be self-employed and engaged in the agricultural sector. However, this comes as no surprise, as the north-eastern states are primarily agrarian-based and still resort to traditional methods of cultivation.

The distribution of north-eastern women in the working age population into various categories according to their usual status activity somewhat confirms the distress-driven nature of employment. The years showing increase in the number of self-employed women also show a simultaneous drop in the domestic and allied activities. Such a pattern was found by Bhalotra and Umana-Aponte in developing economies, where the women make a transition from non-participation to participation in times of distress. While the domestication pattern shows higher participation of rural women in domestic and allied activities, the urban lot mostly remained confined to domestic activities only.

Participation of women workers according to the level of education reflects the national tendency of illiterate and less educated women to be more economically active. Though the participation rates does shoot up at the highest levels of education in the region, there also are high rates of unemployment among the educated lot. This is indicative of proper employment prospects for the educated women of the region.

The study of employment and domestication pattern of the women with respect to their income levels further reiterates the distress-driven feminisation of labour at lower levels of income and the de-feminisation trend wherein women withdraw from the labour force as incomes improve. Also, the trends confirm the inverse relationship between labour force participation and domestic participation. This proves the dual burden of women's work. As the income levels increase, women substitute paid labour with household chores and withdraw from the labour force.

To conclude, however, the trends and patterns of female employment in the NER indicate a distress-driven employment. The high rates of participation of the women in the workforce and large numbers for self-employment confirm the fact. Moreover, the activity status distribution of the women in the working age population over the period 1993–4 to 2011–12 exhibit patterns of counter-cyclical movements from non-participation to participation (as self-employed). However, feminisation of the rural workforce as a result of the occupational shift of the male workers from farm to non-farm sector is *not to be found* in this region. Instead, a shift from farm to the non-farm sector by the workers of both the sexes within the region is evident and found to be more pronounced in the case of the female workers in the state of Manipur. Despite the high sex ratios and high literacy rates in the region, there exists a gender disparity in the employment levels among the educated population.

The employment situation of north-eastern women, as evident from this study, is not encouraging. In the agricultural sector, there was a clustering of women who were found to be mostly self-employed. Thus, despite the fact that the regional average of women's workforce participation exceeds the national average, in terms of employment prospects, women workers of this region cannot be considered any better off than the rest of the states in India. This necessitates the need to improve the work scenario of women by creating appropriate employment opportunities for women, especially for the educated section. Also, the shift of women workers from farm to non-farm sectors should be encouraged and facilitated.

This study attempted to understand the pattern of employment of women. However, it cannot claim to be inclusive of all the factors, as women's work and its accounting is a complex issue determined by interactions between various economic and socio-cultural factors at various levels. The key limitations of the study, as of any another in this area, are the conceptual and definitional limitations of the sources of data used to capture women's work. This chapter aims to study the trends and patterns of female employment in the eight north-eastern states of India (Arunachal Pradesh, Assam, Manipur, Meghalaya, Mizoram, Nagaland, Sikkim and Tripura). The associated literature portrays how complex this issue of women's work is and how varied factors at multiple levels interact with each other to shape the employment patterns of women in a particular region. There appears to exist a constant tug-of-war between economic needs and gendered restrictions which determine how women participate in the labour force at the individual level.

Notes

1 This chapter is an excerpt from her MPhil research on 'Trends and Patterns of Female Employment in the North-Eastern Region of India during the Post-Reform Period'.
2 Shifting (*jhum*) cultivation is a primitive mode of agriculture evolved as a reflex action under the stress of the peculiar geophysical and ecological situations prevailing in the hills of the NER. The system reflects a sort of community farming without heritable rights over the land. The practice starts with selection of forested land, clearing and burning of the forest before the onset of monsoon, planting of various crops in an intimate mixture by dibbling and harvesting. The land is abandoned after cultivation for a period of two to three years, and cultivation is shifted to another site.
3 The feminisation of agriculture refers to women's increasing participation in the agricultural labour force, whether as independent producers, as unremunerated family workers or as agricultural wage workers.
4 Mincer (1962) notes 'given the income elasticity of demand for home goods and for leisure, the extent to which income differentially affects hours of work in the market and household sectors depends on the ease

with which substitution in home production or consumption can be carried out. The lesser the substitutability the weaker the negative income effect on hours of work at home, and the stronger the income effect on hours of work in the market'.

5 Among activities listed by the NSS, the activity status coded 92 refers to those persons 'attending domestic duties Alone', and code 93 refers to persons who 'attended domestic duties and were also engaged in activities like free collection of goods (vegetables, roots, firewood, cattle-feed, etc.) sewing, tailoring, weaving, etc., for household use'.

6 Sanskritisation denotes the process by which castes placed lower in the caste hierarchy seek upward mobility by emulating the rituals and practices of the upper or dominant castes. This term was made popular by Indian sociologist M.N. Srinivas (1966) in the 1950s.

References

Abraham, Vinoj. 2009. 'Employment Growth in Rural India: Distress-Driven?' *Economic and Political Weekly*, 44(16) (April 18–24): 97–104.

Abraham, V. 2013. 'Missing Labour or Consistent "De-feminisation"', *Economic and Political Weekly*, 48(31): 99–108.

Bhalotra, S. and M. Umana-Aponte. 2010. 'The Dynamics of Women's Labour Supply in Developing Countries', Discussion Paper Series/ Forschungsinstitut zur Zukunft der Arbeit, No. 4879.

Blundell, Richard, John Ham, and Costas Meghir. 1998. 'Unemployment, Discouraged Workers and Female Labour Supply', *Research in Economics*, 52(2): 103–131.

Das, M. and S. Desai. 2003. 'Why Are Educated Women Less Likely To Be Employed in India?: Testing Competing Hypotheses', *Social Protection Discussion Paper No. 0313*. Washington, DC: World Bank.

Eswaran, M., B. Ramaswami and W. Wadhwa. 2013. 'Status, Caste, and the Time Allocation of Women in Rural India', *Economic Development and Cultural Change*, 61(2): 311–333.

Goldin, Claudia. 1995. 'The U-Shaped Female Labor Force Function in Economic Development and Economic History', in T. Paul Schultz (ed.), *Investment in Women's Human Capital*, pp. 61–88, Chicago: University of Chicago Press.

Himanshu. 2011. 'Employment Trend in India: A Re-examination', *Economic and Political Weekly*, 46(37): 43–59.

Kingdon, G. G. and J. Unni. 1997. *How Much Does Education Affect Women's Labour Market Outcomes in India?* Gujarat Institute of Development Research.

Klasen, Stephan and Janneke Pieters. 2012. 'Push or Pull? Drivers of Female Labor Force Participation during India's Economic Boom.'

Lundberg, Shelly. 1985. 'The Added Worker Effect', *Journal of Labor Economics*, 11–37.

Mammen, K. and C. Paxson. 2000. 'Women's Work and Economic Development', *Journal of Economic Perspectives*, 14(4): 141–164.

Mathur, A. 1994. 'Work Participation, Gender and Economic Development: A Quantitative Anatomy of the Indian Scenario', *The Journal of Development Studies*, 30(2): 466–504.

Mincer, J. 1962. 'Labor Force Participation of Married Women: A Study of Labor Supply', *Aspects of Labor Economics*, 63–106.

Papanek, Hanna. 1979. 'Family Status Production: The "work" and "nonwork" of Women', *Signs*, 4: 775–781.

Papanek, Hanna and Laurel Schwede. 1988. 'Women Are Good with Money: Earning and Managing in an Indonesian City', *Economic and Political Weekly*, 23, WS73–WS84.

Reddy, D. N. 1975. 'Female Work Participation: A Study of Inter-State Differences: A Comment', *Economic and Political Weekly*, 10(23): 902–905.

Schultz, T. P. 1990. 'Women's Changing Participation in the Labor Force: a World Perspective', *Economic Development and Cultural Change*, 457–488.

Srinivas, M. N. 1966. 'Sanskritization', in *Social Change in Modern India*, Berkeley: University of California Press.

Srivastava, Nisha and Ravi Srivastava. 2010. 'Women, Work, and Employment Outcomes in Rural India', *Economic and Political Weekly*, 45(28): 49–63.

Standing, Hilary. 1991. *Dependence and Autonomy: Women's Employment and the Family in Calcutta*, London: Routledge.

Part II

Work, employment and labour in industries

Chapter 5

Beyond standard outcomes

The state of employment and labour in the tea industry of Assam

*Debdulal Saha, Rajdeep Singha
and Padmini Sharma*

Tea is considered as the second most consumable beverage in the world, after water, and considering the global demand for tea and its consumption, it is one of the most exported agricultural goods (Oxfam 2015). The production of tea is dominated by five countries – China, India, Kenya, Sri Lanka and Turkey – accounting for 76 percent of global production among the 35 tea-producing countries; and the top four major importers are Russia, UK, US and Pakistan (ILO 2015). This industry has witnessed dramatic changes over the last two decades, with a 100 percent increase in production between 2003 and 2013 and a 66 percent increase in quantity, with the export value reaching 168 percent (ibid.). During 2000–5, production prices have declined drastically, with the world market prices for tea declining to half of that in the 1980s (ibid.). In 2008–12, market prices remained high but unstable; since early 2013, tea prices have fallen to pre-2008 levels (ibid.). As the production costs have more or less remained the same, the decline in prices implies a negative impact directly on the working conditions and livelihood of small-scale farmers and plantation workers in several tea-producing countries. Low prices have severely affected producers of the developing countries, where the dismantling and shift from state marketing boards to market exchange and coordination in the tropical product sector have led to the reshaping of income flows and cost burdens, creating intense anxiety among the producer community (Neilson and Pritchard 2009). The decline in prices on account of expatriation of an overwhelming proportion of economic returns to the developed countries has an impact on the human cost involved (ibid.).

Through globalisation of its production network, the tea industry has witnessed many changes in terms of market and production process. A process of economic upgrading, moving from low-value activities to high-value activities (Barrientos et al. 2010), has been evident in the tea estates. In this industry, among the four types of economic upgrading (process, product, functional and chain), process and product upgrading seems to be in the initial phase. Process upgrading is related to the introduction of new methods of production or tools used in plucking, pruning and processing leaves, whereas product upgradation involves a shift towards organic production or certification schemes like the ISO (22000: 20005), ensuring a food safety management system and other such criteria. A number of global governance initiatives in the tea sector, like that of multi-stakeholder roundtables and certification schemes, have been introduced as part of upgradation. The certified scheme is one of the most common forms of corporate social responsibility (CSR) in the tea industry, enabling them to establish standards in the context of environmental, economic and social sustainability. The market share of such certified tea has risen from a mere 1 percent in 2007 to around 12 percent in 2012; Rainforest Alliance[1]-certified tea has undergone the highest growth (Potts et al. 2014). The Ethical Tea Partnership (ETP) works at both ends of the supply chain and in accordance to a particular set of fundamental principles that are in direct reference to ILO's Decent Work Agenda[2] (ILO 2015). In this, members need to report annually on the Fundamental Conventions in addition to the Safety and Health in Agriculture Convention, 2011 (No. 184), and Indigenous and Tribal Peoples Convention, 1989 (No. 169) (ibid.). Fair trade is another instrument to achieve popularity as a certified system for agricultural commodities. In this system, the tea employers are required to comply with fair trade standards set for hired labour in terms of payment. This is fixed according to a country's minimum wage level, assuring access to safe living and working conditions and adherence to minimum environmental norms (Oxfam 2015). In addition to this, certifications like that of SA 8000 are based on principles of international human rights, International Labour Organisation conventions, the Universal Declaration of Human Rights, and United Nations Conventions on the rights of the child seek to introduce economic and social upgrading of the tea plantation workers. However, economic upgrading has not been accompanied by social upgradation of the workers, who are trapped in the exploitative regime of the plantation economy. Thus, quantity and type of employment plays an important role considering labour as a productive factor (Barrientos et al. 2010). In the context of such changes witnessed in the tea plantation economy, it will be interesting to reflect on the scope for social and economic upliftment of the workers in this industry.

In India, tea has traditionally been grown in large plantations that cover several hundreds of hectares. This industry is in the formal sector and it employs a little over 1 million permanent workers, making it the largest employer in the formal private sector. These are situated in mainly four states in the country, namely, Assam and West Bengal in Eastern India and Kerala and Tamil Nadu in Southern India. Assam is the largest tea-growing area, and it produces 50 percent of the country's tea, followed by West Bengal, which makes up 17 percent of the tea produced. The workers in tea plantations usually reside within the plantation premises. The Plantation Labour Act (1951) and other Acts make it mandatory for the plantation management to provide workers with various economic and social entitlements such as minimum wage, bonuses, rations, provident funds, education and health care facilities and others. However, several studies illustrate that, on the contrary, workers are subjected to exploitative work patterns, control mechanisms, low wage payments, deplorable housing and living conditions, an inadequate supply of drinking water and poor levels of welfare benefits, with no provisions of collective bargaining (Bhowmik 1981; Bhowmik et al. 1996; Xaxa 1997; Guha 2012). The workers not only suffer on account of eviction but also face difficulty to search for alternative sources of employment outside the industry.

Since 2000, the consumption of tea in India, the domestic market, has increased at a faster rate compared to its production, which has remained steady at 15–20 million kg annually. The sector's inability to furnish demand has resulted in a steady decline in exports (Sarma et al. 2012). The 'crisis' in the tea industry is more evident in its decline in exports rather than shrinkage of production or price or sale in the domestic market. Hence, the contributing factors could be stiffer competition in the domestic and global market; inadequate investment (ibid.); the closure of tea gardens; and perhaps (more importantly) the quality of tea produced in the international market. In addition, increasing unrest among labourers, often culminating into violent protests, and non-payment of wages and other benefits to the labourers have led to a decline in their living standards and human security in the tea estates (ibid.).

In Assam, many such manifestations have resulted in massive labour unrest among the workers and further degradation of relations between employers and labourers (primarily Adivasis) owing to the non-inclusion of these communities as scheduled tribes of Assam (Gohain 2007). Within the enclave, living conditions are extremely poor, with improper housing and sanitation facilities; such issues have compounded as they fail to comply with the labour legislations meant for the industry.

There is a paradox in the tea industry in India. While various economic upgradations (mainly process and product) are taking place in the sector, the demand is still on the basic issues pertaining to labour standards, basic rights, wage payment and labour welfare. This chapter emphasises on the aspects of labour and employment in the tea industry in Assam, taking into account work and workplace conditions, economic security in terms of wages and compensation, and concerns regarding labourers' welfare and the status of their basic rights.

Four tea estates from Assam have been selected to assess the status of labour and employment. The findings have been analysed against the backdrop of labour legislation like the Plantation Labour Act of 1951, the Minimum Wages Act of 1948 and others to understand the dimensions of economic, social and political exclusion of labourers in the estates. The four estates studied here have been selected to understand labour conditions of tea estates which are situated in different geographical locations. (Tea Estate-1 from lower Assam, Tea Estate-2 from central Assam, and Tea Estate-3 and Tea Estate-4 from upper Assam[3] under Company A)[4]. Tea Estate-1 has the largest area under cultivation, followed by Tea Estate-4, Tea Estate-2 and Tea Estate-3; which opens up a new dimension of looking at working conditions and welfare activities in different categories of tea estates in terms of areas. The aforementioned four tea estates were visited in the period between 2013–16.

The structure of the chapter is as follows. The first section sets the context and objective of the chapter. The second section discusses the origin and conditions of labour and employment and recruitment processes of the tea industry, followed by an exploration of its workplace. The fourth section provides an account of the wage structure and compensation granted in the four estates. The fifth section provides an assessment of the basic welfare benefits against a backdrop of the role of labour market institutions. The last section provides the conclusion of the study.

Labour and employment

A huge workforce which migrated across regional and national boundaries largely met the labour demand of tea plantations at the time of their inception. In North-East India, as colonial rulers set to expand tea plantations in the region, they were stuck with a severe shortage of local workers during the first half of the nineteenth century. The residents of this region were fairly self-sufficient and did not feel the need to accept employment offers by the tea planters (Griffiths 1967). However, according to Ghosh (1999), the notion of such a labour shortage was more perceived than real, as it was the planters who were unwilling to employ local labourers, as they demanded high wages and had control over working hours and their labour use (as cited in Sarma et al. 2012). In 1859, only 10,000 labourers were available as against a requirement of 16,000–20,000 labourers (Xaxa 1985). By 1905–6, the adult labour force on plantations of Assam increased to 417,262, of which a few thousand were locally recruited (ibid.). In the beginning of the twentieth century, there were five systems of recruitment of labourers to tea gardens in the region (Griffiths 1967). A systematic drive towards this process started with the establishment of the Tea Planters Association, which imported workers for a wage of Rs 5 per month (ibid.). This was done through free and unlicensed contractors, but owing to their unscrupulous practices, the Inland Emigration Act of 1863 was passed to control emigration in Assam (ibid.). However, considering its limited scope in protecting labourers after their arrival at the tea garden, the practice of sending garden *sardars* (headmen) or licensed recruiters to the recruiting districts was proposed (ibid.). It was considered to be better, as the sardars understood what the work in tea gardens demanded (ibid.). This was followed by recruitment at Dhubri or the tea garden of 'free labour', where labourers did not have to enter into any contract before arriving in Dhubri and, in theory, could change their minds after seeing the garden and the country (ibid.). The fourth system was based on recruitment of time-expired migrant labourers, contractually covered by Act XIII of 1859 and reinforced by Section 492 of the Indian Penal Code (ibid.). In this case, it was made customary to provide the recruit an advance for binding him under Act XIII for one, two or three years, and in 1886, the Indian Tea Association bonus rules limited the advance to around Rs 6 for a man and Rs 4 for a woman (ibid.). It was followed by recruitment of indigenous labour from Assam, as the government of Assam, in 1953, raised a serious concern about the rising unemployment and shortage of foodstuffs that suggested curtailment of labour recruitment from outside the state of Assam (ibid.). The Indian Tea Association stressed transferring surplus labour from estates of Cachar and Assam to other estates requiring additional labour, and accordingly, by 1959, recruitment from outside Assam had been reduced to negligible proportion (ibid.).

In the context of trends in labour use and employment, as Sarma et al. (2012) depicts, in the northern states, Assam shows a higher rate of employment, at 0.87 for 1998–2004, than West Bengal and other states taken together, at 0.28 for 1998–2004. Subsequently, the labour absorption or trend in labour use per hectare in Assam has increased from 2.24 in 1980 to 2.52 in 1995–7. However, it further declined post-1998 to around 2.27 in 2004 (ibid.). In the 1980s, there was an increase in labour productivity, but it declined considerably from 1991–2004, when it witnessed a negative growth rate of –0.10 percent (ibid.). The composition of labour changed, with a substantial decline in child and adolescent labour, from 14.12 percent in 1980 to 5 percent in 2004, and an increase in the share of adult male labourers (ibid.).

The tea plantation economy, which is considered to be one of the largest employers of organised workforces, has witnessed a transition in terms of a rise in non-standard employment relations in the system. The informalisation and contractualisation of labour serves as a key dimension, as these new categories have restricted access to the quantitative and qualitative aspects of social upgradation at the workplace. Furthermore, the question raised by Sarma et al. (2012) on 'crowding in' of tea garden workers and their families in the tea sector owing to intergenerational immobility of the garden workers can be evaluated to see if this weakness is increasing the precarisation of work within the sector from below. This might be on account of the labourers being exposed to rising unemployment issues at the same time as a lower dimension of employment is being offered to contractually bound or temporary labourers. However, despite all these changes, the workers are excluded from the coverage of social upliftment at work.

The status of workers, in terms of the nature of their employment, defines their ability to benefit from the upgradation process (Barrientos et al. 2010). Reports of Columbia Law School (2014) show how temporary workers in tea estates are denied some essential benefits of basic facilities at the workplace like that of health care. In tea estates, the employment structure can be broadly classified as permanent, temporary/*faltu* and contract labourers. The Plantation Labour Act of 1951 makes no distinction in terms of wages and the provision of basic welfare benefits for all the three categories, though their actual working conditions differ. So there are broadly two types of nonstandardised employment relations within the tea estates, one group directly employed by the tea estates, like that of temporary/faltu labourers, and the other of contract labourers who are hired through a contractor. Hence, there is heterogeneity in employment relations in tea estates not only in terms of standardised and non-standardised employment relationships but even within the non-standardised gamut. The temporary/faltu labourers are enrolled in the estates' payroll; hence, they are entitled to receive pay slips, wages, provident funds, rations, fuel and benefits similar to those received by permanent workers, except a few additional benefits like annual pay, festival advances and bonuses. Moreover, they are provided with digital identity cards of the estates where they work. Initially, they were employed during the peak season of May or June, but due to shortage of man-days they are made to work from the last week of February till the first week of December.

The contract workers, on the other hand, are either hired through a contractor or the locals from the same/nearby areas who approach directly to the management. The estates only deal with the contractor, who often claims to be a government-approved licensed contractor, and pay him a lump sum as wages for labourers. The contractor may not hand over the entire amount to the labourers, and it is always speculated that the contractor deducts a certain amount from the wage as a commission. The contract explicitly prohibits the contractor from hiring an adolescent or a child as a labourer. These contract labourers are not entitled to any other benefits that are obtained by the temporary/faltu labourers. Moreover, unlike temporary labourers, since these contract workers are brought from outside the estate, the contractor receives around Rs 20 (in certain estates) per labourer as a part of transportation costs.

While temporary workers, who usually belong to families of permanent labourers, are entitled to access basic facilities and provisions, contract labourers do not receive any such benefits. Both residential and non-residential labourers are entitled to receive health benefits for injuries of any sort during work, though it is mandatory for them to work for at least 90 days to be eligible for such benefits.

Temporary labourers are employed at both gardens and factories, while contract labourers are usually seen to be engaged in factories or for cleaning drains and the gardens. This is because temporary workers, being a part of the existing families of the estate, are expected to know the skills required for plucking leaves and hence can be safely employed at the gardens. But contract labourers have no direct contact with the tea estates; they might be labourers from other factories or wage workers of any other sort; their skills are not trusted to be employed for plucking activities. As temporary workers know well about the basic structure of a tea estate and the work involved, they are sometimes employed at bungalows, in emergency services like in hospitals, in support services, or as a replacement for a permanent worker.

Drawing from the examples of legal (de jure) and actual (de facto) employees, as introduced by Kalleberg (2000) and Kalleberg et al. (2000), the worker engaged in non-standardised work is exposed to a different power dynamics than a worker involved in a standardised one. As illustrated, the nature of the triangular employment relationship in the tea industry or the absence of any written employment contract with the contract labourers exposes the latter to insecurity and lack of advancement at work. These labourers are basically seasonal workers who toil as per the demands of the actual employers. However, at times they work under another legal employer, as seen in the case of contractor labourers (contractor as the legal employer), who serves as an agent to the real employer and is also not concerned about the rights of the labourers. So, through casualisation and informalisation of these employment relationships, the responsibilities of the employers have been swiftly shrugged off. Hence, such changing dynamics at the workplace further jeopardise the scope for social upgradation of the workers.

Like other industries, recent trends show an inclination towards preference of temporary labourers in the tea industry (see Table 5.1). Needless to mention, there is a clear gain for the management if more temporary workers are employed to do the work, as the former can avoid benefits and facilities that are associated with permanent staffs and their dependents. During peak seasons, every estate needs to appoint temporary workers on a daily wage basis. Both male and female workers are engaged in the factory during the peak season in all shifts. However, female workers are mainly appointed

Table 5.1 Workers' participation

	Estate-1	Estate-2	Estate-3	Estate-4
Resident population	5522	7704	4891	7885
Permanent workers (M/F)	0.48	0.96	1.08	0.93
Temporary workers (M/F)	0.31	0.78	0.47	0.45
Permanent workers/ temporary workers	1.13	1.34	0.81	1.46

Source: Collected from respective estates during fieldwork

at the low-risk zones in the factory, while males operate heavy machineries in the high-risk zone. Females are not allowed to work on the heavy machinery, although the opinion of female workers is different on this matter. Interaction with female workers at the factory shows that given a chance, female workers can also work in the high-risk zone, as they operate drying and sorting machines at the low-risk zone which require even more manual power. Two female workers at Tea Estate-1 mentioned that their assigned work gets accelerated during peak season, when many female workers work together in the factory. Female workers also expressed their willingness to work at the factory as support during peak season.

As per the report of Columbia Law School (2014), there have been both explicit violations of the Plantation Labour Act of 1951 and abuses that fall outside the scope of legislation in the context of the working conditions of tea labourers. As mentioned, the first two dimensions of decent work, encompassing income opportunity and rights at work, have been evaluated in this section to highlight the abysmal working conditions in the four tea estates in Assam. In this, the first dimension, income opportunity, evaluates the wage structure and consumption pattern in addition to the provision of other facilities in kind, followed by a second dimension related to working conditions at the factory and garden that draws our attention towards the provision of basic facilities at work and the maintenance of occupational safety and health.

Work and workplace

An important decent work parameter is conditions at the workplace, and to evaluate it in the context of the present study, the workplace has been divided into two parts – factory and garden. Notwithstanding, the garden is considered as the primary workplace, as the total output is directly associated with the volume of production of tea leaves. The composition of the workforce is dependent on the type of activity, as female workers are seen to be more predominant in the garden and male workers are seen to be engaged in the factory. Thus, working conditions at the factory and garden both have been analysed separately.

Garden

A lot of emphasis has been placed on the health and safety of workers spraying pesticides and other chemicals in the gardens in the amended version of the Plantation Labour Act of 2010. Apart from Tea Estate-4, other estates were seen to be following safety guidelines while spraying pesticides; however, in Tea Estate-4, workers refrained from using masks, safety glasses and aprons. The Act also prescribes provision of basic facilities such as drinking water provision, toilet facilities and other essential amenities at the workplace. However, female workers mainly working in the gardens have expressed the necessity of toilet facilities at the gardens. Most of them urinate in the garden, whereas, as per the Assam Plantation Labour Rules of 1956, latrine accommodations are to be provided in every plantation at the scale of one latrine for every 50 acre of the area under cultivation, and it should have exclusive access for either sex. Moreover, each worker should be entitled to work that is comfortable and free from health hazards but in the case of these estates, pluckers showed discontent regarding the discomfort attached to their work during the plucking of tea leaves. This was basically on account of an umbrella, to be tied to their baskets and which was heavy and difficult to balance. Such issues can be avoided if the management takes workers' safety as its prime concern. In Tea Estate-4, such a problem did not arise, as pluckers were seen to be wearing hats. This was a convenient way to work, and workers were able to enhance their plucking speed. Another important complaint raised by the workers was that the size of plastic bag provided by the management to each plucker has been continuously increasing in the last few years. As a result, workers were facing difficulties filling it up and carrying it. The management has been reportedly facing a shortage of pluckers during peak season; hence, the baskets might have been deliberately made larger in size to fetch more leaves per worker. Excess workloads may have adverse health implications on the workers; such issues are not explicitly covered under the Plantation Labour Act of 1951.

Factory

Workers engaged in the factory are equally exposed to health issues; hence, the examination of labour relations and working conditions at the factory, at every stage of tea manufacturing, is necessary. There are two ways of tea production – the crush, tear and curl (CTC) process and the orthodox method. In the CTC process, the withered green leaves are passed through two rollers rotating in opposite directions, and among the four tea estates, three tea estates, that is, Tea Estate-1, Tea Estate-2 and Tea Estate-4, have only focussed on the CTC process. Tea Estate-3 produces using both the orthodox and CTC methods. More machinery is used in the CTC type, but in the orthodox method, along with machinery, a lot of manual work and constant observation are required; hence, more manpower is also mandated. In a year, the period from May to December is considered to be the peak season of the garden, and work in the factory during this season takes place in three shifts on eight hours' rotation. Since the garden cannot afford any man-day loss, the estates require more manpower. The factory is generally segregated into two zones – high- and low-risk zones. The high-risk zone is mainly the area where CTC machines are located, while drying, sorting, weighing and packaging fall in the low-risk zone that calls for higher manual work.

In addition to the basic facilities, workers are to be provided with the essential amenities to ensure safety and hygiene at the workplace, as per the standards set by the International Organisation for Standardisation (ISO 22000: 2005) and Social Accountability (SA8000). Thus the workers are given mask, gloves, caps, helmets, sandals and aprons; and everyone, including workers, management and visitors are also required to wash their hands and feet before entering the factory. Barring Tea Estate-4, workers from all the other estates reported that they were not provided the basic amenities on a regular basis and were given the aforesaid amenities only during special occasions, such as during visits by auditors and guests. There seem to be clear violations of occupational safety of these workers, who were exposed to dust and pungent smells throughout the day in these factories. Moreover, there were unhygienic practices over using the basic amenities, where workers from Tea Estate-2 and Tea Estate-3 reported that the aprons and other clothes that they received to wear just before auditors or any guest visits were used and unwashed. Once visitors left the premises, workers were told to hand over the amenities to the concerned persons at the factory. On the other hand, workers at Tea Estate-4 expressed a different concern over the usage of aprons. Here, each worker was given only one apron which was washed just once a week, though in practice it needed to be washed every alternate day to maintain hygiene.

As mentioned earlier, mainly male workers are engaged in the production process in the factories, while female workers work at the gardens. The only exception was Tea Estate-1, where two permanent female workers were found at the factory. The two workers also felt exultant and empowered working in the factory along with their male counterparts. When the management was asked about the appointment of female workers at the factory, they expressed their concern over the safety and security of the female workers during night shifts. This is because workers at the factory worked on rotation, where each worker might have to work on a three-shift basis, and most of the labour colonies (known as labour lines) were located far away from the factory. To walk back home, especially in the dark, for female workers was risky. According to the management, male workers were reluctant to work in the tea gardens, especially since 2006.

So there seem to be clear violations of income, security and rights of workers within the framework of decent work. This can be regarded as an economic exclusion of the workers at work, where they are debarred from basic rights and provisions at their workplace.

Wage and compensation

The economic security of estate labourers has been a major concern for a long time. The practice of payment in cash and kind has been questioned on several grounds. One such factor relates to the freedom of workers in the contemporary era to decide about their family's consumption. However, the age-old practice of paying low wages in addition to provision of substandard products jeopardises the economic security of labourers. In reality, the economic security of the labourers can be in question; that is, if they are seen as the means of survival or if they leave the labourers to perish in the enclave economies. This section provides an overview of the economic scenario of the labourers in the four tea estates. The social conditions of the migrant labourers have been devastating, with inhuman working and deplorable living conditions. Being situated in jungles, the estates were highly unhealthy and disease prone. The migrant workers were lured on false promises and were left to struggle in the estates with insufficient nourishment, overwork and unhygienic living conditions like overcrowding, bad housing and an impure water supply, and so on. So these workers, despite having to work under extremely poor compensation and working conditions, had to fight for their basic human rights. Moreover, from an economic perspective, a plantation worker received Rs 4 to Rs 5 per month in some estates and even lower than Rs 4 in others in 1864 (Xaxa 1985). Considering the current wage rate, the increase in absolute terms merely by Rs 90 in a span of 150 years seems to be strange, taking into account the rise in the cost of living index and growth of trade in tea over the years.

Wage structure and consumption pattern

The biggest problem in Assam and West Bengal is that there is no statutory minimum wage for tea plantation labourers (Columbia Law School 2014). The wages are fixed through a tripartite negotiation between the employers' association, trade unions and the state, and unlike the Indian formula of 'need-based minimum wage', which should be sufficient to support two adults and two children, such a system does not seem to be true in the case of the plantation economy (ibid.). It has been proposed that since both men and women work in the plantation system, the aforementioned wages should be halved (ibid.). The daily actual wages of labourers in tea estates of major tea-producing states as of 2014 has been mentioned in Table 5.2.

The wage rate in Assam plantations ranged from Rs 2.50 to Rs. 3.50 per month in the early 1840s and 1850s (Sarma et al. 2012). As per the Directorate of Public Instruction (DPI) of Assam report (1917–18), this rate increased to Rs 8.09 for men and Rs 7.59 for women (including diet rations, subsistence allowance and bonuses) for 1905–6 (ibid.). In this respect, the report of Columbia Law School (2014) shows certain practices in the tea estates have led to further degradation of work. First, by increasing subcontracting of

Table 5.2 Daily rate of wages in major tea-producing states, 2014

Name of the state	Daily rate of wages (in rupees)
Assam	94
West Bengal	95
Tamil Nadu	209.27
Kerala	216.53
Karnataka	228.35

Source: Indian Tea Association, 2015

work to informal labour brokers, wages have degraded below the legal wage rate; second, through a practice of shifting certain core production and operational costs – like costs of tools and those used for pruning – from the company to the workers, wages have diminished. As per the Bipartite Memorandum of Settlement (2005 and 2010) between tea management and the representatives of trade unions, the rate of the incremental wage hike has been summarised in Tables 5.3 and 5.4.

Even before the expiry of the above agreement, dated 3 February 2010, the largest trade union organising labourers in tea gardens of Assam, namely, Assam Cha Mazdoor Sangha submitted a charter of demand seeking an increase in wages in the face of steep regional disparities in wage levels. The Bipartite Memorandum of Settlement dated 1 March 2012 between tea management and the representatives of trade unions. The daily wage of Assam plantation labourers for the period between 2012 and 2017 has been provided in Table 5.4.

In the context of the tea estates under study, the current wage seems to be low where the daily cash income, excluding rations, electricity, firewood and provident funds, stands to be around Rs 94. Compared to wages under the Mahatma Gandhi National Rural Employment Guarantee Act (MGNREGA) schemes and other minimum wages, the tea industry provides a low wage. This drives the workers to move out from the tea estates and search for public work programmes in the locality. However, the mobility of such workers, trapped in enclave economies, is another matter of concern. Moreover, the present cash income is not sufficient to cover consumption of even basic food and nutritional requirements. Discussions with workers from each tea estate revealed that workers normally consume rice (mainly obtained from ration),

Table 5.3 Incremental wage hike as per the Bipartite Memorandum of Settlement, 30 November 2005

Period	Incremental wage hike (Rs per day)
From 01/11/2005 to 30/04/2007	2.60
From 01/05/2007 to 30/08/2008	3.70
From 01/09/2008 to 30/12/2009	3.70
From 01/01/2010 to 31/03/2011	8.00
From 01/04/2011 to 30/06/2012	5.00
From 01/07/2012 to 30/09/2013	5.00

Source: Indian Tea Association, 2015

Table 5.4 Nominal wage of tea plantation labour in Assam

Period	Nominal wage (Rs per day)
From 01/01/2012 to 31/12/2012	84
From 01/01/2013 to 31/12/2013	89
From 01/01/2014 to 31/12/2014	94
From 01/01/2015 to 31/12/2015	115
From 01/01/2016 to 31/12/2016	126
From 01/01/2017 to 31/12/2017	137

Source: India Tea Association, 2015, 2017

lentils, leafy vegetables and *chapattis* (made from wheat flour), with fish or meat on rare occasions and in very small quantity. It is also noticed that the management encourage existing workers to work overtime, as in the case of Estate 3. Labourers who worked overtime only received the overtime wages but no other emoluments or facilities such as rations, which the management should be paying if it employs more temporary workers to cope with increasing work pressure.

Ration and fuel

Payment in kind has always been debated in the context of practicing such a system in present times, but what separates this organised system from other sectors in the economy is its practice of providing rations as a part of the wage at a subsidised rate. The permanent labourers get 1.630 kg each for rice and wheat flour on a weekly basis. In the case of labourers who have worked for more than eight years, the adult dependent get 1.220 kg a week, while minor dependent (2–8 years) gets 610 gm a week. However, it is revealed that the quality of wheat flour was poor, containing large amounts of roughage. Most of the time, the amount of roughage is more than the flour. Along with rations, every worker is also given a certain amount of tea. However, the quantity of tea varies from estate to estate. Workers in all four tea estates complained about the quality of tea; they reported that they were given tea from old unsold stock, often found to be damp and devoid of flavour. So, alienation of labourers from their own produce can be marked as a common feature among these estates. Firewood provided by the company sufficed for a maximum of up to five months, and workers managed on their own by collecting dry leaves, twigs and wood logs from the gardens.

Welfare benefits

In the context of the third dimension, indicators related to conditions of social welfare like hospitals, schools, crèche, living conditions and the provision of water and electricity have been taken into consideration. The company organises various welfare activities under its welfare policies and corporate social responsibilities (CSRs) programmes. These programmes span across outreach programmes, lab-to-land programmes, free health check-up camps (under MMU of NRHM), school health check-ups, free cataract-screening camps and flood relief camps. However, such programmes seem to make less sense when the company fails to safeguard the basic rights and provisions of welfare amenities to its own workers. Moreover, operating as enclave economies, these estates are required to put a lot of emphasis on recreational facilities for their workers. The Plantation Labour Act of 1951 stresses the necessity of having both indoor and outdoor games and the required sports equipment to pursue such activities. In this context, each estate has one labour club in each division with amenities and equipment such as a TV or a carom board, which are very basic and frivolous. Needless to say, labourers do not visit these labour clubs.

Hospital

The Columbia Law School report (2014) acknowledged serious and widespread problems concerning medical care at many estates of Assam. The resentment ranged from absence of doctors and poor quality of care to unexpected costs and the burden of such costs being placed on the labourers when they fall sick (ibid.). The provision of basic health facilities is not only a welfare responsibility of the employer of the tea estate but can be linked to the basic human rights of every individual. In this context, empirical evidence also shows mismanagement and the callous attitudes of the estates towards the responsibilities laid out in the Assam Plantation Labour Rules of 1956. Apart from Tea Estate-2, not even a single dispensary was found in other divisions of other tea estates. Moreover, Tea Estate-1 does not seem to even conform to the beds to workers ratio (15 beds per 1,000 workers) as laid down in the rules. Usage of unsafe practices such as that of using firewood for cooking is being practiced at the hospital of Tea Estate-2. Above all, workers of all estates, except Tea Estate-4, reported that doctors were not available throughout the day, which implies a complete violation under subsections 5 and 6 of Rule 36 under Section 10 of the Assam Plantation Labour Rules of 1956. In such cases, the health assistant prescribes medicine that is objected to by some workers, as the rules prescribes the presence of a full-time qualified medical practitioner (1 per every 1,750 workers or part thereof) assisted by a midwife, trained nurses assistants, a pharmacist and health assistants (see Table 5.5). Estates having links with the National Rural Health Mission (NRHM) were found to be equipped with better resources, such as availability of medicines, ambulances and a baby incubator.

Crèche

The provision of crèche is another basic welfare benefit listed under the Tea Plantation Act of 1951 that can relieve labourers and enable them work at ease, keeping their children in the crèche of the estates. Apart from looking after the children, these crèches are also supposed to provide basic nutrition in the form of fresh milk or milk powder to children below 2 years of age and wholesome solid food to those above 2 years. However, the benefit of crèche is not satisfactory on any of the estates, as the basic infrastructure is extremely poor. They do not adopt any innovative measures and have no learning environment, which prevents the workers from opting for such facilities. Workers are reluctant to send their children to crèches for two main reasons. First, except one crèche which is located close to the factory, all other crèches are far away

Table 5.5 Basic statistics of hospitals

	Tea Estate-1	Tea Estate-2	Tea Estate-3	Tea Estate-4
Resident population/ hospital bed	80.02	154.08	116.45	157.70
Resident population/ doctor	2761	7704	4891	3942.5
Resident population/ nurses	1380.50	2568	1630.33	3942.50
Dispensaries	1	2	0	1

Source: Collected from respective estates during fieldwork

from the factories. Pick up and drop off facilities of children by the tea estates are found to be poor. Second, the quality of food provided at the crèches and the way in which the food gets prepared are not satisfactory. However, as per the Assam Plantation Labour Rules of 1956, the crèche needs to be conveniently accessible for the mothers working on the estates. With regard to food preparation, it is mandatory that the food served to children below 2 years of age is approved by a certified surgeon, but considering the empirical findings of the estates, there is no such case.

Schools

The right to education is a basic right of every child but in the case of tea plantations, it seems to be dubious. The basic issue that has been raised by these workers is the indifferent or rather reluctant attitude of the management towards the promotion of education among the children of plantation labourers. The workers claim that management pays no heed towards the education facilities for these labourers, as they do not want upward mobility in human capital, on account of which they can retain at least the next three to four generations of labourers in their plantation economies. In context of the provision of educational facilities, there is a shortage of classrooms for students and teachers in all the estates (see Table 5.6). For example, in Tea Estate-1, where two classes (Class-I and Class-II) were simultaneously taking place in one room, with the room being partitioned by placing one blackboard in the middle. So the construction of school

Table 5.6 Basic statistics of schools and crèches

	Tea Estate-1	Tea Estate-2	Tea Estate-3	Tea Estate-4
No. of crèches	2	2	1	3
No. of LP schools	2	2	0	2
Pupil/teacher	75.66	63.57	0	48.13

Source: Collected from respective estates during fieldwork

building does not conform to the rules laid out in the Assam Plantation Labour Rules of 1956, which implies lack of basic provisions for the social upliftment of these workers. Hence, this can be claimed to be one of the reasons for restricting development of their capacity for occupational mobility in the future. Apart from Tea Estate-4, where the medium of instruction is Hindi and Assamese, other estates use Assamese and Bengali, as most of the workers have migrated across the country. Moreover, in each of the estates, the tutor to pupil ratio is not in accordance with the prescribed ratio of 1 teacher for every 40 children, as mentioned in the Assam Plantation Labour Rules of 1956. Estates like Tea Estate-3 do not have lower primary schools. When the management was asked about education, responses were that schools are the responsibility of the state government and hence do not fall under the purview of the company or the specific tea estate. Notably, the infrastructure of the government schools is poor. Therefore, a company could partially support school infrastructure by providing chairs or tables or by extending the school buildings. In this, an important institutional support through government towards company-provided schools can be introduced through Sarva Shiksha Abhiyan (SSA) i.e., universalise elementary education, so that students have basic access to their books and other materials for their education, as seen in Tea Estate-4.

Labour quarters

Apart from the inhuman working conditions of these labourers, many studies depict the violation of the Plantation Labour Act of 1951 in terms of housing and sanitation facilities. The Columbia Law report (2014) shows how workers live crowded together in cramped quarters with broken roofs and cracked walls. The incapability of the estates to maintain latrines has turned some living places into a network of cesspools (ibid.). An attempt has been made to evaluate deplorable living conditions of labourers in the four tea estates in terms of variables encompassing the conditions of labour quarters, status of roads and provision of electricity.

Though the section on housing facilities under the Plantation Labour Act of 1951 requires an employer to assume complete responsibility for providing adequate housing arrangement to its labourers, whether the current arrangement can be considered to provide a decent liveable place for the workers seems questionable. There are basically two types of houses in the labour colonies: the old layout and the new one. Under the old layout of houses, the kitchen is built in front of the house, while it is at the rear end under the new layout. Houses in labour colonies undergo no regular repairs and maintenance, unlike what was prescribed in subsection 1 of Rule 63 under Section 16 of the Assam Plantation Labour Rules of 1956. Most houses are repaired by the workers themselves. Houses do not have proper drainage and sanitation facilities. Except for Tea Estate-1 and Tea Estate-4, one toilet covers two labour quarters in some houses. The company is supposed to maintain or clean periodically, but workers mentioned a different reality on the ground. They report to the welfare officer (WO) whenever cleaning and maintenance is required; however, in spite of regular reporting, nothing is done. In some cases, the households that can afford to share the maintenance cost mutually, but as most of the houses cannot bear the cost, they urinate and defecate in the gardens. Human excreta may impact the quality of produce; hence, again the responsibility of the employers to its workers and the market that consumes its products is violated. Added to the condition of the quarters, the accessibility to these colonies in terms of roads is not good. The roads to the labour colonies and the ones inside the colonies are unmetalled. Workers reported that it is very difficult to communicate during the monsoons. Condition of roads from labour colonies to hospitals, schools and crèches, especially in Tea Estate-3, Tea Estate-2 and Tea Estate-1, is not good. As the distance of schools, crèches and hospitals from some of the labour colonies was much more than what was laid out in the acts, labourers are reluctant to send their children to the schools and crèches.

Provision of water

The issue of a safe supply of water is connected to problems of sanitation and sewage in the labour colonies (Columbia Law School 2014).

Throughout the study, scarcity of water remained a common problem of the tea estates; however, the extent of the problem varied (see Table 5.7). For example, Tea Estate-2 suffered from an acute water shortage throughout the year; even the hospital and crèches have limited water supply, while dispensaries and schools have no water supply. In the labour colonies, there are a few working hand pumps which do not work properly during the summer, and consequently, the workers need to go every day to a small rivulet (known as *Jhora*), located quite far away from the garden, for bathing and washing utensils and clothes. In the case of Tea Estate-3, the problem was with the quality of the water, where it was noticed that the drinking water supply was severely affected due to iron deposits inside the water pipe. Hence, the flow of water was very slow, but the time allotted to retrieve water remained the same. Therefore, workers reported that there was an acute scarcity of drinking water at the labour colony. Despite several complaints about this problem, the management paid no heed to workers' concerns. Hence, unlike at management staff quarters, there is either inadequate provision of water taps and latrine facilities among the labour quarters, or, even where it is available, its functioning is not proper. Many of the labourers reported of only one working tap for five households in the labour colony.

Provision of electricity

There are mainly two issues on electricity that have been raised by the workers in all four tea estates. First, the total electricity bill in labour colonies is equally divided among workers. Due to commercial electricity connections, each worker on average ends up paying Rs 300–500 fortnightly, despite having no power connection between 6 a.m. and 4 p.m. at the workers' colony. The electricity

Table 5.7 Basic statistics of labour quarters

	No. of labour quarters	Sources of water	Latrines
Tea Estate-1	1071	563 (taps)	1071
Tea Estate-2	901	103 (taps) + 84 (tube wells) + 96 (wells)	880
Tea Estate-3	754	230 (taps) + 22 (wells)	709
Tea Estate-4	1211	510 (taps)	1211

Source: Collected from respective estates during fieldwork

that is being provided is commercial (not a domestic supply); hence, the rates are high. Workers complained about the ways of metre reading. The electrician concerned normally takes the reading in the afternoon when workers are not present at the houses. Hence, workers are suspicious about the way in which the electricity bill is calculated. This is mainly because houses having just one light (bulb) and one fan are paying almost equivalent the amount paid by houses using consumer durables such as a TV, refrigerator and so on. Labour colonies in Estate C have been deprived of an electricity supply over the last two years which is leading to a hidden agitation among workers. The state can provide or the estate can bargain with the state for subsidised electricity, which currently consumes a huge share of labourers' income.

Conclusion

The main problem with the low standard of living is due to low wages. The low price on the processed tea from the auction market could be one of the reasons behind the low wage payments. Processed tea, manufactured either in the estate or local factories, is sent to the auction centres (Guwahati, Siliguri, and Kolkata for Eastern India). The large tea marketing companies buy from there. It is believed that the cartelisation of buyers in the auctions does not allow tea prices to rise, even though there may be high demand. The cartels comprise a handful of big buyers (most are multi-national companies); thus, they buy tea at lower prices and sell at much higher prices after packaging the product, as the retail price of tea never decreased. Besides being deprived of economic security, the workers are denied too from adequate welfare benefits. For generations, workers in these estates have been associated with these plantations, so they have developed an emotional bonding with the estates. They believe their inherited skills need to be respected by the management; hence, they seek respect not only in terms of economic benefits but even in non-economic aspects. They seek inclusion in the production process to develop a sense of belongingness among the workforce and help them communicate their requirements and needs freely to the management. These estates need to work on the social upgradation of workers by strengthening welfare mechanisms, particularly the quantitative and qualitative aspects. This is so because, unlike other work, plantation economies dwell heavily on workers, who serve as an integral part within the economy. From the limited focus of unions and other interested parties on an increase in wages and the improvement of the quality of rations, the emphasis needs to drift towards the enhancement of welfare mechanisms. Likewise, the provision of health care facilities, schools, crèches and so on needs to be improved, which may be attained through collaboration with other state mechanisms like that of NRHM and Sarva Shiksha Abhiyan.

Notes

1 Rainforest Alliance Certification is provided to farms practicing methods that protect the health of the farmers, their livelihoods, their land and the surrounding waters (Rainforest Alliance, 2015).
2 Decent Work Agenda has been developed by the International Labour Organisation for the community of work looking at job creation, rights at work, social protection and social dialogue (International Labour Organisation).
3 The names of the four tea estates have been changed, and referred to as Tea Estate-1, Tea Estate-2, Tea Estate-3 and Tea Estate-4.
4 The title Company A represents the name of the company whose estates have been considered for this study, and it stands as one of the major tea producers in India.

References

Barrientos, Stephanie, Gary Gereffi, and Arianna Rossi. 2010. 'Economic and Social Upgrading in Global Production Networks: Developing a Framework for Analysis', *Capturing the Gains 2010*, Working Paper 3.

Bhowmik, Sharit K. 1981. *Class Formation in the Plantation System*, New Delhi: People's Publication House.

Bhowmik, Sharit K., Virginius Xaxa, and M. A. Kalam. 1996. *Tea Plantation Labour in India*, New Delhi: Friedrich Ebert Stiftung.

Columbia Law School. 2014. 'The More Things Change . . . The World Bank, Tata and Enduring Abuses of India's Tea Plantations'.

Gohain, Hiren. 2007. 'A Question of Identity: Adivasi Militancy in Assam', *Economic and Political Weekly*, 42(49): 13–16.

Griffiths, Percival, J. 1967. *The History of the Indian Tea Industry*, London: Weidenfeld & Nicolson Publication.

Guha, Amalendu. 2012. *Planter Raj to Swaraj: Freedom Struggle & Electoral Politics in Assam 1826–1947*, New Delhi: Tulika Books.

International Labour Organisation. Decent Work. Retrieved from: www.ilo.org/global/topics/decent-work/lang--en/index.htm. Accessed on 10 June, 2018.

International Labour Organisation. 2015. 'Sectoral Studies on Decent Work in Global Supply Chains: Comparative Analysis of Good Practices by Multinational Enterprises in Promoting Decent Work in Global Supply Chains', in *Sectoral Policies Department (SECTOR)*, Study-3, pp. 101–132, Geneva: International Labour Office.

Kalleberg, Arnei L. 2000. 'Nonstandard Employment Relations: Part-Time, Temporary and Contract Work', *Annual Review of Sociology*, 26: 341–365.

Kalleberg, Arne L., Barbara F. Reskin, and Ken Hudson. 2000. 'Bad Jobs in America: Standard and Nonstandard Employment Relations and Job Quality in the United States', *American Sociological Review*, 65(2): 256–278.

Neilson, Jeff and Bill Pritchard. 2009. *Value Chain Struggles Institutions and Governance in the Plantation Districts of South India*, Oxford: Blackwell Publishing.

Oxfam. 2015. *Fair Trade Tea.* www.oxfam.org.nz/what-we-do/issues/fairtrade/about-fairtrade/fairtrade-tea. Accessed March 2015.

Potts, Jason, Matthew Lynch, Ann Wilkings, Gabriel Huppé, Maxine Cunningham, and Vivek Voora. 2014. *The State of Sustainability Initiatives Review 2014: Standards and the Green Economy*, London: International Institute for Environment and Development. www.iisd.org/pdf/2014/ssi_2014.pdf. Accessed July 2017.

Rainforest Alliance. 2015. *Rainforest Alliance Certified Tea.* Retrieved from: www.rainforest-alliance.org/articles/rainforest-alliance-certified-tea. Accessed on 10 June, 2018.

Sarma, Atul, Deepak K. Mishra, and Vandana Upadhyay. 2012. *Unfolding Crisis in Assam's Tea Plantations: Employment and Occupational Mobility*, New Delhi: Routledge.

Xaxa, Virginius. 1985. 'Tribal Migration to Plantation Estate in North-East India: Determinants and Consequences', *Demography India*, XIV(1): 70–81.

Xaxa, Virginius. 1997. *Economic Dualism and Structure of Class: a Study in Plantation and Peasant Settings in North Bengal*, New Delhi: Cosmos Publication.

Chapter 6

Work, control and mobility in the manufacturing industry

A study of the cement industry in Assam

Piyali Bhowmick

Being a core industry, like iron and steel, cement plays a significant role towards a country's economic development. Demand for cement is one of the key indicators of economic growth, as it signifies the development of infrastructure: building of dams, bridges, schools, hospitals and industries. The industry contributes towards generating employment, direct as well as indirect.

Cement is a powdery substance made from non-metallic minerals like calcium, lime and clay. It is mixed with water to form mortar and with sand, gravel and water to make concrete. Access to abundant supply of limestone or calcium is an essential precondition for the manufacturing of cement. Hence, cement-making plants are located near centres of consumption of finished products or sources of raw materials, namely, limestone and clay (CMA 2012). With technological advancements, the production process has changed from being solely dependent on manpower (labour intensive) to electric power (capital intensive), which has brought forth a reorganisation of labour. Workers have entered into new forms of relationship at the workplace. While casual, contractual, temporary workers are being preferred to full-time employees, new work patterns have been introduced, and labour has been divided into skilled, semi-skilled or unskilled labour force. Several complex issues like wage problem, workers' safety, sharing of profits, adjustment to disputes with co-workers/authority, the provision of social protection and so on need to be considered in the context of these changes.

With regard to the establishment of cement plants, the north-eastern part of India is comparatively new. In 1976, a public sector undertaking run by the Cement Corporation of India was commissioned in Bokajan in Assam (Dikshit and Dikshit 2014). This company was established under the umbrella of the Shyam Group of industries, which dealt with the iron and steel sector in the North-East. Born from this group, the Cement Manufacturing Company Limited (CMCL) entered into the manufacturing of cement under the brand 'Star Cement'. Today, CMCL is the largest cement manufacturer in the North-East. It is located in Lumshnong, 126 km from Shillong on the National Highway to Silchar in Meghalaya (The Shyam Group Corporate Overview, 2017). Its clinkerisation unit is the largest in the North-East, with the capacity to manufacture 0.6 million tonnes of clinker, presumably the highest in the region. The primary concern while setting up the plant was to find a strategic location where limestone, coal and shale, the raw materials required for producing cement, would be easily available. Finally, Meghalaya was selected as the apt place for the plant.

The clinker manufactured in the unit is transported to Guwahati (Sonapur), which is 216 km away, via National Highway 6. At Guwahati the cement is put into the grinding and mixing unit and then finally packaged and transported to other parts of the region. The Guwahati grinding unit has a strategic location with a good network of roads and rail, which makes transport to the bordering areas like Nagaland, Arunachal Pradesh, Bhutan and Nepal (CMCL Annual Report) easier. The robust demand for cement and its long-term potential, increasing investments and attractive opportunities in the north-eastern zone of India have led to a construction boom in the neoliberal era.

Labour relations have undergone changes in recent times, as labour is seen as a commodity to be sold, used and controlled. Along with the management, contractors and supervisors also act as employers in the industry. This has led to a double-edged question in labour relations: who is controlling whom? With the application and introduction of new rules, suppression of union formation, wage reduction and curtailment of promotion for temporary workers, along with the use of technical force, the industry suffers from deskilling and degradation of permanent and temporary workers. At the same time, with increasing urbanisation and globalisation, the need for a huge workforce has prompted many to initiate schemes and experiments to improve labour relations by emphasising employment security, bonus-profit sharing, improvement of performance, teamwork, training, the assignment of decision-making responsibility to the lowest level of the organisation and so on. The data for the study presented in this chapter were collected through field work and interviews. All 56 respondents were selected from a site located at Chamata Pathar, Sonapur, in the outskirts (20 km) of Guwahati. The primary respondents were casual/temporary workers from the grinding unit. The interview schedule was devised in a manner which encouraged every respondent to actively participate in the survey by answering every question. This study targeted workers from various divisions of the industry under the semi-skilled and unskilled category; sampling was done in three stages.

Workers in the production process

The cement industry is not only capital intensive but also manual labour intensive. A large number of workers are appointed in different areas according to their skills. Hence, directly or indirectly, they are involved in the production process. Industry workers include painters, carpenters, drivers, packers, loaders, riggers, operators, electricians, and fly-ash labourers; desk job workers took care of the administration, laboratory and accounts. However, in the civil, mechanical, electronics and instrumentation departments, the number of workers is limited. The process department comprised riggers and fly-ash labourers who cut the bags of raw materials, put the raw materials in the correct proportion into the grinder and then did the packaging. This process requires a huge workforce. However, those involved are mostly temporary workers.

Under CMCL, the clinker produced at the mother plant in Meghalaya is transferred to the grinding unit in Sonapur, adjacent to other markets of the north and north-eastern states. Figure 6.1 shows the structure and the distribution of workers in the Guwahati (Sonapur) grinding unit.

Mechanical, electronics and instrumentation, civil and process are the four units outlined. Each division has its respective head of the department. Human resources, constituting a separate body and not a department, is headed by the deputy manager of the plant. There are one or more supervisors, depending upon the number of temporary workers in each department and the interest of the management. Each division constitutes 15–20 permanent workers. As

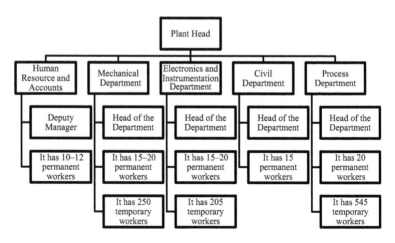

Figure 6.1 Structure and distribution of workers

Source: Based on primary data collected by the author

discussed earlier, various departments have temporary workers like painters, carpenters, drivers, packers, loaders, riggers, operators, electricians and fly-ash labourers. The number of temporary workers at the time the study was conducted is about 1000.

As all workers are males, their dominance is obvious. The level of education differs across the migration category; in fact, it is higher among migrant workers. However, the socio-demographic distribution shows that domination over accommodation is hierarchical. Economic and social exclusion from various steps have proved that workers of the lower level are even deprived of their basic right to be happy. They are cut off not only from their personal space but also from the workplace. Yet workers who have been getting a good salary also receive cash benefits and employee awards owing to their hierarchical position. So, wages, training and safety measures are not properly presented to all workers. While lack of proper training has taken away the workers' rights to learn new skills or improve their present skills and use them to climb up the ladder to a higher position, the absence of stringent methods to implement safety measures or ensure close supervision or implementation of fines for not wearing safety gear make the workers careless regarding safety issues. Workers are not even given transportation facilities like others to reach work on time.

Recruitment process

For the higher ranks, recruitment is made either to fill up vacancies or for new positions. Essentially done through references, via naukri.com or consultancies, the company does not advertise about job hiring. With the help of proper documents and through structured interviews, the higher positions are filled up. However, temporary workers come on their own and submit their bio data. No formal interviews are conducted for their recruitment, but it needs the consent of the human resources staff in the administration. Supervisors, on the other hand, are recruited directly through contractors, who are appointed by the management. The contractor sometimes gives power to supervisors to recruit wage labourers. This means that supervisors are answerable to contractors; wage labourers have a relation with supervisors directly in terms of reporting and with contractors indirectly; contractors report to the management directly. Soon after the second year of its establishment, the employment pattern in the cement industry changed, with the inclusion of casual contract workers in the plant.

Control mechanism

Workers put their effort and labour in the production process, though they do not engage in the process of production directly. Issues like control over working hours and equal distribution of surplus are in the hands of the management. The managerial approach towards controlling labour differs at different points of time depending on the line of control undertaken. As with the labour process, ensuring the usefulness of labour has also been the responsibility of capitalists. In general, workers who are controlled by their superiors depict overt signs of dissatisfaction. This degradation of work affects the social life of the worker as well. The management exercises control to attain maximum work by lowering wages, diminishing interaction between co-workers and encouraging contradictory views between employers and employees (Braverman 1974). The employers, for example, falsely promise promotion and a permanent job; however, only a handful of workers actually get a permanent space or support the decisions of the employers. By implementing more restrictions and creating differences among workers (permanent and temporary) a friction between the workers and the employers is created. This section discusses various forms of the control mechanism practised over workers at different levels of work arrangement.

Experimentation as a control

The duration of the work period for workers at the work station is controlled. The workers have to come to work sharply at the time stated by the management. The in-time is computerised with the help of a punching machine in order to keep a check on workers' punctuality. But the 'out-time' of the workers is neither specified nor recorded; failure to come in on time results in the lowering of their wages. Workers too have no control over the 'out-time'. Although the standard work period is eight hours, the management has made it compulsory for workers to exceed their hours in order to sustain a profit.

Second, workers are kept under surveillance through camera recording. Hence, it is mandatory for workers to restrict their mobility within the workplace premises. The workers cannot go out of the gate, crossing security. Even during lunch break they are under surveillance. Also, control extends to the interaction between co-workers inside the compound. Failure to comply with these rules results in a reprimand, warning, or direct reduction of wages.

The extent to which a worker has control over the work process can be understood from the fact that co-workers interacted in relation to work-related issues only. Thus, to exercise more control, workers are warned of wage cuts if they are seen interacting with one another. Prohibiting interaction also means that social interaction and exchange of information are not entertained, and the scope to learn new skills is deliberately restricted.

Union as a medium of control

It becomes difficult to listen to everyone in a large organisation. Thus, collectively, a body of representatives needs to be chosen through fair election so that problems and grievances of people can be understood in a systematic manner. Six years after its installation, which was accomplished in 2011, there have been protests from the local people. The management recruited a huge number of local people when the industry was set up. The workers joined in the form of casual labour, and the management ensured them that after completion of one year, they would be promoted to hold permanent positions. More than 1000 workers, including unskilled and semi-skilled workers, participated in the protests. In order to keep its reputation, the management decided to grant permanent status to 1000 workers.

The management since then has been trying to replace the old locals with recruits transferred from the Meghalaya Plant or from other states. The new recruitments also included employees from rival companies, luring them with more benefits and salary. Hence, in three years, the management has been able to replace the locals and reduce the number to almost a few hundred. In this process, the voice of workers who have problems like earning a comparatively lesser salary or other issues has been thwarted. The local community in the industry has tried to form a union but has remained unsuccessful, even after taking the legal course. There have been ideological differences between the management and the union. The union wants only the local people to be in it. But the management has a different view altogether. It has selected separate representatives from each department who were experienced and not local. They head their respective departments. Each head of the department becomes the immediate reporting boss for their subordinates. Thus, there are multi-layered power relations. On one hand, the management controls the workers, while on the other hand, department heads have the responsibility to control those working below them.

The management identifies workers who are on their side, can be controlled easily by giving some benefits and can become informers for the management. This practice has enabled the management to decide on the tools to control workers and prevent the formation of a union.

While the collective voice helped workers to gain their rights, these were temporary, as gradually workers who posed a threat were either transferred to the Meghalaya unit or ultimately thrown out of their job. The workers who tried to confront the management individually were threatened by saying: 'eat vegetables now and later you can think of eating chicken/fish/mutton'. During the field study, this was narrated by a local temporary worker who had gone to the management to complain about his low wages. The decreasing collective voice has made workers accept the reality of their woes and stop protesting because of the fear of losing their jobs. A local temporary worker, when asked about the view of forming a union, gave a surprising reply: *'malik jetia 1 taka pabo, ami tetia 25 paisa pam'*, which means 'if the company got a profit of 1 rupee, then workers would get only 25 paisa'. The view suggests that workers have accepted the conditions of work even if they are subjected to various control mechanisms.

Multi-layered control and autonomy

The cement industry needs a huge workforce and outsources the recruitment process of all its workers. The management outsources a large number of temporary workers by giving tenders to contractors. There are about 28 contractors who employ more than 1000 temporary workers in total. The contractors cannot always keep a check on workers. Thus, each contractor appoints more than one supervisor who controls the workers and gives them work. Again, workers are given instruction from their seniors and heads of the department, respectively. Thus, the existence of multi-layered controlling could be seen where, first, the lower rank workers are controlled by their contractors in terms of wage; then by supervisors, seniors and heads of the department on work-related issues; and finally by the management, who controls the overall aspect of the labour process. The employees who are directly appointed by the management are given some autonomy in terms of controlling subordinate workers. Hence, a system of control is created, ensuring maximum supervision of workers in the lower strata and minimum supervision of those in the higher paid jobs.

Conflict and bureaucratic control

With the decline in the number of local workers, there has been a nexus between migrant workers coming from other states and the local people. The local people consider that, as there was only one significant industry in their area, more locals should be recruited to facilitate development. But in due course of time, the management faced competition from other reputed markets, and it realised that to increase production, a skilled labour force would be the ideal. The lower-rank workers are poor and less educated and lack knowledge and skills; hence, gradually, the management decided to hire skilled workers with some work experience from other states. As a result, 90.9 percent of the workers from Sonapur, Assam, get between Rs 5000–10,000 per month, while 25 percent from other states receive between Rs 16,000–20,000. Hence, Table 6.1 shows that the highest paid workers come from other states.

Table 6.1 Migration-wise salary structure (in Rs)

Place of origin	5000–10,000	11,000–15,000	16,000–20,000	Total
Sonapur, Assam	20	1	1	22
Other states	5	1	2	8
Within Assam	22	4	0	26

Source: Based on primary data

Work and its impact on the workers

Overworking hours

The cement industry's grinding unit runs for 24 hours and has four shifts. The different shifts include: general shift (9 a.m.–6 p.m.); A shift (2 p.m.–10 p.m.); B shift (10 p.m.–6 a.m.); and C shift (6 a.m.–2 p.m.). All the shifts include a break time of one hour, in general, which means eight hours of work for every shift. However, workers also worked beyond eight hours. The highest working hours recorded is for 14 hours at a stretch. The workers have strict 'in-time', while clarification from the management is uncertain about the 'out-time' of workers. Among sample respondents, it is found that under the permanent category, 76.9 percent of the workers work for eight hours, while under the temporary category the situation is vulnerable: 33.3 percent and 23.3 percent of the temporary workers work for 12 and 14 hours, respectively (see Table 6.2). Thus, with more working hours, the workers' upgradation of skills and techniques get restricted by the control of the management.

Work-related stress among workers

After working more than the standard stipulated working hours, the workers feel stressed, which results in health problems. The workers have to face problems even outside the workplace. Workers who are breadwinners of the family have to balance financial conditions of their house on the one hand and do more work within a given time, often with no help at the workplace. However, it has been found that longer working hours also lead to more pressure. With the unit's growth in terms of area, production and workforce, work doubled, and workers were expected to work more

Table 6.2 Category-wise working hours of the workers

Category	8 hours	10 hours	12 hours	14 hours	Total
Permanent workers	20	0	4	2	26
Temporary workers	3	10	7	10	30
Total	23	10	11	12	56

Source: Based on primary data

to augment production. Among the sample respondents, it was found that 80 percent of the workers who worked for 12 hours felt pressure during work, and 100 percent of the workers who worked for 14 hours felt pressure because of the work given to them (see Table 6.3). For most of the workers, pressure was experienced during the time when they were given more work. First, the pressure was on punctuality issues, despite owning a vehicle or getting the transport of the company bus. Second, workers felt extremely pressured when they were given extra work which led them to do overtime. Lastly, workers constantly feared a deduction from their salary due to strict/rigid rules set by the manager. The workers also said that during overtime, there were less people employed to help, which made it difficult to conduct a smooth workflow. The supervisor keeps a check on the workers' progress. If any flaw is found, then the supervisor pressures the subordinate workers. Though quarterly health check-ups are mandatory for all workers, the reports of the check-up do not reach them; thereby they assume that they are in good health.

Lack of bargaining power

The preference of the management towards migrant workers has created a threat among the local workers. This threat has kept them alienated from the development of their own skills. A temporary local worker explained in his own words:

> After working for more than five long years, how can I be called an unskilled worker? I have learned how to work by seeing my seniors, but still, getting a promotion is a distant dream. It is the company's fault, not ours. It is their fault to think like that by suppressing our skills.

Table 6.3 Work pressure due to extended working hours

Working hours	Pressure in work	No pressure during work	Total
8 hours	17	6	23
10 hours	8	2	10
12 hours	6	5	11
14 hours	12	0	23
Total	43	13	10

Source: Based on primary data

Notice that even with more working hours, fewer holidays, and unfavourable working conditions, the payment of wages for the temporary workers are acting as a catalyst. Unskilled and semi-skilled workers receive between Rs 5000 and Rs 10,000 per month (see Table 6.4). Contracts are signed for a newcomer for three years. Even if workers work for longer period, they [workers] receive wage fortnightly for 15 days' wages. The unwritten clause is that workers get two weeks wage after working for 30 days. This is mainly because management/contractor keep 15 days wage as caution money. This implies that if any worker wants to leave the job, the company would gain and the workers incur a loss. Hence workers also think before leaving the job in search of better options. For example, a helper who was a temporary worker technically who should get a salary of Rs 5700 per month would receive Rs 2850 instead after 30 days of work. In Sonapur, the village Chamata Pathar had only one industry (a grinding unit), which raised hope to the people to get employment. There was no other way of generating employment apart from farming, which was seasonal. So to earn extra, people residing nearby grabbed the opportunity to get employment.

Grievance mechanism

The grievances of the workers, according to the management, are looked after by the work committee. This is a body of 16 members, four of whom are heads of departments and the rest selected from the administrative staff. A direct meeting between the work committee and the workers is held once every month. The grievances are thereby attempted to be solved within 48 hours. According to the management, there is no need to have a grievance redressal cell, as they think that the work committee is capable of taking care of

Table 6.4 Category-wise salary of the workers

Category	5000–10,000	11,000–15,000	16,000–20,000	Total
Unskilled	29	1	1	17
Skilled	2	5	2	9
Semi-skilled	16	0	0	16
Total	16	0	0	16

Source: Based on primary data

everything in a short span of time. A register is placed beside the attendance register and punching machine, and workers can write their grievances in it. There is a contradiction in terms of inter-action between the management and workers. According to the workers, there is no such committee formed to address their grievances. A collective consciousness amongst workers is not possible to evolve, as interaction is prohibited. No meeting is held between the management and the workers to discuss even work-related issues. The management only applies the rule that wages would be cut if a worker is found interacting with another. The management accepts the fact that no performance evaluation is undertaken for workers working in the industry. But structured feedback has been started recently only at the management level, and there has been no attempt made to engage in a feedback-based improvement model for workers. Essentially, there is a big communication gap between the management and the workers.

Conditions at the workplace

There are long working hours, unfavourable working conditions and immense work pressure, leading to health problems. Transporters who are in charge of the trucks for unloading raw materials and loading the final products work continuously. Helpers are in constant motion from one place to the other in the unit. Fly-ash labourers, who have to cut the bags of raw materials, have to stand and work all the time. Again, technicians, including electricians and other maintenance workers, have to move from one department to the other. However, assistants from different departments are provided with a desk and a chair of their own. Supervisors and office staff, the management, and even security guards have the provision to sit. This implies that a section of workers are not exposed to dust and pollution whereas the other section of workers start and end their day in the dust, in extreme weather conditions.

The findings also reveal that while workers have to work under an extreme controlled environment, the upgrading space is too little or negligible for them to survive. The political role of the management in the workers' consciousness proves that the management does not want the union to be formed. Hence, migrant workers appointed directly by the management in higher positions are selected as representatives for the workers. It further creates an ideological divide among the migrant workers and local workers.

Skill, mobility and upgradation

The labour process is not a new phenomenon. It is the responsibility of employers to control labour through various means. In order to maximise the controlling power, this control is in the hands of the few. De-skilling is a means to enhance control on workers. De-skilling does not imply denuding workers of their skills, but when management enforces steps like the implementation of more working hours, which would subsequently lead to health problems, the power of workers to utilise their skills in their areas of interest becomes limited and work becomes fragmented. Again, control of workers by multiple heads adds up to more pressure in work.

Skill upgradation

In the cement industry, workers in the temporary category join as casual labour, and even if they show specific skills for a particular job, they continue to be a temporary worker. With managerial control over the labour process, the decision to assign skill-based tasks lies with the management. But, even after gaining experience, workers are not promoted. For example, it is found that out of the total sampled respondents, 53.3 percent of the total workers under temporary category has worked for five years, while 36.7 percent of them have been working as temporary workers for six years. Although, over the years, workers gain experience, their skills are kept away from upgrading. During the field work it was found that the all these years temporary workers kept on working without any upgradation, mainly because of the false hope provided by the higher authority that they would get promoted soon. The workers are either engaged in seasonal farming or have been jobless earlier. They have little or no education to get a job, and in order to earn a living, working in the grinding unit appears the best option; getting a job in the city would further push them towards poorer conditions, as the cost of living in the city is higher than in the village, where workers live in their own house and conveyance is easy.

The deputy manager of the plant is responsible for the development of skills for all workers, irrespective of them being permanent or temporary. However, there is no concrete record to show how many workers have developed their skills and upgraded their positions. Among the sampled respondents, 100 percent of workers said that their skills were not upgraded. The permanent workers, who were already skilled or qualified, were appointed by the management to do a certain job related to their utilisation of skills, such as store operation, managing paper work and so on; temporary workers were appointed on the basis of verbal contract, and they were not needed to do anything other than the specified given work, such as looking after the electrical works or working as a helper (see Table 6.5).

A temporary worker while interviewing expressed,

> After working for more than 5 long years, how can I be called unskilled. I have learned so much in these years but still getting promotion is a distant dream. It is the company's fault not ours. It is their fault to think like that by suppressing our skills.

It can be derived from this story that in five years, any unskilled worker would learn at least something to earn a living. But by the workers not being promoted, their scope to uplift their skills gets stuck. Clearly, the management does not want their workers to learn and acquire their rights.

Table 6.5 Experience according to types of workers

Category	1 year	2 years	3 years	4 years	5 years	6 years	Total
Permanent workers	3	6	1	4	8	4	26
Temporary workers	1	1	0	1	16	11	30
Total	4	7	1	5	24	15	56

Source: Based on primary data

Monotonous work

The workers, under the supervision of multiple heads, have to work continuously. For instance, the fly-ash labourers have to do the same work of cutting bags continuously. Again, workers who have an experience of more than four years are also doing the same work on a daily basis. The only difference is that the intensity of working hours is ever increasing, without adding any extra income. Thus, not only is the work monotonous, it also lacked competition. The control over the autonomy of workers is supervised through surveillance cameras, supervisors, seniors and the management.

Vertical and horizontal mobility

Bureaucratic control is exercised by giving promotion impersonally to a few workers who are inclined towards the management. Workers appointed by the management are promoted with more benefits and facilities. Movement upward or downward in the hierarchy is known as vertical mobility. Though promotion of temporary workers is not practised, the management can give orders for their downward mobility. For instance, an operator in the industry sometimes has to work like a helper when the latter is absent from his work. Similarly, a dispensary worker has to look after the work of the helper when such orders are given by the management.

The change in position without a change in hierarchy is called horizontal mobility. It is observed that all workers who are appointed by the management from other states or other places within Assam are given the same position as they were before, with more benefits and better facilities. It can be said that while horizontal mobility is encouraged among the permanent workers, vertical mobility is restricted for temporary workers.

A hierarchy is created based on skill, training and wages, including a substantial class of unskilled labourers. Greater specialisation of tasks subordinates the knowledge, judgement and will of the worker. It is this combination of specialities that led Marx to use the concept of the collective worker to describe the interdependent organisation of labour prior to the use of extensive machinery (Thompson 1989). Every step in the labour process with regard to the lower rank workers is divorced from special knowledge. Meanwhile, the relatively few permanent posts for which special knowledge and training have been reserved are freed as far as possible from the obligations of simple labour. In this way, a structure is created in the labour processes that at its extreme polarises those whose time is infinitely valuable and those whose time is worth almost nothing. This might even be called the general law of the capitalist division of labour (Braverman 1974).

Skill development, behavioural, self-transformation, and safety training is provided to all workers when they are newly recruited. However, the training period is only for the permanent employees appointed by the management directly. The lower level workers who also needed specialised training in some areas are trained by no professional trainer. They work under their seniors and learn by seeing them. Thus, their need to develop their skills remains unfulfilled. Categorising himself as a helper, a worker during an interview said, 'I have learned to work as a technician from my seniors. There was no trainer to train us, but we were kept under the training period'. This reflects that the management indirectly recruits workers under a training period but are unable to provide any trainer. Thus, the worker, in order to earn money, learns all by himself with a hope to get a promotion after learning skills. Unfortunately, the mobility does not transform into a reality.

Safety measures and building up awareness among workers and the management are crucial necessities. The lack of awareness causes frequent accidents. From a qualitative approach, with the increase in years of occupation in the industry, the level of income has not increased. Almost all workers spoke about stagnant work. As per Pearson's correlation of coefficient, the rise in the years of occupation has left no impact on salary (see Table 6.6). The value of correlation of coefficient is (–) 0.614 which is statistically significant at 1 percent. Generally, with years of experience, the salary should have increased, but here it is seen that there is no scope for skills to be upgraded or salary to increase.

Table 6.6 Correlation between years of occupation and income (in Rs)

	Value[a]	Asymp. Std. Error	Approx. T[b]	Approx. Sig.
Pearson's R	−.614	.105	−5.710	.000[c]

Note: a Not assuming the null hypothesis
b Using the asymptotic standard error assuming the null hypothesis
c Based on normal approximation

Conclusion

In this study on the cement industry in Assam, the focus was in the area where workers have been the main force behind the production process. It was found that there has been increasing informalisation of the workforce in the mechanical, electronics and instrumentation and process divisions, where a large number of workers were outsourced. The most striking disparity between the regular/casual workers lay in the average daily earnings of a casual worker, which stood at Rs 240 (after deduction of PF, food cost etc.) and that of a skilled permanent employee, who received above Rs 10,000 per month. The increasing 'informalisation' of employment had gradually eroded the strength of trade unions. With the management's implementation of strategies to control labour, de-unionising posed a challenge. It reflected that the industry was male centric and workers were highly deprived of some basic workplace requirements like holidays and wages and were kept under the control of a multi-layered management structure. This multiple control minimised the upward mobility of positions in the hierarchy. The organisation of work is thus controlled to such an extent that it is reduced to degradation not only at work but also on the social front, where workers get the least time to develop skills and balance their time with their family.

It further revealed that while workers had to work under an extreme controlled environment, the upgrading space was too little or negligible for them to survive. The political role of the management into the workers' consciousness proved that the management did not want a workers' union to be formed. Hence, the migrant workers appointed directly by the management in the higher positions were selected as representatives of the workers. It further created an ideological divide between the migrant workers and the local workers. This reveals that upward mobility in the occupation among temporary workers was controlled. This tendency did not create consciousness among the workers but of course created a mindset of accepting or keeping themselves under the control of superiors – rather, workers consciously preferred being controlled. The cause of this transformation was in the hands of the management, who bought labour power and authority to exert different measures of control.

References

Braverman, Harry. 1974. *Labor and Monopoly Capital: The Degradation of Work in the Twentieth Century*, New York: Monthly Review.

Cement Manufacturers' Association Report. 52nd Annual Report of CMA 2012–2013.

CMA. *Cement Manufacturing Company Limited*, Report 2014–2015. CMA.

Dikshit, Kamal Ramprit and Jutta K. Dikshit. 2014. *North-East in India: Land, People and Economy*, New York: Springer.

The Shyam Group Corporate Overview. 2017. 'Biggest Cement Plant in North–East'. www.shyamgroup.com/corporate_overview.html. Accessed on 14 January 2017.

Thompson, Paul. 1989. *The Nature of Work*, London: Macmillan.

Chapter 7

Fostering employment in the handloom sector in the North-East through cluster development

A case study of Mizoram

Rama Ramswamy

Handlooms constitute a timeless facet of the rich cultural heritage of India. Often considered as the vestiges of the traditional sector, the handloom sector not only represents the rich heritage of India but is also the second largest employment provider after agriculture and has shown great resilience in surviving and sustaining over the ages. Paradoxically, this sector has been weighed down in syndromes of a declining number of weaver households and looms and a shrinking share in total cloth production.

For centuries, India developed a system of specialised concentrations throughout the country where the entire village functioned as a workshop. Traditionally, village enterprises in India were structured in the form of clusters, where specialised products were manufactured with raw material and labour inputs available in the village. The dynamism and economic success of numerous small and medium-sized enterprise (SME) clusters in the 1990s kindled the interest of researchers and policymakers in India, and clustering was revisited as a tool of development of SMEs in India. Cluster development initiatives gathered momentum in India in early 2000 and have sustained the interest of policymakers and academia. In the handloom sector, such cluster development initiatives[1] are undertaken to enable select clusters to become competitive in the globalised economy.

This chapter is based on the mapping of the Thenzawl cluster, a remote town in Mizoram which has developed as an important centre of weaving. The central aim of this chapter is to present a case study of a remote cluster in North-East India where a paradigm shift has occurred in the work pattern of weaving as an occupation, from a domestic chore to a commercial activity, giving remarkable economic returns to the tribal women in the cluster. To this end, the chapter traces the genesis and growth of the Thenzawl handloom cluster in terms of the generation of the number of enterprises, looms, employment, products (innovation) and sales turnover. It also studies the socio-economic profile of the entrepreneurs, the entrepreneurial structure of the cluster on the basis of the number of looms owned and the extent of economic dependence on weaving as an occupation and examines labour aspects of the handloom industry in Thenzawl. Finally, the chapter exhorts the need for state agencies to initiate appropriate cluster intervention strategies to enable this 'made in India' endeavour to be sustained and grow.

Clustering of enterprises: a conceptual framework

Broadly, clusters may be defined as a sectoral and geographical concentration of enterprises faced with common opportunities and threats which can give rise to external economies and favour the emergence of specialised technical, administrative and financial services. Clusters have been defined and conceptualised differently by various scholars and practitioners.[2] Clustering of firms is rooted in Marshal's analysis (1919) of industrial districts. He observed that several advantages such as a pool of specialised labour, access to suppliers of specialised inputs and services, and dissemination of inventions, new ideas and improvements in technology can be derived by enterprises following the same type of business in the same geographical locality.

This conceptualisation of clusters was followed by a lot of research interest stimulated by the success of the 'industrial districts' of Italy, which popularly came to be known as 'Third Italy'. Piore and Sabel (1984) and Becattini (1991) traced the success of the industrial clusters of 'Third Italy' and provided an impetus to research clusters in the 1990s. Becattini (1991) interpreted Marshallian industrial districts as 'socio-territorial entities' which were characterised by the active presence of both a community of people and enterprises in a common area, naturally and historically bound.

Porter (1990) modelled the effect of the local business environment on competition in terms of interrelated influences, graphically depicted in a diamond popularly known as the 'diamond theory'. The theory explained that a cluster is the manifestation of a diamond at work, comprising of three elements, namely, proximity arising from the co-location of companies, customers and suppliers and other institutions.

Different strands of literature, built on the seminal work of Porter and Marshal, focused on different aspects of clustering and specialisation around the globe. Sandee (1994) and Weijland (1999) found specialisation in the production of roof tiles by an entire village in Indonesia. Other works include metal and repair workshops cluster of Takora in Lima, Peru (Villaran 1993); the cluster of Kumasi, a shanty suburb in Ghana; and rattan furniture of Tegalwani, Indonesia (Smyth 1992).

Some well-researched informal rural clusters in India are: the tannery and leather cluster of the Palar valley in Tamil Nadu (Kennedy 2005); small-scale industries clusters (food processing, leather, engineering and chemicals); Khadi and Village Industries Commission (KVIC); handloom and handicrafts in four districts of Unnao, Barabanki, Hardoi and Gorakhpur in Uttar Pradesh (Society for Economic and Social Transition 2005); and five industrial clusters, namely, the brass parts and components cluster of Jamnagar, Gujarat (Awasthi 2004),the brass cluster of Moradabad, Uttar Pradesh, the diesel engine cluster of Rajkot, Gujarat, the sports goods cluster of Meerut, Uttar Pradesh and the cotton knitwear cluster of Tirupur, Tamil Nadu. DuPont (1992) analysed the advantages and drawbacks of industrial clustering in Jetpur, a cluster in Gujarat which has specialised in the dyeing and printing of textiles.

Case studies of artisanal clusters in India examined the functioning of the clusters and their inadequacies and point out the need to extend support to these informal clusters, as in the cases of the low-end artisanal clusters in West Bengal (Biswas 2005), the hand-block printed textile cluster of Jaipur in Rajasthan (Sarkar and Bannerjee 2007), the bamboo and rattan cluster of Kerala (Mathew 2005), the silver filigree cluster of Orissa (Kar 2005) and the leather works cluster of Athani in Karnataka (Chatrapathy 2005).

Twenty handloom clusters from different parts of India were identified by the Office of the Development Commissioner (Handlooms), Ministry of Textiles, Government of India, in the first phase during the Eleventh Plan for cluster development activities on the basis of diagnostic studies prepared on these handloom clusters.

Relevance of clustering

In recent decades, clusters worldwide are being acknowledged as a strategic mechanism through which regions and nations can attain higher levels of industrial development. Industrial clusters have long been associated with productivity and employment creation (Becattini 1991; Becattini et al. 2003; Krugman 1991; Porter 1990, 1998; Piore and Sabel 1984; Sugden et al. 2007). Marshall (1919) expounded several benefits of industrial districts derived from enterprises following the same type of business in the same geographical locality that stem from the presence of a local pool of specialised labour, access to suppliers of specialised inputs and services, and dissemination of inventions, new ideas and improvements in technology. Krugman (1991) further identifies three prominent benefits – labour market pooling, intermediate inputs and technological spillovers. Clusters provide immense benefits to small firms in enhancing productivity and competitiveness in terms of specialised human resources, inducing improved infrastructure (Humphrey and Schmitz 1995; Pitelis and Pseiridis 2007), reducing unit cost economies (Humphrey and Schmitz 1996; Marshall 1919) and encouraging innovation (Baptista and Swann 1998). The success of clusters worldwide has stimulated interest among policymakers the world over to develop policies for local economic development. In fact, the literature suggests that firms within clusters demonstrated greater levels of efficiency, innovation and performance (Rocha 2004). This prods us to understand the relationship between cluster innovation and entrepreneurship.

Clusters – innovation and knowledge systems

Several studies have underlined the relationship between clusters, knowledge spillovers and innovation. There is a growing recognition and evidence that clusters of small firms can be more innovative than large firms. Nick and Pinch (2007) argued that asymmetries in knowledge flows can lead to a competitive advantage for both individual firms and those located in clusters. Marshall's seminal work explicitly explains the role of spatial clusters on innovation and knowledge spillovers. The literature suggests that knowledge spillovers are important for innovation and tend to be spatially restricted (Jaffe 1989; Patel and Pavitt 1991; Feldman 1994; Audretsch and Feldman 1996).

Different strands of the literature delve into varied types of knowledge spillovers in spatial clusters. Polanyi (1966) construed tacit knowledge as knowledge based on the idea that we can know more than we can tell as opposed to codified information that can be formally coded and transmitted. He observed that there are many tasks that involve more skills and insights than can be codified and stored physically. Face-to-face contacts facilitate free flow of exchange of tacit knowledge, which is based on direct observation of products or production processes. This type of knowledge or skills and operational procedures, which do not lend themselves to be presented and defined in either language or writing, does not typically reside in blueprints (Polanyi 1966; Winter 1987). It is in this context that the geographically concentrated industrial configuration has substantial advantage over a diversified configuration (Enright 1994). The process of accumulation and transmission of knowledge is collective in clusters as the storage of knowledge and experience is made largely by collective entities and as per the productive cultural collective traditions of each local system (tacit skills, customs and habits developed locally) (Belussi 1999).

Nick and Pinch (2007) recently moved beyond this distinction of codifiable and tacit knowledge to architectural knowledge to generate new insights into the competitive advantages of a cluster. The concept of milieu,[3] furthermore, discerns the acceleration of knowledge spillover of related industries due to the tendency of tacit knowledge to be embedded in a local milieu. Close multi-directional and complex links of interdependence between local firms result in the formation of cooperation and exchange networks regarding both production and innovation (Dosi 1988; Lundvall 1988). Milieu steers the evolution and transformation of the localised production system and actuates and conducts innovation processes (Camagni and Quevit 1992; Maillat et al. 1993).

In artisanal clusters such as handlooms, family-based apprenticeship knowledge and hereditary systems prevail. This provides a regular supply of highly skilled labour at low costs; the material barriers to entry are also low. Though there is no formal training or curriculum, the emphasis is on systematic learning. Designs are not patented in such systems; hence, imitation is often the key to innovation (Basole 2015). This chapter seeks to understand the knowledge systems in this cluster and the nuances of innovation.

Clusters and entrepreneurship

Entrepreneurship is a human activity which plays an important role in the economic development of regions. Researchers have extolled the role and significance of entrepreneurs in the economic development of nations and regions. Entrepreneurship and innovation are central to economic growth and social transformation, and growth of entrepreneurship is synonymous with the growth and prosperity of any region. Entrepreneurs are believed to be the prime movers of economic growth (Audretsch 2002; Caree and Thurik 2005), and several authors have highlighted the need to foster economic development through the creation of new firms (Birch 1981; Brock 1989; Malecki 1994; OECD 1996; Reynolds et al. 2001; Audretsch and Fritsch 2002). Endogenous or indigenous development relies on the local economic and social system where entrepreneurial firms and innovation play a key role for competitive advantage (Rocha 2004). Several authors argue that regions where strong clusters operate benefit from higher start-up rates. Rocha (2004), furthermore, observed that there is a positive association between entrepreneurship and economic growth, theoretically as well as empirically.

It is argued that clusters foster entrepreneurship by providing established relationships and better information about opportunities; lowering entry and exit barriers; opening up niches of specialisation due to the low degree of vertical integration; promoting a competitive climate and strong rivalry among firms that impose pressure to innovate due to the presence of close competitors; providing role models, particularly local firms that have 'made it'; capturing important linkages, complementarities and spillovers from technology, skills, information and marketing; gathering information on the direction and pace of new business formation and innovation by analysing customer needs that cut across firms and industries; providing access to physical, financial and commercial infrastructure; easing the spin-offs of new companies from existing ones; reducing risk and uncertainty for aspiring entrepreneurs; and providing a cultural environment where establishing one's own business is normal and failure is not a social stigma (Pyke and Sengenberger 1992; Saxenian 1994; Rosenfeld 1997; OECD 1998; Porter 1990 as cited in Rocha 2004). In this study, I have probed into the overarching relationship between cluster processes and the role played, if any, on endogenous entrepreneurial growth.

Clustering in India

A glimpse of the landscape of industrial clusters in India shows that 99.7 percent of the industrial clusters in India are micro-enterprise clusters and traditional manufacturing clusters,[4] while only 0.3 percent are high-tech ones. Furthermore, artisan clusters play an important role in the Indian economy in terms of their size, spread and employment generation. Handloom, handicraft and other clusters, including the coir and village industries sector, have a significant share in the micro-enterprise clusters. The spread of employment in clusters reveals that micro-enterprise clusters contribute to 80 percent and traditional manufacturing clusters contribute to 14 percent of the estimated share of employment in clusters in India, whereas the share of high-tech clusters is only 6 percent of the total employment in clusters (MSME Foundation 2007).

Handloom sector in India: an overview

Handlooms represent an age-old tradition of the rich cultural heritage of India, encompassing the varied hues of its diverse sociocultural expression in its colours, patterns, designs and textures. The Indian weavers' ingenuity deftly combines creativity, traditional knowledge and precision. The handloom sector of India presents a diverse range of products – from carpets and pashmina shawls of Kashmir to the durries of Punjab and Uttar Pradesh and the silk saris of Bhagalpur (Madhya Pradesh), Sambalpur (Odisha), Kanchipuram (Tamil Nadu), Andhra Pradesh (Pochampalli silks) and Madhya Pradesh (Chanderi saris), as well as fabrics of Assam and Manipur, and many more.

This sector is important from the point of view of its size and employment potential. It is the second largest employment provider after agriculture. It provides employment directly and indirectly to 2.78 million handloom households in India, mostly belonging to rural areas (87 percent). Moreover, the sector provides employment to a significant population of the weaker sections of society, namely, Scheduled Castes (SCs), Scheduled Tribes (STs), and Other Backward Castes (OBCs). Women, mostly from rural areas, make up 77.4 percent of the total handloom workforce (NCAER 2010).

The handloom sector plays a vital role in the socio-economic milieu of North-East India. Handloom weaving is a common skill of this region which is passed on from generation to generation through their womenfolk. The north-eastern states of India have the largest concentration of handlooms in the country (more than 65 percent of the total looms), and 50 percent of the handloom workforce and 99 percent of the adult workforce are women.

However, a large majority (more than 62 percent) of the looms in the north-eastern states are engaged in domestic production (NCAER 2010).

Weaving is intricately and inextricably enmeshed in the rich and diverse socio-cultural ethos of the people of the North-East. The myriad handloom products reflect the customs, traditions and identities of the tribes. Assam has the largest number of looms and workforce, followed by Manipur, Tripura, Nagaland, Arunachal Pradesh and Mizoram. Handlooms and handicrafts, in the absence of industries, play a vital role in the economy of Mizoram. Mizoram has a handloom workforce of 41,189 working on 23,938 looms (NCAER 2010).

Production process and labour

Manufacture of handloom products involves three phases – pre-loom, weaving and post-loom.

Pre-loom involves procurement of grey yarn, designing, scouring, dyeing, winding, warping of yarn, sizing, dressing and beaming, and drafting and denting. Normally, hank yarn[5] is consumed in the handloom industry. The *winding* process is done for both warp and pirn winding. Warp winding is the process by which the dyed yarn is woven on small bobbins through *charkas*, while pirn winding is the process of winding the dyed yarn on the pirns to be used as weft yarn during the process of weaving. *Warping* involves winding the required warp threads on the warping machine simultaneously to get a lengthy warp. *Sizing* is the process in which the yarn in the form of warp is applied with sizing mixture. During *dressing* and *beaming*, the yarn, after being sized, is woven on a beam. The pieced warps are stretched to remove the broken threads and the warp is woven on the warp beam. Thereafter, the drawing of each end of the warp thread through the heald[6] as per requirement of designs is called *drafting*. This is followed by the process of drawing the warp yarn threads through the reed[7] and is called *denting* (Government of India 1987).

Weaving is the crucial stage of the production process, where the weaver converts the yarn into different products. Weaving the production involves the final stages of *shedding*, the process where warp is divided into two layers for the passage of the shuttle carrying the weft yarn; *picking*, the process by which the shuttle is moved from one side to the other side with the weft yarn; and *beating*, whereby the thread is beaten to the fall of the cloth (Government of India 1987). *Post-loom* involves cutting, brushing and calendaring the product manually (Khasnabis and Nag 2001).

Handloom workforce

The handloom sector in India is largely household-based, where the family members play an important role in the manufacture of the product. At the outset, we take a look at the composition of the households of the handloom worker in India and their social configurations.

Nearly 2.78 million handloom households are engaged in weaving and allied activities, and the north-eastern states account for 1.68 million (60.5 percent) of the handloom households. Weaver households are classified into four categories on the basis of the type of activity performed by them, namely, weaver households,[8] allied workers' households,[9] idle loom households,[10] and others (households having only minor children engaged in weaving/allied activities). Weaver households constitute the highest share of worker households (81.5 percent), followed by allied workers (14.1 percent) and idle loom households (2.9 percent). Notably, households with no adult workers contribute to 1.5 percent of the total workforce of the handloom sector in the country (NCAER 2010). This reveals that a considerable proportion of minor children are involved in weaving activities in India. The handloom sector provides a livelihood to a significant proportion (72.8 percent) of the weaker section of society such as SCs, STs and OBCs. About 10 percent of handloom working households belong to the SCs, 22 percent to STs and 41 percent to OBCs (ibid.). In spite of its huge employment potential, this sector has witnessed a decline during the past years in terms of the number of looms and weaver households in all states except West Bengal and the north-eastern states.

The total workforce engaged in handloom-related activity is 4.33 million, and more than half of the total workers belonged to the north-eastern states in 2010. About 11.2 percent of the workforce comprises children (below the age of 18); 75.6 percent are engaged in weaving activities; 24.4 percent are allied workers. However, in the North-East, 94.3 percent of adult workers are weavers. Work participation in handloom activity in India is dominated by female workers; 2.99 million (77.9 percent) handloom workers are female, of which a huge majority reside in rural areas. Interestingly,

99 percent of the adult workforce in the north-eastern states are women (NCAER 2010).

Some methodological notes

The information presented in this chapter is mainly derived from primary data which was collected by administering structured questionnaires (in the Mizo language) on a random sample of 175 entrepreneurs out of the 325 entrepreneurs operating their enterprises in the cluster in the month of August to October 2013. Discussions were also held with the president of the Thenzawl Handlooms and Handicraft Association and officers of the government of Mizoram. The research is motivated by the need to find answers to develop industrial bases in the north-eastern states having strong traditional production systems and knowledge systems by presenting a case study of Thenzawl, where fledgling enterprises are embracing entrepreneurship as a viable occupation.

Thenzawl handloom cluster: genesis and evolution

Thenzawl is located in the Serchhip district in Mizoram, with a population of 7219 and at a distance of 93 km from Aizawl, the capital city (Government of Mizoram 2012). The formation of the cluster is rooted in the tradition of weaving. The weavers have a ubiquitous presence in Thenzawl. Invariably, almost every house in Thenzawl has looms, and as one walks the street of Thenzawl, the sound of loom operating can be distinctly heard.

Most of the sample entrepreneurs (88.6 percent) operated their looms in their houses or in the houses of labourers. The houses of small weavers were typically small, with two rooms, one living room with a kitchen attached to it and a bedroom. The looms were usually placed in the veranda, in the living room, or under the stilts in the basement of their house.

The birth of the cluster can be traced back to 1982, when four enterprises started operating eight looms for the commercial production of handloom products. The cluster has traversed a long way since its inception in terms of growth and performance and has emerged as a significant provider of livelihood. It has recorded a remarkable growth in terms of number of units and looms, total production, and sales turnover and employment since the days of its inception. In 1982–5, six more enterprises started commercial weaving activities, increasing the number of looms to 35. Since then, the cluster has been on a growth trajectory, registering an increase in enterprises as well as the number of looms. There has been a steady increase of micro-enterprises – from 205 in 2008 to 325 in 2013. Looms owned by the sample entrepreneurs have increased from merely one in 1982 to 546 in 2013.The number of units sold by sample entrepreneurs increased from 32,198 units in 2010 to 54,678 units in 2013. The product range increased from four in 1982 to 16 in 2013. The total sales of the sample enterprises soared from 40.6 million in 2010 to 53.1 million in 2013. The traditional products – *puanchei*, *siniar* and *puan ropui* have been the most dominant products, with a combined share of about 89 percent of the total sales turnover of sample enterprises in the cluster.[11] The cluster is dominated by small weavers (83 percent), who have created commercially viable enterprises with a few looms (1–3 looms).

Cluster and entrepreneurship

Cluster processes have played a vital role in influencing the decision of the entrepreneurs to set up handloom enterprises in the cluster. There is evidently a positive impact of clusters on entrepreneurship, as the building of cluster relationship and positive synergies derived from linkages with other units in the cluster were the dominant expectations of the entrepreneurs in setting up their own enterprises. Previous experience of weaving, availability of weavers/labourers and ease of setting up business were the predominant factors in facilitating their initiation into entrepreneurship. The networking of firms within the cluster and cluster dynamics were important tools in stimulating entrepreneurship in the cluster, leading to an agglomeration of firms (Ramswamy and Kumar 2011).

The entrepreneurs of Thenzawl

This section studies the organisational structure of the cluster and the socio-economic profile of the entrepreneurs. At the outset, we have traced the commencement of business of the sample enterprises (see Table 7.1).

Table 7.1 shows that 72. 5 percent of the enterprises commenced business operations after 2001, with 45 percent of the enterprises establishing their business in the period 2011–13. The growth of

Table 7.1 Year of commencement of business by the entrepreneurs

Year of commencement	No. of entrepreneurs	Percent
1982–90	28	16
1991–2000	20	11.4
2001–10	48	27.4
2011–13	79	45.1
Total	175	100

Source: Primary data collected in August 2013

total number of enterprises (from 205 in 2008 to 325 in 2013) in the cluster and the growth in the number of sample enterprises in the corresponding period illustrates that the cluster is at the 'rapid take-off' stage of growth.

Membership in handloom cooperatives

Handloom workers in India are currently scattered and work either in isolation or under different mechanisms. Most of the handloom households in India who have reported being members of cooperatives are found in Tamil Nadu (27.6 percent), Andhra Pradesh (18.1 percent), the North-East (16.8 percent), West Bengal (8.3 percent) and Orissa (7.2 percent). Membership in cooperatives societies can protect the rights of weavers and facilitate access to development programmes (NCAER 2010).

However, most of the weavers in Thenzawl are members of an unregistered association, the Thenzawl Handloom and Handicrafts Association, in the cluster. As a cluster intervention strategy, eight cooperative societies were established in the cluster under the aegis of the government of Mizoram in recent years to facilitate the entry of weavers as cooperative members. Only 5.7 percent of the sample entrepreneurs were members of cooperative societies. As the concept of a cooperative society appears to be nascent in the Thenzawl cluster, the government and non-government agencies need to undertake concerted efforts to educate the weavers about the fundamental concept of a cooperative society and the benefits that could be derived from it.

Possession of weavers' identity cards and health cards

The third Handloom Census conducted in 2010 (NCAER 2010) envisaged creating a database of weavers and allied workers throughout the country and facilitated the distribution of photo identity cards to genuine weavers identified by the Census survey. The photo identity cards were issued to ensure that only genuine weavers would get benefits from the various schemes implemented by the Office of Development Commissioner (Handlooms), Government of India. To this end, we made an attempt to find out how many sample entrepreneurs in Thenzawl cluster possessed weavers' photo identity cards. It was distressing to note that only 37.1 percent of the entrepreneurs possessed weavers' photo identity cards. The fact that a majority of the weavers do not possess weavers' photo identity cards exposes the lacunae in the distribution system of weavers' photo identity cards in Thenzawl. The government of Mizoram should plug the gaps in the system.

Furthermore, recognising the need for providing a robust security mechanism by way of health insurance for the weavers and their households, the Government of India launched the Health Insurance Scheme (HIS) (now merged with Rashtra Swasthya Bima Yojana of the Ministry of Labour, Government of India) whereby health cards were distributed to all the weavers in the country.[12] Weavers possessing weaver photo identity cards were eligible to participate in the benefits of this scheme. The government of Mizoram needs to take urgent steps to distribute photo identity cards and health cards to all the weavers in the cluster, strictly adhering to the norms formulated by the Government of India.

Ownership of looms

The cluster is composed of a large number (82 percent) of small weavers owning one to three looms (Table 7.2). About 10 percent of the sample entrepreneurs owned more than seven looms, and

Table 7.2 Number of looms owned by the entrepreneurs

No. of looms	No. of entrepreneurs	Percent
1–3	142	82.9
4–6	15	6.9
7–10	12	6.9
11–20	4	2.3
More than 20	2	1.1
Total	175	100

Source: Primary data collected in August 2013

only about 3 percent of the sample entrepreneurs owned more than 10 looms.

Gender perspective

As mentioned earlier, another distinctive feature of weaving in the north-eastern states is the huge proportion of females in the adult workforce (99 percent) in the handloom sector. Interestingly, all the sample entrepreneurs were women operating their looms on a commercial basis as sole proprietors, substantiating the huge presence of women in the labour force in the North-East. These tribal women have redefined the quintessential 'marginalised woman weaver' as strongly motivated women entrepreneurs who have transformed the role of weaving from being a mere domestic chore to a commercially viable enterprise, notwithstanding the number of looms owned by them. Traditionally, the Mizo girls learn weaving from their mother while the boys go hunting or fishing. The knowledge and skill of weaving is transmitted from mother to daughter as apprenticeship.

Religion, community and caste of entrepreneurs

All the respondents belonged to the Mizo community. It is observed that none of the weavers belonged to the neighbouring country, Myanmar, as is generally found in other parts of Mizoram such as Aizawl and Lunglei. All the respondents belonged to the ST category, and all of them were Christians by religion. Interestingly, all respondents were women entrepreneurs in the present study.

The state of Mizoram is inhabited by a number of tribes who originally belong to the Assam-Burman Group[13] and are believed to have their origins in Chhinlung. The tribes of Mizoram are broadly divided into 9 major and 13 minor tribes and sub-tribes (Verghese and Thanzawna 1997).[14] These tribes and sub-tribes are further divided into a number of clans. Thirty-one different tribes or sub-tribes or clans were involved in the commercial production of handloom products in the cluster. Further, the occupation of weaving is not restricted to specific castes, clans or tribes. It is observed that entrepreneurs from the commoners' clan as well as the chiefs' clan were involved in weaving activities. From the sample entrepreneurs, 15 percent belonged to *Chhakchhuak* (commoners' clan), followed by *Ralte* (sub-tribe) constituting 13 percent and *Sailos* (chiefs' clan) making up 7.5 percent.

Social relationships are not dominated by caste or clan (commoner or chief) dimensions in the Mizo community. This phenomenon seems to be unique to this cluster, since weavers in many parts of India such as Kanchipuram (Tamil Nadu), Varanasi (Uttar Pradesh), Sonepur and Bargarh (Orissa), and Bhalgalpur (Bihar) belonged predominantly to a certain caste, as is evident in research litera-ture.[15] Handloom weaving in the country has remained more or less a traditional caste and family-based occupation. However, unlike in other parts of the country, there are no entry barriers on the basis of clans/tribes/sub-tribes to the weaving occupation in Thenzawl.

Age of the entrepreneurs

Traditionally, the Mizo women learnt the skills of weaving from their mother during early childhood. As shown in Table 7.3, a large number of entrepreneurs (36.6 percent) were in the age group from 31 to 40 years old, followed by the age group of below 30 years old (30.9 percent) and 41–50 years old (20.6 percent). Only five respondents were above 60 years old (2.9 percent).

Educational levels and knowledge system

Mizoram ranked second in literacy rate among all the states in India, with an overall literacy rate of 91.58. The overall literacy rate of Serchhip is 98.76 percent, with the literacy rate among males being 99.24 percent and 98.28 percent among females (Census Report 2011). According to the Census Report of 2011, Thenzawl

Table 7.3 Distribution of age of the entrepreneurs

Age (in years)	No. of respondents	Percent
Below 30	54	30.9
31–40	64	36.6
41–50	36	20.6
51–60	16	9.1
Above 60	5	2.9
Total	175	100

Source: Primary data collected in August 2013

town had an overall literacy rate of 84.81 percent. The literacy rate among males was 84.1 percent, whereas among females it was 85.53 percent. Table 7.4 indicates that almost all the sample entrepreneurs (99.6 percent) were literate in the cluster. Interestingly, the literacy rate among the sample entrepreneurs surpassed the overall literacy rate of the state of Mizoram (91.58 percent), the district of Serchhip (98.76 percent) and Thenzawl village (84.81 percent). Out of the 175 sample entrepreneurs, 89.7 percent attended school, but only 9.7 percent of the sample entrepreneurs had attended college. Among the 175 in the sample, only one entrepreneur was illiterate. The literacy rate in Thenzawl compared favourably with other clusters such as Bhagalpur in Bihar, where the majority of the weavers were illiterate; Barabanki in Uttar Pradesh, where the majority of the weavers had not gone to school; and Nellore in Andhra Pradesh, where 18.26 percent of the weavers were illiterate (Diagnostic Study Reports 1998; Bhaskar Rao and Himachalam 1998).

Though the educational background of the entrepreneur is crucial for his/her success, in the case of craft entrepreneurs, the lack of education does not restrict their entry into entrepreneurship in their field of activity. Moreover, their creative ingenuity, creativity and precision find expression in their products. Notably, all the sample entrepreneurs possessed weaving skills imbibed from their mothers during early childhood, which has encouraged them to initiate themselves to start their own micro-handloom enterprises.

Ramswamy and Jyoti Kumar (2013) observed that the girl children in Thenzawl help out their mothers in weaving, pre-weaving and post-weaving activities while in school and normally drop out of school in the seventh or eighth standard, after attaining competence in weaving handloom products. However, formal education would certainly enable them to manage their enterprise more successfully.

Table 7.4 Educational level of the entrepreneurs

Education	No. of entrepreneurs	Percent
Illiterate	1	0.6
School	157	89.7
College	17	9.7
University	0	0.0
Professional	0	0.0
Total	175	100

Source: Primary data collected in August 2013

The entrepreneurs in Thenzawl lacked managerial skills to operate their enterprises which are crucial for the success of any enterprise. They lacked even the knowledge of maintenance of documents and preparation of basic books of accounts (Ramswamy, 2015). The Indian education system needs to meet the challenges of developing a curriculum that would provide necessary inputs to the artisans without displacing them from their profession.

Knowledge spillovers

The lack of intellectual properties in the cluster makes it easy to imitate through (tacit knowledge) informal exchanges in the cluster. Innovation is evident in the form of new products introduced in the product line and product mix of enterprises. *Puan ropui*, a niche product, was introduced in recent times, and bags, sling bags and purses were introduced in the product line of bags, which previously comprised only the traditional *iptechei*.[16] Other products were added as a new product line consisting of shawls, vest coats and neckties in recent times.

Type and size of family

Handlooms in India are traditionally family-based enterprises where the members of the family engage in ancillary activities. The researcher observed that joint family and nuclear family enterprises co-existed. There were marginally more nuclear families (51.4 percent) as compared to joint families (48.6 percent) among the sample entrepreneurs' families.

The size of the family suggests the number of members dependent on the enterprise. Moreover, as discussed earlier, young Mizo girls learn the weaving skills from their mothers very early and make

Table 7.5 Family size of the entrepreneurs

Family size	No. of entrepreneurs	Percent
Up to 5	93	53.1
6–10	77	44.0
11–15	5	2.9
Above 15	0	0.0
Total	175	100

Source: Primary data collected in August 2013

valuable contributions to the enterprise. Table 7.5 analyses the size of the family of the sample entrepreneurs. It is observed from Table 7.5 that 53.1 percent of the sample entrepreneurs have a family of up to 5 members, 44 percent have 6–10 members and 2.9 percent of the entrepreneurs have 11–15 members in their family.

Main occupation of the entrepreneurs' families

Table 7.6 shows that 72.6 percent of the sample entrepreneurs' families depend on weaving as their main occupation; 15.4 percent of the sample entrepreneurs' families depended on government jobs; 5.1 percent on agriculture and business, respectively; and 1.7 percent of the sample entrepreneurs depended on other occupations.

According to the study conducted by Ramswamy and Jyoti Kumar (2013), weaving was a significant income activity, providing livelihood to 68.04 percent entrepreneurs. Handlooms continue to be an important occupation in the cluster, emphasising the need for promoting this sector in Thenzawl.

Income from the enterprise

Income from a given activity is a strong stimulant to the growth and development of entrepreneurship in that sphere. Profit is an important determinant of success for any enterprise and is important for the sustenance and growth of any enterprise. Table 7.7 shows the annual average income of the sample enterprises from weaving only. An overwhelming majority of the enterprises (91.9 percent) earned an annual income of above Rs 100,000 and above, 6 percent earned Rs 60,001 to 100,000 and 2.2 percent earned Rs 20,000–60,000

Table 7.6 Main occupation of the entrepreneurs

Occupation	No. of entrepreneurs	Percent
Agriculture/Jhumming	9	5.1
Business/trade	9	5.1
Weaving	127	72.6
Government servant	27	15.4
Others	3	1.7
Total	175	100

Source: Primary data collected in August 2013

Table 7.7 Annual average income of entrepreneurs from weaving

Income	No. of weavers	Percent
Rs 20,000	0	0
Rs 20,001–40,000	2	1.5
Rs 40,001–60,000	1	0.7
Rs 60,001–80,000	4	3.0
Rs 80,001–100,000	4	3.0
Above Rs 100,000	124	91.9
Total	135	100

Source: Primary data collected in August 2013

from weaving activities only. None of the sample enterprises earned less than Rs 20,000 annually.

The fact that about 83 percent of the sample enterprises owned few looms (1–3 looms), shows that it is commercially viable to run a handloom enterprise with only a few looms.

Handloom workforce in sample enterprises

As mentioned earlier, the manufacture of handloom products involves three phases – pre-loom, weaving and post-loom. The enterprises in Thenzawl procure dyed yarn for weaving. Thereafter, the design for the product is conceived, which involves deciding the patterns and colour combinations for the product. The weavers themselves were involved in the process of designing the product in Thenzawl. None of the entrepreneurs had any networking with professional institutes of design, namely, National Institute of Fashion Technology (NIFT) or National Institute of Design (NID). The pre-weaving activities are usually performed by the weaver (wage earners and small loom owners) in their households with the help of family members. Warping, dressing and beaming, sizing and dressing and beaming and, thereafter, drafting and denting are performed by the weaver herself with assistance from her family members. Thereafter, the shuttle box is fit in the loom for the next process of weaving.

Small weavers usually do not own warping drums and outsource this activity from weavers owning the warping drums. In Thenzawl, the charges for warping one product were about Rs 30. Lack of warping drums increases the drudgery of the small weavers. Time taken for weaving depends on the intricacy of the designs. Puan

Table 7.8 Distribution of the type of employees and the number of persons employed in sample enterprises

Type of employees (adult)	No. of employees (adult)	Percent
Self-employed	153	26.56
Full-time weavers	340	59.03
Part-time weavers	45	7.81
Allied workers	38	6.6
Total	576	100

Source: Primary data collected in August 2013

ropui, siniar and puanchei demand higher expertise and skills as compared to the plain puan or *puandum*. Table 7.8 illustrates the type of employees and the number of persons employed in sample enterprises.

Table 7.8 shows that 26.56 percent of the employees were self-employed in their own enterprises, 59.03 percent were full-time weavers and 7.81 percent were part-time weavers. The allied workers involved in pre-weaving and post-weaving constituted only 6.6 percent of the total workforce employed in the sample enterprises. The weaver households were usually involved in the allied activities too. The handloom census observed that 94.3 percent of the adult workers in the North-East were weavers and only 5.7 percent of the adult workers reported exclusively working as allied workers. In North-East India, exclusive allied activity is limited, as it is mostly undertaken by the weaver households themselves (NCAER 2010). Notably, 80 minor girl children were engaged in weaving and allied activities in 58 sample handloom enterprises.

Wages

The weavers of the Thenzawl handloom cluster were paid on piece rate system. The wages were paid on the basis of the number of the items produced. The rate of wages differed according to the difficulty, expertise and time required to weave the product. We have analysed the wage rates for the six most important products on the basis of their share in the total sales turnover of the sample enterprises in the cluster, and a comparison has been made to wages paid in the previous years.

The wages for ngotekherh and puandum have also doubled from 1980 to 2008 and registered an increase from 2008 to

Table 7.9 Comparison of the wage rates of select products for the years 1980, 2008 and 2013 (in Rs)

Products	#1980	*2008	2013
Puanchei	150	350	1000
Siniar	150	500	1300
Puan Ropui	–	–	1500
Ngotekherh	100	200	300
Puandum	30	60	100
Tawlhlo Puan	–	–	300

Source: Primary data collected in August 2013

Note: # National Productivity Council (1984), * Ramswamy and Kumar (2012)

2013.[17] Table 7.10 shows the statement of total cost of production of the products having a significant share in the total sales turnover of the sample enterprises.

The select products mentioned in Table 7.10 have a substantial share in the total production of sample enterprises, namely, puanchei (37 percent), siniar (32 percent), puan ropui (20 percent), ngotekherh (5 percent), puandum (3 percent), and tawlhlo puan (1.2 percent); their total costs of production were calculated. As the small weavers do not own the warping drum, they have to pay Rs 30 per product as warping charges. Wages constitute a significant part of the total cost of producing various handloom products in the cluster. It is evident that the crucial factor in deciding wage rate is the time taken to weave and the intricacies of the design of the product. The wage rates for puan ropui, siniar and puanchei are the highest as it involves specific intricate designs and patterns and greater expertise of weaving as compared to tawlhlo puan, ngotekherh and puandum.

In fact, it appears that the high component of wages in the total cost of production lures weavers (wage earners) to start their own small enterprise with a single loom, as the profits that arise from the manufacture of the products accrue to the weaver-owner herself. In the absence of written contracts, it was observed that there is a lot of labour flexibility in the cluster.

Relationship with employers and working conditions

Interestingly, the employer-employee relations were cordial, and there were no complaints from the weavers of exploitation by

Table 7.10 Estimated cost of select products in Thenzawl cluster in 2013

Cost (in Rs)	Puanchei	Siniar	Ngotekherh	Puan Ropui	Puandum	Tawlhlo Puan
Raw material	340* (25.4%)	355* (21.5%)	264* (46.8%)	355* (19.1%)	171* (63.1%)	242* (44.6%)
Labour	1000 (74.63%)	1300 (78.55%)	300 (53.19%)	1500 (80.86%)	100 (36.90%)	300 (55.35%)
Total	1340 (100%)	1655 (100%)	564 (100%)	1855 (100%)	271 (100%)	542 (100%)

Source: Primary data collected in August 2013

Note: * it includes charges for warping in the drum and beam rolling, which is Rs 30 per product

entrepreneurs. All the weavers in the cluster were women, and this cordiality may be attributed to the gendered labour in the cluster. Informal exchanges are very common among the weavers and entrepreneurs, lending each other machinery and inputs in an atmosphere of support and cooperation.

Moreover, as the wages were paid on a piece rate system, there was virtually no monitoring or inspection by the entrepreneurs on the work done by the weavers. Most of the weavers (wage earners) operated their looms in their houses, which facilitated them to look after their household chores along with weaving activities. About 89 percent of the sample entrepreneurs were operating their looms from their houses or the houses of labourers, and only 11 percent were operating their looms in working sheds. In most cases, the looms were housed in the verandah or the basement of their houses below stilts. This poses many difficulties to the weavers. The weavers cited lack of facilities for weaving, storage facilities and a common facilities centre as the foremost infrastructural constraint faced by them. The lack of facilities for weaving is attributed to the lack of sheds for weaving, inadequate warping drums and a lack of space for placing charkhas and other loom accessories. Due to the absence of storage facilities, they store the raw materials in the house itself. There was no common facilities centre (CFC) in the cluster to provide technological support, quality testing and counselling facilities, loom repair services and others. The full-time weavers spent seven to nine hours on average a day in weaving and allied activities, whereas part-time weavers spent four to five hours a day.

Conclusion

The key aspect that emerges from this empirical study is the thriving of entrepreneurship in the cluster rooted in the availability of labour and cluster processes. Cluster processes have played a positive role in endogenous entrepreneurial growth in the cluster, which has created a spin-off of enterprises leading to the formation of a spatial concentration of firms in Thenzawl. The cluster and the firms interviewed have shown remarkable growth in terms of growth of enterprises, total production and sales turnover. The cluster is at the rapid take off rate, with an exponential growth of about 120 enterprises in a span of five years (2008–13).

This study underlines the importance of developing enterprises at the local level leveraging on the knowledge and skills embedded in the socio-cultural systems in tribal societies. In the absence of large industries, artisanal clusters in the North-East can form the base of labour-intensive industrialisation. In fact, the study advises of the need for framing and implementing policies to promote such localised production systems (labour intensive) to provide an impetus to generate employment, creating new enterprises in the region. Appropriate cluster intervention policies should be developed to synthesise endogenous synergies of the region (the labour, gendered skill and social embeddedness of weaving) and translate them into developmental goals for the region. The handloom sector has a huge potential for employment in the North-East. However, in terms of policy inducement, public policy and implementation have not been supportive in the cluster until now. The few NGOs established in the cluster are also working in a fragmented way. Government policy is significant at the national level but rather poor at the local level. The enterprises have not received any support from the state except for a few looms distributed to some entrepreneurs at subsidised rates. In fact, none of the entrepreneurs got any financial assistance from financial institutions.

The handloom sector of India has been caught in the quagmire of chronic problems related to raw materials, marketing, infrastructure and finance, impeding its growth in the last few decades. However, notwithstanding these constraints, clusters such as Kannur (Kerala) and Chanderi (Madhya Pradesh), which were faltering and declining in terms of growth in market and sales, have demonstrated that with the appropriate kind of cluster interventions, they have achieved exemplary growth in terms of quality, sales turnover and market spread and have become benchmark clusters for others to emulate.[18]

Appropriate cluster development interventions such as upgradation of technology, product development, market development, building strong brands and creating networks with NIFT and NID development of infrastructure and banking facilities will enable the cluster to be sustained and grow. However, delay in addressing these challenges would adversely affect the morale of the entrepreneurs and retard the growth of the cluster. The future prosperity of the Thenzawl cluster depends on a combination of successful marketing strategies, continual product innovation and the building of a sound infrastructure through proactive cluster development interventions by both the central and the state government.

Notes

1 The clusters identified were: Bargarh (Orissa), Barabanki (Uttar Pradesh), Bhagalpur (Bihar), Bijoynagar (Assam), Bijnore (Uttar Pradesh), Burdwan (West Bengal), Chirala (Andhra Pradesh), Gadag (Karnataka), Chanderi (Madhya Pradesh), Imphal (Manipur), Kullu (Himachal Pradesh), Kurunjipadi (Tamil Nadu), Madhavaran (Andhra Pradesh), Mubarakpur (Uttar Pradesh), Nadia (West Bengal), Sonepur (Orissa), Thiruvannamalai (Tamil Nadu), Tiruchirapalli (Tamil Nadu), Thiruvanantpuram (Kerala) and Varanasi (Uttar Pradesh).

2 Porter (1998) defined clusters as a geographically proximate group of interconnected companies and associated institutions in a particular field linked by commonalities and complementarities. Clusters encompass an array of linked industries and other entities important for competition, including governmental and other institutions such as universities, standard-setting agencies, think tanks, vocational training providers and trade associations.

3 Milieu is an environment within which physical capital and human capital is created and accumulated over time, which translates into sustainable competitiveness among incumbent firms (Malmberg et al. 1996).

4 Examples of traditional manufacturing clusters: leather and leather products, automotive components, ceramics, etc.

5 Yarn manufactured in spinning mills are of two types – cone yarn and hank yarn. Cone yarn is used by power looms, whereas hank yarn is used by handlooms.

6 The heald is made of a series of vertical cords or wires having in the middle a loop to receive the warp of threads and passing around and between the parallel eyes. It helps in separating the warp thread by which the weft passes smoothly (Dash 1995).

7 The reed is part of a loom and resembles a comb. It is used to push the weft yarn securely into place as it is woven. It helps to separate the threads and keep them in their positions, keeping them untangled, and guides the shuttle as it moves across the loom. It consists of a frame with lots of vertical slits.

8 A household, where it has at least one member who has operated the loom for at least a day in the preceding year (NCAER 2010).

9 Allied workers households do not own looms but are engaged in pre- and post-loom activities (NCAER 2010).

10 Idle loom households are households who own looms, but the looms have not been in operation during the preceding year (NCAER 2010).

11 *Puanchei* is the most colourful traditional dress (*puan*) worn by Mizo women on occasions of weddings and festivals. *Siniar* is a puan enriched by intricate embroidery and *zari* work by the weaver. It comes in varied designs and colours and does not subscribe to any traditional colours. Siniar is one of the most popular dresses worn by the Mizo women. *Puan Ropui* is a niche product woven to cater to the needs of the modern Mizo women. It is richly embroidered with zari and intricate designs and motifs all over the puan. It is the richest and most

highly priced puan produced in Thenzawl (Ramswamy and Kumar 2012).

12 Rashtra Swasthya Bima Yojana is a health insurance scheme launched in early 2008 with the objectives to provide financial protection against catastrophic health costs and improve access to quality health care and expenditure towards hospitalisation for below poverty line households and other vulnerable groups in the unorganised sector.

13 Mizos are said to be the Assam-Burman sub-group who had branched off from the Tibeto-Burman group of the main Tibeto-Chinese race. Some authors have classified them as Tibeto-Burman because of the affinity of the language, even though they have described them as people who once lived in Chhinlung (Verghese and Thanzawna 1997).

14 The major tribes of Mizoram are Lusei or Lutsei (consists of 10 clans and 6 chiefs' clans), Pawi or Lai, Hmar, Lakher or Mara, Paite or Vuite, Ralte (sub-tribe), Chakma or Tsak or Sak, Riang or Tuikuk, and Mogh or Mok or Thakma. The sub tribes are Chawngthu, Chawthe, Ngente, Khawlhring, Khiangte, Pautu, Rawite, Renthlei, Tlau, Vangchhia, Zawngte, Pang and Bawng. The Lusei tribe consists of 10 commoners' and 6 chiefs' clans. The commoners' clans include Pachuau, Chhangte, Chawngte, Hauhnar, Chuango, Chuaungo, Hrashel, Tochhawng, Vanchhawng and Chhakchhuak. The six chiefs' clans are Zadeng, Palian, Thangluah, Rivung, Rokhum and Sailo (Verghese and Thanzawna 1997).

15 Reports submitted to the Development Commissioner (Handloom) Ministry of Textiles, Govt. of India, New Delhi, on some important handloom clusters for adoption under the Integrated Handloom Cluster Development Programme and Arterburn Yvonne (1982).

16 *Ipte* means bag and *chei* means to decorate; it means 'decorated bag' and is woven in typical ethnic Mizo designs.

17 The *ngotekherh* is a traditional Mizo dress also worn for traditional dances like *Cheraw*, the popular bamboo dance, which displays a perfect synchrony of the movements of the footsteps of the Mizo girls to the beats of the bamboo. The ngotekherh usually has white and black stripes, but nowadays fresh combinations of colours like blue and red are being adopted by the weavers to cater to the preferences of the modern Mizo society (Ramswamy and Kumar 2012).

The *puandum* is usually woven in black, red, yellow and green stripes. The puandum traditionally had to be taken by every Mizo girl to her husband's home when she got married, and it was used to cover her husband's body when he died. It is usually worn as a mark of respect to a dead person during mourning and condolence.

The *tawlhlo puan* is an indigo-coloured dress with red and white stripes. It was a traditional dress worn by warriors in ancient times. It symbolises the tribal warriors' undying spirit for defeating the enemy in the battle ground.

18 Some important initiatives taken in the Kannur handloom cluster were: market initiatives such as improvement of the product, design innovations to cater to international markets, imparting supply chain knowledge to manufacturers and exporters and conducting design workshops to give the weavers a perspective of the international demand. This was

achieved through the establishment of four consortia under the cluster project framework who have taken the lead role in the cluster development activities. For example, the Irinavu Handloom Consortium, one of the four consortia, took initiatives to increase productivity and launch new products to cater to the needs of international markets by seeking the services of a German agency, Senior Experten Services. National institutions, business development services (BDS) providers and international support agencies also collaborated with the handloom industry to provide design inputs to weavers and introduced supply chain knowledge to manufacturers and exporters. In fact, an Australian agency conducted a five-day workshop on designs at Kannur to impart knowledge to the weavers to create designs for international markets (Diagnostic Study Reports 1998).

The problems diagnosed at the Chanderi handloom cluster were: lack of credit and technical upgradation, low bargaining power at the weavers' end and poverty in the cluster. However, as a result of the cluster initiatives developed by UNIDO, United Nations Industrial Development Organisation, today this cluster has emerged as a successful cluster. To start with, self-help groups (SHGs) were formed which were again regrouped into a larger federation, namely, Bunkar Vikas Sanstha (BVS) which increased the bargaining power of the stakeholders. Further, with the help of UNIDO, local NGOs, and national and international agencies, the technology of weaving was upgraded, markets were explored and market linkages with wholesaler buyers, including Fab India, a private handicraft retailer with branches all over India were developed (Bedigg 2008).

References

Audretsch, David. B. 2002. 'Knowledge, Globalisation and Regions; A Economist's Perspective', in J Dunning (ed.), *Regions, Globalisation and the Knowledge based Economy*, pp. 63–81, Oxford: Oxford University Press.

Audretsch, David B. and M. P. Feldman. 1996. 'R&D Spillovers and the Geography of Innovation and Production', *American Economic Review*, 86: 630–640.

Audretsch, David B. and M. Fritsch. 2002. 'Growth Regimes over Time and Space', *Regional Studies*, 36(2): 113–124.

Awasthi, D. (2004). 'Labour Process and Productivity in Micro and Small Enterprises (MSES): The Indian Experience', Paper presented at the 46th Annual Labour Economics Conference, Organised by Institute of Development Studies, Jaipur.

Baptista, R. and P. Swann. 1998. 'Do Firms in Clusters Innovate More?' *Research Policy*, 27: 525–540.

Basole, A. 2015. 'Informality and Flexible Specialization: Apprenticeships and Knowledge Spillovers in an Indian Silk Weaving Cluster', *Development and Change*, 47(1): 157–187.

Becattini, G. 1991. 'Italian Industrial Districts: Problem and Perspectives', *International Studies of Management and Organization*, 21(1): 83–90.

Becattini, G., M. Belland'i, G. Dei Ottati, and F. Sforzi. 2003. *From Industrial Districts to Local Development: An Itinerary of Research*, Cheltenham, UK: Edward Elgar.

Bedigg, C. 2008. *Cluster Development Policy Rooted in the Collective Efficiency Approach: an Effective Poverty Alleviation Tool in the Indian Handloom Sector? Case Studies: The Varanasi and Chanderi Handloom Clusters*, Geneva: Graduate Institute of International and Development Studies.

Belussi, F. 1999. 'Policies for the Development of Knowledge Intensive Local Production Systems', *Cambridge Journal of Economics*, 23: 729–747.

Bhaskar Rao, S. and D. Himachalam. 1998. 'Socioeconomic Profile of Handloom Weavers in Nellore Division- A Study', *Small Enterprises Development, Management & Extension Journal*, 25(2): 21–32.

Birch, D. A. 1981. 'Who Creates Jobs?' *The Public Interest*, 6: 3–14.

Biswas, P. K. 2005. 'Organisational Forms, Technological Change and Income Generation: Handloom and Conch Shell Product Clusters in West Bengal', in K. Das (ed.), *Indian Industrial Clusters*, pp. 81–102, Aldershot: Ashgate.

Brock, W. A. and D. S. Evans. 1989. 'Small Business Economics', *Small Business Economics*, 1: 7–20.

Camagni, R. and M. QuéVIT. 1992. *Politiques d'innovation au niveau local (Innovation Policies at the Local Level)*, Padua: University of Padua, GREMÌ.

Caree, M. and A. R. Thurik. 2005. 'The Impact of Entrepreneurship on Economic Growth', in Z. A. Acs and D. B. Audretsch (eds), *Handbook of Entrepreneurship Research: An Interdisciplinary Survey and Introduction*, pp. 437–472, New York: Springer.

Chatrapathy, M. M. 2005. 'Transforming Artisans to Entrepreneurs through Group Enterprise: the Footwear Cluster of Athani, Karnataka', in K. Das (ed.), *Indian Industrial Clusters*, pp. 199–206, Aldershot: Ashgate.

Dash, S. N. 1995. *Handloom Industry in India*, New Delhi: Mittal Publications.

Diagnostic Study Reports. 1998. Indian Handloom Clusters. Retrieved from www.indianhandloomscluster-dchl.net/introduction.asp. Accessed on 4 April 2010.

Dosi, G. 1988. 'Sources, Procedures and Micro Economic Effects of Innovation', *Journal of Economic Literature*, 26: 1120–1171.

DuPont, V. 1992. 'Impact of In-migration on Industrial Development: A Case Study of Jetpur in Gujarat', *Economic and Political Weekly*, 27(45): 2423–2436.

Enright, M. J. 1994. 'Regional Clusters and Firm Strategy'. Paper presented at the Prince Bertil Symposium on The Dynamic Firm: the Role of Regions, Technology, Strategy and Organization, Stockholm, 12–15 June.

Feldman, M. P. 1994. *The Geography of Innovation*, Dordrecht: Kluwer Academic Publishers.

Foundation for MSME Clusters (FMC). 2007. *Policy and Status Paper on Cluster Development in India*, New Delhi: FMC. http://fmc.org.in/wp-content/uploads/2012/10/Policy-and-Status-Paper1.pdf. Accessed 5 September 2009.

Government of India. 1987. *Report on the Working and Living Conditions of Workers in the Handloom Industry in India, Unorganised Sector Survey Series Labour Bureau*, Chandigarh: Ministry of Labour, Government of India.

Government of India. 2011. *Census Report*, New Delhi: Ministry of Home Affairs.

Government of Mizoram. 2012. *Statistical Handbook Mizoram*, Aizawl: Directorate of Economic and Statistics.

Humphrey, J. and H. Schmitz. 1995. 'Principles for Promoting Clusters and Networks of SMEs.' Small and Medium Enterprises Programme Discussion Paper 1, Vienna: UNIDO.

Humphrey, J. and H. Schmitz. 1996. 'The Triple C Approach to Local Industrial Policy', *World Development*, 24(12): 1859–1877.

Jaffe, A. B. 1989. 'Real Effects of Academic Research', *American Economic Review*, 79: 957–970.

Kar, G. C. 2005. 'The Silver Filigree Cluster in Cuttack, Orissa: What Ails it?' in K. Das (ed.), *Indian Industrial Clusters*, pp.161–170, Aldershot: Ashgate.

Kennedy, L. 2005. 'Variations on the Classical Model: Forms of Cooperation in Leather Clusters of Palar Valley, Tamil Nadu', in K. Das (ed.), *Indian Industrial Clusters*, pp. 102–122, Aldershot: Ashgate.

Khasnabis, R. and P. Nag. 2001. 'Labour Process in the Informal Sector – a Handloom Industry in Nadia District', *Economic and Political Weekly*, 36(52): 4836–4845.

Krugman, P. 1991. 'Increasing Returns and Economic Geography', *The Journal of Political Economy*, 99(3): 483–499.

Lundvall, B. A. 1988. 'Innovation as an Interactive Process: from User-producer Interaction to the National System of Innovation', in G. Dosi (ed.), *Technical Change and Economic Theory*, pp. 349–369, London: Pinter Publishers.

Maillat, D., M. Quévtt, and L. Senn. 1993. *Réseaux d'innovation et milieux innovateurs: un pari pour le développement regional (Innovation Networks and Innovative Environments: A Bet for Regional Development)*. Neuchâtel: EDES.

Malecki, E. J. 1994. 'Entrepreneurship in Regional and Local Development', *International Regional Science Review*, 16: 119–153.

Malmberg, Anders, Sölvell Örjan and Zander Ivo. 1996. 'Spatial Clustering, Local Accumulation of Knowledge and Firm Competitiveness', *Geografiska Annaler. Series B, Human Geography*, 78(2): 85–97.

Marshall, A. 1919. *Industry and Trade*, London: Macmillan.

Mathew, M. 2005. 'Flexible Specialization for Rural Industries? A Study of the Bamboo and Rattan Sub-Sector', in K. Das (ed.), *Indian Industrial Clusters*, pp. 143–160, Aldershot: Ashgate.

National Productivity Council. 1984. *In-depth Studies in Handloom and Handicraft Industries in Mizoram Handloom*, Guwahati: National Productivity Council.

NCAER. 2010. *Handloom Census of India*, New Delhi: NCAER.

Nick, H. and S. Pinch. 2007. 'Knowledge and Clusters', in C. Pitelis, R. Sugden and James R. Wilson (eds), *Clusters and Globalisation: The Development of Urban and Regional Economies*, pp. 114–132, Cheltenham, UK: Edward Elgar.

OECD. 1996. *SMEs: Employment, Innovation and Growth: The Washington Workshop*, Paris: OECD.

OECD. 1998. *Fostering Entrepreneurship*, Paris: OECD.

Patel, P. and K. Pavitt. 1991. 'Large Firms in the Production of the World's Technology: An Important Case of Non-Globalization', *Journal of International Business Studies*, 22(1): 1–21.

Piore, M. J. and C. F. Sabel. 1984. *The Second Industrial Divide – Possibilities for Prosperity*, USA: Basic Books.

Pitelis, C. and Pseiridis, A. 2007. 'A Conceptual Framework for Firm Cooperation and Clusters, and their Impact on Productivity', in C. Pitelis, R. Sugden and James R. Wilson (eds), *Clusters and Globalisation: The Development of Urban and Regional Economies*, pp. 17–60, Cheltenham, UK: Edward Elgar.

Polanyi, M. 1966. *The Tacit Dimension*, New York: Doubleday.

Porter, M. 1990. *The Competitive Advantage of Nations*, London: Macmillan.

Porter, M. 1998. 'Clusters and the New Economics of Competition', *Harvard Business Review*, 76(6): 77–91.

Pyke, F. and W. Sengenberger. 1992. *Industrial Districts and Local Economic Regeneration*, Geneva: International Institute for Labour Studies.

Ramswamy, Rama. 2015. 'Challenges of Managing Traditional Craft Enterprises: A Case Study of Thenzawl Handloom Cluster in Mizoram', in R. K. P. G. Singha (ed.), *Development Perspectives in North East India: Micro and Macro Studies*, pp. 75–82, New Delhi: Lakshi Publishers.

Ramswamy, Rama and N. V. R. Jyoti Kumar. 2013. 'Women Weavers in Mizoram: Sustaining Livelihood through Cluster Development', *Indian Journal of Gender Studies*, 20(3): 435–452.

Ramswamy, R. and N. V. R. J. Kumar. 2011. 'Impact of Clusters on Entrepreneurship: A Case Study of Thenzawl, Mizoram', *Small Enterprises Development, Management & Extension Journal*, 39(2): 110–115.

Ramswamy, Rama and N. V. R. J. Kumar. 2012. 'Marketing of Handloom Products: A Case Study of Thenzawl Cluster in Mizoram', *Indian Journal of Marketing*, 42(12): 34–41.

Reynolds, P. D., S. M. Camps, W. D. Bygrave, E. Autio, and M. Hay. 2001. *Global Entrepreneurship Monitor – 2001 Executive Report*, USA: Kauffman Center for Entrepreneurial Leadership.

Rocha, Hector O. 2004. 'Entrepreneurship and Development: The Role of Clusters', *Small Business Economics*, 23: 363–400.

Rosenfeld, S. 1997. 'Bringing Business Clusters into the Mainstream of Economic, Development', *European Planning Studies*, 5: 3–23.

Sandee, H. 1994. 'The Impact of Technological Change on Inter-firm Linkages: A Case Study of Clustered Small-Scale Roof Tile Enterprises in Central Java', in P. O. Pedersen, A. Sverrisson and M. P. van Dijk (eds), *Flexible Specialization: The Dynamics of Small-scale Industry in the South*, pp. 84–96, London: Intermediate Technology.

Sarkar, T. and S. Bannerjee. 2007. 'Artisan Clusters – Some Policy Suggestions', *The Innovation Journal*, 12 (2): 3–14.

Saxenian, A. 1994. *Regional Advantage: Culture and Competition in Silicon Valley and Route 128*, Cambridge, MA: Harvard University Press.

Smyth, I. 1992. 'Collective Efficiency and Selective Benefits: The Growth of the Rattan Industry of Tegalwangi (Indonesia)', *IDS Bulletin*, 23(3): 51–56.

Society for Economic and Social Transition. 2005. Report on Rural Cluster Development: A Case Study, New Delhi: Society for Economic and Social Transition.

Sugden, R., Ping Wei and R. W. James. 2007. 'Clusters, Governance and Development of Local Economies: A Framework for Case Studies', in C. Pitelis, R. Sugden and James R. Wilson (eds), *Clusters and Globalisation: The Development of Urban and Regional Economies*, pp. 61–88, Cheltenham, UK: Edward Elgar.

Verghese, G. and R. L. Thanzawna. 1997. *A History of the Mizos, Volume–I*, New Delhi: Vikas.

Villaran, F. 1993. 'Small-scale Industry Efficiency Groups in Peru', in B. Späth (ed.), *Small Firms and Development in Latin America: The Role of Institutional Environment, Human Resources and Industrial Relations*, Geneva: International Institute of Labour Studies, ILO.

Weijland, H. 1999. 'Micro-enterprise Clusters in Rural Indonesia: Industrial Seedbed and Policy Target', *World Development*, 27(9): 1515–1530.

Winter, S. G. 1987. 'Knowledge and Competence as Strategic Assets', in David J. Teece (ed.), *The Competitive Challenge-Strategies for Industrial Innovation and Renewal*, pp. 159–184, Cambridge, MA: Ballinger.

Chapter 8

From craft to industry

Understanding the dynamics of handloom weaving in Manipur[1]

Otojit Kshetrimayum

This chapter examines the dynamics of society, work and employment in the handloom sector of Manipur with its transition from a traditional craft to an industry. Exploring the sociology of work in the handloom sector in Manipuri society, it highlights the gender construction of weaving within its social structure and examines weaving as an occupation in the social hierarchy and the extent weaving undergoes feudalisation as an occupational craft. From employment aspects, the study underlines the socio-economic dimensions of the handloom industry in Manipur. A case study of women handloom entrepreneurs is also carried out to examine how the segregation of weaving according to sex has empowered these women through entrepreneurship.

Each aspect of Manipuri life finds vivid reflection in its material culture. Manipur's ethnic identity, social hierarchy, aesthetic attainment and religious concepts are rooted in the cultural ethos of any of its ethnic groups (Roy 1979). For example, there are a number of myths in Manipur that talk about the introduction of the cotton plant and the art of weaving. This account of the origin of the cotton plant and the art of weaving, as given in the ancient texts, signifies the sacredness of weaving as a practice. Handloom weaving in Manipur refers to the evolution of an industry from a mythical foundation to a commercial activity. Weaving among the Meiteis of Manipur was part of their culture and tradition. Receiving royal patronage, the industry flourished further. This was followed by a period of feudalisation during which the weaving of certain clothes was sorted out as per particular lineage group and sex, leading to the social seclusion of weavers. Colonial rule had brought about the modernisation of the weaving tradition. It initiated the process of institutionalisation of this craft. After the state merged with the independent Indian Union, post-independence, handlooms in Manipur underwent 'cooperatisation'. Figure 8.1 outlines a framework of the evolution of handloom weaving in Manipur.

The weaving industry in Manipur is not just an economic activity that can be explained only from an economic perspective. There is a concomitant relationship between its origin as an industry and the cultural demands of society (Kshetrimayum 2016). The industry is sustained, as there is a need for costumes by different clans to mark their distinct identity and for various secular and religious occasions. So weaving became a medium which serves as a repository and transmitter of culture and civilisation. The costumes serve as narratives of a different kind, which is neither oral nor literate but one which inheres and tells the history, cultural identity, social structure, gender roles and ethos of the society. This means that there is a deeper structure cloistered in handloom work apart from its utilitarian function. Owing to these cultural connotations, weaving is an important site for sociological enquiry.

Manipur: an overview

Manipur is a name given to this land after the declaration of Hinduism as a state religion in the beginning of the eighteenth century, during the time of the great ruler of Manipur, Pamheiba or Garibniwaza. In early times, the state was known by different names such as Kanglei Pungmayol, Kangleipak, Meitrabak and Poirie Meitei. Manipur was also known by a variety of names in the neighbouring

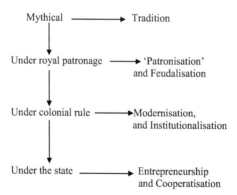

Figure 8.1 Evolution of handloom weaving in Manipur

areas. The Burmese called it Kathe, the Assamese called it Meklei, the Cacharis, Monglei, and the Shans termed it Kassay. Today, Manipur is one of the eight north-eastern states of India. It is bounded on the east by Burma (Myanmar), on the west by the Cachar district of Assam and on the north by Nagaland and the Chin hills of Burma. It has a geographical area of approximately 22,327 sq. km, out of which one-tenth is in the plains (valley); the rest are in the hills. There are 33 tribes spread over the hill areas, whereas there are only 6 ethnic groups – the Meiteis, Lois/Chakpas, Yaithibis, Meitei Bamons (Brahmins), Bishnupriyas and Meitei Pangans (Muslims) – in the valley. Of the six ethnic groups in the valley, the Meiteis, Lois/Chakpas and Yaithibis claim to be of endogenous origin, and the Bamons, Bishnupriyas and Pangans are of exogenous origin.

The prehistoric caves of Khangkhui and Tharon and the Palaeolithic tools and Neolithic sites at Napachik indicate the great antiquity of Manipur's civilisation, which predates Christ by a few thousand years. The various proto Meitei tribes of Manipur valley were politically and socially integrated into a political and social entity by the powerful Ningthouja (Mangang) kingdom founded by Pakhangba (AD 33–154) in the first century AD. Animism was believed to be the ancient belief of the Meitei. The evolution of the Meitei state from a tribal or lineage-based polity to a full-fledged feudal state in the fifteenth century during the reign of Kyamba (1467–1508) was a significant chapter in the political history of Manipur. In the seventeenth century, Khagemba (1597–1652) further expanded and strengthened the kingdom of Manipur. The Royal Chronicle, *The Cheitharol Kumbaba*, which recorded the day-to-day happenings/events of more than 74 kings, shows that King Khagemba had to contend with Manipur's neighbours – the Shans, Burmese, Chinese, Bodo states of Tripura, Dimasa Kachari, Ahoms and the Muslims (Singh and Singh 1989).[2]

Manipur reached the climax of its glory in the eighteenth century during the reign of Garibniwaza (1709–48) when he conquered upper Burma and also accepted Hinduism and declared it as the state religion, leading to a process of 'Hinduisation' of Manipur's religious, social and cultural life. The conflicts with Burma and internal differences greatly weakened the Kingdom of Manipur in the early nineteenth century, leading to the Burmese conquest of Manipur, locally known as *Chahi Taret Khuntakpa*, the Seven Years Devastation (1819–26). The threat from the Burmese led Manipur to look towards the British East India Company for liberation from the Burmese. Gambhir Singh (1825–34), the king at that time, entered into an elaborate political treaty with the British for trade and military alliance. In 1827, the British government installed their first political agent, equivalent to an ambassador, in Manipur. Later, during the period of Chandrakirti (1850–86), the relationship between the two governments was based on mutual trust. After the death of Chandrakirti, there was bitter conflict among the heirs, and as a result, in 1891, British sovereignty extended its tentacles over the once independent kingdom. Manipur was to remain under British rule for 56 years, that is, from 1891 to 1947. Then it became independent till the Maharajah signed the merger agreement with the Indian Union on 15 October 1949 (Kamei 1991). On 21 January 1972, Manipur was elevated to full statehood within the Indian Union.

Manipur has three major communities: Meiteis, Nagas and Kukis. Both the Nagas and the Kukis are umbrella terms for various tribes. They constitute the STs in Manipur. There are 34 STs in Manipur. They are Aimol, Anal, Angami, Chiru, Chothe, Gangte, Hmar, Kabui, Kacha Naga, Koirao, Koireng, Kom, Lamgang, Mizo, Lushai, Maram, Maring, Mao, Monsang, Moyon, Paite, Ralte, Sema, Simte, Suhte, Tangkhul, Thadou, Vaiphei, Zou, Poumei Naga, Tarao, Kharam, any Kuki tribe and Mate. They lived mostly in the five hill districts of Manipur, namely, Ukhrul, Senapati, Churachandpur, Tamenglong and Chandel, and the majority of them follow Christianity as their religion. The Mao tribe is mostly concentrating in the Senapati district, the Tangkhuls in the Ukhrul District, the Kabuis in the Tamenglong District, the Anals and Maring in the Chandel District, and the Thadous and Kukis in the Churachandpur District. The Meiteis are concentrated in the four valley/plain districts of Manipur, namely, Imphal East, Imphal West, Bishnupur and Thoubal.

As per the Census 2011, the total population of Manipur is 2,570,390. Of this, the rural population is 1,736,236 and the urban population 834,154. In absolute numbers, out of the total increase of 403,602 added in the last decade, the rural contribution is 145,416 and that of the urban area is 258,186. The total ST population in the Census 2011 is 902,740. Of this, 791,126 are in rural areas and 111,614 in urban areas. In terms of proportion, the ST population constitutes 35.1 percent of the total population. The highest proportion of ST members has been recorded in Tamenglong district (95.7 percent) and the lowest in Thoubal district (0.4 percent). The highest number of ST members has been recorded in the Churachandpur district (254,787) and the lowest in the Thoubal district (1808).

In the context of this chapter, we have confined our study to the Meitei community of Manipur. Unlike weaving in other parts of India, weaving in Manipur is entirely the work of women. Weaving formed an integral part of their domestic duties. The majority of the weavers in the state are self-employed artisans who carry on the profession in their own homes with the assistance of their family members in the pre-loom and post-loom processes. During the pre-plan period, all the cottage and village industry in Manipur, especially the handloom industry, was independently run by the workers themselves with the help of family members. The craft which initially started to meet the limited demand of families soon developed into a profession for certain groups of people, and ideas of commercialisation and marketing of products as an economic activity entered the field. This transition was further accelerated by the extension of cooperatives in the handloom sector by the state. The art of weaving in its contemporary form has become a modern economic enterprise in Manipur.

It is in this context that this chapter examines the dynamics of society, work and employment in the handloom sector in Manipur, with its transition from a traditional craft to an industry. Exploring the sociology of work in the handloom sector in Manipuri society, it highlights the gender construction of weaving within its social structure. It also examines weaving as an occupation in the social hierarchy and the extent of feudalisation of weaving as an occupational craft. From the employment aspects, the study underlines the socio-economic dimensions of the handloom industry in Manipur. A case study of women handloom entrepreneurs is also carried out to examine how the segregation of weaving by sex has empowered these women through entrepreneurship.

Handloom sector: an overview

Though the handloom sector is decentralised, unorganised and rural-based, it is one of the largest economic activities in India and plays an important role in the country's economy. The contribution of the handloom sector towards textile production, employment and export earnings is significant. India occupies a prominent place in the world as far as the number of handlooms and the varieties of traditional handloom products are concerned. India produces 85 percent of the handlooms of the world, producing a variety of products using all kinds of fibres and yarns of varying counts to produce the widest range of products.

As per the Handloom Census of 2009–10, there are 2.37 million handlooms employing 4.33 million handloom weavers and allied workers in the country. Nearly 2.78 million handloom households are engaged in weaving and allied activities in India, out of which 87 percent are located in rural areas and the remaining 13 percent in urban areas, implying that the handloom sector is predominantly a rural-based industry. The handloom sector supports a large section of weavers and allied workers, who belong to economically weaker sections like SCs, STs and OBCs.

In India, the majority (82 percent) of handloom-working households are weaver households, which means that at least one member of every such household is engaged in weaving activities. In North-East India, 90 percent of the handloom worker households are weaver households, whereas in the states outside the region, 29 percent of the total handloom worker households are allied worker households. Nearly 28 percent of the handloom worker households are into purely domestic production and mostly located in the north-eastern states. There are major differences in the gender composition of the adult handloom workforce between the north-eastern states and other parts of India. The north-eastern states have a predominantly (99 percent) female adult workforce. In states outside the North-East, male handloom workers are present in significant numbers (44 percent).

There are major differences in the employment structure of adult handloom workers in the North-East and other states. In the North-East, 96 percent of all adult handloom workers work in independent production systems, though a large proportion of them are domestic workers. In comparison, 76 percent of all adult handloom workers are contract workers in other states – 66 percent work under master weavers or private owners, and 10 percent work under institutions. A large majority of looms in the north-eastern states engage in domestic production (62 percent), and a relatively smaller (34 percent) proportion is into mixed production. In states outside the North-East, 82 percent of the looms are purely for commercial production and 14 percent for mixed production.

An analysis of the trends of the handloom sector in India and Manipur is highlighted by examining the three handloom censuses in India. From Table 8.1, it is observed that there had been a growth of 12.3 percent of handloom weaver household units in Manipur from the first (1987–8) to the second (1995–6) handloom census, whereas there was negative growth of 17.5 percent at the all-India level. From the second (1995–6) to the third (2009–10) handloom census, there was negative growth both in Manipur and India, with 18.5 and 10 percent, respectively. It is significant to note that the number of handloom weaver household units in Manipur decreased drastically from the second to the third handloom census. In the case of the country as a whole, there was a decreasing trend from the first to the third handloom census. It is, therefore, a matter of great concern for the survival of this sector.

Regarding the number of handloom household workers (Table 8.2), there was again a decreasing trend from the first to the third handloom census at the all-India level. However, in the case of Manipur, there was a growth of nearly 36 percent from the first to the second census and massive negative growth of about 52 percent from the second to third census.

In the case of a number of handloom household and non-household looms (Table 8.3), there was a huge decline of nearly 32 percent both in Manipur and at the all-India level from the second to the third handloom census.

Manipur has a predominantly (99 percent) female adult workforce, as represented in all the three handloom censuses (Table 8.4). At the all-India level, male handloom workers are present in

Table 8.1 Distribution of handloom weaver household units in Manipur and all India

Distribution of handloom weaver household units					
States	1987–8	1995–6		2009–10	
	No. of units	No. of units	Growth (% age)	No. of units	Growth (% age)
Manipur	192,138	215,801	12.32	175,977	−18.45
All India	3,060,090	2,524,512	−17.50	2,268,008	−10.16

Source: Data based on Census of Handlooms in India, 1987–8, 1995–6 and 2009–10

Table 8.2 Distribution of handloom household workers in Manipur and all India

State-wise distribution of handloom household workers in India

State	1987–8	1995–6	Growth rate (% age)	2009–10	Growth rate (% age)
Manipur	334,626	454,599	35.85	218,753	–51.88
All India	6,342,523	5,197,482	–18.05	4,331,876	–16.65

Source: Data based on Census of Handlooms in India, 1987–8, 1995–6 and 2009–10

significant numbers (22 percent). The exclusive dominance of women as weavers in Manipur, therefore, needs an enquiry.

It is a matter of great concern, as the trends of the growth of the handloom sector both in India and Manipur are not very bright. There has been a huge decline in the number of handloom weaver household units, handloom household workers, and handloom household and non-household looms, as observed from the three handloom censuses.

Occupational stratification of weaving in Manipur

In this section, we try to understand the social, cultural and political dynamics of weaving in Manipur. This has been discussed by examining the occupational stratification of weaving through (a) segregation of weaving according to sex; (b) weaving as an occupation in social hierarchy; and (c) the 'feudalisation' of the weaving craft.

Segregation of weaving by sex

The dress and the mode of dressing form a significant part of the Meitei traditions of Manipur. The Meitei cultural tradition of the art of weaving is based on a mythical foundation. According to mythology, it was the supreme goddess who introduced the art of weaving. It is believed that Chitnu Tamitnu, a goddess and primaeval celestial ancestress of the Meitei, discovered cotton and produced yarn out of it. When the threads were ready for weaving she arranged the required equipment and constructed the 'Sinnaishang'

Table 8.3 Distribution of handloom household and non-household looms and their working status in Manipur and all India

Distribution of HH and non-HH looms and their working status

States	1987–8			1995–6				2009–10			
	Working	Idle	Total	Working	Idle	Total	Growth rate (percent)	Working	Idle	Total	Growth rate (percent)
Manipur	266,915	3346	270,261	267,470	14,026	281,496	4.16	186,707	3931	190,634	−32.28%
All India	3,611,513	279063	3,890,576	3,137,138	349,171	3,486,309	−10.39	2,146,436	230,899	2,377,331	−31.81%

Source: Data based on Census of Handlooms in India, 1987–8, 1995–6 and 2009–10

Table 8.4 Number of adult weavers by gender in Manipur and all India

	Male	Female	Total
Handloom census 1987–8			
Manipur	77 (0.03%)	281,454 (99.97%)	281,531
All India	1,555,270 (37.08%)	2,638,497 (62.92%)	4,193,767
Handloom census 1995–6			
Manipur	2412 (0.57%)	415,563 (99.43%)	417,975
All India	1,222,201 (36.74%)	2,103,887 (63.26%)	3,326,088
Handloom census 2009–10			
Manipur	1,577 (0.77%)	202,742 (99.23%)	204,319
All India	848,473 (22.05%)	2,998,362 (77.95%)	3,846,835

Source: Data based on Census of Handlooms in India 1987–8, 1995–6 and 2009–10

(work shed). It is also believed that the goddess Panthoibi once saw a spider producing fine threads and making cobwebs, and from it she derived the idea and thus started the art of weaving. The goddess Panthoibi represents wealth and prosperity. Again, the feminity of the deity who introduced the art signifies the association of this occupation with females (Devi 1998: 106).

Weaving was so culturally esteemed in the traditions of the Meitei that in the community ritual of Lai Haraoba, the dance performed by the *Maibi*s (priestess) symbolically conveys the art of weaving to the young girls. Traditionally, it was a practice for the parents to give a set of weaving apparatus to their daughter as an indispensable part of the marriage gift on her wedding. It would also be worthwhile to note that when selecting a girl for a daughter-in-law, the Meitei parents gave priority to the prospective bride's proficiency in the art of weaving. Until recently, it was compulsory for every female in Meitei society to be trained in the art of weaving. Females who do not possess adequate knowledge and skill in weaving are viewed as lacking in the quality of womanhood, and for that matter, they do not have a source of wealth and prosperity. That is why the knowledge and skill of weaving were compulsory for every Meitei female. Acquiring knowledge of the art of weaving was thus viewed as the greatest asset that a girl of marriageable age needed to possess. It is the women who provided their families with all the necessary household cloths and garments worn by the members by making the items themselves. It has been reported that every Meitei household had at least a set of weaving looms, either the loin loom (*Khwang Iyong*) or the throw-shuttle loom (*Pang Iyong*) type. A Meitei girl is initiated into the art at a tender age, and throughout her life, she practices this art. Not only does she supply clothing to her family members but also makes it a source of family industry. It is said that the development of this industry by women is linked to the men's continuous engagement in wars. Women, therefore, not only had to supply men with the uniforms but also had to maintain their families by selling the product of this industry (Roy 1979: 13).

The fact that various types of clothes were in use is revealed in the *Puyas* (ancient handwritten manuscripts), though no date has been mentioned. Besides, the oral traditions of the Meiteis such as legends, folk tales, etc., clearly suggest that the various items used in the weaving of clothes formed part of the dowry[3] of the princesses and daughters of royal families. For example, at the daughter's marriage, different weaving tools such as the Khwang Iyong (loin loom), Pang Iyong (throw shuttle loom), etc., were some of the essential items of a dowry. There is also a reserved room known as the *Ningol Ka* (daughter's room) in the *Yumjao* or traditional Meitei house. The unmarried girls of a particular locality would bring the different items used in weaving like the *Tareng* (spinning wheel) to assemble in this room and perform the work of spinning till late at night and engage themselves in a sort of competition with each other to bring out the best design and product. This tradition of coming together in a single house to weave and work is known as *Sinnaipham Kaba* (going to work). This was done on a rotation basis from one house to the other every other day. Since the Second World War, this practice has dwindled.[4] Up to the present, it is still considered to be a taboo for men to touch the *phanek* or the loin cloth of women, and definitely weaving has remained an exclusive activity for women. There is, therefore, a strong culture of segregation of weaving by sex in Manipuri society.

Weaving as an occupation in social hierarchy

Social hierarchy in Manipuri society is based on the king's assignment of occupations to various lineages. Based on the lineage-based status stratification model, Manipuri society can be classified into three social categories: (a) *Achou Ashang Mee*, (b) *Meecham* and (c) *Hanthaba Mee*.

Achou Ashang Mee, or the aristocrats, helped the king in formulating customary laws and in provisioning judicial, administrative and military services. Hanthaba Mee, or degraded people, were assigned certain occupations which were considered derogatory and were not performed by the common or aristocratic Meiteis. These included silk manufacturing, smelting of iron, distilling of spirits, making of earthen vessels for storing water or for cooking, manufacturing of salt, fishing and making provisions of grass for the king's ponies, etc. Some of them also served as scavengers.

Weaving as an assigned occupation was performed by the meecham, or common people. The common Meiteis can be divided into occupational and non-occupational groups. The non-occupational groups were those who settled in the northern fertile land and enjoyed physical and social proximity to the kings. The occupational group had one occupation assigned to each of them. These occupational lineages were again bifurcated into artisans and non-artisans. There were some *yumnak*s (lineages) who used to supply primary requirements to the king. They were known as Primary Artisan Lineages. There were also some lineages that supplied secondary requirements to the king called *Khutnaiba*, which may be referred to as Secondary Artisan Lineages. The non-artisan lineages included *Lairikyengbam*, who were assigned clerical works in the king's courts. In the social hierarchy, the non-occupational lineages were at the top, followed by the non-artisans and the artisan lineages, respectively. Among the artisans, the primary artisans had higher status than the secondary artisans.

Weaving as an occupation belongs to primary artisans, since clothing is considered a primary requirement for the king. Thus, in the status hierarchy, lineages that were assigned weaving as an occupation were part of the primary artisan lineages and above the degraded lineage, though below the aristocratic lineage.

'Feudalisation' of weaving craft

The Manipuri society was a feudal[5] society with the dominance of institutions like *lallup*[6] and *loipotkaba*.[7] However, since the beginning of the twelfth century, there has been a process of 'feudalisation' of weaving in this society. The two major factors that have contributed to this process were the enforcement of the royal decree

Loyumba Shilyen in AD 1110 and the adoption of Hinduism as the state religion in AD 1714. The feudalisation of Meitei society was associated with the king taking control over labour, assigning specific occupations to each lineage group. This process also gave rise to sex role differentiation of labour and the formalisation of hierarchy by ascribing different values to different occupations. In traditional Indian society, one's occupation depended on caste. Textile production is also determined by certain castes or sub-castes.[8] However, in Manipur, a family acquires an occupational unit by virtue of the fact that that particular occupation was assigned by the king. For instance, a particular job was assigned to a particular *yumnak* (lineage). Thus, the names of each yumnak would normally indicate the occupation assigned to them traditionally. Though weaving for domestic use was the function of every household, the alliance of lineages with productive labour processes was formally institutionalised in the early twelfth century during King Loyumba's reign (AD 1074–1112) (Hodson 2003: 27). The king's control over the economic production of the artisans is clearly embodied in the royal decree *Loyumba Shilyen* issued by the king himself in AD 1110. The code was based on the earlier codes and conventions current during the previous reigns. The decree is regarded as the first written constitution of Manipur. Later kings like Kyamba (1467–1508), Khagemba (1597–1652), Garibniwaz (1709–48), Bhagyachandra (1763–98) and Chourjit (1803–13) further expanded and strengthened the decree.

Loyumba Shilyen deals with the distribution of occupations according to yumnak (lineage); assignment of duties to priest and priestess (*Maiba*s and *Maibi*s); responsibilities for the maintenance of the abode of deities (*Umanglai*s) to selected sages; creation of administrative departments (*Loishang*s); duties and functions of kings and queens; royal etiquette, titles and decorations awarded to nobles; administration of justice; keeping of standard time; and many other things. The decree was basically written for two purposes: one was to organise the division of labour and to avoid social conflict within the community and even outside it, and the other was to maintain royal control over the subjects. In the case of well-developed industries like handloom and dyeing, the weaving of different types of clothes was assigned to different yumnaks or sageis belonging to various *Yek-Salai*s (clans).[9] These occupations were distributed to 34 lineages. It is further reported that most of the traditional dyes were produced and developed under Loyumba's patronage. The tasks of dyeing were distributed to eight lineages. It is mentioned in the *Mashin* (a manuscript dealing with the duties allotted to the people) that the colour of the yarn used in weaving the *Ningthouphi* (King's cloth) was dyed in diverse colours by different lineages (Devi 1998: 87). The assigned occupations of the lineages were not interchangeable. Those who failed to conform to the orders of the king were punished by sending them into exile and reducing them to a degraded class or status of Loi. This system of strict specialisation is a vivid example of 'patriarchal feudalism'. It did not give the women weavers the freedom to engage in diverse weaving crafts. Table 8.5 gives the list of the names of lineages with their respective assigned crafts:

Table 8.5 List of *yumnak* (lineages) with their assigned crafts

Name of lineage	Weaving craft
Thingucham	Mungphi
Lairellakpam	Laiphi
Kaswam	Wana Katang Phi
Chakpa Thiyam	Laiphi Tonkap
Chakpa Lampam	Phiren
Kongpacham	Langtomphi
Thonngkabam	Yarongphi
Khumallabam	Chamiphi
Haokhom	Tungkap Phi
Laikhuram	Sarong Phi
Salchiram	Leirum Phi
Wahengbam	Dolai Kup Phi
Kabacham	Dolai Thanaba Phi
Apucham	Phiren Phi
Haodijam	Heikoi Phi
Thodingcham	Singkap Phi
Thongpam	Laiyek Phi
Kongbam	Purum Phi
Chingkhalpam	Tarao Phi
Thinpam	Pumthit Phanek
Taibangcham	Phimu Yekpa Phi
Yumlenpam	Nongphi
Wokthiyambam	Khunung Musum Phi
Chakpram	Phiren
Thoudam	Phagang Phi
Nongthombam	Ningthouphi
Ahongsangbam	Embroidery work

(Continued)

Table 8.5 (Continued)

Name of lineage	Weaving craft
Ninghthoujam	Chinphi
Khoirisumbam	Khunung Chumkhun Phi
Yumnak Sangbam	Chingkhong Phi
Khoisnam	Phimu Lanphi
Singkhangbam	Khunung Mathang Phi
Chingkhwapam	Korou Phi Phingang
Wangpacham	Shangmi Lanmu Phi

Source: Devi (1998)

The hierarchy in society found expression in the products of the female craftsperson. To differentiate the chief from the serf, the craftsmen (craftswomen in this context) had to produce goods of superior appearance and durability in terms of colour, design and quality. This put the craftswomen continuously on the attempt to improve their skills and engage in constant experimentation with vegetable dyes and different variant threads, namely, cotton, silk, etc., to attain excellence (Haobam 1991: 207).

It is further reported that most of the traditional dyes were produced and developed under Loyumba's patronage. The tasks of dyeing were distributed to eight lineages, as mentioned in Table 8.6:

Table 8.6 List of *yumnak* (lineages) engaged in yarn dyeing

Name of lineage	Colour of yarn
Akangcham	Leirel Khoipaklei (light pink)
Chingakham	Chengsang Muyumlei (light brown)
Irom	Ureirom Makhong Meiri (flame red)
Khumanthem	Higok Nanou Lei (light blue)
Khumukcham	Kumlang Kumpal Lei (black)
Ipusangbam	Chingya Napu Lei (yellow)
Washiyampam	Sanglen Yaichu Lei (deep green)
Phijam	Loirang Thangchulei (black)

Source: Devi (1998)

An important dimension that calls for examination here is the culture of silk production that took place after the adoption of Hinduism. The production of silk was entirely in the hands of the Lois, whose low social position permitted them to practice many remunerative forms of employment which custom denied to the Meiteis (Hodson 2003: 27–8). This is because after the adoption of Hinduism as the state religion in the early eighteenth century, the concept of purity and pollution had attained a major significance in Manipuri society. As per the 'new Hindu value system', since harvesting of silk involves killing of the silk larvae, it is considered as a polluted activity.[10] Thus, production of silk was on a very limited scale. However, today anyone can engage in silk culture. This activity has become one of the main occupations and major sources of income among the women in Manipur with the commencement of the sericulture project funded by the Japanese government.

Though weaving was primarily a female occupation, male weavers were called to the weaving house of the palace if particular clothes had to be made for the kings and queens (Mutua 1997: 12). The weaver of Ningthouphi had to be a male and was generally the chief of the weavers in the state. Women were excluded from weaving the royal apparel since they menstruate and therefore were considered polluted. This whole arrangement raises the question of sex role differentiation, since weaving was generally an activity of womenfolk in Manipuri society. This also bears the imprint of the patriarchal social structure where the main weavers (women) were deliberately relegated to a powerless position. During the days of the Maharaja, under British domination, there were idiosyncratic rules but not oppression. For example, Maharani Dhanamanjuri Devi liked the '*thambal machu phanek*' (pink lotus-coloured Manipuri sarong dress of ladies), and no one was permitted to wear it except the Maharani.[11]

From the beginning of the twentieth century, there was a major transition in Manipur's handloom industry under the patronage of British rule. The industry became much more 'secular' and organised than before. Colonial rule had brought about modernisation in the weaving tradition. It initiated a process of institutionalisation, which paved the development of the craft into an industry.

Handloom sector in Manipur: employment perspective

The socio-economic dimension of the handloom industry in Manipur is highlighted in this section by examining the Handloom Census of India, 2009–10, a report published by the National Council of Applied Economic Research and Development Commissioner (Handloom), Ministry of Textiles. Regarding the number of handloom worker households, Manipur stands in the fourth position and constitutes 6.43 percent of the total handloom worker households in India. In Manipur, 84 percent of the handloom worker households are located in rural areas and nearly 16 percent in urban areas. Thus, the handloom sector in the state is predominantly a rural activity. Manipur occupies the sixth position among workers, constituting about 4.7 percent of the total handloom workers in India. Manipur has the third highest number of looms, with nearly 8 percent of the total number of looms in India, after Assam and West Bengal. Thus, Manipur is a significant contributor to the handloom sector in India (see Tables 8.7–8.9).

Economic status

As seen from Table 8.10, 5.3 percent of the handloom worker households belong to the poorest of the poor category, and 30.1 percent belong to the BPL category. Only 11.6 percent of the households

Table 8.7 Number of handloom worker households in select states in order of ranking

Sl. No.	State	Number of handloom worker households	Percentage share to total household (2,783,271)
1	Assam	1,240,817	44.58
2	West Bengal	406,761	14.61
3	Tamil Nadu	189,069	6.79
4	Manipur	178,975	6.43

Source: Third National Handloom Census of India, 2009–10

Table 8.8 Number of handloom workers in select states in order of ranking

Sl. No.	State	Number of handloom workers	Percentage share to total workers (4,331,876)
1	Assam	1,483,864	34.25
2	West Bengal	665,006	15.35
3	Tamil Nadu	318,512	7.35
4	Andhra Pradesh	306,465	7.07
5	Uttar Pradesh	217,015	5.00
6	Manipur	204,319	4.71

Source: Third National Handloom Census of India, 2009–10

Table 8.9 Number of looms in select states in order of ranking

Sl. No.	State	Number of looms	Percentage share to total workers (23,77,331)
1	Assam	1,111,577	46.75
2	West Bengal	307,829	12.94
3	Manipur	190,634	8.01

Source: Third National Handloom Census of India, 2009–10

Table 8.10 Number of handloom worker households by type of ration card owned

Location	AAY*	BPL*	APL*	No ration card	Total
Rural	7682	45,199	17,507	80,724	151,112
Urban	1810	8641	3285	14,127	27,863
Total	9492	53,840	20,792	94,851	178,975
Percentage	**5.30**	**30.08**	**11.61**	**52.99**	**100**

Source: Third National Handloom Census of India, 2009–10

Note: * Antyodaya Anna Yojana (AAY); Below Poverty Line (BPL); Above Poverty Line (APL)

hold APL cards. It is also likely that many households belonging to the 'No Ration card category' may be very poor. A sizeable number of the handloom households (53 percent) do not hold any ration card. It is evident that as compared to the national average poverty level of 22 percent as per the Planning Commission's estimate for 2011–1, the incidence of poverty among the handloom worker households is much higher, at more than 35.4 percent.

House ownership

Table 8.11 shows that 41.5 percent of total handloom worker households live in *kuchcha* dwellings; 56 percent lives in semi-*pucca* dwellings. This is indicative of their poor economic condition; the majority of handloom worker households (97.5 percent) live in semi-pucca or kuchcha dwellings. Both the kuchcha and semi-pucca houses are mostly located in the rural areas. Only 2.5 percent of the households have *pucca* houses. About 93 percent of the

Table 8.11 Number of handloom worker households by type of dwelling unit

Location	Kuchcha[12]	Semi-pucca[13]	Pucca[14]	Total
Rural	65,357	82,302	3453	151,112
Urban	8984	17,980	899	27,863
Total	**74,341**	**100,282**	**4,352**	**178,975**
Percentage	**41.5**	**56**	**2.5**	**100**

Source: Third National Handloom Census of India, 2009–10

handloom workers live in their own dwelling units. Only 4 percent of the workers live in rented premises (see Tables 8.11 and 8.12).

Under-age workers

Out of the total handloom workers of 218,753 in Manipur, nearly 7 percent are below 18 years of age. The reasons for existence of large number of under-age handloom workers may be due to the large-scale incidences of poverty among the handloom worker households, predominantly the domestic nature of handloom production and low level of educational attainments among the handloom worker households.

Out of the total adult handloom workers, nearly 98 percent are weavers, and 2 percent are allied workers. Nearly 84 percent of the adult handloom workers belong to the rural areas, and 16 percent are located in the urban areas (see Tables 8.13–8.14).

Gender

Handloom weaving in Manipur is exclusively the work of the womenfolk. This has been validated from Table 8.15, showing that that nearly 99 percent of the total adult handloom workers are women, with only a miniscule number comprising men, the majority of whom are allied workers. Most of the women handloom workers, nearly 86 percent, belong to the rural areas, signifying that the handloom sector is a major occupation for the rural women in Manipur.

Social Groups

As represented in Table 8.16, the percentage of Schedule Castes (SCs) in Handloom Worker Households is 4.6, while those of Scheduled

Table 8.12 Number of handloom worker households by ownership of dwelling

Location	Owned	Rented	Others	Total
Rural	139,150	7645	4317	151,112
Urban	26,858	177	828	27,863
Total	**166,008**	**7822**	**5145**	**178,975**
Percentage	**92.75**	**4.37**	**2.87**	**100**

Source: Third National Handloom Census of India, 2009–10

Table 8.13 Number of total handloom workers by age group

Location	Total workforce (all ages)	< 18 years	18 years & above
Rural	184,088	11,780	172,308
Urban	34,665	2654	32,011
Total	**218,753**	**14,434 (6.59)**	**204,319 (93.40)**

Source: Third National Handloom Census of India, 2009–10

Table 8.14 Total workforce by type of handloom workers

Location	No. of adult weavers	No. of adult allied workers	Total adult workers
Rural	169,878	2430	172,308 (84.3)
Urban	30,729	1282	32,011 (15.7)
Total	**200,607**	**3712**	**204,319**
Percentage	**98.2**	**1.8**	**100**

Source: Third National Handloom Census of India, 2009–10

Table 8.15 Number of adult[15] handloom workers by gender (2009–10)

Location	Male	Female	Total
Rural	1261	171,047	172,308
Urban	316	31,695	32,011
Total	**1577**	**202,742**	**204,319**
Percentage	**0.8**	**99.2**	**100**

Source: Third National Handloom Census of India, 2009–10

Table 8.16 Number of handloom worker households by social groups

Location	Scheduled Castes (SCs)	Scheduled Tribes (STs)	Other Backward Castes (OBCs)	Others	Total
Rural	5825	38,505	39,819	66,963	151,112
Urban	2415	424	8104	16,920	27,863
Total	**8240**	**38,929**	**47,923**	**83,883**	**178,975**
Percentage	**4.60**	**21.75**	**26.77**	**46.86**	**100**

Source: Third National Handloom Census of India, 2009–10

Table 8.17 Number of adult handloom workers by social groups

Location	Scheduled Castes (SCs)	Scheduled Tribes (STs)	Other Backward Castes (OBCs)	Others	Total
Rural	6421	43,545	45,451	76,891	172,308
Urban	2701	466	9295	19,549	32,011
Total	**9122**	**44,011**	**54,746**	**96,440**	**204,319**
Percentage	**4.46**	**21.54**	**26.79**	**47.20**	**100**

Source: Third National Handloom Census of India, 2009–10

Tribes (STs) and Other Backward Castes (OBCs) are 21.8 and 26.8, respectively. It shows that 53 percent of the total handloom worker households belong to socially disadvantaged groups such as SCs, STs and OBCs. Similarly, 53 percent of the total adult handloom workers belong to these disadvantaged groups (Table 8.17). This social group status is also closely linked to the incidence of poverty among handloom workers.

Education

The educational status of the workers also indicates their capacity to break the vicious cycle of poverty. As shown in Table 8.18, about 17 percent of the total adult handloom workers have never attended school. A vast majority of them, that is, 83 percent, have an educational level of high school and below. Interestingly, nearly

Table 8.18 Educational attainment of adult handloom workers

Location	Never attended school	Below primary	Primary	Middle	High school/ secondary	Higher secondary	Graduate & above	Others	Total
Rural	29,389	11,926	24,693	54,425	29,482	14,293	6342	1758	172,308
Urban	1524	4793	3103	9654	6507	3833	2329	268	32,011
Total	**34,182**	**13,450**	**27,796**	**64,079**	**35,989**	**18,126**	**8671**	**2026**	**204,319**
Percentage	**16.7**	**6.6**	**13.6**	**31.4**	**17.7**	**8.8**	**4.2**	**1.0**	**100**

Source: Third National Handloom Census of India, 2009–10

4 percent have graduation or higher qualification. This implies that this sector is not only confined to women who are illiterates or have lower educational attainment.

Employment

On average, the handloom workers are employed for 211 days a year. While weavers get 211 days of work, the allied workers get work for only 189 days. A slight difference exists in the number of days worked in rural and urban areas. While the weavers in rural areas work for 210 days, those in urban areas work for 220 days. The allied workers in rural areas work for 190 days and those in urban areas work for 188 days.

It is observed that nearly 97 percent of the total adult handloom workers are independent workers, followed by workers working under master weavers, private owners, the State Handloom Development Corporation (SHDC), cooperative societies and the Khadi and Village Industries Commission (KVIC). Nearly 84 percent of the total adult handloom workers are working full-time, while 16 percent are engaged part time. These details are highlighted in Tables 8.19, 8.20 and 8.21.

Income

The average annual earning of the handloom households is Rs 56,261 in Manipur and Rs 36,498 at the all-India level (see Table 8.22). Thus, the state has higher average annual handloom household income than at the national level. However, it is found that the share of handloom income to total handloom

Table 8.19 Total and average number of person-days worked per year

Location	Total days worked (weaver + allied)[16]	Average days per household	Average days per worker	Average days per weaver	Average days per allied worker
Rural	36,094,646	239	209	210	190
Urban	7,011,327	252	219	220	188
Total	**43,105,973**	**491**	**428**	**430**	**378**

Source: Third National Handloom Census of India, 2009–10

Table 8.20 Number of adult handloom workers by employment status

Location	Independent[17]	Under master weavers[18]	Under SHDC*	Under KVIC*	Under a cooperative society	Under private owners	Total
Rural	166,639	3834	57	29	50	1699	172,308
Urban	31,256	204	3	5	7	536	32,011
Total	197,895	4038	60	34	57	2235	204,319
Percentage	96.85	1.97	0.02	0.01	0.02	1.09	100

Source: Third National Handloom Census of India, 2009–10

Note: * State Handloom Development Corporation (SHDC), Khadi and Village Industries Commission (KVIC)

Table 8.21 Number of adult handloom workers by nature of engagement

Location	Full-time[19]	Part-time[20]	Total
Rural	145,647	26,661	172,308
Urban	26,870	5141	32,011
Total	**172,517**	**31,802**	**204,319**
Percentage	**84.43**	**15.56**	**100**

Source: Third National Handloom Census of India, 2009–10

Table 8.22 Average earning of handloom households (Rs/annum)

Location	Weaver households	Allied households	All households
Rural	55,672	53,927	55,675
Urban	59,078	70,559	59,442
Total	**114,750**	**124,486**	**115,117**

Source: Third National Handloom Census of India, 2009–10

household income in the state is only 9.53 percent across all handloom households, while it is 30.2 percent at the all-India level (see Table 8.23). This sharp discrepancy can be attributed to the fact that most of the households in Manipur do handloom weaving generally for commercial production at a very subsistence level and primarily for domestic purposes. The average annual income from handloom activity across all households in the state is Rs 5361 which again is much lower than the Rs 11,015 per annum at the national level.

Loom and yarn

As represented in Tables 8.24–8.28, there are 190,634 looms in Manipur, out of which about 98 percent are in working order, while the remaining 2 percent are in idle status. Only 12 percent of the working looms are into commercial production, and about 87 percent of the looms are into domestic and commercial production.

Almost 97 percent of the looms use mill-spun yarn, implying that the state exclusively depends on other states for its yarn requirement. Out of the total households procuring hank and dyed yarn for their looms, about 96 percent receive it from the open market,

Table 8.23 Contribution of handloom to total household income in percentage

Location	Percent share of income from handloom
Rural	9.42
Urban	10.08
Total	**19.50**

Source: Third National Handloom Census of India, 2009–10

Table 8.24 Number of looms by working status

Location	Working[21]	Idle[22]	Total
Rural	158,783	3204	161,987
Urban	27,920	727	28,647
Total	**186,703**	**3931**	**190,634**
Percentage	**97.93**	**2.06**	**100**

Source: Third National Handloom Census of India, 2009–10

Table 8.25 Number of working looms by purpose of usage

Location	Commercial[23]	Domestic[24]	Both domestic and commercial	Total
Rural	19,708	980	138,095	158,783
Urban	3132	35	24,753	27,920
Total	**22,840**	**1015**	**162,848**	**186,703**
Percentage	**12.23**	**0.54**	**87.22**	**100**

Source: Third National Handloom Census of India, 2009–10

Table 8.26 Number of working looms by type of yarn

Location	Mill-spun yarn	Hand-spun yarn	Total
Rural	153,888	4895	158,783
Urban	27,328	592	27,920
Total	**181,216**	**5487**	**186,703**
Percentage	**97.06**	**2.93**	**100**

Source: Third National Handloom Census of India, 2009–10

Table 8.27 Number of households reporting major source of input: hank yarn

Location	Open market	Master weaver	Cooperative society	SHDC*	Others	Total
Rural	118,629	2685	29	33	1690	123,066
Urban	21,252	132	4	12	617	22,017
Total	**139,881**	**2817**	**33**	**45**	**2307**	**145,083**
Percentage	**96.41**	**1.50**	**0.02**	**0.03**	**1.59**	**100**

Source: Third National Handloom Census of India, 2009–10

Note: * State Handloom Development Corporation (SHDC)

Table 8.28 Number of households reporting major source of input: dyed yarn

Location	Open market	Master weaver	Cooperative society	SHDC*	Others	Total
Rural	132,283	2868	42	28	2822	138,043
Urban	23,819	138	11	3	545	24,516
Total	**156,102**	**3006**	**53**	**31**	**3367**	**162,559**
Percentage	**96.02**	**1.84**	**0.03**	**0.02**	**2.07**	**100**

Source: Third National Handloom Census of India, 2009–10

Note: * State Handloom Development Corporation (SHDC)

followed by supply from other sources, master weavers, the State Handloom Development Corporation (SHDC) and cooperative societies. It shows that the handloom households are very much susceptible to market volatility and risks. Frequent road blockades and closure of markets due to political unrest in the state has also drastically affected this industry.

Empowering women through handloom entrepreneurship

A case study of women handloom entrepreneurs or master weavers of Manipur was carried out. The study was conducted among the 50 handloom master weavers of the Imphal East district. These respondents were chosen through snowball sampling, and interviews were conducted. The main objective is to study the entrepreneurial functioning of the handloom entrepreneurs and examine whether it leads to their empowerment.

Establishing an enterprise

There are two ways to establish an enterprise. The first route is to inherit a part of the family enterprise. Handloom weaving is primarily a family or kin-oriented business. The second route is that taken by weavers who, after working for intermediaries – cooperatives, NGOs or a master weaver – for a while, set up their own firms with financial support from family or elsewhere.

The most challenging part of starting one's own enterprise is to raise the required capital and to recruit weavers, as most of them would be under the aegis of another master weaver. An important factor in creating an enabling environment for new start-ups is the macro environment surrounding the village or cluster. Regarding the age of the selected women entrepreneurs, a maximum of 42 percent belonged to the 31–40 age group. Surprisingly, 10 percent of the entrepreneurs were between the ages of 18–20 years. The youngest entrepreneur was 18 years old, while the oldest was 76; 40 percent of the respondents were graduates; only 10 percent had no formal education. This indicates the direct correlation between education and entrepreneurship in this case.

Regarding the nature of the organisation, single ownership accounted for 60 percent, whereas 40 percent of the enterprises were running as partnerships. The study shows that 62 percent and 14 percent of the enterprises had established the units in their own and rented buildings, respectively. However, it is interesting to observe that 24 percent of the enterprising units did not own or rent buildings. Instead, they operated their businesses from their own homes.

Start-up process of the enterprises

Among those surveyed, there were more fresh start-ups (66 percent) than splinter firms, that is, an extension of the already established enterprise. This implies that given certain conditions, independent weavers do have possibilities of coming out of the 'clutches' of master weavers to establish their own ventures. It is the demand for a particular product as well as the influence of their social networks that seem to create an enabling environment for weavers to set up their own ventures. It was seen that the urge to supplement the family income and unemployment had motivated 66 percent of the entrepreneurs to start up their handloom enterprises. On the other hand, the reasons stated by 34 percent of the entrepreneurs for establishing the enterprises were passion for work and to take up their traditional occupation.

Investment and financial assistance

It is observed that 80 percent of the entrepreneurs invested Rs 10,000–50,000 initially for the establishment of the enterprise. There were only 8 percent and 6 percent who had initially invested below Rs 10,000 and above Rs 50,000, respectively. It is interesting to note that the initial source of funding for 60 percent of the entrepreneurs came from themselves while the remaining 30 percent and 10 percent from family and loans from banks, respectively.

The study has shown that 70 percent of the enterprises have received financial assistance from cooperative banks, the Department of Industry and Commerce, the Prime Minister's Rozgar Yojana[25], the nationalised bank, the post-office, or private finance agencies. However, 30 percent of them did not receive financial assistance from any sources.

Spheres of operation

Any entrepreneur has to engage in two separate spheres of operation – production and marketing. The finance and design of new products play an important role in both. The clients of the entrepreneurs are the owners of textile stores in various urban and semi-urban areas, and it is through them that the products reach their retail customers. The main raw material in the handloom industry is yarn, which is imported mainly from outside the state, particularly from Guwahati. Dyed yarn in different colours is given to the weaver, who prepares the warp and the weft, which are then woven to form the required fabric.

The enterprises employed some weavers on permanent basis. Moreover, 74 percent of them employed weavers both on a contractual and permanent basis. The permanent weavers see to those weavers who were working in the workshed provided by the entrepreneurs, while the contract weavers see to those who were working from their homes.

Handloom production can be viewed as a two-pronged operation comprising management of raw material and procuring finished products. The weaver, after receiving the yarn, initiates the weaving process with pre-loom activities like sizing the warp, preparing the weft, etc. The variations in the organisation of pre-loom activities differ according to the place of production. In certain areas, these pre-loom activities are carried out by women and children of the house and from the neighbourhood and there is no explicit payment. In other areas, specialists do the pre-loom activities and are paid directly by the master weavers.

It is interesting to note that all the enterprises were heavily dependent on the production through traditional looms. Regarding the nature of the looms being used by the weavers, all the enterprises were using fly shuttle looms, while 54 percent and 38 percent of them were also using throw shuttle looms and loin looms, respectively. The only innovative method of production that they had introduced was the use of double-seated throw shuttle looms.

The fabric was mostly made in the weaver's home. When the weaver returned the finished goods, she was paid based on the complexity of work and labour involved. The entrepreneur deducted some amount for the repayment of the loan before making the payment to the weaver. The entrepreneur meticulously maintained a ledger where she recorded all financial dealings with her weavers. The weaver kept a small passbook which was updated as and when the exchange of goods and money took place. Once financial matters were settled, designs for the next batch of production were given. If the designs were simple, then the details were orally conveyed to the weaver. Complex designs, on the other hand, were provided on a graph paper. In either case, intricate details were not gone into, giving room for the weaver to use her own creative skills. Since interactions between various stakeholders were conducted regularly, there were codes to describe basic patterns and colour combinations.

The competitive advantage for entrepreneurs in this phase comes by keeping their transaction costs low. The key function in their operation was what could be termed as 'rotation of cash'. Entrepreneurs continuously manipulated various stakeholders in order to survive. They tried to extract longer credit periods from the raw material suppliers and also withhold payments to weavers or pay in parts.

Marketing

The study shows that 74 percent of the enterprises sold their products by cash, 64 percent by credit and 26 percent by instalment. It is also observed that 38 percent of the enterprises sold their products through their own showrooms. The enterprises also used retail stores, agents, exhibitions-cum-sales, and door-to-door vendors for selling their products.

Generally, the clients were retail store owners in various parts of the state. If they purchased regularly, they were considered to be core clients; there were others who were irregular or occasional clients. The interactions between new clients and master weavers usually started small, and the transactions were conducted in cash. After a few such instances, there was a possibility that some clients may switch to purchasing products on credit.

Sales promotion techniques were adopted through advertisements (newspapers and cable TV), agents, door-to-door campaigns, and pamphlets; 16 percent of the enterprises had used all these modes of sale promotion. In order to market her products and recover her credit, the entrepreneur made a trip to each of the core clients' locations at least once a month. Although clients were allowed a credit period of one month, most entrepreneurs were able to recover the credit in this period. Since handloom sales happened in cycles, going up during the festival and marriage seasons and going down during the monsoon, the entrepreneur had the upper hand during the peak season, when she got payments on time, and the clients had an upper hand during the lean season, when she got an extended credit period. In order to survive, an entrepreneur had to skilfully balance her time and energy between her clients, her suppliers and her weavers. This is where her individual social capital in the form of access to resources (cash flows, credit periods, information) along with her history of interactions comes into play.

While visiting her clients, an entrepreneur also tried to gauge the market demands. Each store had a different clientele, depending on its location, with different customers requiring different product ranges. If the customers did not find the product they wanted, they were likely to indicate this while interacting with the salesperson. This information was informally collated and passed on to the entrepreneur, who then decided which new designs were to be produced. It is this market feedback channel that more or less ensured the production of marketable products.

Many of the handloom designs replicated things from nature like birds, animals, flowers, etc. Thousands of interactions between customers, store owners, entrepreneurs and weavers took place over a course of several years to develop techniques and designs for handloom products. None of this was codified and remained in a tacit form. Hence, social networks become an important conduit to convert tacit knowledge into products. In addition to the tacit knowledge that resided in handloom clusters, entrepreneurs also reproduced designs and colours from books and magazines or copied from currently popular mill-made fabric. Once an entrepreneur decided to produce a particular design, it was translated into concrete weaving terms. For this, the entrepreneur or weaver used graph paper.

After the product was made, the entrepreneur, with her knowledge of what kind of product sells where, selected specific products for specific clients. Sometimes the clients wanted a particular design or even developed a design series that supported their proprietary product. Although it is possible to customise designs for clients, entrepreneurs are reluctant to experiment unless it is paid for, as any change from the norm involves extra capital and labour. An entrepreneur will develop a new set of designs only when she feels that the existing ones may not have future markets.

Problems encountered

The problems encountered by handloom entrepreneurs were related to the shortage and high price of yarn, lack of investment, unorganised marketing system, and stagnation of finished products. The enterprises had problems regarding the non-availability, high cost and poor quality of yarn. The main reasons for these problems were frequent economic blockades/strikes in Manipur in general and Imphal in particular, the dependence on yarns imported from outside the state, and control of yarn trading by businessmen from other parts of the country. Issues like lack of adequate funds, the expensive cost of machinery and demands for higher wages for the labourers have been encountered by most of the enterprises. Inadequate sales promotion, less demand and inferior quality were the major marketing problems. Moreover, poor quality, high cost and old stock had led to stagnation of the products.

When entrepreneurs were asked about their plans in the near future, all of them expressed that they aspired to expand their units and increase the level of production by introducing the latest machinery and trained personnel. They had plans to improve their sales promotion techniques and marketing process. They also wished to introduce new varieties of garments according to the requirements of the consumers.

Empowering lives

It is significant to observe that all the respondents felt that they were economically empowered in the sense that they were making an attempt to start their own entrepreneurship for generating income, not only for themselves but also for the people involved in their enterprises. Besides this, some of them, that is, 18 percent, expressed that they were both economically and politically empowered. They were leaders and active members of the *Meira Paibi* (torch bearers, an informal women's group for social order), while some were Pradhan, Panchayat members[26], etc. There were others, that is, 24 percent, who felt that they were also socially empowered. They opined that their family members and others started respecting and encouraging their enterprise. Their views on various issues began to be heard and considered. There was another group, consisting of 16 percent of the respondents, who felt that they were economically, socially and politically empowered. They had received freedom and confidence and were not hesitant to visit places outside the state for business purposes, like participation in fairs.

Conclusion

This chapter examines the social, cultural and political dynamics of sex segregation in the handloom sector in Manipur, as weaving as an occupation has characteristics which are highly consistent with typical female stereotypes in society at large. There is a strong culture of segregation of weaving by sex in Manipuri society, as emphasised in their mythology, socialisation and social taboo. However, this gender stereotype has provided an avenue for employment and income generation to women of the state, as the handloom sector is a major industry in the state. The chapter has observed that women entrepreneurship in the handloom industry in Manipur is associated with the changing social and political structures and the expansion of the market on the supply side and the attributes of the culture of weaving on the demand side. It has shown that the emergence of women entrepreneurship in the handloom industry has definitely brought about some positive changes in the social, economic and political status of the women, though many problems associated with the industry are yet to be addressed. It is therefore apt to mention what Anker (1998) had argued, that sex segregation of occupations is not always bad for women, nor is it always good for men.

Notes

1 The present chapter is an adaptation of my study of *Women and Entrepreneurship in North East India: Handloom as an Enterprise in Manipur* published by V. V. Giri National Labour Institute in 2016.

2 The Royal Chronicle of Manipur, *Chaitharol Kumbaba*, is the most important indigenous literature of Manipur, which records the historical events of nearly 2000 years, covering the reign of 78 kings from the accession of Pakhangba in AD 33 to Bhodhachandra (1941–55). It provides only an account of day-to-day political events, with less emphasis on the social aspects. But enough accounts are given on the religious aspects; especially the king's initiation into Hinduism is narrated in detail.

3 Dowry here refers to a kind of gift to the bride at the time of marriage. It generally consists of items needed to start a family. The choice of items is solely decided by the bride's parents. However, there are certain items which should be included as per the custom of the society.

4 Ibid. p. 9.

5 Feudalism flourished between the tenth and thirteenth centuries in Western Europe. At its core, it was an agreement between a lord and a vassal. A person became a vassal by pledging political allegiance and providing military, political and financial services to a lord. A lord possessed complete sovereignty over the land or acted in the service of another sovereign, usually a king. If a lord acted in the service of a king, the lord was considered a vassal of the king. The meaning of feudalism has expanded since the seventeenth century, and it now commonly describes servitude and hierarchical oppression.

6 *Lallup* was the highest state militia, which literally means 'war association' (*Lal* means war and *Lup* means association). It was a feudal service rendered by the subjects to the king. Originally, it was a military service, which was extended to other non-military or economic activities of the state. The general system of lallup was based on the assumption that it was the duty of every male from 16 to 60 years old to attend Loishang (the royal office) and render his service according to his skill and grade for 10 days of every 40 days to the state.

7 Loipotkaba literally means paying of tribute to the king, a service mainly rendered by the Lois. It also included the performance of heavy duties for the king. These were the least honoured activities performed by the degraded section of the Meiteis, i.e., the Loi/Chakpa, Bishnupriya and the Yaithibi. They did not perform Lallup but paid tribute to the king.

8 Saliya (or Chaliyan or Sali or Sale) is an erstwhile Malayali weavers' caste of northern Kerala and southern coastal Karnataka. The main weavers' castes of South India are Sale, Devanga and Kaikkolar. Among these, the first two castes are native to Kannada and Telugu-speaking

regions, as is evident from inscriptions. Kaikkolar community is native to the Tamil-speaking region, while Padmashali is a Telugu weavers' caste or social group found largely in Andhra Pradesh. Ramdasia Sikh is another caste, and members of this community are engaged in the profession of weaving. They may at times also be referred to as *julaha*, meaning a weaver in Punjabi and Hindi. They are found in the states of Punjab, Haryana, Delhi, Rajasthan, Uttar Pradesh, Uttarakhand and Himachal Pradesh.

 9 The main feature of the social structure of the Meiteis is the institution of Yek-Salai. It is a large exogamous unit, each tracing itself to a common mythical ancestor who is part of the Meitei Divine Pantheon. It can be loosely translated as 'clan'. Meitei society has seven patrilineal units known as Yek-Salais. These seven Yek-Salais are *Mangang, Luwang, Khuman, Moirang, Angom, Khabanganba* and *Sarang-Leishangthem* (also called *Chenglei*).

10 Silk moths lay eggs on specially prepared paper. The eggs hatch and the caterpillars (silkworms) are fed fresh mulberry leaves. After about 35 days and four moltings, the caterpillars are 10,000 times heavier than when hatched and are ready to begin spinning a cocoon. A straw frame is placed over the tray of caterpillars, and each caterpillar begins spinning a cocoon by moving its head in a 'figure 8' pattern. Two glands produce liquid silk and force it through openings in the head called spinnerets. Liquid silk is coated in sericin, a water-soluble protective gum that solidifies on contact with the air. Within 2–3 days, the caterpillar spins about 1 mile of filament and is completely encased in a cocoon. The silk farmers then kill most caterpillars by heat, leaving some to metamorphose into moths to breed the next generation of caterpillars.

11 We could also see a differentiation existing among the weavers in the contemporary Manipuri society, although not well demarcated. Those weavers who are engaged with the weaving of more intricate designs are considered to be at the higher status among the artisans. Thus, the status of weavers is determined by the designs of the clothes they produced. Those weavers engaged with weaving clothes used in social functions like *Wangkhei Phi, Phanek Mayek Naibi, Phige*, etc., were considered important than those involved in weaving ordinary clothes for daily wear.

12 A *kuchcha* house is one whose walls and roof are made of non-*pucca* materials. Non-pucca materials include unburnt bricks, bamboo, mud, grass, leaves, reeds, thatch, etc.

13 A semi-pucca house is a structure that has either the walls or the roof – but not both – made of pucca materials.

14 A pucca house is a structure whose walls and roof are made of pucca materials such as cement, concrete, oven-burnt bricks, stone, iron, timber, tiles, slate, plywood and artificial wood of synthetic material.

15 Adult workers comprise workers who are aged 18 years and above.

16 An allied worker is one who has undertaken pre-loom (dying of yarn, warping/ winding, weft winding, sizing, testing, etc.) and/or post-loom activities (dying of fabric/calendaring/printing of fabric, made-ups,

etc.), even for one day in the last year (preceding the survey date), either within the premises of the house or outside the household premises.

17 An independent worker describes a production system in which the worker purchases raw materials from the market, makes cloth or an allied activity product/service (warp product, weft product, sizing, calendaring, made-ups, etc.) and sells the woven finished products or services in the market independently, all on his own.

18 A master weaver refers as a generic term to people who get the yarn sized, supply beams to smaller owners and get the fabric woven and the cloth processed. This system has evolved over years. In the past, master weavers used to advance yarn to weavers working in their own houses. In recent years, many master weavers have set up common sheds for weaving, where hired weavers come and undertake production activities.

19 Persons who operate looms or work on allied work on a full-time basis, that is, those who engage exclusively on handloom activity, are treated as full-time workers.

20 Part-time handloom workers are persons engaged in occupations other than weaving or allied handloom work and who operate looms or undertake handloom-allied activity only during their leisure hours or when the regular weavers/allied workers are out on lunch, tea, etc.

21 A working loom is defined as a complete loom that has been operated at least for one day during the last year or is at present working.

22 A complete but idle loom is defined as the loom that has not been used for even a single day during the last year.

23 Handloom work – including weaving and allied work – that is undertaken as an occupation in which the product or service is primarily made for market consumption may be regarded as commercial handloom activity.

24 Handloom work that is undertaken primarily for noncommercial purposes such as making fabrics for domestic consumption may be regarded as domestic handloom activity.

25 Prime Minister's Rozgar Yojana (PMRY) for providing self-employment to educated unemployed youth has been in operation since 2 October 1993. The Scheme aimed at assisting the eligible youth in setting up self-employment ventures in industry, service and business sectors.

26 A gram panchayat (village council) is the only grassroots-level of panchayati raj formalised local self-governance system in India at the village or small-town level, and has a Pradhan as its elected head. The gram panchayat is divided into wards and each ward is represented by a Ward Member, also referred to as a Panch or Panchayat Member, who is directly elected by the villagers.

References

Anker, Richard. 1998. *Gender and Jobs: Sex Segregation of Occupations in the World*, Geneva: International Labour Organization.

Census of Handlooms in India 1987–88, Ministry of Textile, GOI.

Devi, Sobita. 1998. *Traditional Dress of the Meiteis*, Imphal: Bhubon Publishing House.

Handloom Census of India, 2009–10, New Delhi: NCAER.

Haobam, Sukumar. 1991. 'Arts and Crafts of Manipur', in N. Sanojaoba (ed.), *Manipur: Past and Present*, New Delhi: Mittal Publications.

Hodson, Thomas Callan. 2003. *The Meitheis*, Delhi: Low Price Publications.

Kamei, Gangumei. 1991. *History of Manipur (Pre Colonial Period)*. Vol. 1, New Delhi: National Publishing House.

Kshetrimayum, Otojit. 2016. *Women and Entrepreneurship in North East India: Handloom as an Enterprise in Manipur*, Noida: V. V. Giri National Labour Institute.

Mutua, Bahadur. 1997. *Traditional Textiles of Manipur*, Imphal: Mutua Museum.

Roy, Nilima. 1979. *Art of Manipur*, Delhi: Agam Kala Prakashan.

Singh, Ibungohal and Khelchandra Singh. 1989. *Cheitharol Kumbaba* (second edition), Imphal: Manipur Sahitya Parishad.

Part III

Migration and labour mobility

Chapter 9

Employment potential of migrant workers in Meghalaya

An empirical exploration

Jajati Keshari Parida

Meghalaya is one of the most progressive north-eastern states of India. It covers an area of about 22,000 sq. km and has a population of about 30 *lakh* (a lakh = 100,000) (Census[1] 2011), or about 0.25 percent of the total population of India. Endowed with nature's gifts, Meghalaya, with the collective endeavour of the inhabitants of the state, has attained economic stability (Ministry of Tourism, Government of India 2003). Since 2000–1, Meghalaya had been passing through a phase of rapid economic growth (about 7.3 percent per annum). This rapid growth of GDP was accompanied by structural changes in both output and employment. The share of GDP changed for agriculture from 42.7 to 16.6 percent, for industry from 15.3 to 29.4 percent, and for services from 42 to 54 percent over the period from 1980–1 to 2010–11. The share of employment in agriculture decreased from 73.5 to 56.5 percent, in industry increased from 8.1 to 11.8 percent, and in services increased from 18.5 to 31.6 percent from 2004–5 to 2011–12. In the process of structural change, it is expected that rural to urban migration would increase (Lewis 1954).

However, given the geographical location and socio-political and cultural environment of Meghalaya and the North-Eastern Region (NER), the nature and structure of migration are different. Meghalaya is not an exception. It is a land-locked region, with Assam covering the east and north perimeter and Bangladesh the western and southern sides; therefore, any disturbance to the socio-economic balance of Assam tends to affect Meghalaya. For decades, militant outfits like NSCN (IM), ULFA, ANVC, NDFB, etc., in the NER have encouraged the growth of other militancy outfits, which in turn have brought about large-scale migration in this region. Ethnic conflicts became endemic in post-colonial times (Dasgupta and Dey

2010). Such conflicts not only referred to differences between the state and ethnic insurgent groups but also inter-ethnic and intra-ethnic clashes that displaced a considerable number of people from the hills and valleys of Assam, Manipur, Nagaland and Mizoram (Shimray 2004; Dasgupta and Dey 2010; and Ramesh 2012), as well as the Garo-hills region of Meghalaya.

More recently, a study by Ramesh (2012), however, claims that large-scale out-migration from the NER is driven by employment and aspiration for higher education. This study also stated that increasing educated and youth unemployment, an abysmally lower level of industrialisation, the lower expansion of modern service sector occupations in the region, and perceived employment prospects in other states collectively prompt aspirant youths to migrate to other states to explore better opportunities. Given the new directions of the migration process in the periods of high growth in Meghalaya, it is important to know about the (a) volume and pattern of out-migration and driving factors in Meghalaya and (b) skill composition of out-migrants and their employment patterns. This chapter tries to answer these questions using the national level migration survey data collected by the National Sample Survey (NSS) organisation.

This chapter is organised into seven sections: the second section discusses the theoretical background; the third section provides the sources of data; the fourth section explores the recent trends and patterns of internal migration within India and from North-Eastern India; the fifth section provides the trends and patterns of migration and reasons for out-migration from Meghalaya; the sixth section explains the employment patterns of both in- and out-migrants in Meghalaya and tries to identify the employment-generating sectors that absorb migrants within and outside Meghalaya; and finally, the seventh section focuses on the conclusion and policy recommendations.

Theoretical perspectives

It is difficult to arrive at a conclusion regarding a particular theory which shapes the out-migration pattern from Meghalaya. Rather, a combination of theoretical arguments is important. Though social networks have a role in both international and internal migration processes, the economic motive of migration often plays a dominant role. When we discuss the role of poverty and unemployment in Meghalaya and the availability of job opportunities and better livelihood conditions in other states of India, we need to believe the push-pull framework developed by Ravenstein (1885) and Lee (1966). Furthermore, when we discuss the movement of people from rural areas (labour surplus regions) to urban areas (labour scarce regions) during a structural transformation process, often we say Lewisian transition (see Lewis 1954) is taking place. According to the 'new economic theory of migration' (see Stark and Bloom 1985), migration is an outcome of the household's utility maximisation process. With the recent improvement in the mean years of schooling statistic and the rising share of relatively better educated migrants in Meghalaya, it can be argued that the 'human capital theory' (Lucas 1988) of migration is at work. However, in Meghalaya, political insurgency and ethnicity conflicts could also play an important role in this process. As a result, a large number of people have been forced to go out of Meghalaya during the past couple of decades.

Though these migration theories are more or less relevant in the case of Meghalaya, the economic factors behind migration are more emphasised in this chapter, from time to time. The chapter also projects the simultaneous working of push-pull factors along with the Lewisian transition and the roles they play in driving out-migration from Meghalaya and the employment patterns of the migrants.

Sources of data

This study is based on secondary data. The unit data collected by the National Sample Survey (NSS) of India – namely, the 55th (1999–2000) and 64th (2007–8) rounds of migration-specific surveys – are used for the analysis. These surveys provide a comprehensive national coverage: a sample size of 819,013 persons (509,779 in rural and 309,234 in urban areas) in 1999–2000 and 572,254 persons (374,294 in rural areas and 197,960 in urban areas) in 2007–8 at the national level. For the entire NER (eight states), these surveys covers 87,670 persons (62,838 in rural areas and 24,832 in urban areas) in 1999–2000 and 88,167 persons (63,077 in rural areas and 25,090 in urban areas) in 2007–8. In Meghalaya, the sample size covers 8,754 persons (6,472 in rural areas and 2,282 in urban areas) including 4357 males and 4397 females in 1999–2000. In 2007–8, it covers 11,081 persons (8777 in rural areas and 2304 in urban areas) including 5731 males and 5350 females.

These surveys provide information on numerous socio-economic variables at the household and individual level, including age, sex, caste, religion, landholding, monthly expenditures, migration status, current and last residence, state of domicile, level and types of education, employment status, occupation and industry of employment, etc. The absolute volume of migration is estimated and adjusted to the census population to get the exact approximation. The data on the poverty head count ratio is taken from the estimates of the planning commission (2004–5), whereas the average expenses (from 2003–4 to 2006–7) on subsidising agricultural equipment (a proxy for mechanisation in agriculture) and state-wise minimum wages of unskilled agriculture workers are taken from the ministry of agriculture. Based on the place of last residence information, in- and out-migrants are defined. Those who reported that their place of last residence (at least six months ago) is the same as their current residence are defined as non-migrants. But those who reported that their place of last residence is different from their current residence are defined as migrants. Furthermore, those migrants (currently residing in Meghalaya) who reported that their place of last residence was in other states of India (excluding the state of Meghalaya) are defined as in-migrants in Meghalaya. Conversely, those migrants (currently residing in other states of India excluding Meghalaya) who reported that their place of last residence was Meghalaya are defined as out-migrants from Meghalaya. Based on these classifications of migrants, the employment status of in- and out- migrants of Meghalaya is examined.

Exploring migration patterns in India and north-eastern states

All-India level migration trends

At the all-India level, migration trends are showing an increasing share of rural to urban migration and a decreasing share of rural to rural migration (see Figure 9.1). This is because of the transformation that is taking place along with rapid economic growth in recent years (also see Parida et al. 2015). The share of rural to rural migration has decreased significantly from 62 percent to about 38 percent from 1999–2000 to 2007–8, whereas the share of rural to urban and urban to urban migration have increased from 19 percent to about 23 percent and 13 percent to 19 percent from 1999–2000 to

1999–2000   2007–8

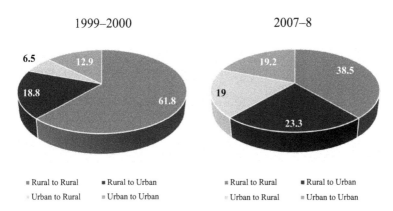

Figure 9.1 Sector-wise migration flows in India, 1999–2000 and 2007–8
Source: Author's estimation based on NSS unit data (55th and 64th) migration rounds

2007–8. The absolute number of rural out-migrants has increased by about 42 million (23.7 percent increase), from 175.3 million in 1999–2000 to 216.8 million in 2007–8 (see Table 9.1). Both absolute numbers of out-migrants and out-migration rates are very high in most of the agriculture-dependent and relatively poorer states like Odisha, Bihar, Uttar Pradesh, Madhya Pradesh, Andhra Pradesh, Chhattisgarh, Jharkhand, Rajasthan, West Bengal, Gujarat, Tamil Nadu and Maharashtra. In terms of the number of rural out-migration, Uttar Pradesh stands at the top. About 1.3 million additional people have migrated out from rural Uttar Pradesh from 1999–2000 to 2007–8 (from 35.6 million to 37 million). Maharashtra registered the second highest number of rural out-migrants, followed by Andhra Pradesh, West Bengal, Rajasthan, Bihar, Madhya Pradesh, Karnataka, Odisha and Tamil Nadu in 2007–8. In terms of the percentage increase in out-migration, Chhattisgarh is followed by Andhra Pradesh, Rajasthan, West Bengal, Maharashtra and Bihar. It is important to note that the states with a relatively high poverty head count ratio (HCR) are showing a large number of rural out-migration in India.[2] These findings are similar to the findings of Parida et al. (2015) and Parida (2016), which claim that socio-economic distress plays an important role in the out-migration process.

Table 9.1 State-wise rural out-migration and the factors affecting it in India, 1999–2000 and 2007–8

Name of the state	Poverty HCR in 2004–5 (%)	Agricultural wage[3] rates (Rs)	Avg. expenses on mechanisation[4] (Rs in lakh)	Rural literacy rates (%)		Rural unemployment (CDS) rates (%)		Number of people out-migrated from rural areas (million)			Rural out-migration rate (%)	
				1999–2000	2007–8	1999–2000	2007–8	1999–2000	2007–8	Change	1999–2000	2007–8
Andhra Pradesh	29.9	112	1335	42.2	49.6	1.8	5.3	12.5	18.7	6.2	22.7	29.7
Arunachal Pradesh	31.1	NA	205	47.7	58.2	0.3	1.2	0.07	0.02	-0.06	9.7	2.2
Assam	34.4	100	93	61.4	74.2	1.9	3.1	1.6	2.8	1.2	7.8	12.1
Bihar	54.4	114	613	35.1	46.4	1.0	3.6	12.8	14.4	1.6	15.1	20.3
Goa	25	157	27	73.5	73.1	4.5	2.5	0.18	0.10	-0.08	25.7	15.9
Gujarat	31.8	100	299	54.3	60.5	0.8	2.1	9.3	11.0	1.7	28.9	32.1
Haryana	24.1	167.23	288	56.0	61.2	0.8	2.4	3.7	5.1	1.4	25.2	31.1
Himachal Pradesh	22.9	110	156	65.7	73.4	0.8	2.9	1.7	2.5	0.8	32.0	40.2
Jammu & Kashmir	13.2	110	192	52.7	58.1	1.1	1.7	1.2	1.5	0.3	19.3	21.5
Karnataka	33.4	133.8	988	48.2	58.2	0.8	3.7	9.9	10.6	0.7	26.4	29.3
Kerala	19.7	200	31	81.6	85.2	4.3	6.7	6.5	7.7	1.2	30.1	30.1
Madhya Pradesh	48.6	114	368	43.9	57.7	0.8	2.9	14.7	14.0	-0.7	23.4	29.1
Maharashtra	38.1	120	295	58.4	67.6	1.4	4.4	18.7	20.9	2.2	32.3	34.0
Manipur	38	81.4	135	63.0	76.4	0.9	1.5	0.03	0.04	0.01	2.2	2.6
Meghalaya	16.1	100	82	65.4	84.2	0.2	0.4	0.05	0.1	0.05	3.3	4.1
Mizoram	15.3	132	152	81.8	88.6	0.6	0.3	0.013	0.067	0.05	3.7	11.6
Nagaland	9	80	77	74.1	82.0	1.3	2.8	0.09	0.1	0.01	18.5	10.9
Orissa	57.2	90	540	46.8	57.2	1.3	3.4	7.0	9.7	2.7	22.7	29.0
Punjab	20.9	148	110	57.8	63.3	0.9	3.7	4.5	5.6	1.1	29.0	32.5

Rajasthan	34.4	135	512	40.1	47.4	0.7	1.9	10.6	14.7	4.1	28.2	31.8
Sikkim	31.1	NA	23	66.8	76.7	1.1	1.8	0.2	0.1	0.0	39.6	25.3
Tamil Nadu	28.9	100	259	59.2	64.8	1.8	10.8	10.1	9.7	-0.4	25.7	23.4
Tripura	40.6	100	118	72.8	70.1	0.4	8.1	0.2	0.3	0.0	9.3	8.7
Uttar Pradesh	40.9	100	300	43.3	51.1	0.6	1.8	35.6	36.9	1.3	26.1	26.3
West Bengal	34.3	120.5	269	54.2	64.6	2.6	5.4	13.3	16.7	3.4	21.6	25.3
Delhi	13.1	234	6	73	76.3	1.4	1.3	0.63	0.57	-0.07	22.2	61.1
Chhattisgarh	49.4	100	194	NA	58.5	NA	2.1	NA	6.4	6.4	NA	30.0
Jharkhand	45.3	111	25	NA	54.3	NA	3.9	NA	3.9	3.9	NA	17.9
Uttaranchal	32.7	113.68	193	NA	63.2	NA	3.0	NA	2.3	2.3	NA	33.4
Other UTs	NA	NA	8	64.2	71.4	2.1	7.7	0.3	0.3	0.0	44.2	26.2
All India	**37.2**	**NA**	**263.1**	**48.9**	**58.1**	**1.3**	**3.8**	**175.3**	**216.8**	**41.5**	**24.0**	**27.1**

Source: These data are taken from multiple sources like the Planning Commission (poverty) and Ministry of Agriculture (wages and expenses) and the rest are estimated using NSS unit data

The continuous growth of rural population and lack of non-farm employment opportunities in rural areas have caused a huge increase in agricultural employment in 2004–5, with most of it being unpaid family members (Parida 2015). After 2004–5, periods with growing mechanisation[5] in agriculture on the one hand and the increasing rural unemployment[6] rate (current daily status (CDS)) on the other have pushed huge segments of the rural population to migrate out. Increasing rural literacy rates, particularly at the secondary and above levels (due to the 'Right to Education') during these periods would also have enabled a large segment of the rural educated youth to migrate out for better opportunities in the urban areas.

Migration trends in north-eastern states of India

In the entire NER, increasing trends of migration are observed from 1999–2000 to 2007–8 (see Table 9.2). The absolute number of migrants in the NER has increased from 26 lakh to 48 lakh during this period. The percentage of migrants to the total population has also increased from 9 percent to 12 percent. This implies the

Table 9.2 Migration scenario in north-eastern states of India, 1999–2000 and 2007–8

Name of the state	% of migrants to total population		Absolute number of in-migrants (in lakh)		Absolute number of out-migrants (in lakh)	
	1999–2000	2007–8	1999–2000	2007–8	1999–2000	2007–8
Arunachal Pradesh	1.8	1.3	0.16	0.15	1.1	0.34
Assam	8.2	13.3	19.72	36.37	2.8	2.5
Manipur	0.8	0.9	0.15	0.19	0.45	0.64
Meghalaya	1	3.7	0.19	1.16	0.53	0.44
Mizoram	1.4	15.9	0.08	1.71	0.14	0.24
Nagaland	26.3	13.4	1.85	1.66	0.54	0.37
Sikkim	23.3	34.1	1.14	2.03	1.2	0.4
Tripura	10.2	11.5	3.06	4.38	0.83	0.31
North-East total	**9.1**	**11.8**	**26.4**	**47.7**	**7.6**	**5.2**
All-India total	**26.6**	**29.3**	**2689.6**	**3357.86**	**299.7**	**365.8**

Source: Author's estimation based on NSS unit data (55th and 64th) migration rounds

fact that people from outside the NER are finding this region as a suitable destination to migrate. The states that attracted most of the migrant population in 1999–2000 were Assam (20 lakh), Tripura (3 lakh), Nagaland (2 lakh) and Sikkim (1 lakh). As the volume of migration increased in 2007–8, Assam (36.4 lakh) again absorbed the highest number of migrants. Assam is followed by Tripura (4.4 lakh), Sikkim (2 lakh), Mizoram (1.7 lakh), Nagaland (1.6 lakh) and Meghalaya (1.16 lakh) in 2007–8.

In terms of percentage of migrants to the total population, Nagaland shows the highest percentage of migrants (26 percent) in 1999–2000. Nagaland is followed by Sikkim (23 percent), Tripura (10 percent) and Assam (8 percent) in 1999–2000. However, in 2007–8, Sikkim (34.1 percent) registered the highest percentage of migrant population, which is followed by Mizoram (16 percent), Nagaland (13.4 percent), Assam (13.3 percent), Tripura (11.5 percent) and Meghalaya (3.7 percent). Furthermore, Assam stands at the top in terms of the number of out-migrants going to other states from the NER. The other NE states from which large numbers of migrants are going to other parts of India are Sikkim, Arunachal Pradesh, Tripura, Meghalaya and Nagaland.

The sectoral migration flow from north-eastern states to other states of India shows (see Figure 9.2) that rural to rural migration flow is the most dominant stream (70 percent). Though the percentage of rural to urban migration has increased from 13 percent to

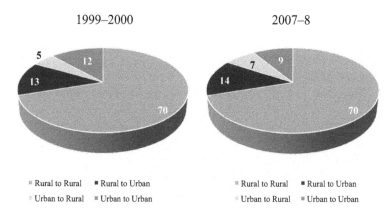

Figure 9.2 Sector-wise migration flows in north-eastern states of India, 1999–2000 and 2007–8

Source: Author's estimation based on NSS unit data (55th and 64th) migration rounds

14 percent from 1999–2000 to 2007–8, its share is negligible. The dominant share of rural to rural migration implies the fact that the process of structural transformation (particularly in employment) in the north-eastern states has not yet started. Since most of the north-eastern states are agrarian and industrially backward states, it is important to increase investment on education and skill development on one hand and expansion of the manufacturing and service sectors on the other. This would not only help to initiate the process of structural transformation but also boost output and economic growth in these states.

Since the government of Meghalaya has initiated the process of skilled development with the help of the Asian Development Bank in recent years, it is important to know the current trends and patterns of migration (both in- and out-migration) from Meghalaya and what migrants' employment potential is in other states of India using the national level survey data.

Trends and patterns of migration in Meghalaya

Both the absolute number and percentage of migrants in Meghalaya increased from 1999–2000 to 2007–8 (see Table 9.2). Only about 1 percent of Meghalaya's population constituted migrants in 1999–2000, which increased to 3.7 percent in 2007–8. The absolute number of migrants increased from 0.19 lakh to 1.16 lakh during the same period. This huge increasing number of migrants within the territory of Meghalaya could be an outcome of the structural transformation that begun in the last decade. The number of persons who migrated out to other states of India, however, declined slightly from 0.53 to 0.44 lakh. This implies the fact that during this period migration is heavily concentrated within Meghalaya.

The states that attracted most of the out-migrants from Meghalaya in 1999–2000 include West Bengal (49 percent), Assam (15.4 percent), Uttar Pradesh (13 percent), Maharashtra (10.6 percent) and Odisha (about 8 percent). This trend has shifted slightly in 2007–8, with the highest percentage of out-migrants in Assam (47 percent). Tamil Nadu attracted the second highest share (19 percent) of out-migrants from Meghalaya, which is followed by Maharashtra (8 percent) and West Bengal (7.5 percent). Most of the female migrants were found in neighbouring states or states with relatively less distance from Meghalaya (see Table 9.2). The highest share of male out-migrants is found in states like Maharashtra,

Tamil Nadu, Uttar Pradesh, West Bengal and Assam (see Table 9.3). It is important to note that three of the largest metro cities of India belong to these states. The young migrants with a better education are believed to be attracted to the large cities in search of better employment or education opportunities.

Age group-wise distribution of the out-migrants from Meghalaya implies that the share of those younger than 25 is increasing over the years (see Table 9.4). An important reason behind the migration of youth from the NER is 'educational and employment considerations' (Ramesh 2012). It is widely understood that despite a high literacy rate, the region is characterised by a visible lack of adequate avenues for higher or technical education or vocational training. The weak local educational system, especially in terms of meeting the requirements of the new economy occupations and professional

Table 9.3 Migration flows from Meghalaya, 1999–2000 and 2007–8

Name of the state	Out-migrants from Meghalaya staying in other states of India (in %)					
	1999–2000			2007–8		
	Male	Female	Total	Male	Female	Total
Assam	13.7	16.3	15.4	61.4	7.8	47.0
Mizoram	0	0	0	0.6	9.8	2.8
Nagaland	1.9	0.6	1.1	1.7	6.9	3.1
Tripura	0	2.8	1.8	2.3	12.7	5.0
Bihar	0	0	0	0.3	0	0.3
Gujarat	2.2	0.6	1.2	0	0	0
Karnataka	0	0	0	2.3	0	1.6
Maharashtra	30.3	0	10.6	5.4	15.5	8.1
Orissa	11.3	6.0	7.9	0	0	0
Punjab	0	0	0	0	12.7	3.4
Tamil Nadu	0	0	0	25.6	0	19.0
Uttar Pradesh	36.3	0.5	12.9	0	0	0
West Bengal	4.3	72.8	49.0	0	29.0	7.5
Jharkhand	0	0	0	0.6	5.7	2.2
Other states/ UTs/countries	0	0.3	0.1	0	0	0
Total	100	100	100	100	100	100

Source: Author's estimation based on NSS unit data (55th and 64th) migration rounds

Table 9.4 Distribution of out-migrants from Meghalaya by age groups and sex, 1999–2000 and 2007–8 (in %)

Age groups	1999–2000			2007–8		
	Male	Female	Total	Male	Female	Total
Below 15 years	2.1	0.3	0.9	5.8	2.0	4.8
15 to 24 years	0.5	41.0	26.9	34.3	14.6	29.2
25 to 34 years	7.7	25.8	19.5	8.1	11.7	9.0
35 to 59 years	89.7	32.0	52.0	51.5	69.8	56.2
60 & above	0.0	1.0	0.6	0.4	2.0	0.8
Total	**100**	**100**	**100**	**100**	**100**	**100**

Source: Author's estimation based on NSS unit data (55th and 64th) migration rounds

service sector, compels the youths to migrate for better educational opportunities in other states.

From the distribution of out-migrants by their level of education, it is also revealed that the share of skilled migrants is increasing over the years, with a declining share of illiterates (see Table 9.5). The share of illiterates among migrants was 52 percent in 1999–2000, which decreased to only 31 percent in 2007–8. The share of migrants with a secondary and above level of general education increased from 36 percent to about 55 percent from 1999–2000 to 2007–8. The increasing share of migrants in the 35–59 age group (see Table 9.4) implies the fact that there exists a mismatch between the demand and supply in the job market. Along with this, the inadequate economic infrastructure may have definite implications on the migration decisions of educated and ambitious youth to urban centres for higher learning. The lower labour absorption capacity of local labour markets and perceived employment prospects in the urban centres together prompt the aspirant youth to migrate to cities for exploring better opportunities.

The reason for migration in Meghalaya reveals that employment and education are the major reason for male migration, whereas marriage and movement with an earning member of the family are the major reason for female migration. The same is true in the case of out-migrants from Meghalaya to other states (see Table 9.6). About 52 percent of male migrants changed their usual place of residence (migrated) for employment-related reasons in 1999–2000.

Table 9.5 Distribution of out-migrants from Meghalaya by level of education and sex, 1999–2000 and 2007–8 (in %)

Level of education	1999–2000			2007–8		
	Male	Female	Total	Male	Female	Total
General education						
Illiterate	13.8	72.1	51.8	38.0	9.7	30.7
Primary	0.0	13.1	8.6	12.7	16.7	13.7
Secondary	74.9	6.3	30.2	44.1	17.2	37.1
Higher secondary	1.4	6.6	4.8	3.6	48.0	15.0
Graduate & above	0.5	1.9	1.4	1.6	8.5	3.3
Technical/vocational education						
Below graduate	8.4	0.0	2.9	0	0	0
Graduate & above	1.0	0.0	0.3	0.1	0.0	0.05
Total	100	100	100	100	100	100

Source: Author's estimation based on NSS unit data (55th and 64th) migration rounds

Table 9.6 Reasons for migration by sex in Meghalaya, 1999–2000 and 2007–8 (in %)

Reasons	1999–2000			2007–8		
	Male	Female	Total	Male	Female	Total
In-migrants to Meghalaya						
Employment	72.1	10	52.4	60.6	16.1	39.3
Education	6.0	4	5.4	28.8	0	15.0
Marriage	0	75.4	23.9	2.1	63.8	31.7
With family	0	4.3	1.4	8.3	20.1	13.9
Other socio-political & economic problems	21.9	6.3	17.0	0.2	0	0.1
Total	100	100	100	100	100	100
Out-migrants from Meghalaya staying in other states						
Employment	29.9	0	10.4	1.6	6.7	3
Education	0	0	0	29.6	7.5	23.9
Marriage	0	90.5	59	0	50.6	13.1
With family	2.1	7.4	5.6	2.9	24.4	8.4
Others	68	2.1	25.1	65.9	10.7	51.6
Total	100	100	100	100	100	100

Source: Author's estimation based on NSS unit data (55th and 64th) migration rounds

This figure had declined slightly to 39 percent in 2007–8, but still it remains the major reason for male migration in Meghalaya. About 5.4 percent of male migrants in Meghalaya reported that they migrated to acquire education in 1999–2000. The share of migrants who reported education as the cause increased drastically to 15 percent in 2007–8. Moreover, among male out-migrants, about 0 percent reported education as the reason in 1999–2000, which showed a radical change in 2007–8, with 29.6 percent of male migrants reporting education as the reason for leaving Meghalaya. The findings of Srivastava and Bhattacharyya (2002) and Deshingkar and Akter (2009) in recent years also show a sharp increase in urban mobility, with a significantly larger percentage of male migrants reporting economic and employment-related reasons for mobility in India. Given the intricacy of this phenomenon, it is important to find out the individual and household-level factors that drive rural to urban migration decision of individuals and their workforce participation in urban India.

The study of inter-sectoral migration flow is important from a wider perspective. First, increasing rural to urban flows provide an indication of the structural transformation that is popularly known as the Lewisian (1954) transition, which is a manifestation of the transition that is taking place in the rural and urban sectors because of high economic growth. Migration from rural to urban areas also explains how uneven economic growth may emerge as a consequence (Harris and Todaro 1970). Labour market forces like unemployment and expected wage differentials often act as driving forces behind migration decisions (Harris and Todaro 1970). The urban to urban migration, on the other hand, partly explains the cost-of-living and income differentials across regions that is reflected through migration decision of households in a dynamic general equilibrium setting.

The increasing share of rural to rural and urban to urban migration flows from Meghalaya to other states of India (see Figure 9.3) indicates that a horizontal transformation is taking place. This flow is unlike that of either a Lewis or Harris and Todarian transition. Rather, human capital formation plays a major role in driving a large segment of the migrant population to go out of Meghalaya for exploring better opportunities, which is later reflected by the labour market outcomes. Earlier studies on migrant labour like Connell et al. (1976), Joshi and Joshi (1976), Dupont (1992), Kundu and Gupta (1996), Srivastava (1998), Bhattacharya (2002), Singh

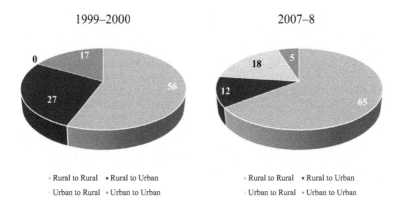

Figure 9.3 Sector-wise out-migration flows from Meghalaya to other states of India, 1999–2000 and 2007–8

Source: Authors' estimation based on NSS unit data (55th and 64th) migration rounds

(2002), Mitra (2003), Vijay (2005) and Deshingkar and Akter (2009) have found that poor households participate extensively in the migration process, and these groups of people migrate either permanently or semi-permanently between lagging and developed regions and between rural and urban areas, mostly being absorbed in the unorganised sector of the economy.

Employment patterns of in- and out-migrants from Meghalaya

Out of the total migrant workers in 1999–2000 in Meghalaya, the share of self-employed workers was about 45 percent, the share of regular salaried workers was about 18.5 percent and the share of casual workers was 13 percent; 0.7 percent were job seekers and 23 percent were not part of the labour force (see Table 9.7). In 2007–8, the share of self-employed remained constant, but the share of casual workers had increased, with a declining share of regular salaried workers. This a reflection of the informalisation process that is taking place at the all-India level after 2004–5. At the all-India level, though there had been an increase in employment opportunities in the organised sector, it is mainly for informal[7]

Table 9.7 Employment status of out-migrants from Meghalaya, 1999–2000 and 2007–8 (in %)

Employment status	1999–2000			2007–8		
	Male	Female	Total	Male	Female	Total
Migrants staying in Meghalaya						
Self-employment	54.9	2.0	45.4	47.8	39.9	44.7
Regular salaried workers	20.5	9.1	18.5	12.5	9.6	11.4
Casual labourers	15.4	1.1	12.9	27.1	6.3	18.9
Job seekers	0.8	0.0	0.7	0.3	0.1	0.2
Others	8.5	87.8	22.6	12.3	44.1	24.8
Total	**100**	**100**	**100**	**100**	**100**	**100**
Out-migrants from Meghalaya staying in other states						
Self-employment	19.0	6.7	11.0	42.4	14.6	35.2
Regular salaried workers	66.2	1.9	24.3	4.3	0.0	3.2
Casual labourers	0	0		18.5	12.7	17.0
Job seekers	12.7	0	4.4	1.2	0.6	1.0
Others	2.1	91.4	60.3	33.6	72.1	43.6
Total	**100**	**100**	**100**	**100**	**100**	**100**

Source: Author's estimation based on NSS unit data (55th and 64th) migration rounds

workers. Their share rose from 32 percent in 1999–2000 to 54 percent in 2004–5 to 67 percent in 2011–12 (Mehrotra et al. 2014). In Meghalaya, the percentage share of self-employed migrant workers remained constant at 45 percent, whereas the share of regular salaried workers declined from 18.5 percent to 11.4 percent and the share of casual workers increased from 12.9 percent to 18.8 percent from 1999–2000 to 2007–8. The unskilled and semi-skilled worker from rural areas are most likely to work either as casual labourer or are self-employed by opening small shops or engaging themselves in petty trade, street vending, rickshaw pulling or auto rickshaw driving etc.

The employment pattern of out-migrants from Meghalaya is showing an interesting trend. The share of regular salaried workers was 24.3 percent in 1999–2000, which declined to only 3.2 percent in 2007–8 (see Table 9.7). The share of regular salaried workers among male migrants was 66 percent, which declined massively to only 4.3 percent. About 11 percent of out-migrants were self-employed in 1999–2000, which significantly increased to 35 percent in 2007–8. Furthermore, the share of casual workers among out-migrants increased from 0 to 17 percent. This is again a reflection of the informalisation process that is taking place at the all-India level. At the all-India level, of the 60 million new jobs generated during that period, 52 million were created in the unorganised segment of enterprises (Mehrotra et al. 2014). The unorganised manufacturing sector added 9 million jobs during the period from 1999–2000 to 2004–5, while the unorganised services sector created 16 million jobs between 2000 and 2005, driving an employment increase in the first half of the decade (Mehrotra et al. 2014). This rise in unorganised employment is mainly due to the lack of opportunities in the organised sectors, and the existence of various kinds of business constraints[8] that encourage the employer to hire contract or temporary workers.

The industry-wise distribution of out-migrants reveals that about 36 percent of the out-migrants were employed in the agriculture and allied sectors in the destination states in 1999–2000 (see Table 9.8). The share of employment in agriculture and allied sectors had declined slightly to 31 percent in 2007–8. About 12 percent of the out-migrants were engaged in the manufacturing sector in 1999–2000, which became 0 percent in 2007–8. The afore-mentioned reasons might have been responsible for this drastic change. The share of employment in social services like education, health, etc., sectors was about 69 percent. In 2007–8, the share of employment in the social service sectors, however, declined massively to only 12 percent, with an increasing share of emerging sub-sectors in the service sector such as real estate, finance, hotel, trade, transport and communication. This increasing share of service sector employment among out-migrants is expected, since the services sector has emerged as a major contributor to economic growth in India in recent years, though it is highly heterogeneous in terms of its range of services, the size of value added, capital investment, composition and level of employment. The share of service sector output in GDP has been increasing from 38 percent in 1980–1 to about 58 percent in 2011–12 (Mehrotra et al. 2014; Mehrotra and Parida 2017).

Sector-wise distribution of in-migrants in Meghalaya also reveals a similar pattern, with an almost constant share of employment (about 51 percent) in the agriculture and allied sectors from 1999–2000 to 2007–8 (see Table 9.8). The share of manufacturing employment is quite low but increased from 1 percent to about 3 percent, reflecting increasing manufacturing activities in the state in recent years. In the service sector, sub-sectors like hotel, trade,

Table 9.8 Migrants' industry of employment, 1999–2000 and 2007–8 (in %)

Industry of employment	1999–2000			2007–8		
	Male	Female	Total	Male	Female	Total
Migrants staying in Meghalaya						
Agriculture & allied	52.0	25.5	51.2	49.1	57.8	51.6
Mining & quarrying	0	0	0	6.9	0	4.8
Manufacturing	1.0	0	1.0	4.3	0.2	3.1
Electricity, gas and water	0	0	0	0	0	0
Construction industry	2.2	0	2.2	7.4	0	5.2
Hotel, trade & restaurant	15.3	0	14.8	13.5	14.4	13.8
Transport & communication	14.7	22.4	15.0	2.5	0.1	1.8
Real estate & finance	1.0	0	0.9	0.4	5.9	2.0
Education, health and other services	13.8	52.1	14.9	16.1	21.6	17.7
Total	**100**	**100**	**100**	**100**	**100**	**100**
Out-migrants from Meghalaya staying in other states						
Agriculture & allied	20.6	0	17.4	35.5	53.3	31.0
Mining & quarrying	0	0	0	0	0	0
Manufacturing	0	77.6	12.4	0	0	0
Electricity, gas and water	0	0	0	0	0	0
Construction industry	0	0	0	0	0	0
Hotel, trade & restaurant	1.7	0	1.4	0.4	0	7.1
Transport & communication	0	0	0	2.1	0	1.8
Real estate & finance	0	0	0	54.9	0	47.9
Education, health and other services	77.7	22.4	68.9	7.2	46.7	12.2
Total	**100**	**100**	**100**	**100**	**100**	**100**

Source: Author's estimation based on NSS unit data (55th and 64th) migration rounds

education, health, transport and communication absorbed a significant share of migrant workers in 1999–2000 and 2007–8.

Conclusion

As the emerging trends of out-migration from Meghalaya are driven by better employment opportunities outside the state, which in turn is often directed by the availability of better education. Generating skills at various dimensions through appropriate policy initiatives would have a long-term socio-economic implication for the state as a whole. The issue of skill development goes well beyond making the young masses employable. Young men/women, too, face employability issues that derive from their poor level of skills and need adequate training, which was observed in this chapter. Most migrants are engaged as casual labourers outside Meghalaya. Had they been trained, they would have been found employed either as regular salaried workers or as self-employed workers in manufacturing or service sectors.

Though service sectors are generating quite a significant share of employment and absorb a large share of migrants, the manufacturing sector is lagging behind. The stagnant manufacturing sectors in Meghalaya need to be focussed on generating employment, which in turn would drive economic growth on a sustainable basis. For manufacturing to grow and generate employment faster than other sectors of the economy, the rate of gross capital formation needs to be higher. Good physical infrastructure in terms of improved transportation, an uninterrupted power supply and adequate land along with flexible regulations (with respect to bureaucratic controls) regarding safety, pollution, inspections, licensing and labour conditions are needed to improve the competitiveness of manufacturers in Meghalaya.

Notes

1 Population Census, Government of India; www.censusindia.gov.in/ 2011census, accessed on 1 June 2011.
2 The estimated correlation coefficient between the poverty head count ratio (HCR) and rural out-migration is positive (0.43).
3 State-wise Daily Rates of Minimum Wages for Unskilled Agricultural Workers under the Minimum Wages Act of 1948 in India, as of 31 March 2011. In the states where more than one wage rate prevails, the highest value of the wage rate is taken in to consideration.
4 State-wise Financial Outlay for Agricultural Equipment to Farmers at Subsidised Rates under Centrally Sponsored Schemes of Macro Management in India (2003–4 to 2006–7).
5 This could be evident from the increase in average government expenses on subsidising agricultural equipment to farmers across the states in India. This chapter finds a positive correlation (0.52) between mechanisation in agriculture and rural out-migration.
6 As the correlation between rural unemployment and out-migration is positive (0.06).

7 As per the NCEUS definition,

> Informal workers consist of those working in the informal sector or households, excluding regular workers with social security benefits provided by the employers and the workers in the formal sector without any employment and social security benefits provided by the employers.

8 Labour laws and other regulations have often hindered expansion of employment in organised manufacturing. There are 45 different national and state-level labour laws in India (Panagariya 2008). Labour laws apply in practice mainly to the organised sector. As the size of a factory grows, it increasingly becomes subject to more legislation. In order to avoid rigidity on account of these regulations, firms often employ casual labour or turn more capital intensive.

References

Bhattacharya, Prabir C. 2002. 'Urbanization in Developing Countries', *Economic and Political Weekly*, 37(41): 4219–4228.

Connell, John, Biplab Dasgupta, Roy Laishley, and Michael Lipton. 1976. *Migration from Rural Areas: The Evidence from Village Studies*, New Delhi: Oxford University Press.

Dasgupta, Geetisha and Ishita Dey. 2010. 'State of Research on Forced Migration in the East and North-East', *Economic and Political Weekly*, 45(21): 37–41.

Deshingkar, Priya and Shaheen Akter. 2009. 'Migration and Human Development in India', *Human Development Research Paper*, No. 2009/13, UNDP.

Dupont, Veronique. 1992. 'Impact of In-Migration on Industrial Development: Case Study of Jetpur in Gujarat', *Economic and Political Weekly*, 27(45): 2423–2436.

Harris, John R. and Michael P. Todaro. 1970. 'Migration, Unemployment and Development: A Two Sector Analysis', *American Economic Review*, 60(1): 126–138.

Joshi, Heather and Vijay Joshi. 1976. *Surplus Labour and the City: A Study of Bombay*, Bombay: Oxford University Press.

Kundu, Amitabh and Shalini Gupta. 1996. 'Migration, Urbanization and Regional Inequality', *Economic and Political Weekly*, 31(52): 3391–3398.

Lee, Everett S. 1966. 'A Theory of Migration', *Demography*, 3(1): 47–57.

Lewis, W. Arthur. 1954. 'Economic Development with Unlimited Supplies of Labour', *Manchester School of Economic and Social Studies*, 22: 139–191.

Lucas Jr, Robert E. 1988. 'On the Mechanics of Economic Development', *Journal of Monetary Economics*, 22(1): 3–42.

Mehrotra, Santosh and Jajati Keshari Parida. 2017. 'Why Is the Labour Force Participation of Women Declining in India?' *World Development*, 98: 360–380.

Mehrotra, Santosh, Jajati Parida, Sharmistha Sinha and Ankita Gandhi. 2014. 'Explaining Employment Trends in the Indian Economy: 1993–4 to 2011–12', *Economic and Political Weekly*, XLIX(32): 49–57.

Ministry of Tourism, Government of India. 2003. *India Tourism Statistics*, New Delhi: Market Research Division, Ministry of Tourism Government of India.

Mitra, Arup. 2003. *Occupational Choices, Networks and Transfers: An Exegesis Based on Micro Data from Delhi Slums*, New Delhi: Manohar.

Panagariya, Arvind. 2008. *India: The Emerging Giant*, New York: Oxford University Press.

Parida, Jajati Keshari. 2015. 'Growth and Prospects of Non-farm Employment in India: Reflections from NSS Data', *Journal of Industrial Statistics*, 4(2): 154–168.

Parida, Jajati Keshari. 2016. 'MGNREGA, Distress Migration and Livelihood Conditions: A Study in Odisha', *Journal of Social and Economic Development*, 18(1): 17–39.

Parida, Jajati Keshari, Sanjay Kumar Mohanty, and K. Ravi Raman. 2015. 'Remittances, Household Expenditure, and Investment in Rural India: Evidence From NSS Data', *Indian Economic Review*, 50(1): 79–104.

Ramesh, Babu P. 2012. 'Migration from North-East to Urban Centres: A Study of Delhi Region', *N L I Research Studies Series*, No. 094/2012.

Ravenstein, Ernst Georg. 1885. 'The Laws of Migration', *Journal of the Statistical Society of London*, 48(2): 167–235.

Shimray, U. A. 2004. 'Socio-Political Unrest in the Region Called North-East India', *Economic and Political Weekly*, XXXIX(42).

Singh, C. S. K. 2002. 'Daily Labour Market in Delhi: Structure and Behaviour', *Economic and Political Weekly*, 37(9): 884–889.

Srivastava, Ravi. 1998. 'Migration and the Labour Market in India', *Indian Journal of Labour Economics*, 41(4): 583–616.

Srivastava, Ravi and Sangeetha Bhattacharyya. 2002. 'Globalisation, Reforms and Internal Labour Mobility: Analysis of Recent Indian Trends'. Paper presented at a seminar 'Labour Mobility and Globalising World: Conceptual and Empirical Issues' during September 2002, V. V. Giri National Labour Institute. New Delhi.

Stark, Oded and David E. Bloom. 1985. 'The New Economics of Labor Migration', *American Economic Review*, 75(2): 173–178.

Vijay, Gudavarthy. 2005. 'Migration, Vulnerability and Insecurity in New Industrial Labour Markets', *Economic Political Weekly*, 40(22/23): 2304–2312.

Chapter 10

Out-migration and labour mobility

Case studies from Assam

Snehashish Mitra

'So, where does your son work?' I asked. 'Hajirabad', replied Ghan-shyam Thapa, who belongs to the Nepali community residing in Bhutankhuti village. Confused initially, I said that it's Hyderabad, the capital of newly formed Telangana state in southern India; in vain, though. 'Yes, that place – Hajirabad', replied Ghanshyam. Later that day, it dawned in my mind that the apparent linguistic travesty of Ghanshyam Thapa inadvertently represented the stark reality of his village, Bhutankhuti, along with most of the villages of the region falling under Baksa district in north-western Assam. *Hajira* in Assamese roughly translates to 'labour' in English, hence Hyderabad, being a city which has a large number of migrants from North-East India, logically becomes 'Hajirabad' to Ghanshyam Thapa, because it is where his son is working in a guest house. Bhutankhuti is the last village in India before the Bhutan border, lying 21 km north of NH 31. Ghanshyam's son is one of the many migrants from the village. A random interview with members of the households of the nearby villages across the communities would provide a similar story of out-migration. According to the Census of India, the total number of migrants from the North-Eastern Region (NER) to other parts of India increased from 0.6 million in 1991 to 1.1 million in 2001 (Chyrmang 2011). Migration provides insights into the changes taking place in the North-East itself. It is to be noted that more people are leaving the North-East than ever before, and the heightened scale of migration is relatively new, especially since the second half of the 2000s (McDuiera 2012).

This chapter aims to understand the phenomenon of out-migration from Assam by selecting two particular field sites in the districts of Baksa and Nalbari in Western Assam, by taking into account the challenges of livelihood that have emerged in the sites along with the socio-political spectrum of the region, which heavily hinges on ethnicity and identity. Through the ethnographic narratives, I make an attempt to showcase the 'hidden transcript of the subaltern class' (Scott 1990). Decades of insurgency and counterinsurgency have resulted in a militarised society in much of the NER, which serves as a major catalyst for migration to other parts of India. While the findings of the chapter confirm to that phenomenon, it moves beyond the overwhelming focus on militarisation and delves into the environmental changes and different resource extraction patterns of the communities. The analysis of environmental resource management would be central to the argument by bringing in different facets of the discipline 'political ecology'. Works of David Arnold (1993) and Jean Drèze (1988) have shown how the different grids of power surrounding management of environmental resources have been crucial in influencing the relationship between ecology, politics and survival in colonial India. Ranabir Samaddar (1998), in his work on the *Junglemahals* in West Bengal and Jharkhand, has investigated the politics of community formation and how environmental happenings would churn the different kinds of social reaction through unrest, revolt and migration.

We begin with a short history of migration in North-East India in the upcoming section, followed by the case studies encountered in Baksa and Nalbari districts. In the subsections, the issues of conflict have been discussed in detail, along with how it influences migration. While observations have been illustrated throughout the chapter, an evaluation of the theoretical and empirical queries has been presented in the conclusion. Wherever possible, the findings have been fitted into relevant concepts or similar findings elsewhere, but the temptation to venture into the dialectics or to conceptualise every experience shared by the respondents and situations encountered on the field has been avoided.[1] Generalisations of the social dynamics across regions could be considered as the strength of a thesis, as James Scott had done through his influential work *The Art of Not Being Governed* (Scott 2009); however, it risks losing out on the specificities of particular places (Karlsson 2013) to which this chapter attempts to cater.

Assam's migration pattern: colonial and post-colonial narratives

The region recognised as today's North-East India has been historically deemed as rich in resources, given its endowment of natural resources. The resources have provided sustenance to both indigenous and migrant communities while serving as objects of extraction for British and Indian states. Different communities like Ahoms, Bodos, Misings, Mizos and Nagas have historically transcended different parts of North-East India and settled down as inhabitants. The pattern of in-migration took a different version with the advent of the British in the territories of Assam after the Treaty of Yandabo was signed on 22 February 1826. As a part of the colonial project, the tribal communities from Central India were forced and the Bengali peasants from Mymensingh were endorsed to migrate to the tea gardens and the riverine plains of Assam, respectively. The Partition of India in 1947 and the Bangladesh Liberation War of 1971 gave rise to subsequent tides of migrants into Assam from Bangladesh.

In this context, out-migration from a space which has been a destination of migrants and witnessed politics over in-migration poses a puzzle in front of us which perhaps demands new ways of negotiating with the issue. A survey released in early 2011 by a small nonprofit organisation, the North-East Support Centre and Helpline (NESCH), puts the number of migrants from the North-East to outside the region at 414,850 between 2005 and 2010 (NESCH 2011: 10). The increasing trend of out-migration from the region can be conceptualised through the pattern of India's economic growth, especially in the post-liberalisation period. Jan Breman observes that in the last decade urban India's growth has been greater than that of rural India, which is a major shift from the earlier trend and is caused by the flight away from land and agriculture (Breman 2013: 23). The urbanisation rate in North-East India has been significantly lower than the national average; for example, according to the census of 2001, the level of urbanisation in the North-East was 21.5 percent, while the national figure stood at 27.78 percent.[2] According to the 2011 census, 18.26 percent of the population in North-East India lived in urban centres, while the national figure was 31.17 percent nationwide; within the north-eastern states, Assam ranked the lowest in terms of urban population, with 14.1 percent.[3] Therefore, out-migration perhaps ought to be natural, from a region which has been recognised as under-developed/backward in the post-colonial period, with the statistical evidence confirming the same. However, the historical context of in-migration in the region justifies having a deeper understanding of out-migration from the region under a supposed welfare state which has given special attention to the region in recent years through policies like that of 'Look East'.[4] Also, in contrast to today's trend, an early British report stated that it would be rare for an Assamese living at a distance to leave his home for the mere purpose of working in a tea plantation (Sharma 2011: 63). Till now, scholars have been far more concerned with migration into the North-East during the colonial and post-colonial eras, which is seen as permanently rupturing the demographics of the region and launching the grievances that have sustained armed struggle (Baruah 1999; Hazarika 2000). Migration from the North-East to other parts of India is on a much smaller scale when compared to the sample size of other migration studies in India and lacked scholarly attention until recently; however, the lack of literature should not be equated with lack of significance (McDuiera 2012).

Foothill migrants – out-migration from Baksa

The district of Baksa lies in the foothills of the eastern Himalayas, bordering Bhutan. The popular assumption is that Baksa is the misspelt form of *Bangsa* – a Dzongkha word meaning a farmhouse and a corridor, as it is known that the Bhutanese king and subjects used this area for trade and passage to the plains. Now, the name Baksa is officially taken and used.[5] The Baksa district falls under Bodoland Territorial Council (BTC).[6] The Baksa block is one of the blocks of the Baksa district, where I conducted my fieldwork based from a small town called Nikashi. Nikashi and the villages around it boast several different communities like Bodos, Nepalis, Adivasis,[7] Bengalis and Assamese.

Bhutankhuti village (see Figure 10.1), is predominantly occupied by the Nepali community, with a few households of Bodos, Axamiyas and Adivasis.[8] The original livelihood character of the village is captured in the etymology of Bhutankhuti.[9] The Nepalis have been renowned for their dairy farming in the region. However, the last *khuti* of the village closed down around 1985, and people had started to change their livelihood from khuti to agriculture since the 1960s. The khutis eventually ceased to exist due to the expansion of human settlements and deforestation caused by changing land-use patterns among the villagers. According to Ishwaria Gautam, headmaster of a local government school, 'Now in Bhutankhuti, you will be served with black tea', he said with a tone of sarcasm. He remarked:

> When the khutis were at their prime, villagers would walk for around 9 km to the nearby Dumni market, adjoining the Dumni Tea Estate. Milk products like ghee and cream were

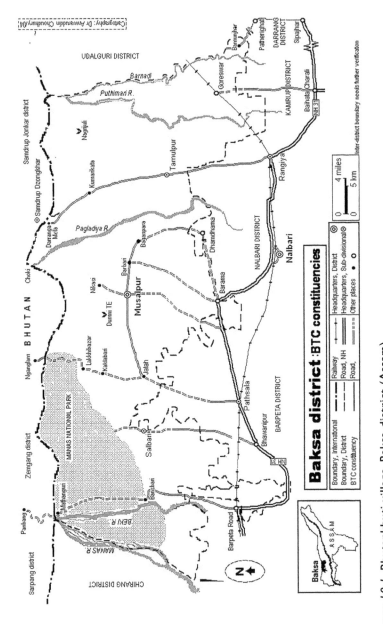

Figure 10.1 Bhutankhuti village, Baksa district (Assam)

Source: http://baksa.gov.in/map/map2.jpg, accessed on 28 October 2017

mainly sold along with milk. Ironically, on the contrary, today one would have to buy Amul Taza milk carton coming from as far as Gujarat in the Nikashi town, in the black market. Khutis allowed us to lead a comfortable lifestyle, but as people started to attain education, a social consciousness arose against being a *garakhia*/milkman. Earlier, every boy who took birth was destined to be a garakhia, ascribing to our traditional livelihood.

Such accounts confirm that from being the conserver of tradition, education became the means to promote and reinforce change in outlook, values and norms (Kumar 2014). From the narratives, it could be deduced that the trend of out-migration started within the timeframe when khutis ceased to be a viable livelihood. During the season of harvest, the villagers face regular raids of elephants and monkeys, leading to rising human-animal conflict. Such conflicts are understandable, as forest coverage in the area has been reduced to a large extent due to the illegal timber business and expansion of settlements. Some of the respondents blamed the Bodo Movement (1985–2003)[10] for deforestation; such narratives are often rooted in the collective agreement and tacit consensus reached within the community, which provides a window onto collective priorities and groups (Robbins 2012: 137).

Kamal is one of the early migrants from the village who shuttles between farming at Bhutankhuti and working in Bengaluru and Meghalaya as a wage labourer.[11] He would come back during the rainy season of four months and then engage in agriculture at home. Sponsoring his children's education is the major reason for Kamal's frequent migration. Kamal's younger brother has already left for a job in Meghalaya's sawmill despite owning 7 bighas[12] of land and having five family members to support. In Bhutankhuti, it is possible to harvest only once a year due to the lack of irrigation facilities. The amount of rainfall has decreased over time, and the disappearance of khutis has led to the reduction of soil fertility. According to Kamal:

A household needs rice worth Rs 20,000 per year, this amount can be arranged by working a few months outside. Hence, people prefer to trade their labour outside. Fragmentation of land is also a factor of discouragement; my father had 12 bighas which was divided among me and my brother. Now I have 5 bighas which will be later divided among my two sons in future;

will they be doing agriculture then? From Bhutankhuti, several youths are now going to Guwahati, where they are being trained in security/hospitality sectors by government-approved agencies and then going out for jobs; the wages are not at par with the labour.

The respondents in Bhutankhuti took pride in the fact that almost every household has a graduate, unlike villages dominated by other communities nearby. However, there is barely any scope of jobs for the educated populace in Bhutankhuti, except a few schools and a medical dispensary. Some of the degree holders work in educational institutes of Nikashi, while others venture out in search of jobs. As Béteille (1969) pointed out, control over land, capital and labour determines who takes advantage of the new opportunities that arise in the village itself. Those who have nothing but education to help them must go elsewhere, i.e., to a city, to seek a better life. In other words, they must escape from the village. In Bhutankhuti, even the families which possess land holdings are facing out-migration of family members as well, due to the lack of adequate income-generating means locally. During focussed group discussions, people recounted the days of militant activities wherein they frequently faced extortion from multiple groups; people would then form village defence committees to ward off such practices. The following section delves into the narratives of conflicts in length.

Conflict memories and narratives

Nepali residents of Bhutankhuti had a mixed response to the different aspects of the Bodo Movement. Most of them are appreciative of the infrastructural developments in the area after the formation of the BTC, especially roads. Moon Singh Brahma, the local executive member of Dihira constituency, is held in high regards by some of the respondents. A different insight about the situation of Baksa was narrated by Sunil Sharma, who returned to Bhutankhuti after working for several years in Punjab and Maharashtra. Now he is back at home, making ends meet by cultivating his lands and maintaining a dozen bovine cattle. After a cup of tea, Sunil opened up about the situation of the region.

Baksa is considered as a peaceful district under BTC and rightly so. However, it is peaceful in a comparative sense and not in an actual one. During the Movement, we had to face the brunt of both the army and militants. Once the cadres came to collect money from the villagers, we got hold of them and handed them over to the police. A retired army officer from the village gave them some third degree prior to that. Next day, those same guys came in a police van and took away five young boys from the village. The next day we went to the police station, most of us were armed with whatever we could gather, *khukri*[13] being the common weapon. We found that the young boys have been tortured physically and the mob was on the boil to ransack the police station. However, we restrained ourselves and got the boys back to the village. If there is such a blatant blurring of lines between the state agents and the extremists, how can the people remain in peace? It is unfortunate that despite living in close proximity to each other for so many years, the Bodos despise us. The Bodo kids would hurl verbal abuse at Nepali kids, the kids are innocent with no political understanding, hence, such mentality must be prevailing among the household elders. This is a disturbing trend. We have also faced discrimination in government jobs, our candidates don't get the jobs despite scoring adequate marks in exams like TET,[14] but their candidates (understandably Bodo) would get the job despite scoring low marks. After BTC formation, roads have developed but I don't consider that to be actual development. You must know that Nepalis are the earliest settlers in the areas in and around Nikashi and the word Nikashi has Nepali roots. During the heydays of the khutis, the bovine cattle were occasionally let out of the khutis, so that the khutis could be cleaned up. Nikashi was the place where the cattle used to be left out (this activity roughly translates into 'nikash' in Nepali and other languages derived from Sanskrit). Hence, the place got its name Nikashi.

Sunil's account ostensibly represented the opinions of differences held by one community towards another and poses an urgent question about the politics of autonomy practised by the Bodo political class, wherein the claim of indigeneity overarches other considerations. Representation of such narratives, however, is not aimed at demonising any community but rather to reemphasise that the trajectory of governance also showcases the tendencies of turning into a majoritan ethnocracy[15] in a region prone to ethnic divisions and conflicts. If we bring in the readings of partition scholarship, this part of the Baksa district shows the marks of micro-partition – of neighbourhoods, villages and community (Samaddar et al. 2005). As the non-Bodo communities in the BTC demand to move out of the BTC, it points towards a trend of balkanisation,[16] with inevitable implications on security and livelihood. The nature of governmentality in the BTC, albeit with limited autonomy, has not created enough job opportunities for the educated people in the region; neither has it adequately addressed the issues faced by traditional livelihood opportunities like dairy and agriculture.[17] Over the last few years the political spectrum of the region has been organised and reorganised along ethnic lines; however, the issue of labour out-migration is yet to be addressed; so is the issue of sustainable peace and security.

Signs of conflict are intermittently present in Baksa, due to insurgent activities and inter-party squabbles. A burnt down office of a political organisation in front of the house where I was staying in Nikashi town was a testament to the palpable tension scenario of the area. The politics of the region has manufactured distrust among the communities. On the eve of my arrival in Baksa, Manoj Das, a caste Assamese (non-Bodo) who raised his voice against the Bodo hierarchy in the area several times, was murdered. The curfew was placed from 6 p.m. to 5 a.m. for several weeks to prevent any sort of nuisance. The December 2014 massacre in Kokrajhar and Sonitpur districts[18] was followed by a series of curfews. Such untoward incidents were inevitably followed by a strike or two by different outfits. On average, there was at least one strike per week during my stay in the field; such realpolitik creates bottlenecks in the social and daily life of the local communities. The mobility of the people gets restricted due to a conflict-ridden situation which also limits their potential of economic activities and income.

Locating Nalbari: in the context of history

Nalbari district is located to the south of the Baksa district (see Figure 10.2); it is situated between the hills of Bhutan and the Brahmaputra River. Nalbari has numerous water channels crisscrossing through its landscape, as water from the hills moves downstream to join the Brahmaputra River in form of streams and rivers. This has led to the creation of a large number of water bodies in Nalbari which have sustained the *machmoria* or the fishing community

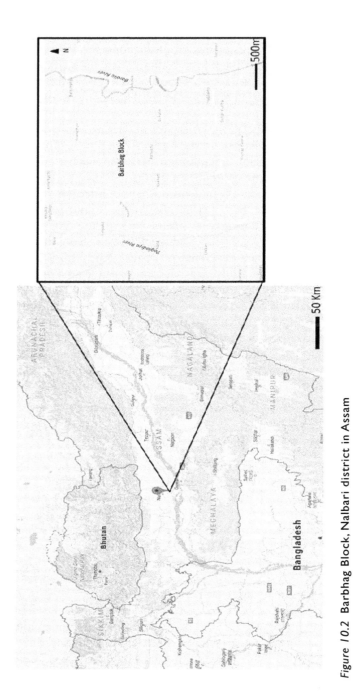

Figure 10.2 Barbhag Block, Nalbari district in Assam

Source: Google Maps, 2017, accessed on 10 October 2017[20]

(henceforth referred to as machmoria) in the district. Agriculture is the mainstay of the major section of the populace. Proximity to Guwahati city (around 70 km from Nalbari town, the district head-quarters of Nalbari) and the early spread of education had created a working class involved in the governmental and non-governmental service sectors.

In Nalbari, I conducted my fieldwork in the Barbhag block (see Figure 10.2). According to Prithibhushan Deka, a member of a local non-governmental organisation Gramya Vikash Mancha (GVM), the term Barbhag originated during the Ahom rule to indicate a greater area under the undivided Kamrup district, in between Rangia, Hajo and Nalbari. During the Ahom period, farmers of the area paid maximum tax, mostly in kind, to the central storage of the king; 'bar' means big and 'bhag' means share; this indicates that a high amount of revenue was paid by the farmers during those days. During the British period, farmers of the area regularly revolted against tax impositions. According to a report published in *Hindoo Patriot* on 5 February 1894 (Guha 2014), the British government found it difficult to collect land revenue in *tehsils*[19] of Patidarang, Nalbari, Barama, Bajali and *mouzas* of Upar Barbhag (present Barbhag). Farmers of the Barbhag region organised *Raiz Mel* (people's convention) against the British government, which indicates a strong control of the farmers over local politics in the colonial period.

Conflict continuous and migration

In continuance with the rebellious attitude during the colonial period, Nalbari was a hub of United Liberation Front of Assam (ULFA)[21] since the 1970s/80. Under the influence of ULFA, Nalbari temporarily turned into a liberated zone by the late 1990s. This had several implications with migration from the region. At the latter stage of my fieldwork, when people were well acquainted with me, they came up with the stories of conflict and their own experiences.

> I fear the police more than the army, as I grew up with the army; I was regularly slapped by the army when they came for search operations. They made us stare at the sun continuously and drink water from the tube well continuously. But the policemen are more dangerous; they would book you silently

which would create problems later on. Army slaps a guy, and the case rests there itself. Many times we had to leave home when the army came looking for ULFA cadres.

(A villager)

Three guys were shot down in front of me. Army burnt down my entire house. There is no house in Nalbari where the ULFA cadre had not stayed and had food.

(Former ULFA cadre)

He joined ULFA when he was studying in Nalbari college. For the last several years there has been no trace of him. We consider that he has expired. We have had different stories about his disappearance. It is said that he went to Myanmar to collect arms and fell sick on his way back in Manipur. We wrote to the ULFA high command three times, but even they couldn't provide his whereabouts. Army took away my younger brother several times, I had to arrange money to free him.

(Brother of a former ULFA cadre)

Subsequently, several relationships emerged between migration and conflict from the narratives of the respondents. Initially, the thieves and burglars of the area left the area in fear of the ULFA, and due to the presence of ULFA throughout Assam, they left the state and went to places like Bangalore and Chennai, where they found out there was a market for labour. Later, this group of former thieves and burglars facilitated the labour movement out of Nalbari by helping them to secure jobs in different cities of Southern India. After the ULFA weakened in the late 1990s and early 2000s, many youths fled the villages in the apprehension of army harassment and persecution by the state.

Krishna Namasudra belongs to the machmoria[22] community. Belonging to the community of fisher folks Krishna possesses a boat, which was used by him to ferry ULFA cadres from his village to a nearby village at night time. This led to the army's setting its sight on Krishna's house:

The army suspected my son due to the black blanket they found in my house. ULFA cadres used such blankets at night to travel from one place to another over our boats. However, my son didn't join the ULFA, and I cleared all doubts about him in the local police station with the help of a local army personnel. Despite that, I asked him to migrate as I thought the army might come back for him.

Krishna's son has been working in a fish packaging unit in Gujarat for the last 12 years; he is married and has a son. Krishna hopes that his son will come back with his family, as he is concerned about the fact that his grandson will not be able to learn Assamese in the schools of Gujarat. The first choice of migrants like Krishna's son was Guwahati, as it was the biggest city nearby. However, in Guwahati, the migrants were met with apathy due to several factors. The ULFA activities had shot Nalbari into the national headlines, which created a negative stereotype against the people from Nalbari in places like Guwahati. People of Guwahati were unwilling to employ and rent their homes to Nalbari's migrants. Added to this were the language dynamics. Prithibhushan explained:

> The dialect of Assamese language in Nalbari is Nalbaria or Kamrupia. This is different from the Assamese written script and the language which is spoken in the districts of Upper Assam; as the Muslim invaders, including the Mughals, could proceed only till the Hajo-Nalbari belt, the language got influenced by foreign lingos here. Hence even if a candidate from Nalbari has a better credential, it is most likely that he/she will be turned down in favour of a candidate from Upper Assam who speaks the apparent polished dialect.

Conflicts in Nalbari, therefore, made migration a popular choice among the people. In the early days, if someone left their villages in Nalbari, it used to be major news in the locality for a month preceding the migration, and ceremonies were carried out for the same. Similar ceremonies in the form of separation rituals are also practised in China (Stafford 1999). The villages under the Barbhag block have undergone multiple environmental changes since the 1950s which have been detrimental to the livelihoods of the region. The intensity of change varies from one hamlet to another within a village, and so does the pattern of migration. The upcoming section deals with the details.

From prosperity to perniciousness: Barbhag's livelihood trajectory

Barbukia village

Barbukia is one of the villages in the Barbhag block. The village comprises four hamlets, one inhabited by Hindu upper castes, another by Hindu scheduled castes and the other two by Assamese Muslims. The pattern of out-migration is different among the hamlets owing to their community structure, land ownership patterns and their location with regards to the water bodies and *mathauri*s (embankments). Birendra is a farmer from the Barbukia village; he observes:

> Farming is like a lottery out here; if it floods early we can't even harvest the crops. Even if it rains less out here, but more in Baksa, the water bodies will get filled up and flood the area. On the other hand, if the Brahmaputra exceeds its carrying capacity, it will push back water through Pagladia river.

The Barbhag block is bounded by two rivers, Pagladia in the west and Baralia in the east (see Figure 10.2). The rivers originate in Bhutan, flow through Baksa and Nalbari and eventually join the Brahmaputra. Till the 1950s, villages like Barbukia were prosperous in nature due to flourishing agriculture and fish yields from the water bodies. Though flooding was a regular occurrence in villages like Barbukia, it used to recharge the water bodies, which helped in maintaining the livelihood and hygiene of the villages. Agriculture and fisheries flourished simultaneously. In the 1950s, the government put up embankments along the Pagladia and Baralia rivers in the name of controlling floods, despite the opposition of the local people. As in most other instances, opposition of local communities was considered as irrational by the state planners. Similar acts of resistance against the imposition of control over commons in Africa were viewed as irrationalism by an ecologically destructive and ignorant native population (Grove 1990). Initially, the embankments in Barbhag block served the purpose; however, with time, the embankments suffered infringement due to lack of maintenance.[23] In 1990, the Baralia River was channelled southwards, which made the river seasonal instead of perennial in the stretch of

Barbukia village and left the area under the whims of the Pagladia River. During the monsoons, when the Brahmaputra would exceed its carrying capacity, it would push back sand-filled water through Pagladia and flood the villages under the Barbhag block, which led to two significant outcomes:–

• The embankments hindered the free flowing of the flood water and resulted in inundation of farmlands.
• The sand-filled water of Pagladia eventually filled up the water bodies, which severely compromised the livelihood of the scheduled caste community. As the sands increased the height of water beds, it further aggravated flood problems by delaying the water passage during monsoon.

The series of transformation of environmental landscapes over the years created challenges of sustainable livelihood in villages like Barbukia. Government interventions of similar kinds have been analysed deeply in the 'hazards approach', an important building block of the discipline of 'political ecology'. Focussing both on natural and technological problems faced by human communities, hazards research took as its goal the rational management and amelioration of risk (Robbins 2012: 33). Gilbert White challenged the conventional way of thinking about and dealing with floods. Writing his thesis in the 1940s, White concluded that the traditional way of dealing with flood hazards – building more engineered structure, as done in Barbhag – is expensive, irrational and does little to solve the human problem. Rather, he called for better land use and change in people's behaviour to mitigate future impacts of natural flood events (White 1945). Farmers like Birendra in Barbhag echo the observations of White, in a different place and time. However, such floodplain investment, which defies the logic of local people, can be better understood by delving into the political economy behind it, the role of capital in agricultural development and the control of legislative processes through normative ideologies, vested interests and campaign finance (Robbins 2012: 35). The externalities of the investments have resulted in unsure remuneration from the traditional livelihoods, thus triggering out-migration from the area. Initiatives are being taken by organisations like Gramya Vikash Mancha (GVM) to undo some of the faulty management of natural resources by constructing small-scale irrigation canals (see Figure 10.3); successful implementation of such initiatives has plugged the stream of out-migration to a considerable extent.[24]

From catching fish to packing fish

The machmorias in Nalbari belong to the *namasudra* community.[25] In the early days, the namasudras used to be the only community to be engaged as fisher folk, an occupation that was looked down upon by the social hierarchy. As Weber (1978) stated, it has long been observed that different people are expected to carry out different kinds of work and are allowed control over different environmental goods; the local natural water bodies were/still are accessed by the namasudra community exclusively. The impartment of education created a shift in the mindset of the namasudras. Prabhat Namasudra, from Barsimulia village, elaborates this mindset shift:

> As the namasudras started getting educated, they realised that being a machmoria is not a worthy profession. A consciousness

Figure 10.3 'Diversion Based Irrigation' canals constructed by Gramya Vikash Mancha (GVM) with participation of the villagers in Nagrijuli Block, Baksa district

Source: Photograph taken by the author during fieldwork

developed among us that it is also not respectable for the women of the family to be a machmoria, as the women of the other communities didn't indulge in any such task. Hence, the participation of women as the machmoria ceased to exist. Earlier, only we used to catch fishes, while other communities abstained from the same, as it was not socially sanctioned for them. But now even the Brahmins and Bengali Muslims are involved in the fish trade.[26]

Prabhat's narrative brings out an inverse relation between education and traditional livelihood, a stark continuation of the phenomenon which I came across in Bhutankhuti. This trend is in continuance with findings from different studies which suggest that *ceteris paribus*, labour force participation of women declines with initial impartment of education and increases again only at higher levels of education (Kingdon and Unni 1997; Das and Desai 2003). The changing gender roles of the namasudra perhaps could have a direct/indirect implication on migration, as income of the household was bound to decrease once the social protocol prevented the namasudra women from being involved as a machmoria. Further empirical research can unravel the correlation. Namasudras possess limited land holdings, as they primarily depended on catching fish for their livelihood; therefore, the prospect of sustaining themselves through agriculture remains limited. Also, the yearly flood makes agriculture a risky affair.

Barsimulia has a unique migration pattern: a considerable number of migrants migrate to Golaghat, a district in Upper Assam. The migrants mainly work in the eateries of Golaghat town. Besides going to upper Assam, a good share of migrants from the Barsimulia villages work in the fish packaging units of Gujarat and Andhra Pradesh. From being machmorias, namasudras have turned into fish traders and fish packers in their locality and faraway places, respectively. The transition is pregnant with issues of landscape alteration, changing gender roles and diluting the monopoly of namasudras over fish trade.

Dokoha: confronting the puzzle

Dokoha is the southernmost village of the Barbhag block and shares its border with the village of Bullud, which is situated in the Kamrup (Rural) district. Bullud is a village predominantly inhabited by Bengali-speaking Muslims. Narratives about Bullud and its people, shared by the villagers of Dokoha, hold the potential to give some idea about, if not unlock, the puzzle of in-migration and out-migration in Assam, as referred to in the beginning of the chapter. While ethnicity plays a major role in the narratives of the respondents, one needs to be cautious in order to locate the fine line between specificity and general trends while making sense of the narratives. In Dokoha, I carried out fieldwork in three hamlets, namely:

1 Majhorsuppa
2 Dakhinpara
3 Chutiapara

From the field interviews, I gathered that there are around 25 outmigrants from 90 households in Majhorsuppa. Most of the migrants work in the sandal-making units in Kerala. The migrants who are involved in casual labour in the sandal units earn around Rs 6000/month, while the ones involved with the machinery earn Rs 12,000/month. A significant indicator of the migrants in these households was the calendars from the sandal company (see Figure 10.4). Suresh and Ramesh are two migrants from the hamlet who work in the sandal-making unit of Kerala. The duo shared a story in reference to the 2012 exodus of north-eastern migrants to southern India against the backdrop of Bodo-Bengali Muslim riots in western Assam:

> We had to return to the village, as there were no young guys in the village to stand up against any sort of unwanted incidents. The train which we boarded was packed to its last inch; people were stuffed even in the toilet. The train was turned into a medical express; it was allowed to pass by unhindered with no delay. It didn't stop at the big stations, apprehending attacks on us.[27] It only stopped at small stations or in the middle of no-man's land. At one station in Andhra Pradesh we were served fried rice by volunteers of Bajrang Dal.[28] In one of the evenings there were few Bihari Muslims who were making an attempt to manoeuvre some space to read *namaz*.[29] This enraged some of us as we were travelling in pathetic condition and it was mainly due to the brethren of those Muslims. Hence they ended up being manhandled.

Figure 10.4 Calendars of the sandal-making units in Kerala adorning the walls of a migrant's household in Majhorsuppa hamlet of Dokoha village, Nalbari

Source: Photograph taken by the author during fieldwork

Such narratives enable us to trace the different experience of migrants from Assam. While conflict is one aspect which they aspire to leave behind, the implications of the same cannot be avoided at times, as most of the migrants have their family and landholding back at their native place. Significantly, the migrants didn't feel safe enough under the Indian state outside the region, nor could they entrust the state with the security of their family members back in Assam, as a result of which they had to bear the collective journey back home. The reaction to the namaz on the train explicitly portrays the mistrust and xenophobic attitude which has been perpetrated in the public psyche. While the boundaries of the Indian state allow the Assamese labourers to migrate outside North-East India, their terms of participation in the broader labour market are bounded with ethnopolitical considerations.

Competition of land and culture of labour

Dakhinpara hamlet of Dokoha village lies on the south of the river embankments and, hence, evades the inundation of water during monsoon. The hamlet is inhabited by Hindu upper caste and 'Other Backward Caste' (OBC) categories. Rajani Bezbaruah is a farmer owning 40 bighas of land. As a result, he is busy with agriculture for most of the year. To interact with Rajani, I accompanied him in his fields and offered him some unskilled labour, as he was preparing his land for rice cultivation. After a while, we sat down to take a rest, and Rajani pointed to the southward village of Bullud. Rajani holds the opinion that most of the residents of Bullud are originally from Bangladesh. Rajani stated:

> People from Bullud are now buying land in our hamlet at Rs 20,000/bigha, whereas in other parts of Barbhag the price of land is around Rs 30,000/bigha. Axamiyas[30] these days are unwilling to toll in the field; hence they are keen to sell off their land.

Rajani appreciates the culture of labour among the Bengali Muslims in the following account, as he smokes up a *bidi*[31]:

> You see this bidi? The male children of the Bengali Muslims are groomed for labour through this bidi. When they are 8 to 9 years old, the father would give them a fag or two of the bidi, which would create an addiction for bidi among the child. However, he wouldn't be entertained with any money. Hence, the boy would venture out in the neighbourhood and indulge in small-scale labour jobs like cleaning the gardens, collecting cow dung, etc. After earning a few bucks, the boy would buy a packet of bidi and give the remaining balance to their parents. Also, every member of their household works as labour in the agricultural fields, while in Axamiya households like mine, only I would venture out to trade my labour. The women from the Bengali Muslim household come to our houses to attend to household chores like cleaning up the house and its premises, at a wage rate of Rs 150/day; they are also employed as *rouni*[32] in the field at the rate of Rs 600/bigha. The *mians*[33] practice pisciculture along with crop cultivation. It is near impossible for me

to own a fishery, as it requires constant supervision to prevent theft. The Bengali Muslims, however, would guard their fisheries throughout the night.

Rajani's emphasis on the different cultures of labour was central to the narratives in Chutiapara hamlet as well, which is inhabited by Axamiya Muslims. There are around 107 households, and most of the out-migrants (around 50) work in the fish-packaging units of Andhra Pradesh. Tayijuddin is a landless person who owns a woodcutting enterprise; his son once out-migrated to Andhra Pradesh. One of Tayijuddin's sons is a graduate; now he drives a tractor within the locality, as Tayijuddin couldn't arrange the bribe which ensures an entry point in a government job. Such narratives find resonances in other parts of Southeast Asia, as encountered by Murray Li in the Sulawesi highlands of Indonesia (Murray Li 2014: 40). Such instances also show that investment in education is risky, as jobs in the formal sector are so scarce that they have to be bought, and people like Tayijuddin do not have the money asked as an entrance fee to the formal economy (Breman 2013).

As Chutiapara hamlet is inhabited by Axamiya Muslims, I was curious to know about their perception and opinion about the neighbouring Bengali Muslims of Bullud. As I floated the idea in the courtyard of Darbesh Ali's household, Darbesh emphasised on the culture of labour among the Bengali Muslims, as Rajani did:

> They are now selling cabbage at Rs 2/kg these days, it's possible, as every member of their household puts their labour behind the agricultural activities. They can make a meal out of rice, chilli and salt, which is unthinkable among us. People from our hamlet don't migrate to Guwahati, as the labour market there is also completely dominated by the Bengali Muslims. They also work for Rs 180/day at times instead of the actual wage rate of Rs 200/day; they wouldn't complain even if they didn't receive payment for a day or two. We can't put ourselves through such a regimen; hence, the contractors prefer them these days. They don't need to worry about sending money back home, as the females are also earning through labour works. These people have no time to die even, such is their labour capacity.

A visit to the local weekly market in Bijulighat confirmed that both the vegetable and fish market in the Barbhag block and in areas beyond them is predominantly under the control of Bengali Muslims. How much of this phenomenon can be attributed to the 'culture of labour' of the Bengali Muslim community remains a significant question. Taking into account the difference of the culture of labour, there is a need to look back to a few historically significant trends surrounding labour in Assam. Sharma (2011) elaborates on this trend and represents the colonial attitude of attributing the indolence of the Assamese peasants to their addiction to easily accessible opium. They acquired the epithet of *lahe* (slowly slowly). Their laziness was compounded with the fertile soil in which all crops, particularly opium, grew with easy profusion. Colonial officials like Captain Rowlatt articulated the new colonial orthodoxy about the lazy native when he stated that opium is the element which induces great laziness and adds to the peculiar characteristics of the Assamese people.[34] In comparison, the peasants from East Bengal and their subsequent generations have been undertaking rigorous labour, as confirmed by some of the narratives shared. It's a possibility that the presence of different scales of labour in the same place in conjunction with the non-performing/dysfunctional state churns out multiple factors for migration in order to avoid a precarious situation.

Collective observations, findings and analysis

Given the geopolitical location of North-East India, the recent focus of the Indian state on the region hinges on its agenda of expansion of bilateral ties with its eastern neighbours. As a result, there has been an emphasis on developing the infrastructure of the region through widening roads, expanding air connectivity, extending railway networks, opening new and reactivating old dormant trade routes, and facilitating border trade and transit points. Such activities have serious implications on the use and extraction of the resources of the region, along with occasioning changes in the composition of the labour market and mobility. Therein lies the need to understand the changes which the region would undergo and locate the relation between recent events and relevant changes, in which migration and labour mobility figure prominently.

According to the National Skill Development Council, 14 million labourers are to move out from the North-East between 2011 and 2021, as 2.6 million more jobs are to be generated against a labour demand of 17 million.[35] Inward remittances obtained from

0.8 million youth settled outside Assam is 2800 million (2012–13 financial year); 0.3 million of the out-migrants are employed as a security guard (in industries and commerce departments, government of Assam). From the account of out-migration from Baksa and Nalbari, it emerges that livelihood challenges and issues of citizenship, conflict and security are essential in interrogating the pattern of labour mobility. While 'son of the soil' has been a major political issue, wherein public sentiments have tilted against the participation/presence of alleged Bangladeshis in the labour market, today one finds that the sons are moving away from the soil, leaving a question mark over the earlier claims of indigenous rights and valid citizenship. It seems that the reconfigured environmental landscape has reconfigured the labour market, which also holds the potential to reconfigure the questions in Assam's political spectrum.

Small land-holdings and reduced demand for local labour are factors behind out-migration, as income is both inadequate and uncertain from agricultural activities in the field sites, which is typical of the situation in the subcontinent. As Breman observes:

> Increasing pressure on agrarian resources caused by land fragmentation in tandem with the progressive mechanisation of production has made off-farm employment a must especially for those with little or no landholdings. For many households working on the land is not any more the prime livelihood as it has been for the generations preceding them. Farmers have become cost conscious and may engage labourers for half a day only. Agricultural labour remains important, but often as a subsidiary activity for youngsters in particular. While males and females in the older age brackets still tend to hang on to what has been or still is their main occupation – working in the fields – their sons and daughters only do so if no other employment is available
>
> (2013: 44).

While Breman did his fieldworks in the terrains of southern Gujarat, the issues highlighted have much wider resonance, as South Asia is at the epicentre of the informal economy. If one pays a cursory visit to the villages under the Baska block, one would see that most of the labourers in the agricultural field are either women or elderly males of the house, in line with the assertion of Breman (2013: 45). It seemed like the case of 'missing men'. In the global

context, increased awareness of women's work resulted in an explo-
sion of development programmes directed specifically at women:
the 'Women in Development' approach to international aid. As a
result, the Mahila Kisan Sahastrikaran Pariyojana (MKSP)[36] programme is implemented in a large scale in the villages of the Baska
block. MKSP aims to promote women participation in the agricultural sector, which seems to be a necessity given the migration of
the men from the region. A similar trend of women's participation
in agricultural practices is prevalent in other parts of India as well;
for example, in the Jharkhand region, for each 80 days of human
labour required per acre annually, female workers supply 65 days
of labour (Sharan and Dayal 1993). Migration also includes a surge
in trafficking labour, sex, human organs, weaponry, etc., once again
suggesting a different kind of connectivity – the other site of official
globalisation today (Samaddar and Mitra 2016). Several cases of
trafficking persist, especially among the Adivasi community, Delhi
being a favourite destination for the traffickers. Guwahati, being the
nearby largest city, is a transit point for such trafficking mobility.

The alteration of landscapes, in Baksa and Nalbari, holds the
potential to enhance some productive resources, while other
resource extraction patterns might be hindered; the results will
inevitably impinge differently on different groups, potentially creating or increasing conflicts and struggles. Subsequently, as one
section of the population migrates or perhaps is being forced to
migrate, out-migration/exit from the place of origin is the standard
remedy for impoverishment by the development planners. Planners
know well that increased efficiency in agriculture will squeeze out
farmers who can't compete, but they argue the squeeze is necessary (Murray Li 2014). It is the so-called 'creative destruction' upon
which increased productivity and economic growth depend. The
improved statistics, however, gulp down livelihood opportunities of
many, particularly the ones participating in the informal economy,
as an opportunity cost, giving rise to a situation of 'social Darwin-
ism' in which a person unable to compete locally is forced to exit
the scene and play along with the script of the development planners. It might be oversimplifying to state that the increased desire/
capacity to toil as labour among Bengali Muslims, in comparison
to the Axamiyas,[37] are pushing the latter out of the state, but it
could be factored into the analysis, and the hypothesis can be tested
with further research. However, such a trend is on par with the
view of World Bank experts; farmers who cannot compete should

be encouraged to sell their land to people who can use it more productively.

One such 'productive' trend is the setting up of fisheries in Barbhag. Earlier practised mainly by Bengali Muslims, the demonstration effect has started to roll in other communities. While investment in fisheries might earn a profit individually, given the topography and environmental nuances of the area, it holds the potential to negatively affect agriculture by further delaying the water passages and eventually leading to further migration from the Barbhag block, constraining local resource extraction pattern. Such tendencies of extraction from natural resources are central to the theme of marginalisation theory in political ecology. Marginalisation is a process whereby the politically and socially marginal people are pushed into ecologically marginal spaces and economically marginal social positions, resulting in their increasing demands on the marginal productivity of the ecosystems and in a degraded landscape returning less and less to an increasingly impoverished and desperate community (Robbins 2012: 91).

As the account of Tayijuddin showed us, gaining education does not ensure an entry into the job market. Nalbari, for instance, has been in the news for massive recruitment scams.[38] The school dropouts depict a worst-case scenario, as they are neither employable in the formal sector, nor do they feel inclined to indulge in agriculture. Excepting Manipur, the dropout rates of the northeastern states are higher than the national figure of 49.3 percent in standards 1–10. Assam and Meghalaya top the dropout rate, with 77.4 percent ('Basic Statistics of North Eastern Region 2015': 282). Coupled with the economic and environmental challenges, an incomplete education eliminates the prospect of pursuing traditional livelihoods such as being a garakhia and machmoria from the mental landscape of the community; an alternate means of income generation is barely feasible given the bureaucratic set-up, which acts as a major push factor for out-migration. Therefore, in several households, there was an appreciation of the fact that a household member has migrated.

Besides the precariousness of livelihood, the ethnic conflicts and the prospect of conflicts in the region manufacture a dysfunctional state of affairs, which negates the prospect of churning out sustainable livelihood practices from the locally available resources. Such political developments have shifted the communities far away from the collective identity of being an Axamiya, which was mainly endorsed and created by the Ahom dynasty and involved the assimilation of different communities under its regime (1228–1826). Warnings of such fragmentation were forecasted in the writings of the late Parag Kumar Das, a journalist and activist of Assam, wherein he had critiqued the non-inclusive governance of the Assam Gana Parishad government (1986–91 and 1996–2001) in Assam, which came to power in 1986 riding on the sub-nationalist sentiments of the Assam Movement (Das 1996). The most problematic outcome of such a discourse of politics, enmeshed with such high octaves of ethnic overtones, is the intercommunity clashes or one-sided massacres which have occurred intermittently in the present BTC areas. The extent to which conflict is correlated to migration in a place like Baksa would require further in-depth research.

Does the prevalent trend of migration call for any government initiatives and interventions? The earlier sections have pointed out how the government-sponsored investments behind altering the landscapes have already created a flow of out-migrants, and, unless reviewed, the investments would worsen the situation. Similar state-sponsored disaster had also taken place in Odisha, where the Jersey breed of cow was given to poor households and the traditional Khariar bull, well suited to the local climate, was biologically extinct, as they were culled to maintain the purity of the Jersey breed. The project, intended to reduce out-migration from the region, actually increased it, forcing more independent producers into low-wage labour (Sainath 1996). Such collective experiences of policy failure represent the state to be a deterrent in the community's lifestyle as it dismantles the existing set-up in exchange for a new network of capital, resource extraction and labour which makes them vulnerable. My argument is not to do away with the state or paint out-migration as a negative phenomenon, but rather to stress participatory policy formulation by taking into account the opinions of the local communities who sustained themselves by extracting natural resources much prior to the existence of the Indian state, so that migration is not forced, stemming from desperation, whereby migrants are forced to accept exploitative terms of employment in their workplace.

The lives of the migrants from the North-East Region once captured the headlines in 2012 during their panicked exodus from different states of southern India in 2012, in the backdrop of riots in the Bodoland Territorial Council (BTC).[39] Otherwise, mention of such people is seldom found in the media unless a mishap occurs involving them. On 14 November 2014, it was reported that an Assamese migrant was killed by miscreants in Kerala as the migrant protested against his wife being eve-teased; on 30 December 2014, a report was published in the vernacular daily *Axamiya Pratidin* that three Assamese girls were rescued from a train in Kokrajhar while they were trafficked; on 3 February 2015, Deben Kalita from Baksa was reported to be missing in Chennai, where Deben went in search of jobs. Occasionally, such news of the migrants would appear in the local dailies. On the other hand, advertisements have started to emerge in the same dailies about security personnel in Chennai with a remuneration of Rs 8000–12,000; also, posters are now found in Guwahati, seeking security guards for a salary of Rs 12,000, with accommodation and insurance (see Figure 10.5).

It is with great expectation and partial apprehension that people are looking forward to the changes that North-East India is specu- lated to undergo under the pretext of India's 'Look East and Act East Policy'. Therein lays a possibility that the series of activities would usher in a new regime of labour participation by reconfig- uring labour skills and mobility. Whether the changes would free the people and migrants of Baksa and Nalbari from the circle of insecurity, or give rise to a new series of contentions over ethnicity, indigenous rights and citizenship in India's north-eastern frontier would determine the evaluation of India's new regime of govern- ance in North-East India.

Figure 10.5 Fliers on the walls of Guwahati

Source: Photograph taken by the author during fieldwork

Notes

1 I am indebted to the members and volunteers of Gramya Vikash Mancha (GVM), a non-governmental organisation actively pursuing livelihood and women empowerment schemes in the Baksa and Nalbari districts. It would not have been possible to conduct fieldwork in Baksa without the help of my good friend and GVM employee, Bipul Dewri.

2 The figures are from the Census of India 2001, reproduced in Hoque (2013).

3 The figures are from the Census of India 2011, reproduced in Devi (2012): 272–276; also see www.journalcra.com/sites/default/files/2197. pdf, accessed on 20 September 2016.

4 For details on the Look East policy with a focus on Northeast India's logistics and infrastructure, see Mitra and Samaddar (2016).

5 The etymology is referred from http://baksa.gov.in/, accessed on 26 July 2016.

6 BTC was formed in 2003 to safeguard the due rights and ethno-economic interests of the indigenous Bodo community. It can also be considered as an expression of self-assertion intending to differentiate from the identity of being an Assamese, within the state of Assam.

7 Adivasis refer to the tribes of Central India who were brought into Assam and North Bengal by the British administration in order to employ them as labourers in the tea gardens.

8 Bodos are an ethnic and linguistic aboriginal group spread across North Bengal and Northeast India. At present they are heavily concentrated in Western Assam. The Bodos are classified as a plains tribe in the Sixth Schedule of the Indian Constitution. *Axamiya* literally means the language of the Assamese people and the citizens of Assam.

9 *Khuti* means grazing fields with stables of bovine cattle in the local languages.

10 The Bodo movement was aimed against the hierarchy of Assamese culture in the Bodo-dominated areas. There have been diverse demands by different Bodo-dominated political organisations ranging from a separate nation to a separate state. Varied notions of sovereignty and autonomy have led to infighting within the Bodos. The movement has had both violent and non-violent expressions over the time.

11 Jowai has several coalmines and sawmills; it is situated in the state of Meghalaya.

12 1 bigha = 14,440 square feet; www.lawyersclubindia.com/experts/ Extent-Bigha-101196.asp#.VwzBQ9R94_4, accessed on 11 April 2016.

13 A *khukri* is a sharp, pointed weapon, a signature of the Nepali community.

14 The Teacher Eligibility Test conducted to recruit teachers for government schools.

15 An ethnocracy is a type of political regime in which the state apparatus is appropriated by a dominant ethnic group (or groups) to further its interests, power and resources. On ethnocracy, see Samaddar et al. 2005: 22.

16 Balkanisation describes the process of fragmentation or division of a region or state into smaller regions or states that are often hostile or uncooperative with one another. The region known as the Balkans is commonly thought to include Albania, Greece, Romania, the European portion of Turkey and often surrounding areas. The decline of the Ottoman Empire in the eighteenth century led to a series of revolts that accelerated the fracturing of the region into a number of smaller states whose unstable coexistence led to violence that came to a head in World War I. Since 1919, 'balkanise' and its related noun, 'balkanisation', have come to refer to the kind of divisive action that can weaken countries or groups, as well as other things.

17 On details of the autonomy discourse in BTC, Barbora (2005) has elaborated on the construction of frontiers and negotiation of political space within it. Barbora comments that the functioning of the autonomous council in the North-East has given rise to a statist discourse which has not delivered justice.

18 Refer to www.thehindu.com/news/national/other-states/assam-toll-rises-as-violence-spreads-to-kokrajhar/article6724739.ece, accessed on 2 April 2016.

19 *Tehsils* and *mouzas* refer to different administrative divisions in different regions of South Asia.

20 The author gratefully acknowledges Sonia Das, Research Scholar, NIAS, Bengaluru, for guidance with the map.

21 ULFA was formed in 1979 to carry out an armed struggle against India to form a socialist Assam.

22 *Machmoria* refers to the livelihood of catching fish from water bodies, mainly practised by the scheduled caste community in different parts of India.

23 See 'No repair work done for 3,700 km dykes: Patowary', Assam Tribune, 3 August 2016; www.assamtribune.com/scripts/mdetails.asp?id=aug0416/at057, accessed on 16 August 2016.

24 Refer to http://infochangeindia.org/agriculture/stories-of-change/nal bari-farmers-resume-cultivation-after-25-years.html, accessed on 11 April 2016.

25 The *namasudra* caste is situated in the lower rung of Hindu caste hierarchy, historically subjected to discrimination on the basis of their caste. In Barbhag they mostly have 'Namasudra' as their title; for example, Prabhat Namasudra.

26 Fish are still mainly caught by the namasudras; the other communities are involved in fish trade in the market.

27 Suresh and Ramesh meant attacks on the train by the Muslim community, who were enraged because their community members were mostly on the receiving end of violence during the riot.

28 Bajrang Dal is a right-wing organisation operating in India in the name of the Hindu religion.

29 Namaz refers to ritual prayers prescribed by Islam.

30 Rajani uses the term *Axamiya* to differentiate between himself and the Bengali Muslims, which is unlikely to be accepted by the Bengali-speaking Muslims, as they speak Assamese as well and have been inhabiting Assam for over a 100 years now.

31 Bidi is a locally made cigarette made from unprocessed tobacco rolled in leaves. Bidi is mostly consumed by the working class across India.
32 *Rouni* refers to a kind of labour which involves sowing the crop.
33 Male Bengali Muslims are termed as mians in colloquial Assamese language.
34 Selections from the Records of the Government of Bengal, 'Evidence from District Collectors'. Authority of the Board of Revenue, Bengal, Superintendent, Government Printing Bengal Government Press, Alipore, Bengal 1944, reproduced in Sharma (2011).
35 Refer to http://timesofindia.indiatimes.com/city/guwahati/14mn-to-migrate-from-Northeast-by-2021-in-search-of-jobs-as-demand-fails-to-meet-supply-Study/articleshow/11611220.cms, accessed on 2 August 2016.
36 Refer to www.mksp.in/, accessed on 3 April 2016.
37 I adhere to Rajani's advertent categorisation in this case (see fn 30); adherence, however, shouldn't be equated with agreement.
38 Refer to www.assamtimes.org/node/7707, accessed on 20 April 2016.
39 Refer to www.thehindu.com/opinion/op-ed/home-is-hardly-the-best/article3796017.ece, accessed on 1 April 2016.

References

Arnold, David. 1993. 'Social Crisis and Epidemic Disease in the Famines of Nineteenth-century India', *Social History of Medicine*, 6(3): 385–404.
Barbora, Sanjay. 2005. 'Autonomy in the Northeast', Ranabir Samaddar (ed.), *The Politics of Autonomy*, pp. 187–198, New Delhi: Sage.
Baruah, Sanjib. 1999. *India against Itself: Assam and the Politics of Nationality*, Philadelphia: University of Pennsylvania.
Basic Statistics of North Eastern Region 2015. 2015. Shillong: North Eastern Council Secretariat.
Béteille, Andre. 1969. 'Ideas and Interests: Some Conceptual Problems in the Study of Social Stratification in Rural India', *International Social Science Journal*, 21(2): 219–234.
Breman, Jan. 2013. *At Work in the Informal Economy of India: A Perspective from the Bottom Up*, New Delhi: Oxford University Press.
Chyrmang, Rikil. 2011. 'Magnitude of Migration from North Eastern Region of India', in Sebastian I. Rajan (ed.), *Migration, Identity and Conflict: India Migration Report*, pp. 72–94, New Delhi: Routledge.
Das, Maitreyi B. and Sonalde Desai. 2003. *Why Are Educated Women Less Likely to be Employed in India?: Testing Competing Hypothesis*, Washington, DC: Social Protection, World Bank.
Das, Parag. 1996. 'Axom'r Jonojatiyo Raijor Xomosya, Udayachol aru Onyanyo', in Udayaditya Bharali (ed.), *Parag Kumar Das'r Nirbachito Rochonaboli*, Guwahati: Udangshri Prakashan.
Devi, Bimolata Kh. 2012. 'A Study on Urbanisation in North Eastern India', *International Journal of Current Research*, 4(10) October: 272–276.

Drèze, Jean. 1988. *Famine Prevention in India*, Helsinki, Finland: World Institute for Development Economics Research of the United Nations University.

Grove, Richard H. 1990. 'Colonial Conservation, Ecological Hegemony and Popular Resistance: Towards a Global Synthesis', in J. M. Mackenzie (ed.), *Imperialism and the Natural World*, pp. 15–50, Manchester: Manchester University Press.

Guha, Amalendu. 2014. *Planter Raj to Swaraj: Freedom Struggle and Electoral Politics in Assam*, New Delhi: Tulika Books.

Hazarika, Sanjay. 2000. *Rites of Passage: Border Crossings, Imagined Homelands, India's East and Bangladesh*, New Delhi: Penguin Books.

Hoque, Azimul. 2013. 'Urbanization Pattern in NE India: Strategic Overview', *Two Circles: Mainstream News of the Marginalized*. http://twocircles.net/2013may24/urbanization_pattern_ne_india_strategic_overview.html#.WEYp9vl97IV. Accessed 1 December 2016.

Karlsson, Bengt G. 2013. 'Evading the State: Ethnicity in Northeast India through the Lens of James Scott', *Asian Ethnology*, 72(2): 321–331.

Kingdon, Geeta and Jeemol Unni. 1997. *How Much Does Education Affect Women's Labour Market Outcomes in India?* Ahmedabad: Gujarat Institute of Development Research.

Kumar, Krishna. 2014. 'Rurality, Modernity and Education', *Economic and Political Weekly*, 49(22): 38–43.

McDuiera, Duncan. 2012. *Northeast Migrants in Delhi: Race, Refuge and Retail*, Amsterdam: Amsterdam University Press.

Murray Li, Tania. 2014. *Land's End: Capitalist Relations on an Indigenous Frontier*, London: Duke University Press.

North-East Support Centre and Helpline (NESCH). 2011. *Northeast Migration and Challenges in National Capital Cities*, Delhi: NESCH.

Robbins, Paul. 2012. *Political Ecology: A Critical Introduction*, West Sussex, UK: Wiley-Blackwell.

Sainath, Palagummi. 1996. *Everybody Loves a Good Drought: Stories from India's Poorest Districts*, New Delhi: Penguin.

Samaddar, Ranabir. 1998. *Memory, Power, Identity: Junglemahals: 1880–1950*, Hyderabad: Orient Longman.

Samaddar, Ranabir, et al. (eds). 2005. *Partitions: Reshaping States and Minds*, Oxon: Frank Cass.

Samaddar, Ranabir and Snehashish Mitra. 2016. *Bridge of Spaces: East by Rear East, Ah! The Northeast*, Calcutta Research Group Research Paper Series, Policies and Practices 76. Kolkata: Calcutta Research Group.

Scott, James. 1990. *Domination and the Art of Resistance: Hidden Transcripts*, New Haven, CT: Yale University Press.

Scott, James. 2009. *The Art of Not Being Governed: An Anarchist History of Upland Southeast Asia*, New Haven, CT: Yale University Press.

Sharan, Ramesh and Harishwar Dayal. 1993. 'Deprivation of Female Farm Laborers in Jharkhand Region of Bihar', *Social Change*, 23(4): 95–99.

Sharma, Jayeeta. 2011. *Empire's Garden: Assam and the Making of India*, Durham, NC: Duke University Press.

Stafford, Charles. 1999. 'Separation, Reunion and the Chinese Attachment to Place', in *Internal and International Migration: Chinese Perspectives*, Chinese Worlds, Vol. 1. London: Curzon Press.

Weber, Max.1978. *Economy and Society*, Berkeley: University of California.

White, Gilbert F. 1945. 'Human Adjustments to Floods: A Geographical Approach to the Flood Problem in the United States', University of Chicago, Department of Geography, Research Paper No. 29.

Part IV

Employment diversification

Chapter 11

Rural non-farm employment in North-East India

A temporal and spatial analysis

Bhagirathi Panda

The manifestation of the current state of economic development of any economy is essentially an anecdote of processes of structural transformation in the spheres of income and employment. An analytical study of the nature of such evolutionary processes, over time and across space, in any given developing economy can provide important broad insights to map out the future course of economic and developmental policies for this economy. Noted economists such as Fisher (1939), Clark (1940), Nurkse (1953), Lewis (1954), Myrdal (1957), and Hirschman (1958), Chenery (1960) and Kuznets (1966) have attributed the development of an economy to structural transformations. Structural transformation primarily implies a continuous reallocation of labour (it can also be other resources including capital) as an important factor of production from low productivity sectors to high productivity sectors. Developing countries like India still continue to reveal the relevance of cross-sector labour reallocation in a framework of traditional-modern sector/rural-urban dualism as advocated by Lewis (1954) and Ranis and Fei (1963). In the initial works of Lewis and Ranis and Fee, it was implicit that traditional-modern and rural-urban dualisms were synonymous. However, with the coming up of formal and informal dualism and emergence of unemployment and under-employment in urban space and consequent revision of the dualism framework by Ranis (2004), this dualism gets more familiar with farm and non-farm in the rural set-up and formal and informal in the urban set-up. While the dualism in the urban economy more or less resembles the Lewis and Ranis and Fee-type in terms of productivity differences, the rural situation of farm and non-farm categorisation does not exhibit a dualism based on obvious productivity differentials, entailing a universal structural transformation that would promote increased economic growth and development. This is precisely because of the heterogeneity of the rural non-farm sector in terms of productivity and a transformation of its labour market based on both developmental as well as distress factors.

Structural transformation, North-East and rural non-farm employment

The economy of the North-Eastern Region (NER), even today, is predominantly rural. However, it exhibits a lot of distortions and is undergoing significant transformations in many of its economic dimensions. As mentioned earlier, one of the important means of promoting economic development in developing countries happens to be structural transformation of its income and employment space in terms of reallocation of labour from low productivity sectors to relatively high productivity sectors. This kind of structural transformation makes the labour market efficient, with an increase in productivity. Since the North-East was and still continues to be a predominantly agrarian rural economy, with approximately 60 percent of its workforce engaged in the farm sector, improvements in education and other dimensions of human development, an increase in agricultural productivity because of modernisation of agriculture and an expansion in physical infrastructure through government initiative across the board, it was presumed that the Lewis and Ranis-Fee-type structural transformation would happen in the region. It is time to question if such a transformation has happened for the region. Studies undertaken, including some by this author, bring out the fact that considerable employment diversification has happened in the region after economic reforms (Panda 2012). However, can this diversification process be called a structural transformation of the type postulated by Lewis (1954), Chenery (1960), Ranis and Fei (1961), and Kuznets (1966)? Does it confirm the agricultural productivity-led growth thesis of the rural non-farm sector propounded by Mellor (1976)? Has this diversification process strengthened and made the rural labour market in the region efficient? These are some of the valid questions that need to be answered through systematic analytical studies. This chapter is an attempt to answer some of these questions with the help of the available secondary data and published works of authors/institutions, including the present author himself. Secondary data on employment and unemployment have been collected from various rounds of surveys conducted by the National Sample Survey Organisation (NSSO). They have been used to describe and explain the growth and sectoral composition of the employment diversification process over time and across states. Primary data are used to test if the diversification process has happened through developmental factors like an increase in agricultural productivity, urbanisation, literacy, commercialisation of agriculture etc., thereby confirming the positive structural transformation process propounded by Lewis and others.

The chapter is presented in five sections. The introductory section briefly presents the all-important theory of structural transformation enunciated by the previously cited noted economists, having a close relationship with employment diversification. The second section contextualises this theoretical framework with the developments in the economy of the North-East and testing some relevant research questions in subsequent sections. The third section presents the growth and nature of rural non-farm employment (RNFE) in the region over time and across gender and regions. The fourth section analyses the factors responsible for the growth in rural non-farm employment, thereby qualifying the nature of structural transformation taking place, that is, whether it is the Lewis and Ranis-Fee type or not. The fifth section makes a conclusion with some policy suggestions.

Concept, growth and nature of RNFE in the North-East

Concept of RNFE

Although there is no clear classification of RNFE, most authors follow the World Development Report (1995), which defines all economic activities in rural areas, except the ones in agriculture, livestock, fishing and hunting, as non-farm. To make it explicit, in the Indian context, in most studies undertaken using secondary data, RNFE is defined to include all types of household/individual employment in rural areas in industries like mining and quarrying, household and non-household manufacturing, processing, repairs, construction, trade and hotel, transport, storage and communications, and community, as well as personal services. In this chapter, we go by this definition.

Growth of RNFE

Traditionally, the Census and NSSO have been two important sources that provide data for an analysis of the growth and nature of RNFE in the region. However, census data for the classification of people on the basis of their detailed sectoral economic activities for the region and individual states are yet to be published for the latest census year, 2011. Therefore, we have used NSSO usual status quinquennial data (ps+ss) on industrial classification of activities collected in different rounds for estimating the share of RNFE and its various sub-sectors during the period 1993–4 to 2011–12. The same is reproduced in Figure 11.1.

Figure 11.1 and its accompanying figures clearly show that both the NER as well as the country as a whole have undergone considerable diversification of employment from farm to non-farm activities in rural sectors since the beginning of economic liberalisation. However, the North-East, except for the period 2004–5, has consistently maintained a slight edge over the country in terms of share of RNFE. Its share of RNFE has increased from 24.7 percent in 1993–4 to 36.5 percent in 2011–12, as compared to from 21.6 percent to 35.99 percent for the country as a whole during the same period. Therefore, the region after economic reforms vis-à-vis the country has undergone comparatively increased diversification of its rural employment space. Whether this diversification process confirms Lewis and Ranis and Fee-type structural transformation is another story to be examined in subsequent sections.

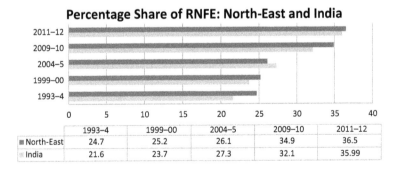

Percentage Share of RNFE: North-East and India

	1993–4	1999–00	2004–5	2009–10	2011–12
North-East	24.7	25.2	26.1	34.9	36.5
India	21.6	23.7	27.3	32.1	35.99

Figure 11.1 Temporal growth of RNFE in India and the NER

Source: Author's estimation based on NSSO reports of 50th, 55th, 61st, 66th, and 68th rounds

Spatial-temporal dimensions of RNFE

Next we come to the spatio-temporal dimension of RNFE in the region. Table 11.1 clearly shows the unevenness with respect to the share of RNFE across states and over time in the region. During 2011–12, Tripura's share of RNFE, at 68.4 percent, was the highest, and Arunachal Pradesh's share, at 21.5 percent, was the lowest in the region. This explains the heterogeneity in employment diversification and the rural labour market in the region. At the beginning of economic liberalisation during 1993–4, there were four states having shares of RNFE less than the regional average. After almost two decades, there are five states having shares of RNFE less than the regional average. Hence, the catching-up effect is missing in the field of spatial concentration of RNFE in the region. Of all the seven states[1], Nagaland has not displayed any kind of diversification over the past two decades. Assam also does not present any appreciable degree of continuity and universality in this regard.

Gender and RNFE

Study of employment diversification with respect to gender can provide valuable insights to better understand the rural labour market and the process and nature of structural transformation. A close look at Table 11.2 and Figure 11.2 illustrates that in the

Table 11.1 State-wise share of rural non-farm employment in the NER

State/NSSO rounds	50th round (1993–4)	55th round (1999–2000)	61st round (2004–5)	66th round (2009–10)	68th round (2011–12)
Arunachal Pradesh	13.6	16.6	18.1	24.3	21.5
Assam	20.8	32.3	25.7	29.5	35.4
Manipur	36.2	24.7	30.7	46.6	54.3
Meghalaya	14	13.5	18.2	29.3	33.0
Mizoram	11.1	14.5	12.6	19.4	24.2
Nagaland	25.1	20.3	20.7	25.9	23.3
Tripura	52.4	54.3	56.8	69.4	68.4
North-East	24.7	25.2	26.1	35	36.5

Source: Author's calculation based on NSSO reports of 50th, 55th, 61st, 66th, and 68th rounds

Table 11.2 Male–female employment in the rural non-farm sector in the NER and India

NER/ India	Male/female	Percentage share of RNFE				
		1993–4	1999–2000	2004–5	2009–10	2011–12
NER	Male	28.2	27.7	30.1	35.8	39.0
	Female	18.6	20.0	19.3	33.9	35.6
	Gender gap (percentage points)	9.6	7.7	10.9	1.9	4.6
India	Male	25.9	28.6	33.5	37.2	40.6
	Female	13.8	14.6	16.7	20.6	25.1
	Gender gap	12.1	14.0	16.8	16.6	15.5

Source: Author's calculation based on various census reports for 1991 and 2001 and NSSO reports of 50th, 55th, 61st, 66th, and 68th rounds

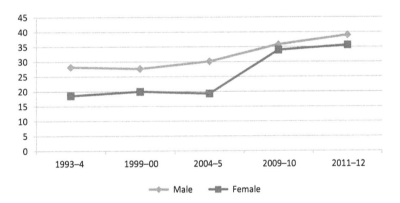

Figure 11.2 Male-female employment in the rural non-farm sector in the NER and India

Source: Data from Table 11.2

whole of the 1990s and up to 2005, the NER has not experienced any kind of increased employment diversification in its rural sector with respect to women. Subsequent to mid-2000, there had been a significant increase in the share of women's employment in the rural non-farm sector. The gender gap in RNFE, which was 9.6 percentage points in 1992–3, had almost closed in 2009–10. It has marginally increased to 4.6 percentage point during 2011–12. For the country as a whole, this gap maintains an undesired continuity and stands at 15.5 percentage points in 2011–12. There are states like Tripura and Manipur having very high proportion of the female workforce (80.9 and 75.9 percent, respectively) undertaking non-farm employment in the rural sector. There are also states like Arunachal Pradesh and Nagaland where the proportions of women undertaking non-farm activates in the rural sector happen to be in percentages of single digits. This kind of huge variation across states necessitates critical analysis. Such a critical explanation requires a detailed analysis of the factors responsible for the growth of RNFE individually for each state. It is most difficult to undertake such an analysis for each individual state in this chapter, and moreover this is not the mandate of this chapter. The objective of this chapter is to present a pan-North-East picture.

Table 11.3 makes it abundantly clear that the average share of RNFE for women in the North-East is much higher than the share of RNFE for women for the country as a whole. There can be different reasons for it in development theory. Some can be because of genuine development factors, and some is owing to distress factors. As seen from Table 11.4, during the period 1993–4 to 2011–12, this region has undergone a high degree of casualisation of employment for women in the rural sector.

Casual employment of women as part of total women's employment in the rural North-East has significantly increased, by 12.1 percentage points, from 11.4 percent in 1993–4 to 23.5 percent in

Table 11.3 Gender and RNFE in the North-East across states, 2011–12

States/region	Share of RNFE in percentage	
	Males	*Females*
Arunachal Pradesh	28.9	9.6
Assam	41.4	20.9
Manipur	44.1	75.9
Meghalaya	39.2	26.3
Mizoram	23.5	25.3
Nagaland	31.3	9.8
Tripura	64.9	80.9
North-East	39.0	35.6
All India	40.6	25.1

Source: Author's calculation based on NSSO report of 68th round

Table 11.4 Employment types for rural women in the North-East: 1993–4 to 2011–12

State/region	1993–4			2011–12			Percentage point increase/decrease		
	SE	RE	CE	SE	RE	CE	SE	RE	CE
Arunachal Pradesh	94.3	5.2	0.5	89.5	5.6	4.8	−4.8	0.4	4.3
Assam	49.1	18.2	32.7	64.3	17.5	18.2	15.2	−0.7	−14.5
Manipur	92.9	4.5	2.6	50.3	4.6	45.1	−42.6	0.1	42.5
Meghalaya	85.6	2.8	11.6	75.6	8.9	15.6	−10	6.1	4
Mizoram	97.5	2.2	0.3	81.3	4.3	14.4	−16.2	2.1	14.1
Nagaland	89.8	7.9	2.3	94.9	2.9	2.2	5.1	−5	−0.1
Tripura	61.2	9.1	29.7	27.2	8.2	64.5	−34	−0.9	34.8
North-East	81.5	7.1	11.4	69	7.4	23.6	−12.5	0.3	12.1
India	58.6	2.7	38.7	59.3	5.6	35.1	0.7	2.9	−3.6

Source: Author's calculation based on NSSO reports of 50th and 68th rounds

Note: SE = self employment, RE = regular employment, CE = casual employment

2011–12. The same statistic for the country during the corresponding period has witnessed a reverse trend by 3.6 percentage points. Self-employment for women in the North-East has undergone a significant decline, by 12.5 percentage points, whereas regular wage/salaried employment has almost remained unchanged. Table 11.5 makes this position explicit. Casual employment for women in the non-farm sector in the NER during the period 1993–4 to 2009–10 has undergone a huge 133.4 percentage point increase, whereas self-employment in the non-farm sector during the same period has experienced a significant 32.8 percentage point fall. The share of contributing women family workers (CWFW) has significantly increased both in the farm as well as non-farm sectors, by 95.5 and 125.9 percent, respectively.

These developments of a large increase in casual female employment, substantial decrease in self-employment and stagnancy in regular wage/salaried employment after economic reforms, examined with the nature of changes in the shares of different segments of RNFE (discussed in the subsequent section), indicates the fact that the distress factor could be one of the important reasons for the growth in female rural non-farm employment in this region. Hence, it can be reasonably argued that the rural labour market in the North-East for women continues to remain in a state of distress,

Table 11.5 Share (%) of farm and non-farm employment types in total female employment by region

Region	Type of employment among female workforce, 2009–10							Percentage change in type of employment among female workforce, 1983–4 to 2009–10						
	SE		CFW		RE	CE		SE		CFW		RE	CE	
	F	NF	F	NF		F	NF	F	NF	F	NF		F	NF
North-East	12.1	7.3	39.6	3.2	14.2	12.0	11.6	−59.5	−32.8	95.5	125.9	−27.0	−8.6	133.4
India	10.7	8.0	29.0	4.6	10.5	28.4	8.8	−46.5	44.4	−2.9	14.5	70.3	−5.	95.0

Source: Author's calculation based on NSSO reports of 50th, 55th, 61st, 66th, and 68th rounds

Note: SE = self-employment, CFW = contributory family workers, RE = regular wage/salaried employment, CE = casual employment, F = farm sector, NF = non-farm sector

showing low productivity and lack of any meaningful structural transformation. It also reminds us of an emerging situation of gender vulnerability in the region, notwithstanding the fast reduction/ elimination of a gender gap in the RNFE space. This gender deprivation is visible when more and more rural women in the workforce are pushed to undertake supportive, residual and casual work in the region.

Statewide, when we scan through the nature of rural employment for women given under Table 11.4, we again come across diverse trends and high degrees of variation. Five out of the seven states in the region, namely, Manipur, Tripura, Mizoram, Arunachal and Meghalaya, have experienced an increase in casual employment for women. Of these five, the magnitude of the increase in casual employment is very high for Manipur and Tripura (42.5 and 34.8 percent, respectively). These are also the five states which have experienced a very high to moderate fall in self-employment. Tripura, Nagaland and Assam are the three states which exhibit a fall in the proportion of regular wage/salaried employment, and the other four states show marginal increases in such proportional shares. This provides us an important insight that the rural labour market for women in the region exhibits both elements of uniformity and heterogeneity. The uniformity dimension is reflected in the broad casualisation trend, and the heterogeneity aspect is visible when states like Assam and Nagaland show significant deviations to this trend. Women's employment in the rural economy of Assam over this period of 18 years shows a moderate fall (14.5 percentage points) in casual employment and almost an equal percentage point rise in self-employment. This, again, at least in terms of the rural labour market for women, validates the often advocated theoretical and practical construct of two economies in the region, i.e., a hill economy without Assam and an economy with Assam.

Sectoral composition of RNFE

Temporal aspects of composition of RNFE

RNFE, as a theoretical construct in economics of development and as an analytical category in development practice, is not homogeneous. It consists of a number of subcategories/sectors/segments. A careful analysis of its composition can bring out a number of stylised facts having implications for rural labour markets and structural transformation theory, practice and policy in developing countries. For the NER, this type of analysis is more critical, as with such a breakdown on the basis of temporal, spatial and gender characteristics, hitherto invisible dynamics of the rural labour market can be presented in terms of focussed stylised facts having immediate implications for economic and development policies for the region. Table 11.6 gives a detailed regional picture of the temporal progression of the various segments/subcategories within the RNFE space for males and females taken together and compares the same with the all-India situation. Two important developments as seen from Table 11.6 are (a) a continuous and considerable fall in the share of public administration, education, community service, etc., from 49 percent in 1993–4 to 25 percent in 2011–12 as a segment of RNFE and (b) a sudden spurt of construction segment from a moderate share of 14.1 percent in 2004–5 to a much more visible share of 36 percent in 2011–12. The construction sector, during this period, also appears to have experienced the highest average annual growth rate, at 9.8 percent. In fact, public administration, education, community service, etc., as a segment or industrial category, has experienced a decline, as reflected in the negative annual growth rate of 1.3 percent. Another disheartening development is the gradual fall in the share of manufacturing employment, from a moderate percentage of 13.9 in 1993–4 to a low of 9.2 percent in 2011–12. A decline in the share of public administration, education, community service, etc., is understandable, as the state is gradually withdrawing from some of these related areas. Moreover, as an economy experiences more population growth and human development, varied segments of jobs are required to be created in the private sector. What is worrisome is the secular decline in employment in the manufacturing segment and an abnormal growth in the construction segment. Two of the states that have experienced a high degree of diversification in to the construction sector are Tripura and Manipur, and a more careful observation here shows that much of this diversification has happened because of casual jobs in the construction activities undertaken through public employment programmes like MGNREGA, PMGSY, etc. This gets credence for the fact that up to 2004–5, only 14.1 percent of working persons found employment in the construction sector in the region. This share suddenly increased to 31.3 percent in 2009–10 and continued to surge till 2011–12, at 35.8 percent. MGNREGA as a wage employment programme was introduced in the region in 2006 and

Table 11.6 RNFE and its different segments in the North-East and India as per usual status (ps+ss) (in percentage): persons

RNFE segments	NER				India				Growth rate: North-East
	1993–4	2004–5	2009–10	2011–12	1993–4	2004–5	2009–10	2011–12	1993–4 to 2011–12
Mining & quarrying	0.8	1.1	2.0	1.4	2.8	1.8	1.9	1.2	5.7
Manufacturing	13.9	13.0	10.0	9.2	32.4	29.7	22.4	22.8	0.2
Electricity, water, etc.	1.2	1.1	0.6	0.8	0.9	0.7	0.6	0.6	0.0
Construction	10.2	14.1	31.3	35.8	11.1	17.9	29.3	29.3	**9.8**
Transport, storage and communication	5.3	6.6	6.6	5.7	6.5	9.2	9.1	17.1	2.8
Trade, hotel & restaurant	18.8	23.4	21.3	21.8	19.9	22.3	19.9	7.9	3.3
Fin. inter, business act. etc.	0.8	0.8	1.1	0.2	1.4	1.8	1.9	0.9	–5.0
Public admn., education, community service etc.	49.0	39.9	27.1	25.1	25.0	16.6	14.9	20.3	–1.3

Source: Author's calculation based on NSSO reports of 50th, 55th, 61st, and 68th rounds

continues to be operational in the region to date. Tripura reports a high degree of women's employment in MGNREGA, and average person days created per household in MGNREGA has always remained above 85 in this state. In 2015–16, the average person-days of work in MGNREGA was 94.66. When such a high magnitude of person-days is reported in MGNREGA and simultaneously the construction sector in RNFE reports a high share of employment post-MGNREGA implementation and the state reports the highest magnitude of casualisation of rural employment, it can safely be presumed that there is a correspondence between these two developments. This again reconfirms our earlier supposition that distress factors are more at play when it comes to diversification of rural employment in the NER.

Further, notwithstanding the obvious secular fall in the share of employment in the RNFE space, subsector of public administration, education, community service, etc., still constitutes one-fourth of the total RNFE and remains as the second biggest RNFE subsector after construction in terms of share of employment. This implies that government and public sector regular employment still remains an important source of employment for people in the North-East vis-à-vis the country (see Table 11.6). The overall situation of (a) declining share of employment in the manufacturing, financial insurance, business activities and transport storage and communication sectors and (b) the sizable but falling share of employment in the government and community services sectors, coupled with the ever-increasing employment share in the construction sector, clearly brings out the fact that rural non-farm sector in the North-East is yet to emerge as an autonomous productive form of employment confirming the structural transformation thesis of economic development and migration.

Gender aspects of composition of RNFE

Table 11.7 very clearly illustrates the vulnerability of women in RNFE in the NER of India. During 2011–12, 50 percent of its female workforce in the RNFE is engaged in the construction sector, as against only 30 percent of the male workforce. Female employment has undergone negative growth during the period 1993–4 to 2011–12 in four of the important subsectors of RNFE, that is, manufacturing; transport, storage and communications; financial insurance, business, etc.; and public administration, education,

Table 11.7 RNFE and its segments in the North-East and India as per usual status (ps+ss) (in percentage): males and females

RNFE segments	Gender	North-East			India			Growth (North-East)
		1993–4	2004–5	2011–12	1993–4	2004–5	2011–12	1993–4 to 2011–12
Mining & quarrying	Male	1.0	1.3	1.9	2.7	1.8	1.3	5.1
	Female	1.6	0.5	0.9	2.8	1.8	1.1	0.5
Manufacturing	Male	9.6	7.7	7.3	27.1	23.6	20.0	0.3
	Female	35.3	29.0	13.2	49.6	50.2	36.8	-1.7
Electricity, water, etc.	Male	0.7	1.7	1.0	1.2	0.6	0.8	3.9
	Female	0.5	0.0	0.3	0.7	0	0.3	1.2
Construction	Male	11.0	15.7	29.8	12.3	20.2	32.2	**7.6**
	Female	5.9	7.8	50.2	6.5	8.9	24.8	**16.7**
Transport, storage and communication	Male	6.4	8.3	8.0	8.5	11.3	10.4	3.1
	Female	1.0	0.5	0.4	0.7	1.1	0.6	-2.2
Trade, hotel & restaurant	Male	20.6	22.0	23.1	21.2	24.8	19.7	2.5
	Female	14.5	20.2	16.0	15.1	14.8	11.1	4.2
Fin. insurance, business, etc.	Male	1.5	1.0	0.3	1.5	2.1	1.0	-6.9
	Female	0.5	0.5	0.0	0.7	0.6	0.5	-21.0
Public adm., education, community service etc.	Male	49.2	42.3	28.7	25.5	15.6	14.5	-1.2
	Female	40.7	41.5	19.0	23.9	22.6	24.8	-0.8

Source: Author's calculation based on NSSO reports of 50th, 61st, and 68th rounds

community service, etc. All these four subsectors of RNFE are supposedly the more productive sectors. When we compare this situation with the males, it shows that males are in a better position. They are predominantly engaged in the productive subsectors of public administration, education, community services; transport, storage and communication; and trade, hotel and restaurants, and all through the period 1993–4 to 2009–10. What we read from the situation is about the pushing-up effect for women in rural areas in the field of employment because of distress and (maybe) societal influences leading to choice constraints. This illustrates a situation of despondency, choice constraint (because of capability limitations) and unevenness and structural rigidity in the rural labour market.

Spatial aspects of composition of RNFE

Spatial dynamics of composition of RNFE in the region is explained in Table 11.8 (for females) and in Table 11.9 (for males). During 2011–12, in three of the states, that is, Tripura, Manipur and Mizoram, more than 50 percent of the female workforce in the RNFE are engaged in the construction subsector of RNFE. These are also three states where MGNREGA has provided higher days of average man-days per household. This certainly makes us deduce, subject to subsequent confirmation through productivity studies, that distress factors are more at play in these three states when it comes to diversification of employment for women. When it comes to employment in trade, hotel and restaurant category, for females, the states of Meghalaya and Nagaland do well. For Meghalaya, this may be because of its nature of being a state for tourists and its floating population from the neighbouring state of Assam. For males, the states of Assam, Meghalaya and Arunachal Pradesh have a high share of employment in this sector. The public administration, education and community services subsector has a predominately higher share in RNFE for women in the state of Arunachal Pradesh (68.38 percent), followed by the states of Assam (48.11percent) and Meghalaya (35.18 percent). This may be because of the predominance of government initiatives in Arunachal Pradesh in the spheres of education, health, infrastructure and public services and the dominance of the government, churches, etc., in providing education and health services in the state of Meghalaya, and a sizable number of women working as domestic help in the state. For the

Table 11.8 RNFE and its segments in north-eastern states as per usual status (ps+ss) (in percentage): males, 2011–12

Industry	Arunachal	Assam	Manipur	Meghalaya	Mizoram	Nagaland	Tripura	North-East
Mining & quarrying	0.00	1.11	0.60	3.78	2.51	0.00	0.00	0.90
Manufacturing	0.42	16.06	23.02	7.12	0.81	12.60	12.56	13.11
Electricity, water, etc.	0.00	0.00	0.91	0.20	0.41	0.20	0.00	0.34
Construction	14.44	15.1	53.73	14.17	53.65	26.12	74.55	50.21
Transport, storage and communication	2.72	1.37	0.05	0.35	0.00	1.52	0.05	0.35
Trade, hotel & restaurant	17.05	18.23	14.88	42.98	28.44	34.96	1.79	16.07
Fin. inter, business, etc.	0.00	0.00	0.00	0.00	0.00	0.00	0.01	0.00
Public adm., education, community service, etc.	65.38	48.11	7.41	35.18	16.69	24.59	11.03	19.02

Source: Author's calculation based on NSSO report of 68th round

Table 11.9 RNFE and its segments in north-eastern states as per usual status (ps+ss) (in percentage): females, 2011–12

RNFE Segments	Arunachal	Assam	Manipur	Meghalaya	Mizoram	Nagaland	Tripura	North-East
Mining & quarrying	0.87	0.39	0.80	9.19	0.21	0.86	0.68	1.87
Manufacturing	3.95	14.27	7.14	6.56	7.10	1.82	7.61	7.31
Electricity, water, etc.	1.66	0.05	0.09	0.59	1.36	5.37	0.08	1.03
Construction	19.95	17.53	31.49	21.38	22.03	10.29	58.02	29.76
Transport, storage and communication	4.92	9.39	9.50	13.57	6.13	9.78	3.92	8.00
Trade, hotel & restaurant	25.67	35.39	16.37	26.05	19.18	23.05	18.30	23.10
Fin. inter, business, etc.	0.17	0.65	0.70	0.08	0.00	0.00	0.22	0.28
Public admn., education, community service, etc.	42.81	22.33	33.90	22.58	43.98	48.82	11.18	28.66

Source: Author's calculation based on NSSO report of 68th round

state of Assam, it could be due to the dominance of the government, church, communities and other religious and social institutions, as well as a sizable number of women working as domestic help. Therefore, the composition analysis of RNFE in terms of its different sectors demonstrates a situation of heterogeneity, with some degree of core uniformity, with respect to employment in the sectors of construction and trade, hotel and restaurants.

RNFE and its determinants

The most important part is to answer the question: what are the important factors that have led to the diversification of employment in the rural economy of the North-East? It is not easy to answer this question, going by the heterogeneity in RNFE in the North-East with respect to gender, space and composition. However, to answer some of the research questions that we raised in the second section, we need to undertake some economic analysis to find out critical factors that could have caused the growth of RNFE in the North-East. Again, we have in the course of our discussion and analysis in the third section partially answered some such questions. However, these answers need also to be reconfirmed through some kind of appropriate quantitative economic analysis.

In the literature of development and labour economics, these factors are broadly classified as pull (development) and push (distress) factors. Some of the identified and tested pull factors happen to be: (a) agricultural growth (Mellor 1976; Gaiha and Imai 2008), (b) urbanisation (Unni 1989; Hazell and Haggblade 1991), (c) literacy (Reardon 1998; Reardon et al. 2001; Ranjan 2009), (d) commercialisation of agriculture (Vaidyanathan 1986) and (e) infrastructure (World Bank 1978; Jonasson and Helfand 2010). The important push or distress factors that have been found to influence the growth of RNFE are: (a) declining land to man ratio and unemployment (Vaidyanathan 1986; Verma and Verma 1995), (b) poverty (Srivastav and Dubey 2002) and (c) the unemployment rate (Vaidyanathan 1986; Bhaumik 2002).

In the context of the North-East, along with the studies undertaken by the present author, Panda (1999, 2012), Mishra (2007), and Srivastav and Dubey (2002) have identified agricultural growth, literacy and urbanisation to be important pull factors for the growth of RNFE in the region. They have also identified the size of the land-holding and poverty to be important push factors for the growth of RNFE. Undertaking an economic analysis of factors responsible for the growth of RNFE in the North-East based on secondary data requires either cross-sectional or time series data. Time series data are not reported by any agency, that is, neither by census nor by NSSO. What is reported by them are cross-sectional data at different periods of time. Here also, census authorities have not yet released data for economic classification of household activities for the latest census year of 2011 for all the north-eastern states. NSSO data on economic activities in its reports are usually provided at the level of the states but not at disaggregated levels. This thus poses a problem in undertaking such an intended economic analysis. To overcome this problem, here we report, with little modification, an economic analysis that we had earlier undertaken in 2012 based on field data collected as a part of a research project from VVGNLI, NOIDA. In this analysis, we present a binary logit model that estimates the coefficients of factors governing the probability of participation of households in RNFE. These data were collected from 1000 households spread over 10 villages and five districts in Assam and Meghalaya (details given in Appendix at the end of the chapter). The determining factors through collected data were grouped into two classes – pull or push. Key pull factors included in the model are urban proximity, agricultural growth, access to credit and education of the head of the household. In the push category, household poverty and land ownership were taken in. Household poverty is taken as a binary variable based on whether the sample household belongs to a poor class or not. Households having an annual gross income of Rs 30,000 or less have been classified as living below poverty. This is based on the prevailing practice in both the states in classifying households if they are poor or not. The variable details are given as follows:

a   Dependent variable, that is, engagement in primary occupation (PO): PO = 1, if engaged in non-farm, otherwise 0
b   Independent variables:

- EDUHEAD = Education of the head of household measured in terms of number of years of
- HHSIZ = Size of the household in terms of members
- HHIAL = Household annual income from agriculture (proxy for agricultural growth)
- LDOWN = Land owned by the household

- ACCRDT_D = Access to credit dummy = 1 if the household has access to credit; = 0, otherwise
- HHPOV = Household poverty dummy, = 1 if the household is a BPL household; = 0 otherwise, that is, if an APL household
- DISTNUC = Distance of the household from the nearest urban centre, measured in terms of km

The regression run gives the following result reported in Table 11.10.

The model offers a robust prediction. Both the Cox & Snell, as well as Nagelkerke R square values are reasonably high. The model makes it obvious that probability of participation of the households in non-farm activity is significantly influenced by household income from agriculture, access to credit, household poverty and distance from the nearest urban centre. Expansion in rural income derived from agriculture is presumed to have impacted positively the growth of RNFE, primarily through enhanced consumption demand. Access to credit and urban proximity (measured as distance from nearest urban centre) are also found to positively impact the growth of RNFE and the coefficient values are statistically significant. The implication of a statistically significant value of ACCRDT_D coefficient is that the households who have access

Table 11.10 Determinants of participation of households in non-farm activity: binary logistic regression results

Variable	B	SE	WALD
EDUHEAD	.036	.040	.777
HHSIZ	.102	.061	2.826
HHIAL	.000*	.000	187.511
LDOWN	−.034	.032	1.125
ACCRDT_D	1.329*	.450	8.708
HHPOV	2.297*	.388	34.975
DISTNUC	−.049*	.013	13.787
Constant	2.595*	.568	20.862
N	1000		
−2 Log likelihood	407.555		
Cox & Snell R square	.581		
Nagelkerke R square	.806		

Source: Data collected from 1000 households spread over 10 villages and five districts in Assam and Meghalaya

Note: * Significant at 1 percent level

to credit have ventured to undertake non-farm activities. A negative but statistically significant value of DISTNUC implies that the less the distance of the household from the nearest urban centre, the greater is the likelihood of the household's participation in non-farm activities. Education of the head of household and household size although are positively related to RNFE expansion, the value of their coefficients are not statistically significant. Education coefficient being positive but not statistically significant implies that either education level in the study area has not reached that critical level to make the desired impact on pursuing non-farm activities or much of the employment type in the study area is not high-end non-farm activities requiring higher educational qualifications. Poverty status of the household is an important dummy variable affecting the household's capacity to undertake more non-farm activities. Therefore, the growth of RNFE in the North-East can be attributed to both pull as well as push factors. However, this result of ours is based on micro data collected through a field survey. Hence, generalisation for the whole region based on limited field survey data may not be very adequate.

Critical findings, conclusion and suggestions

Based on this analysis and discussion, we present some critical findings here, followed by our concluding remarks and suggestions for policy.

Critical findings

The critical findings can be listed as:

- The rural economy of the North-East at the macro level, based on analysis of data with respect to the nature of the changing activity profile of the workforce and the sectoral composition of RNFE, shows no appreciable signs of confirmation to the structural transformation theory. Alternatively, its rural labour market remains inefficient and heterogeneous and signals the presence of distress diversification and casualisation of employment. Micro study undertaken at the household level presents a mixed picture. It finds both the pull factors and push factors being responsible for the growth of RNFE in the region, thereby confirming to both Mellore's thesis of positive diversification through increase in agricultural productivity and Vaidyana-than's thesis of distress diversification because of poverty.

- Post economic reforms, this region vis-à-vis the country has undergone comparatively increased diversification of its rural employment space. However, this diversification is marked by unevenness with respect to the share of RNFE across states and over time.

- Subsequent to mid-2000, there has been a significant increase in the share of women's employment in the rural non-farm sector. The gender gap in RNFE which was very visible in the early 1990s, had almost closed in 2009–10 and marginally increased in 2011–12. However, the rural labour market in the North-East for women continues to remain in a state of distress, marked with low productivity and lack of any meaningful structural transformation. This reminds us of an emerging situation of gender vulnerability in the region, notwithstanding the fast reduction/elimination of the gender gap in the RNFE space. Further, there is a pushing-up effect for women in rural areas in the field of employment because of distress and perhaps societal influences leading to choice constraints in the rural labour market.

- The rural labour market for women shows a spatial dualism validating the often advocated theoretical and practical construct of two economies in the region, that is, a hill economy without Assam and an economy with Assam.

- In the composition front of RNFE, three very important developments are discernible. These are: (a) there is a continuous and considerable fall in the share of public administration, education, community service as a segment of RNFE, (b) the sudden spurt of the construction segment in RNFE, (c) a secular fall in the share of manufacturing employment in RNFE.

- The overall situation of (a) declining share of employment in manufacturing, financial insurance, business activities, and transport storage and communication sectors and (b) the sizable but falling share of employment in the government and community services sector coupled with the ever-increasing employment share in the construction sector clearly brings out the fact that the rural non-farm sector in the North-East is yet to emerge as an autonomous productive form of employment confirming the structural transformation thesis of economic development and migration.

Conclusion, suggestions and limitations

As the RNFE space for women reflects gender vulnerability, distressed pushed diversification, increased casualisation, and hill-non hill spatial dualism, there is an urgent need to improve the quality and productivity of women's employment in the region through measures of intervention and inducement. These measures should aim at reducing and eliminating capability and choice constraints for women through the involvement of multiple establishments like the government, market, community and civil society.

Since the diversification process in rural employment in the region is primarily distress-driven and to a less extent development-driven, and the rural non-farm sector in the North-East is yet to emerge as an autonomous productive form of employment confirming the structural transformation thesis of economic development and migration, sectoral productivity studies need to be undertaken to find out the productivities of each sector – the reasons for them being unproductive/less productive – and possible ways of calibration to make them productive. The production linkage aspect of agricultural growth needs to be primarily focussed on. Thus, to propel positive growth in the non-farm sector, it is essential to undertake immediate regional, state and central-level action plans to increase agricultural productivity through crop diversification, commercialisation, market expansion, and transfer of labour to selected potential high productive non-farm sectors. One important limitation of this chapter is the lack of productivity estimates for different segments of the rural non-farm sector. In future, this aspect of RNFE can be taken up for a detailed study.

Note

1 Sikkim has not been included in this study as Sikkim became a part of North-East Council in 2002.

References

Bhaumik, Shankar Kumar. 2002. 'Employment Diversification in Rural India: A State Level Analysis', *The Indian Journal of Labor Economics*, 45(4): 719–769.

Chenery, H. B. 1960. 'Patterns of Industrial Growth', *American Economic Review*, 50(4): 624–654.

Clark, C. 1940. *Conditions of Economic Progress*, London: Macmillan & Co Ltd.

Fisher, A. G. B. 1939. 'Production: Primary, Secondary and Tertiary', *Economic Record*, 15(1): 24–38.

Gaiha, R. and K. Imai. 2008. 'Do Institutions Matter in Poverty Reduction? Prospects of Achieving the MDG of Poverty Reduction in Asia', *Statistica & Applicazioni*, 4(2): 129–160.

Hazell, P. B. and Haggblade, S. 1991. 'Rural – Urban Growth Linkages in India', *Indian Journal of Agricultural Economics*, 46(4): 515–529.

Hirschman, A. O. 1958. *The Strategy of Economic Development*, New Haven, CT: Yale University Press.

Jonasson, Erik and Helfand Steven. 2010. 'How Important are Locational Characteristics for Rural Non-agricultural Employment? Lessons from Brazil', *World Development*, 38(5): 727–741.

Kuznets, S. 1966. *Modern Economic Growth: Rate, Structure and Spread*, New Haven, CT: Yale University Press.

Lewis, W. A. 1954. 'Economic Development with Unlimited Supplies of Labour', *The Manchester School*, 22(2): 139–191.

Mellor, J. W. 1976. *The New Economics of Growth: A Strategy for India and the Developing World*, London: Cornell University Press.

Mishra, D. 2007. 'Rural Non-Farm Employment in Arunachal Pradesh-Growth, Composition and Determinants', *NLI Research Studies Series*, (075) June.

Myrdal, G. 1957. *Economic Theory and Underdeveloped Regions*, London: University Paperbacks, Methuen.

NSSO (National Sample Survey Organisation). 1994. *Reports on Employment and Unemployment, 50th Round*, Department of Statistics.

NSSO (National Sample Survey Organisation). 1999. *Reports on Employment and Unemployment, 55th Round*, Department of Statistics.

NSSO (National Sample Survey Organisation). 2005. *Reports on Employment and Unemployment, 61st Round*, Department of Statistics.

NSSO (National Sample Survey Organisation). 2010. *Reports on Employment and Unemployment, 66st Round*, Department of Statistics.

Nurkse, R. 1953. *Problems of Capital Formation in Underdeveloped Countries*, Oxford: Basil Blackwell.

Panda, B. 1999. 'Growth, Composition and Determinants of Rural Non-Farm Employment in Arunachal Pradesh', *The Indian Journal of Labor Economics*, 42(2): 283–289.

Panda, B. 2012. 'Growth, Composition and Determinants of Rural Non-Farm Employment in North East India', *NLI Research Studies Series* (097).

Ranis, G. 2004. 'Labour Surplus Economies', *Discussion Paper* (900), Yale University. December.

Ranis, G. and J. C. H. Fei. 1961. 'A Theory of Economic Development', *The American Economic Review*, 53(3): 452–454.

Ranjan, S. 2009. 'Growth of Rural Non-farm Employment in Uttar Pradesh: Reflections from Recent Data', *Economic and Political Weekly*, 44(4): 63–70.

Reardon, T. 1998. *Rural Non-farm Income in Developing Countries, in FAO, The State of Food and Agriculture*, Rome: FAO.

Reardon, T., J. Berdegue and G. Escobar. 2001. 'Rural Nonfarm Employment and Incomes in Latin America: Overview and Policy Implications'. *World Development*, 29(3): 395–409

Srivastav, N. and A. Dubey. 2002. 'Rural Non Farm Employment in India: Spatial Variations and Temporal Change', *Indian Journal of Labour Economics*, 45(1): 745–758.

Unni, J. 1989. 'Changes in Women's Employment in Rural Areas 1961–1983', *Economic and Political Weekly*, 24(17): 23–31.

Vaidyanathan, A. 1986. 'Labour Use in Rural India: A Study of Spatial and Temporal Variation', *Economic and Political Weekly*, 21(52): A130–146.

Verma, B. N. and V. Neelam. 1995. 'Distress Diversification from Farm to Non Farm Employment Sector in the Eastern Region', *Indian Journal of Agricultural Economics*, 50(3): 422–429.

World Bank. 1978. *Rural Enterprise and Non-Farm Employment*, Washington, DC: World Bank.

Appendix

Details of sample selection

Meghalaya	Districts	Village	Farm	Non-farm	Total
1	Jaintia hills	a. Ummulong	53	47	100
		b. Nongbah	43	57	100
2	Ribhoi	a. Byrnihat	63	54	117
		b. Lawbyrwa	47	36	83
Total of Meghalaya			206	194	400
Assam					
1	Nagaon	a. Halowa	30	70	100
		b. Niz-Narikoli	40	60	100
2	Jorhat	a. Tarajan Gayan	2	98	100
		b. Azan Gaon	13	87	100
3	Kamrup	a. Beztula	0	100	100
		b. Nadia	46	54	100
Total of Assam			131	469	600
Grand Total			337	663	1000

Source: Field Data

Chapter 12

Trends, composition and determinants of rural non-farm employment in Assam and its implication for rural income distribution

Anamika Das

With the increasing pressure of population growth on agricultural land and the failure of large-scale industrialisation policies adopted by developing countries, the importance of the rural non-farm (RNF) sector in absorbing surplus rural labour has increased immensely in recent decades. Till the 1960s, development economists emphasised the dual-sector growth model forwarded by Lewis in 1954 and Ranis-Fei in 1961, which states that surplus labour from the backward agriculture sector would be uninterruptedly absorbed by the steadily expanding modern (largely urban-based and capital-intensive) industrial sector (Chadha 1993). But the ineffectiveness of the dual-sector model in reducing rural unemployment and the gradual expansion of rural non-farm activities made policymakers to look at the RNF sector as an alternative source of rural employment. The RNF sector is defined as the sector which includes all economic activities in rural areas except agriculture, livestock, fishing and hunting (Lanjouw and Lanjouw 1995). It is a heterogeneous sector that includes activities undertaken by farm households as independent producers in their home; urban-based firms subcontracting work to farm families; non-farm activities undertaken in villages; and rural-town enterprises (ibid.). Rural workers commuting to their place of work, which may not be rurally located, also fall under the purview of our study.

In the context of developing countries, the importance of the RNF sector is manifold. The RNF sector not only contributes to the growth of rural employment but also to the growth of output and minimises rural to urban migration. Since the 1980s, the importance of the RNF sector has been growing in Asian countries such as China, Malaysia and Indonesia. China witnessed the growth of

RNF workers from 11 percent of total rural employment in 1980 to 20 percent in 1986. Town and village enterprises of China experienced 23.4 percent and 12.7 percent of the annual rate of growth of real output and employment, respectively, over the period 1978–6 (ibid.). In Malaysia, 50 percent of rural labour was in the non-farm sector in 1980 (Islam 1987). In Indonesia, rural services, commerce, manufacturing and construction absorbed more rural labour than agriculture during the period from 1971 to 1980 (Islam 1987). Farm management surveys and time allocation studies of South African households reported that 15–65 percent farmers had a secondary occupation in the non-farm sector and 15–40 percent of the total family labour hours were spent on income-generating non-farm activities (Haggblade, Steven, and Hazell 1989).

The importance of the RNF sector in India is visible both in terms of its share in rural employment and rural income. There has been an increase in the share of RNFE from 27.3 percent in 2004–5 to 35.9 percent in 2011–12, as evident in NSS 61st and 68th rounds data. Further, about 48 percent of the average rural household's income comes from the non-farm sector (Dubey 2008).

In a country like India, where the poverty level is very high, growing interest among academia and policymakers in the non-farm sector stems from the implication of the RNF sector on poverty. Composition of employment status in the non-farm sector has also undergone changes in the post-reform period. There is a decline in self-employment and an increase in casualisation of labour over the period from 1972–3 to 1993–4 (Chadha 1997; Unni and Rani 2005). There is a continuous decline of regular employment in the post-reform period (Jatav and Sen 2013).

Therefore, it is important to identify the people joining the non-farm sector, their quality of work and what prompts rural people to join the non-farm sector. Some researchers emphasise that the RNF sector acts as a residual sector absorbing those rural workers who are pushed out of agriculture (Chadha 2002; Sahu 2003; Himanshu 2007). These unskilled workers join the non-farm sector as casual labour. This pattern of shifting from agriculture to the non-agriculture sector has little impact on poverty reduction.

This essay has made an attempt to study the trends, composition and determinants of RNFE and distributional aspects of RNF income, drawing on evidence from Assam, a north-eastern state of India. RNFE in Assam has increased from 21 percent in 1993–4 to 38 percent in 2011–12 (NSS 50th and 68th round data). Assam is one of the least urbanised states in India, with seven out of every eight people still living in rural Assam (HDR Assam 2003). In comparison to the all-India figure of 25.7 percent, as many as 33.89 percent of the population lived below the poverty line in rural Assam in 2011–12 (Planning Commission 2013). The shift from traditional farming and largely subsistence-oriented systems to modern, technologically advanced and market-oriented agriculture has taken place slowly in the state and is uneven in its spread. Most importantly, uncertainties and vagaries of nature such as the regular occurrence of flooding continue to overwhelm agriculture. Therefore, it would be interesting to examine the role that the non-farm sector plays in improving rural livelihoods, especially when the capacity of agriculture to support it is limited.

After describing data sources and the methodology, the trends and composition of RNFE in Assam are examined, followed by the determinants of RNFE in this chapter. We then study its impact on income distribution and the conclusion that can be derived.

Data sources and methodology

Our study is based on both primary and secondary data. We have studied the trends and composition of RNFE in Assam in terms of its share in total rural workers using unit-level data obtained from NSS 50th, 61st and 68th round. We have considered both total as well as non-farm workers, taking their principal and subsidiary status together. Non-farm workers are those who work in industries other than agriculture and allied activities, as given by NIC codes. Taking the cue from existing literature such as Chadha (1997), Seth (1992) and Jatav (2013), we have also included those who reside in rural areas but commute to nearby urban centres for work within the category of rural non-farm workers.

We have studied the determinants of RNFE in Assam using both primary and secondary data. The secondary data used in the study pertains to NSS unit-level data for the period 2011/12. We have run logit regression to study the factors which influence an individual's decision to join the RNF sector. The logit equation we have used is

$$\ln [p/(1 - p)]_i = \beta_1 + \beta_2 X_{2i} + \ldots\ldots + \beta_7 X_{7i} + U_i$$

- p is the probability that the event Y (dependent variable) occurs, $p(Y = 1)$; i.e., $Y = 1$ if the worker joins the non-farm sector
- $p/(1 - p)$ is the 'odds ratio'
- $\ln[p/(1 - p)]$ is the log odds ratio, or 'logit'
- α is the intercept term and βs are the coefficients of independent variables X_i
- U_i are the error terms

The dependent variable is a dichotomous variable that takes 1 if the person joins the non-farm sector and 0 otherwise. The independent variables considered in our model while using secondary data are sex, level of education, caste, amount of land cultivated and ratio of dependent member (age below 15 and above 60) in the family of rural workers. To understand the effect of local factors on non-farm participation, we have used the village dummy in addition to the variables mentioned earlier while studying the determinants based on primary data.

We have examined the question of distribution of RNF income and its impact on overall income distribution using only primary data. The rationale for relying on primary data is that income data is not available with the secondary data source, such as the NSS and census data. Moreover, secondary data sources such as the NSS and census underestimate the share of non-farm employment in rural areas. Though the NSS fully captures labour allocation patterns throughout the year, it tends to overlook local factors determining rural workers' participation in the non-farm sector.

For primary survey, we have used simple random sampling. Using census data for the year 2011, we have divided the districts of Assam into high, medium and low categories, based on the percentage share of rural non-farm employment[1] (see Figure 12.1). For the primary survey, we randomly selected the Barpeta district from the medium category district. Two villages named Salekura and Borbarijar were selected randomly from the district, and from each village, a sample of 60 households were selected randomly. Two pre-tested semi-structured schedules were implemented, one at the household level and the other at the individual level, for those engaged in non-farm jobs.

We have studied the distribution of non-farm income across different landholding classes. To study the impact of RNF income on overall rural income inequality, the Gini decomposition method has been used.

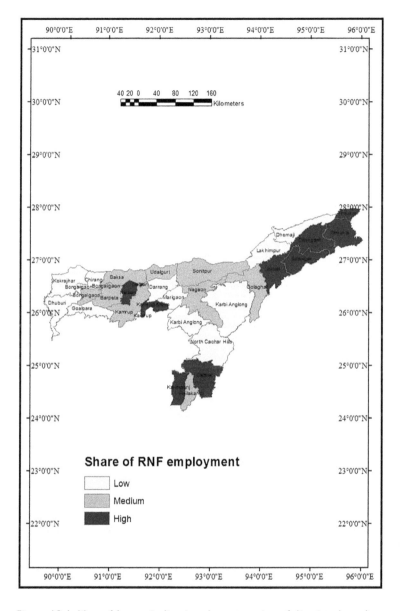

Figure 12.1 Map of Assam indicating the categories of districts based on the share of RNFE

Source: Author generated map based on Census data of the year 2011 using ARCGIS software

The equation for the Gini decomposition method can be represented as:

$$G = \sum S_k G_k R_k, \text{ } k \text{ takes the value from 1 to } k.$$

Here,

S_k signifies how important the income source is with respect to total income

G_k signifies how equally or unequally the income source is distributed

R_k signifies how the income source and the distribution of total income are correlated (if Rk is positive and large, it means that the income source is unequally distributed and flows disproportionately to those who are at the top of income distribution)

Trend of rural non-farm employment in Assam

The share of RNF workers in total employment was very low in Assam during the 1970s and 1980s, particularly compared to the states which witnessed high agricultural growth (Chadha 1997). Though RNFE showed an upward trend towards the end of the 1980s, the trend got reversed in the early years of reforms. The ratio of male workers engaged in the RNF sector to total male rural workers declined to 21.8 percent in 1993–4 from 23.5 percent in 1987–8. The ratio of female workers engaged in the RNF sector to total female workers, though considerably lower than the male counterparts, exhibited a similar trend, with the share declining from 17.7 percent in 1987–8 to 16.8 percent in 1993–4 (ibid.).

In the post-1993 period, the state saw a rebound in rural non-farm employment, with its share increasing from 20.8 percent in 1993–4 to 37.97 percent in 2011–12 (NSS 50th and 68th round reports). The share of non-farm workers compared to total male rural workers in Assam increased over this period. The share of non-farm workers compared to total female rural workers, however, declined from 16.8 percent in 1993–4 to 11.7 in 2004–05, but again increased in 2011–12. This indicates rural females had been moving in and out of agriculture during this time period.

In terms of industrial composition of the RNF sector, construction emerged as the most important sector, accounting for the bulk of the employment generated in the non-farm sector. The sector witnessed the highest positive percentage change for both male and female workers. Within the RNF sector, male employment was more diversified compared to female employment. Participation of females was mostly concentrated in 'other services' and trade and hotels in 2011–12 (see Table 12.1).

Within the non-farm sector, the employment status of rural workers varied from worker to worker. Most of the studies focussing on RNFE in India indicate that with the introduction of economic reforms in 1991, the share of regular salaried employees started declining alongside an increasing share of casual workers in India. It is evident in Table 12.2 that rural non-farm employment in Assam also showed the same trend over the period from 1993–4 to 2011–12. Self-employment had a dominant share in the RNF sector, accounting for more than 50 percent. However, during the period from 1993–4 to 2011–12, the female share of both salaried and casual workers in the non-farm sector increased in Assam.

Education and caste profile of farm and non-farm workers in Assam

Education level and caste profile act as entry barrier for workers in joining the non-farm sector (Jatav and Sen 2013). In Table 12.3, we have reported the education of farm and non-farm workers for the period 2011–12. More than 70 percent of illiterate workers in rural Assam were in the farm sector. The share of workers in the non-farm sector was higher as the level of education was higher. However, a significant share of illiterate and less-educated workers in the non-farm sector raised the question of the quality of jobs generated in the non-farm sector.

Most of the casual workers engaged in the non-farm sector are either illiterate or have a low level of education (Table 12.4). The same trend can be seen in the case of self-employed. However, workers with a medium or higher than medium level of education have better access to salaried jobs. This indicates that illiterate workers and workers with a low level of education are mostly engaged in low-quality jobs.

Both male and female workers from each of the social groups witnessed a higher share of jobs in agriculture than in the non-agricultural sector. However, in the case of ST and OBC, rural workers in agriculture sector recorded a much higher share than other categories (see Table 12.5).

Table 12.1 Trend of percentage share of rural workers (principal + subsidiary) across different broad industry categories

Industry	1993–4			2004–5			2011–12			Percentage change in the share of employment over the period		
	Persons	Male	Female	Persons	Male	Female	Persons	Male	Female	Persons	Male	Female
Agriculture and allied activity	79.2	78.2	83.2	74.3	69.6	88.3	62.03	58.6	79.04	−21.68	−25.06	−5
Non-farm sector												
Mining and quarrying	0.2	0.2	–	0.3	0.3	–	0.18	0.16	0.25	−10	−20	–
Manufacturing	3.5	2.2	8.7	3.1	2.9	3.7	5.49	5.91	3.4	56.86	168.64	−60.92
Electricity	0.3	0.3	–	0.1	0.2	–	0.02	0.02	–	−93.33	−93.33	–
Construction	0.7	0.8	0.1	2.5	3	0.8	6.57	7.26	3.13	838.57	807.5	3030
Trade, hotel and restaurant	6.9	8.2	1.9	9	11.6	1.1	12.84	14.66	3.8	86.09	78.78	100

Source: Calculated from NSS (50th, 61st and 68th rounds) unit-level data

Table 12.2 Distribution of rural non-farm workers (defined by principal and subsidiary status) in Assam according to their usual employment status

Usual employment status	All			Male			Female		
	1993–4	2004–5	2011–12	1993–4	2004–5	2011–12	1993–4	2004–5	2011–12
Self-employed	53.43	54.02	51.82	51.98	55.89	53.61	60.82	39.25	34.21
Regular salaried/wage employee	31.09	19.28	19.61	32.83	18.88	17.97	22.23	22.44	35.7
Casual wage labour	15.47	26.7	28.57	15.19	25.23	28.42	16.94	38	30.09

Source: NSS 50th, 61st, 68th reports

Table 12.3 Distribution of rural workers with different levels of education across farm and non-farm sector for the period 2011–12

Education level	Farm	Non-farm	Total
Illiterate	73.82	26.18	100
Literate without formal schooling, below primary or primary education	68	32	100
Medium and secondary	59.34	40.66	100
Higher secondary and diploma holder	29.47	70.53	100
Graduate and above	25.81	74.19	100

Source: Calculated from NSS (68th round) unit-level data

Table 12.4 Distribution of RNF workers with different status of work across education levels for the period 2011–12

Education	Self-employed	Salaried	Casual
Illiterate	6.6	4.26	24.97
Literate without formal schooling, below primary and primary education	37.7	12.7	34.96
Medium and secondary	43.5	31.1	34.02
Higher secondary and diploma holder	9.49	27	4.12
Graduate and above	2.76	24.9	1.92
Total	100	100	100

Source: Calculated from NSS (68th rounds) unit-level data

Table 12.5 Distribution of rural workers of different social groups in the farm and non-farm sectors in Assam (2011–12)

Social group	All		Male		Female	
	Farm	Non-farm	Farm	Non-farm	Farm	Non-farm
ST	74.01	25.99	69.73	30.27	89.66	10.34
SC	57.07	42.93	55.16	44.84	67.24	32.76
OBC	66.73	33.27	62.74	37.26	80.41	19.59
Others	55.57	44.43	53.25	46.75	73.55	26.45

Source: Calculated from NSS (68th round) unit-level data

Determinants of RNF participation

The present section will focus on the determinants of RNFE. We have examined the determinants of non-farm participation by rural workers in Assam, using the NSS 68th round data, i.e., for the period 2011–12.

The result of logistic regression shows that sex, level of education, and land cultivated influence non-farm participation of rural workers in Assam (see Table 12.6). The negative sign of the coefficient of the variable sex indicates that compared to males, females are less likely to join the non-farm sector in Assam. Inadequate access of females in the non-farm sector has been documented in the extant literature (Chadha 1997; Unni and Rani 2005; Binswanger 2013; Jatav and Sen 2013; Binswanger-Mkhize 2013).

The probability of participation of rural workers in the non-farm sector increases with the improvement of education level, indicating

Table 12.6 Results of logit regression to analyse the determinants of rural non-farm employment

Independent variable	Coefficient	Std. Err.	P > z	Marginal Effects(dy/dx)
Sex: Male (RC)	−0.98***	0.13	0.00	−.18
Education level: Illiterate (RC)				
Primary	0.52***	0.15	0.00	.09
Medium and secondary	0.91***	0.15	0.00	.17
Higher secondary and diploma	2.23***	0.20	0.00	.43
Graduate and above	3.01***	0.26	0.00	.55
Caste: ST (RC)				
SC	−0.05	0.16	0.76	−.01
OBC	−0.03	0.13	0.81	−.005
Others	0.13	0.12	0.29	.02
Land cultivated	(−) 0.001***	0.00	0.00	−.0002
Land cultivated squared	0.00***	0.00	0.00	1.44e − 08
Dependency ratio of household	0.19	0.21	0.37	.04
Constant	−0.12	0.52	0.00	

No. of observations = 2836; LR chi squared (11) = 738.30; Prob > chi squared = 0.000; Pseudo R squared = 0.1915;

Source: NSS 68th Round Data

Note: RC means reference category; coefficients with *** are significant at 1%

that a low level of education acts as an entry barrier for rural workers who join the non-farm sector. A similar trend has also been noted in the extant literature (Chadha 1997; Unni and Rani 2005; Jatav and Sen 2013; Binswanger-Mkhize 2013). The negative coefficient of land cultivated indicates that rural workers with less cultivable land are more likely to join the non-farm sector. Thorat (1993) also finds the inverse relationship between landholding and the share of rural households engaged in the non-farm sector for 1977–8, 1983–4 and 1987–8.

However, the positive sign of the square term of land cultivated indicates a non-linear relationship between landholding and non-farm participation. This suggests that the relationship between RNF participation and land cultivated is a U-shaped curve. Such a relationship between RNF participation and asset holding has also been noted in Kenya and Vietnam (Evans and Ngau 1991). As the asset holding/income of the household rises, the tendency of diversifying towards the RNF sector decreases until a threshold level is reached. After crossing this asset/income level, any increase in assets/income results in the tendency to invest the surplus in RNF sector activities.

Interestingly, caste and ratio of dependent members do not have any impact on RNF participation.

The overall results depict a mixed picture, showing the significance of both push and pull factors. As the level of education of rural workers improves, they are more likely to join the non-farm sector for higher returns. However, a U-shaped relationship between land cultivated and non-farm participation indicates that rural workers with less cultivable land are pushed out of agriculture, but beyond a threshold of land ownership, the workers probably are driven by the motivation to invest their surplus income and join the non-farm sector.

Insight from the village studies

We have defined our sample households of both the villages in terms of members working in farm and non-farm sectors. We have used the same definitions of workers and non-farm workers as those we used for NSS data, mentioned in the methodology part. The important non-farm occupations in the two villages are wage labour, driver, tailor, small trader, shopkeeper, carpenter, weaver, cook, ASHA (Accredited Social Health Activist) worker and government servants such as teacher, anganwadi[2] worker and other government jobs. The dominant occupation in the non-farm sector is wage labour, which accounts for 30 percent of the total non-farm workers, followed by carpenters (11 percent) and traders (11 percent). The qualitative study indicates another dominating source of non-farm income of rich households or households with higher land size is interest earning. Rich rural people lend money to poor, landless rural people at exorbitant rates of interest. Most of these poor are Muslims.

Taking a cue from the extant literature (Seth 1992; Chadha 1997; Jatav and Sen 2013), we consider RNF workers as those whose place of residence is rural, but they commute to urban centres for work. We have divided the households into three categories/types. Type (i) households having members working only in the non-farm sector, Type (ii) households with members working only in agriculture and allied activities. In type (iii) households where some of the members work in farms while others work in the non-farm sector. The interviews with key informants, including the *Gaonburha* (the village head), suggest that most households in the two villages earn their livelihood from their engagement in both farm and non-farm sectors. Almost all the households in the sample have livestock to support their consumption needs; however, few maintain them as a commercial venture.

Land is an important asset of rural households, and degrees of non-farm participation vary across landholdings (Table 12.7). A significant share of both marginal and small landholding households

Table 12.7 Percentage distribution of households with different amounts of land across varied non-farm participation

Group of cropped areas	Households			
	Type (i)	Type (ii)	Type (iii)	Total
Landless	91.89(34)	2.7(1)	5.41(2)	100(37)
Marginal (up to 2.5 acres)	2.82(2)	19.72(14)	77.46(55)	100(71)
Small (up to 5 acres)	0	22.22(2)	77.78(7)	9
Semi-medium, medium and large (above 5 acres)	0	0	100(3)	3

Source: Primary Survey

Note: Type (i) households are those where all the working members of the households work in the non-farm sector.
Type (ii) households are those where all working members work in the farm sector.
Type (iii) households are those where members work in both the farm and non-farm sectors.

diversify their livelihood. Households with a large farm size are also the households with members working in farm and non-farm sectors.

Across the two villages, our sample consists of 280 workers as defined by usual principal and subsidiary status taken together. Taking usual principal and subsidiary status together, 44 percent of workers work in the farm sector and 56 percent work in the non-farm sector. As many as 59 percent of the male workers work in the non-farm sector, while only 48 percent of female workers participate in the non-farm sector.

A higher share of illiterate workers are found to be involved in the non-farm sector compared to the farm sector (see Table 12.8). A similar trend is also noted for workers with education level more than higher secondary. It indicates that rural workers in these villages with a very low level of education join low-quality non-farm jobs due to distress factors. However, educated rural workers are more likely to get remunerative non-farm jobs. This trend is, however, at variance with what we observe at the all-Assam (refer to Table 12.3) state level, where most illiterate workers are found to be engaged in the agriculture sector.

The distribution of non-farm workers across different levels of education also indicates the significant presence of illiterate workers in the non-farm sector. Almost 50 percent of the male workers engaged in the non-farm sector are either illiterate or educated up to the primary level (Table 12.9). More than 40 percent of the female workers engaged in the non-farm sector report a similar education

Table 12.8 Distribution of workers with different levels of education across the farm and non-farm sectors

Level of education	All		Male		Female	
	Farm	Non-farm	Farm	Non-farm	Farm	Non-farm
Illiterate	47.31	52.69	46.03	53.97	50.00	50.00
Up to primary	45.83	54.17	40.00	60.00	75.00	25.00
Middle and secondary	45.24	54.76	39.39	60.61	66.67	33.33
Higher secondary and diploma	31.25	68.75	33.33	66.67	20.00	80.00
Graduate and above	34.78	65.22	42.11	57.89	0.00	100.00

Source: Primary Survey

Table 12.9 Percentage distribution of non-farm workers across different levels of education

Level of education	All	Male	Female
Illiterate	31.01	32.95	26.77
Up to primary	16.46	18.18	18.90
Middle and secondary	29.11	29.55	31.50
Higher secondary and diploma	13.92	10.23	14.17
Graduate and above	9.49	9.09	8.66
Total	100	100	100

Source: Primary Survey

status. Thus, the significant presence of illiterate or less educated workers in the non-farm sector indicates that jobs taken up by the sample workers in the region are of poor quality and devoid of any skills.

The distribution of non-farm workers in the sample reflects a pattern, with self-employment being the most important mode of employment, followed by wage labour and salaried workers. As much as 51 percent of non-farm workers are self-employed, and 29 percent are wage labour. Salaried non-farm workers constitute only 20 percent of the total non-farm workers. The distribution of workers, when disaggregated over male and female, reflects a similar pattern.

As mentioned earlier, degrees of non-farm participation vary across landholdings. Higher participation in the non-farm sector is noticed among the landless as well as workers with more than 5 acres of cultivated land. In contrast, moderate participation in the non-farm sector is noticed among workers with medium and small size of land (Table 12.10). This tentatively suggests the U-shaped relation between the cultivated land and non-farm participation.

The degree of non-farm participation also varies across the age of workers. Younger workers have better access to the non-farm sector than the older ones. In our sample, rural workers in the 14–40 age group have a higher share in the non-farm sector than the farm sector. However, workers above 40 years have a higher share in the farm sector.

In the sample, a significant percentage of workers from STs and other categories join the non-farm sector. As much as 82 percent of ST workers in the sample are in the non-farm sector. This contrasts with the overall situation in the state, where workers in the STs tend to be concentrated in the farm sector.

Table 12.10 Percentage distribution of workers with different sizes of land cultivated across the farm and non-farm sectors

Land cultivated	Farm	Non-farm	Total
Landless	9.59	90.41	100
Marginal (up to 2.5 acres)	53.66	46.34	100
Small (2.5–5 acres)	69.70	30.30	100
Semi-medium, medium and large (above 5 acre)	40	60	100

Source: Primary Survey

Determinants of rural non-farm employment

The re-examination of the same question using primary data lends credence to the results noted in the secondary data. The results of logistic regression using village data confirms the importance of land scarcity, sex, age and the education of rural workers in non-farm participation (Table 12.11). Compared to illiterate rural workers, workers with higher secondary and diploma-level education are more likely to join the non-farm sector. The negatively significant coefficient of the variable sex indicates that compared to males, females are less likely to join the non-farm sector. The age of rural workers also has a significant impact on non-farm participation. Generally, old rural people do not want to leave their traditional occupation, i.e., agriculture. Besides, young workers have higher adaptability to learn skills to join the non-farm sector. Binswanger-Mkhize (2013) states that young and educated rural workers, particularly males, have better access to the non-farm sector. Primary data also confirms the U-shaped relationship between cultivated area and non-farm participation.

When we control the region-specific factor through the region dummy (with Borbarizar as a reference category), the coefficient of the region dummy is found to be positive and significant. This suggests that workers from Salekura, a village frequently ravaged by flood, are more likely to join the non-farm sector. This can be explained in terms of the insight from Ellis (2000), which argues that rural people diversify their livelihood for desperate reasons such as a natural disaster (e.g., flooding), when the chance of crop failure is very high.

Interestingly, compared to SCs, STs and workers from other categories are more likely to join the non-farm sector. Our results

Table 12.11 Result of logit regression

Independent variable	Coefficient	Std. Err.	P > z	Marginal effects (dy/dx)
Education level: Illiterate (RC)				
Up to primary	0.083	0.436	0.849	0.02
Middle and secondary	−0.083	0.379	0.827	−0.02
Higher secondary and diploma	0.876*	0.510	0.086	0.16
Graduate and above	0.803	0.560	0.152	0.15
Total cultivated area	−1.935***	0.327	0	−0.36
Total cultivated area square	0.277***	0.054	0	0.05
Sex: Male(RC)	−0.863**	0.360	0.016	−0.16
Village dummy: Village Borbarizar (RC)	0.841**	0.381	0.027	0.15
Age	−0.029***	0.011	0.009	−0.01
Caste: SC(RC)				
ST	1.576**	0.687	0.022	0.28
OBC	0.000	(empty)		
Others	0.233*	0.410	0.57	0.05
Constant	2.731***	0.871	0.002	

Number of observations = 275; LR Chi^2(11) = 71.48; Prob > chi^2 = 0.000; Pseudo R^2 = 0.1903

Source: Primary Data

Note: Coefficients with single, double and triple stars indicate level of significance at 10 percent, 5 percent and 1 percent, respectively. RC means reference category.

indicate that caste acts as an entry barrier in non-farm participation. However, ST workers who are economically and socially backward might join low-quality non-farm jobs due to distress factors. However, this is at variance with our results at the all-Assam level, which show that the caste of an individual rural worker does not have any significant impact on his non-farm participation.

Distribution of non-farm income across landholding classes

The distribution of non-farm income across households with different sizes of landholding indicates that workers with more than 5 acres of land have a disproportionate claim over the income accruing from the non-farm sector. While they account for about 40 percent of the total non-farm income, the remaining 60 percent is distributed among the landless, marginal and owners of small landholdings, indicating a skewed distribution of rural non-farm income (Table 12.12). However, non-farm workers with more than 5 acres of land account for only 4 percent of the total non-farm workers (Table 12.12). The share of non-farm income in the total household income declines as the size of landholding of a household increases, even though the absolute level of non-farm income increases (Table 12.13). Reardon (1998) has noted this trend in a number of case studies. As already noted in the review, landless, low-skilled rural workers face substantial entry barriers in the remunerative non-farm activities (ibid.). They join the non-farm sector in low-paid casual jobs with little time for farm work. Though their share

Table 12.12 Distribution of RNF workers across landholding classes

Land owned	Share of RNF workers
Landless	41.77
Marginal (up to 2.5 acres)	48.1
Small (2.5–5 acres)	6.33
Semi, medium and large (above 5 acres)	3.8
Total	100

Source: Calculated from primary survey

Table 12.13 Distribution of average non-farm income and the share of average non-farm income in the average household income across households with different landholdings

Land owned	Average non-farm income	Percentage of total non-farm income	Share of average non-farm income in the average household income
Landless	61,837.84	18.28	87.47
Marginal (up to 2.5 acres)	69,652.8	20.6	69.00
Small (2.5–5 acres)	73,200	21.64	51.32
Semi, medium and large (above 5 acres)	133,500	39.47	44.54

Source: Calculated from primary survey

of non-farm income in total income is high, absolute income from the non-farm sector is low.

Effect of non-farm income on overall income distribution

The Gini decomposition method has been used to see the impact of farm and non-farm income of households on the total income inequality. The equation for Gini decomposition method can be represented as

$$G = \sum S_k G_k R_k, \ k \text{ takes the value from 1 to } k.$$

Here,

S_k signifies how important an income source is with respect to total income

G_k signifies how equally or unequally distributed the income source is

R_k signifies how the income source and the distribution of total income are correlated (if Rk is positive and large, it means that the income source is unequally distributed and flows disproportionately to those who are at the top of income distribution)

The result shows that non-farm income is less unequally distributed with a G_k value of 0.54 than farm income with a G_k value of 0.65. But the positive percentage change in overall income inequality (0.05), others being constant, due to a 1 percent increase in non-farm income indicates that non-farm income increases overall income inequality (see Table 12.14).

Table 12.14 Gini decomposition by income source

Total income variable: Total income of the household

Source	S_k	G_k	R_k	Share	Percent change
Farm income	0.28	0.65	0.58	0.24	−0.05
Non-farm income	0.72	0.54	0.89	0.76	0.05
Total income		0.45			

Source: Calculated from primary survey data

The percentage change shows the effect of a small change in a particular income source on inequality.

However, we find that a 1 percent increase in farm income, others being constant, reduces income inequality (negative percentage change). The favourable effect of farm income on overall income distribution may be because of an increase in the agricultural labour wage following the expansion of RNFE.

The Gini correlation between non-farm income and total income (R_k) is as high as 0.89, indicating that non-farm income favours the rich more than the poor. Similar evidence was noted in Burkina Faso, Tanzania and Nigeria (Matlon 1979; Reardon and Taylor 1996). However, the evidence for reducing the effect of non-farm income on overall rural income inequality was found in Ecuador, Pakistan, Taiwan, the southern zone of Burkina Faso and Punjabi villages of India (Chinn 1979; Chadha 1986; Adams 1995; Reardon and Taylor 1996; Lanjouw and Stern 1998).

The unfavourable impact of RNF income on overall income distribution indicates that non-farm employment may increase the absolute income of the poor, but not to the same extent as it increases the income of the rich because of the entry barrier of poor, unskilled rural workers in remunerative non-farm jobs.

However, it is difficult for researchers to attribute the increase in overall income inequality to RNF income, as there is no information about the distribution of overall income in the absence of non-farm income. If those currently employed in the non-farm sector were engaged as farm labour, the wage might be even lower due to an increase in labour supply, leading to increased overall income inequality (Reardon 1998).

Conclusion

This chapter examines the trends, composition and determinants of RNFE using NSSO unit-level data. Given that there may be local region-specific factors which may influence participation in the non-farm sector, the essay also revisits the same question using primary data collected from two villages chosen from the Barpeta district. Further, the question of distributional aspects of non-farm income cannot be answered by relying on the secondary data, as it does not have information on the income earned by rural households from different sources. The chapter makes an attempt to answer this question using household survey data collected in the two villages.

Assam has witnessed an increasing trend in the share of RNFE over the period from 1993–4 to 2011–12. The state has witnessed an increase in rural employment in all the industrial categories of the non-farm sector except mining and electricity. The construction sector accounts for the highest percentage change in the share of rural employment in the state, followed by trade, hotel and restaurant. In the non-farm sector, workers are mostly self-employed. There has been an increase in the share of casual workers in the non-farm sector, with a continuous decrease in the share of salaried workers.

A disaggregation of RNFE in terms of sex shows that male RNFE has witnessed the highest positive percentage change in the construction sector, followed by the manufacturing sector. As regards female participation in RNFE, the positive percentage change in female participation in RNFE is highest in the construction sector over the period from 1993–4 to 2011–12, but the percentage change in their participation in the manufacturing sector has been negative over the same period. On the whole, the manufacturing sector in Assam accounts for only 5.49 percent of rural workers in 2011–12.

The study of determinants of RNFE at the individual level signifies that both push and pull factors are in operation when it comes to participating in the non-farm sector. As the level of education of rural workers improves, they are more likely to join the non-farm sector for higher returns. However, a U-shaped relationship between land cultivated and non-farm participation indicates that rural workers with little or no cultivable land are being pushed out of agriculture, and those with higher cultivable land may be lured to the non-farm sector by the possibility of higher potential returns of their investment of surplus generated in the agriculture sector.

What is the distributional consequence of non-farm participation? Evidence generated in the primary data points towards unequal distribution of RNF income, which is more likely to be concentrated among the households with a larger size of land compared to those with a smaller size of landholding.

The results of Gini decomposition suggest that income from the non-farm sector raises the overall income inequality. The results may suggest that rural workers with better access to resources and skills are benefited more than their poorer counterparts, who face entry barriers in remunerative non-farm jobs. However, farm income has a favourable effect on overall income distribution. The favourable effect of farm income on overall income distribution may be because of an increase in agricultural labour wages due to the expansion of RNFE.

Though there has been an expansion of RNFE in Assam during the study period, the quality of jobs generated in the sector is of concern. There is hardly any job creation in the traditional non-farm sectors such as weaving, manufacturing of silk and brass utensils. Most of the expansion of jobs in RNF has occurred in construction and trade, hotel and restaurant, where most of the workers are casual and self-employed.

The U-shaped relationship between land cultivated and non-farm participation indicates that some resource-poor rural people are joining low quality non-farm jobs to support their fragile livelihood, but the relatively better off people with access to resources, both physical and social, take up more remunerative non-farm jobs. This necessitates actions and programmes by the government to impart education and skills to rural workers so that the movement of workers from the farm to the non-farm sector is driven by higher earnings and better standards of living.

Notes

1 In the 2011 census, economic activities of workers are classified as cultivators, agricultural labourer, working in household industries and other work. We define non-farm workers for the 2001 and 2011 census as those who are working in household industries and other jobs.
2 Anganwadi was set up in 1985 in India as a centre for rural mother and child care. It is part of the Integrated Child Development Services program to combat child hunger and malnutrition (http://healthopine. com/the-anganwadi-workers-of-india-connecting-for-health-at-the-grassroots/).

References

Adams, R. H., Jr. 1995. *Sources of Income Inequality and Poverty in Rural Pakistan: Research Report 102*, Washington, DC: International Food Policy Research Institute.
Assam Human Development Report. 2003. Planning & Development Department, Government of Assam.
Binswanger-Mkhize, Hans P. 2013. 'The Stunted Structural Transformation of Indian Economy Agriculture, Manufacturing and the Rural Non-farm Economy', *Economic and Political Weekly*, 47: 26–27.
Chadha, Gopal Krishna. 1986. 'The Off-farm Economic Structure of Agriculturally Growing Regions: A Study of Indian Punjab', in R. T. Shand

(ed.), *Off-farm Employment in the Development of Rural Asia*, Canberra: Australian National University.

Chadha, Gopal Krishna. 1993. 'Non-Farm Employment for Rural Households In India : Evidence vs. Prognosis', *The Journal of Labour Economics*, 36(3).

Chadha, Gopal Krishna. 1997. 'Access of Rural Households to Nonfarm Employment: Trends, Constraints and Possibilities', in G. K. Chadha and Alakh N. Sharma (eds), *Growth, Employment and Poverty: Change and Continuity in Rural India*, New Delhi: Vikash Publishing House Private Limited.

Chadha, Gopal Krishna. 2002. 'Rural Non-farm Employment in India: What Does Recent Experience Teach Us?' *The Indian Journal of Labour Economics*, 45(4): 663–694.

Chinn, Dennis L. 1979. 'Rural Poverty and the Structure of Farm Household Income in Developing Countries: Evidence from Taiwan', *Economic Development and Cultural Change*, 27: 283–301.

Dubey, Amresh. 2008. *Consumption, Income and Inequality in India. Background*, paper prepared for India Poverty Assessment Report, Washington, DC: World Bank.

Ellis, Frank. 2000. 'The Determinants of Rural Livelihood Diversification in Developing Countries', *Journal of Agricultural Economics*, 51(2): 289–302.

Evans, Hugh Emrys and Peter Ngau. 1991. 'Rural – Urban Relations, Household Income Diversification and Agricultural Productivity', *Development and Change*, 22(3): 519–545.

Haggblade, Steven and Peter Hazell. 1989. 'Agricultural Technology and Farm Nonfarm Growth Linkages', *Agricultural Economics*, 3: 345–364.

Himanshu. 2007. 'Recent Trends in Poverty and Inequality: Some Preliminary Results', *Economic and Political Weekly*, 42(6): 497–508.

Islam, Rizwanul. 1987. *Rural Industrialisation and Employment in Asia*, New Delhi: ILO-ARTEP.

Jatav, Manoj and Sucharita Sen. 2013. 'Drivers of Rural Nonfarm Employment in Rural India', *Economic and Political Weekly* 48(26, 27): 14–21.

Lanjouw, Jean O. and Peter Lanjouw. 1995. 'Rural Non-Farm Employment: A Study', *Policy Research Working Paper 1463*, Washington, DC: World Bank.

Lanjouw, Peter and Nicholas Stern. 1998. *Economic Development in Palanpur Over Five Decades*, Oxford: Oxford University Press.

Matlon, Peter J. 1979. *Income Distribution among Farmers in Northern Nigeria: Empirical Results and Policy Implications*, East Lansing: Department of Agricultural Economics, Michigan State University.

Reardon, Thomas. 1998. *Rural Non-farm Income in Developing Countries*, in FAO, The State of Food and Agriculture, Rome: FAO.

Reardon, Thomas and J. E. Taylor. 1996. 'Agro Climatic Shock, Income Inequality and Poverty: Evidence from Burkina Faso', *World Development*, 24: 901–914.

Sahu, Partha Pratim. 2003. 'Casualisation of Rural Workforce in India: Analysis of Recent Trends', *The Indian Journal of Labour Economics*, 46(4): 927–939.

Seth, Ashwani. 1992. *The Rural Non-farm Economy: Processes and Policies*, Geneva: ILO.

Thorat, Sukhdev. 1993. 'Land Ownership Structure and Non-Farm Employment of Rural Households in India', *The Indian Journal of Labour Economics*, 36(3).

Unni, Jeemal and Uma Rani. 2005. 'Gender and Non-farm Employment', in Rohini Nayyar and Alak N. Sharma (eds), *Rural Transformation in India – The Role of Non-farm Sector*, New Delhi: Institute for Human Development.

Chapter 13

Employment diversification in Tripura

Rajdeep Singha

The process of development is largely associated with the movement from a low-wage subsistence economy, mainly agriculture, to the more productive manufacturing or service sector. Writers of modern growth theories like Arthur Lewis (1954), Simon Kuznets (1955)[1] and many other development economists argue that this process, after all, results in higher wages and household income and thereby lowers of the poverty level. Such development patterns were visible in Western Europe in the eighteenth and nineteenth centuries and again in South Korea, Taiwan, Malaysia and Thailand in the twentieth century. However, in the developing countries, agriculture remains an important sector, and historical evidence in developing countries suggests that growth in agricultural productivity has remained the prerequisite to sustained economic development (DFID 2002). For instance, India is expected to become the world's largest population in the next 15–20 years, and as a result an increase in the demand for food will need to be met through higher agricultural productivity. Agriculture also provides labour for the non-agriculture sector. Due to 'surplus' labour in the traditional sector or agricultural sector, the social opportunity cost is very low and can be utilised for non-agricultural activity. In India, the opportunity for a productive job is the key to productivity improvement. In developing countries, labour power is the only asset for large numbers of the poor (Deb 2000). Developmental policies are closely associated with the nature of the labour market. The capacity of a larger macro-economic environment to create new jobs with higher than subsistence level wages is always the key to the success of any policy.

The International Labour Organization (ILO) recently put forward the concept of 'decent employment'. It is the quality and not the quantity of a job that matters for the economic and social development of a country. In India, there is a large segment of unemployed labour force. In the backdrop of a volatile international global economic environment, the performance of the Indian economy in terms of economic growth has remained outstanding in the last two decades. India's economic growth is among the highest in the world. According to the economic survey of GoI (2015–16), the main factor behind India's performance is its macro-economic stability. But the major challenge for the economy is to create enough 'good' jobs that are at least safe and well-paid. Between 1999–2000 and 2009–10, the employment elasticity of the India sector is only 0.19 (Misra and Suresh 2014); i.e., for every 10 percent increase in GDP, the employment growth is around 2 percent. This is termed as a period of 'jobless growth' (Aggarwal 2016).

In comparison to other developing countries, the incident of unemployment is less in India; under-employment and low wages seem to be greater problems. Up to the present, a large portion of the Indian labour force is occupied in agriculture and allied activities, which yields low remuneration. Wages for non-farm professions like carpentry, drivers, blacksmiths, etc., are at least 15–20 percent higher than in agricultural; industrial wages compared to agriculture are more than 1.5 times higher (FICCI 2015). With erratic weather and the neglect of policymakers, the agricultural sector presents an uncertain future to the labour market. The rise of capital-intensive technology and changes in the production techniques within a labour-intensive sector have largely influenced the labour market (Aedo et al. 2013; Singha 2008). As the opportunity in the formal sector is also declining day by day, more than half the labour force is self-employed, and another one-third are casual workers (Mamgain 2017).

Labour market indicators reveal that the condition of socially disadvantaged groups like women, Scheduled Tribes (STs), Scheduled Castes (SCs) and minorities is poor. Their presence in any well-paid job is limited. This low presence can be attributed to different factors including lack of education, skills, information, etc. This chapter tries to project the occupational diversification and segregations evident in the state of Tripura. Tripura has an essentially agrarian economy, characterised by high rate of poverty, low percapita income, low capital formation, inadequate infrastructure, geographical isolation and communications blocks, inadequate exploitation of forest and mineral resources, low progress in the industrial field, and a high unemployment problem (*Economic Review of Tripura*, 2014–15). Beginning with a discussion on the data sources and the demographic profile of Tripura, the chapter analyses empirical findings and other related issues and describes the magnitude of occupation segregation in the state.

Data sources

This chapter uses a unique unit-level data set from the India Human Development Surveys (IHDS) of 2004–5 and 2011–12. The IHDS is the first of its kind, where the data has been obtained by revisiting households. The re-contact rate for the IHDS was 83–90 percent in rural areas and around 72 percent in urban areas. Comparison of IHDS data with other reputable data sources such as the Census, National Sample Surveys (NSS) and National Family Health Survey (NFHS) shows that the IHDS compares well with these sources on common items like literacy rate, poverty ratio etc. (Barik et al. 2015). The IHDS is one of the first surveys to collect detailed income data. Most surveys depend on consumption expenditures or household assets to measure a household's economic level. Apart from collecting such data, the IHDS has measured household income as well. Over 50 different income sources were queried. This data presents a complex combination of rural and urban samples. To calculate population estimates from a sample at the India level or for individual states' levels, weights are used in all analyses in this chapter.

State profile

Tripura is situated in the southwest of India's North-Eastern Region (NER). The capital of Tripura, Agartala, is connected with Assam by the National Highway (NH-44); flights operate between Agartala and Kolkata as well as Guwahati. The distance between Guwahati and Agartala is about 587 km. The distance between Agartala and Siliguri, West Bengal (which is considered the entry point to the North-East), is about 1065 km (Economic Review of Tripura, 2013–14). Tripura shares 856 km of its border with Bangladesh, which is about 84 percent of the total length of its border. The direct distance between Agartala (Tripura) and Kolkata (through Bangladesh) is only about 350 km.

With a total area of only about 10,492 sq. km, the cultivated area of Tripura is only about 27 percent, and 60 percent of the area is occupied by hills and forests. The government of Tripura reorganised its administrative units in 2012 by creating four new districts, six new subdivisions and five new blocks in order to decentralise the administration further for better and more effective delivery of services and effective implementation and monitoring of development programmes. The state now has eight districts, 23 subdivisions, 58 blocks, and 1 Tripura Tribal Areas Autonomous District Council (TTAADC) created under the Sixth Schedule of the Constitution.

The state has a total population of about 36.74 *lakh* (1 lakh = 100,000) (Census 2011), which is the second highest in the NER, after Assam (see Table 13.1). The density of population has increased by 45 points (measured in people per square kilometre) to reach 350 (Census 2011), as compared to 305 (Census 2001). The growth of population in the state during 2001–11 was 14.75 percent, showing an increase in male and female population by 13.98 percent and 15.55 percent, respectively; however, in India, the growth rate in the same decade had been 17.64 percent, with 17.19 percent and 18.12 percent growth of the male and female population, respectively.

The sex ratio has increased by 13 points in the state and reached 961 in 2011 compared to 948 out 1000 men in 2001, which is higher than the national level (which has increased by 7 points and reached 940 in 2011 compared to 933 in 2001). The literacy rate of Tripura has gone up, from 73.19 percent in 2001 to 87.75 percent in 2011, showing an increase of 14.56 percent (the national level literacy rate has gone up from 64.83 percent in 2001 to 74.04 percent in 2011). Among the top four districts out of the total eight districts of the state, the Dhalai district (22.78 percent) has the

Table 13.1   Key vital statistics of Tripura: 1951–2011

Year	Population (in lakh)	Density of population (per sq. km)	STs (lakh)	SCs (lakh)
1951	6.46	62	2.37	0.4
1971	15.56	148	4.51	1.93
1981	20.53	196	5.84	3.1
1991	27.57	263	8.53	4.51
2001	31.99	305	9.93	5.56
2011	36.73	350	11.66	6.54

Source: Census Reports, RGI, Government of India

highest growth rate in population, while West Tripura (12.50 percent) shows the lowest.

Trend in employment

According to the National Industrial Classification Code[2] (1 digit) presented by the Central Statistical Organisation (CSO), the whole economy can be subdivided into three sectors – primary (including agriculture, hunting, forestry and fishing, and mining and quarrying), secondary (essentially manufacturing), and tertiary/service (including construction, transport, financing etc.). From Table 13.2, it is clear that in Tripura the trend has changed between 2005 and 2012. In 2004–5, 43.79 percent of the sample population was engaged in the primary sector, but this was reduced to 10.38 percent in 2011–12. The same trend can be observed in the manufacturing sector, too. The service sector is emerging as the single largest in Tripura. The employment rate in the service sector is on the rise, from around 45 percent (2004–5) to around 80 percent (2011–12). Within the service sector, the highest employment is in the construction sector. The growth of the construction sector is around tenfold. Other than construction, transport, storage and communication are the only sectors where employment has increased during the period of this study.

Table 13.2 Change in the industrial pattern of workers (in percentage)

Types of industry*	2004–5	2011–12
Agriculture, hunting, forestry and fishing	43.79	10.38
Mining and quarrying	0.65	0.00
Manufacturing	10.33	8.44
Electricity, gas and water	1.56	0.45
Construction	4.36	43.14
Wholesale, retail trade and restaurants, hotel	4.93	4.53
Transport, storage and communication	8.15	13.64
Financing, insurance, real estate and business services	3.37	1.85
Community, social and personal services	22.85	17.58
Total	100	100

Source: IHDS 2004 and 2012

Note: * NIC (1 Digit)

According to the National Occupation Classification (NOC) code, all occupations are classified into seven major occupational groups. It is possible to place them into a hierarchical order (Mamgain 2017). Professional, technical and related workers top the hierarchy, while production and related workers, transport equipment operators and labourers remain at the bottom of the list. The middle categories comprise sales and service workers (see Table 13.3). Interestingly, jobs from the topmost category have decreased from 14.06 to 10.36, due to a decrease in availability of government jobs and the absence of an active private sector in the state. There has been a decrease in middle-level jobs (like clerical or sales jobs) as well. As already pointed out, the diminishing role of agriculture is evident from Table 13.3. As a result, much of the labour force has shifted towards the bottom of the hierarchy. The nature of such jobs is primarily informal, and workers in this rank earn low wages, with no provision of social security. In other words, changes in the labour market structure are making workers more vulnerable.

The changing pattern of female workers in various industries is different from their male counterparts. As per Census 2011, in Tripura, out of 10,77,019 main workers around 83 percent are male and only 13 percent are female. However, there is an overall increase in the female participation rate, from 19.67 percent to 29.15 percent (see Table 13.4). But the highest withdrawal of

Table 13.3 Change in the occupational pattern of workers (in percentage)

Types of occupation*	2004–5	2011–12
Professional, technical and related workers	14.06	10.36
Administrative, executive and managerial workers	0.41	0.67
Clerical and related workers	8.55	7.01
Sales workers	4.82	4.23
Service workers	5.87	3.64
Farmers, fishermen, hunters, loggers and related workers	43.38	10.77
Production and related workers, transport equipment operators and labourers	22.91	63.33
Total	100	100

Source: IHDS 2004 and 2012

Note: * NCO (1 Digit)

Table 13.4 Change in the industrial pattern of workers by sex (in percentage)

NIC (1 Digit)	2004–5		2011–12	
	Male	Female	Male	Female
Agriculture, hunting, forestry and fishing	72.35	27.65	95.95	4.05
Mining and quarrying	100	0	0	0
Manufacturing	81.56	18.44	85.39	14.61
Electricity, gas and water	100	0	100	0
Construction	67.33	32.67	55.1	44.9
Wholesale, retail trade and restaurants, hotel	100	0	80.23	19.77
Transport, storage and communication	100	0	84.06	15.94
Financing, insurance, real estate and business services	100	0	100	0
Community, social and personal services	81.46	18.54	71.21	28.79
Total	80.33	19.67	70.85	29.15

Source: IHDS (2004 and 2012)

female workers is in the farm sector. The female presence in agriculture is reduced from 27.65 percent to merely 4 percent. On the other hand, the participation rate of male workers in agriculture has increased from 72 percent to 95 percent. The trend is reversed in the construction sector, where female participation has increased from 33 percent to 45 percent. Other than 'construction', 'wholesale, retail trade and restaurants', and 'financing, insurance, real estate and business services', participation of female workers has been mainly in 'community, social and personal services', increasing from 18.54 percent (2004–5) to 28.79 percent (2011–12).

It is widely established that the gender gap is not only about the employment rate but also in terms of income disparity between males and females (Boulet and Lavallée 1984; Kemp and Beck 1986; Sorensen and McLanahan 1987). It is evident from different studies that the nature of inequality exists in the whole world irrespective of developed and developing countries (e.g., Effroni 1980; Toren and Kraus 1987). There are essentially two explanations behind such disparity. One, women select occupations that are supportive in nature, where the wage is also low. Two, the differences in wage are the outcome of discrimination. Limited access to or 'crowding' of an occupation may result in an oversupply of labour in that occupation (Bergmann 1974).

As evident from Table 13.5, the percentage of female workers increases as one climbs up the hierarchy of occupation.[3] In the professional, technical and related workers' categories, female workers have increased from 19.26 percent (in 2004–5) to 31.48 percent (in 2011–12). However, there has been a parallel increase of female works in the lower strata, that is, as production and related workers and transport equipment operators, as well as labourers (from 14.54 in 2004–5 to 36.11 percent in 2011–12). The probable reason for this may be the level of effective education among the women.

In contrast to rural Tripura, sectors like manufacturing, construction, wholesale, retail trade, restaurants, hotel, transport, storage and communication have grown in urban areas. The percentage of workers in financing, insurance, real estate and business services has increased in the rural area from 0 to 48.53 percent (see Table 13.6). But in this sector, the female presence is almost nil, which means that new opportunity in this sector is benefiting the rural male workers only. This means that issues related to women's employment are qualitatively different from those of male workers

Table 13.5 Change in the occupational pattern of workers by sex (in percentage)

NCO (1 Digit)	2004–5		2011–12	
	Male	*Female*	*Male*	*Female*
Professional, technical and related workers	80.74	19.26	68.52	31.48
Administrative, executive and managerial workers	100	0	100	0
Clerical and related workers	94.46	5.54	83.24	16.76
Sales workers	100	0	100	0
Service workers	82.02	17.98	77.6	22.4
Farmers, fishermen, hunters, loggers and related workers	72.09	27.91	95.95	4.05
Production and related workers, transport equipment operators and labourers	85.46	14.54	63.89	36.11
Total	80.33	19.67	71.45	28.55

Source: IHDS (2004 and 2012)

Table 13.6 Change in the pattern of workers by rural–urban (in percentage)

NIC	2004–5		2011–12	
	Rural	*Urban*	*Rural*	*Urban*
Agriculture, hunting, forestry and fishing	99.00	1.00	100.00	0.00
Mining and quarrying	100.00	0.00	0.00	0.00
Manufacturing	74.44	25.56	52.23	47.77
Electricity, gas and water	71.79	28.21	0.00	100.00
Construction	89.91	10.09	84.43	15.57
Wholesale, retail trade and restaurants, hotel	64.33	35.67	40.69	59.31
Transport, storage and communication	62.22	37.78	73.74	26.26
Financing, insurance, real estate and business services	100.00	0.00	51.47	48.53
Community, social and personal services	78.82	21.18	74.53	25.47
Total	86.36	13.64	77.16	22.84

Source: IHDS (2004 and 2012)

(Beneria and Sen 1981; Melkas and Richard 1998; Ghosh 2009). Increase in employment does not always mean an improvement in the conditions of women workers, since it can lead to a double burden[4] upon women whose household obligations still have to be fulfilled (Ghosh 2014).

In terms of changes in occupational pattern, there is clear-cut rural-urban division. The urban areas are taking away 'good' jobs from rural areas. As is visible from Table 13.7, Numbers of jobs in the urban areas are more as one goes higher up the hierarchy, in comparison to the rural area. For example, the percentage of workers in professional, technical and related jobs has increased in the urban area by 10 points, while the percentage of workers in sales in the rural area has increased from 27 to 54 (see Table 13.7).

Nature of the occupational patterns among social groups

It will be interesting to understand how the nature of occupation has changed over this period of time for different social groups.

Table 13.7 Change in the occupational pattern of workers by rural–urban (in percentage)

NCO (1 Digit)	2004–5		2011–12	
	Rural	Urban	Rural	Urban
Professional, technical and related workers	87.48	12.52	77.58	22.42
Administrative, executive and managerial workers	100	0	100	0
Clerical and related workers	79.41	20.59	66.85	33.15
Sales workers	72.63	27.37	45.15	54.85
Service workers	62.52	37.48	61.68	38.32
Farmers, fisherman, hunters, loggers and related workers	98.99	1.01	100	0
Production and related workers, transport equipment operators and labourers	73.11	26.89	75.8	24.2
Total	86.36	13.64	76.32	23.68

Source: IHDS (2004 and 2012)

In the IHDS data, social groups are categorised in four different groups. Brahmins and other upper castes were grouped into a single category, while the rest were classified as SCs, STs and OBCs. Participation of all social groups, except STs, was apparent in agriculture, hunting, forestry and fishing. The involvement of ST workers reduced from 63.97 percent to only 14 percent. The other social groups occupied themselves in much more diverse functions. In 2004–5, as well as in 2011–12, a majority among the SCs were employed in both occupation categories – 'farmers, fishermen, hunters, loggers and related workers' and 'production and related workers, transport equipment operators and labourers' (see Table 13.8). On the other hand, between 2004–5 and 2011–12, there was a major change in the occupational pattern of STs. The ST workers are moved out from the farm sector and pushed to production and related workers' groups, as well as the transport equipment operators and labourers' sectors. These patterns suggest the change in landholding patterns and the consequent shift from land-based occupation to different types of daily wage jobs. Thus, like many other data (NSSO), this data set also shows that the relative position of the marginalised group and

Table 13.8 Occupational patterns of workers by their social group (in percentage)

NCO (1 Digit)	2004–5				2011–12			
	OBCs	SCs	STs	Others	OBCs	SCs	STs	Others
Professional, technical and related workers	13.69	15.68	22.97	47.66	8.41	12.90	29.78	48.91
Administrative, executive and managerial workers	0.00	100.00	0.00	0.00	0.00	0.00	58.94	41.06
Clerical and related workers	21.55	5.52	45.08	27.85	18.25	10.15	20.90	50.70
Sales workers	32.05	9.12	0.00	58.82	0.00	31.55	16.31	52.14
Service workers	7.50	31.10	22.00	39.40	22.40	39.91	15.29	22.40
Farmers, fishermen, hunters, loggers and related workers	7.50	31.10	22.00	12.63	19.61	39.67	16.58	24.14
Production and related workers, transport equipment operators and labourers	23.45	34.15	11.94	30.46	23.27	20.40	30.55	25.78
Total	17.93	16.26	39.12	26.69	19.82	22.02	27.32	30.84

Source: IHDS (2004 and 2012)

Table 13.9 Occupational patterns of workers among social groups (in percentage)

NCO (1 Digit)	2004–5				2011–12			
	OBC	SC	ST	Other	OBC	SC	ST	Other
Professional, technical and related workers	10.74	13.56	8.26	25.11	4.40	6.06	11.29	16.43
Administrative, executive and managerial workers	0.00	2.52	0.00	0.00	0.00	0.00	1.45	0.89
Clerical and related workers	10.28	2.90	9.85	8.92	6.45	3.23	5.36	11.52
Sales workers	8.62	2.71	0.00	10.63	0.00	6.06	2.53	7.16
Service workers	2.45	11.23	3.30	8.67	4.11	6.59	2.03	2.64
Farmers, fishermen, hunters, loggers and related workers	37.95	18.97	71.60	20.53	10.65	19.39	6.53	8.43
Production and related workers, transport equipment operators and labourers	29.96	48.11	6.99	26.15	74.39	58.66	70.81	52.94
Total	100	100	100	100	100	100	100	100

Source: IHDS (2004 and 2012)

OBCs are over-represented in low-end jobs and under-represented in the high-end ones. By comparing the period, the situation is not favouring the marginalised groups. Between 2004–5 and 2011–12, participation of 'Others' in 'production and related workers, transport equipment operators and labourers' has decreased from 30 percent to 25 percent, whereas that of STs has increased from 12 percent to 30 percent.

Changes in income

Though the majority of the population in developing countries like India is employed, the proportion of what the employed earn is extremely low. The general unemployment rates in developing countries are low because the poor cannot afford to remain unemployed. The outcome is high incidence of poverty. In India, though the unemployment rate is 5 percent, poverty is more than 30 percent (Deb 2000). One of the major challenges for the majority of the population is a lower number of options available for employment or the prevalence of a narrow labour market. The presence of a narrow labour market leads to different types of problems, including low wages. The types of labour market also differ significantly between the rural and urban. Access to different types of employment can determine 25 percent of poverty levels in India. This is also true for Tripura. The NSSO data suggests that in Tripura around 44 percent of the poor are farmers (in 2004–5). Table 13.10 suggests that in 2004–5, workers whose income is less than Rs 5000 are mostly farmers. But according to Table 10.11, workers of the same category (less than Rs 5000) were employed in construction work in the period 2011–12. Hence, there is a movement from agriculture to construction, primarily involving female workers, though the net effect on their income has remained insignificant. It is also to be noted that there is inequality within the construction sector. There is no doubt that there is a rise in income within the construction sector, but its benefits are enjoyed by only a few. Though workers are moving from agriculture to other sectors in search of a better livelihood, the outcome is not encouraging. On the other hand, the number of farmers in the high income group has also decreased from 19 percent in the year 2004–5 to 10.7 percent in the year 2011–12 (see Tables 13.10 and 13.11).

Table 13.10 Income of the workers by industries (in percentage), 2004–5

Industry	Less than 5000	5001– 10,000	10,001– 20,000	20,001– 50,000	More than 50,000	Total
Agriculture, hunting, forestry and fishing	100	82.25	65.67	56.06	19.00	43.79
Mining and quarrying	0	0	0	0	1.59	0.65
Manufacturing	0	17.75	4.78	16.69	7.02	10.33
Electricity, gas and water	0	0	0	0	3.84	1.56
Construction	0	0	8.73	5.88	1.17	4.36
Wholesale, retail trade and restaurants, hotel	0	0	5.49	6.3	3.81	4.93
Transport, storage and communication	0	0	2.19	7.3	12.48	8.15
Financing, insurance, real estate and business services	0	0	0	0	8.3	3.37
Community, social and personal services	0	0	13.14	7.78	42.8	22.85
Total	100	100	100	100	100	100

Source: IHDS (2004 and 2012)

Table 13.11 Income of the workers by industries (in percentage), 2011–12

Industry/ Income	Less than 5000	5001– 10,000	10,001– 20,000	20,001– 50,000	More than 50,000	Total
Agriculture, hunting, forestry and fishing	0	0	0	10.89	10.7	10.38
Mining and quarrying	0	0	0	0	0	0
Manufacturing	0	0	0	7.06	9.32	8.44
Electricity, gas and water	0	0	0	0	0.62	0.45
Construction	100	100	100	58.95	34.93	43.14
Wholesale, retail trade and restaurants, hotel	0	0	0	1.36	5.85	4.53
Transport, storage and communication	0	0	0	12.94	14.54	13.64
Financing, insurance, real estate and business services	0	0	0	1.22	2.15	1.85
Community, social and personal services	0	0	0	7.59	21.89	17.58
Total	100	100	100	100	100	100

Source: IHDS (2004 and 2012)

Magnitude of occupation segregation

Segregation among occupations is often cited as one of the main reasons behind the continuing gap between different groups (Blau and Marianne 1987). Various studies conclude that the 20–40 percent earning gap between men and women can be eliminated if equal opportunity is offered to females (Teiman and Hartmman 1981; Goldin 1990; Mamgani 2017). One way of establishing whether there is segregation, if jobs are distributed in a group form, is by looking at whether certain jobs are more likely to have a larger percent of a certain type of employees. For example, is this job more likely to be a male or female one? This can be measured through the use of the segregation index. The index attempts to review if there is a 'larger' than expected presence of a certain group in any given job category.

This section tried to capture the similarities or dissimilarities among different groups by using Hutchens' 'square root' segregation index (Hutchens 2001, 2004). Hutchens shows that index S satisfies seven desirable properties for a good numerical measure of segregation. In particular, S is additively decomposable by population subgroup: total segregation may be expressed as the sum of within-group segregation (a weighted sum of S across sub-groups) plus between-group segregation. S lies on the unit interval, with 0 representing complete absence of segregation and 1 representing complete segregation.

The index is defined as:

$$H = \sum_{i=1}^{S} \left[\left(\frac{P_i}{P} \right) - \sqrt{\frac{P_i}{P} \cdot \frac{r_i}{R}} \right].$$

where P is the number of the worker in occupation and R is the social group. This study calculates this index for each type of pairing, such as female vs male, STs vs Others, SCs vs Others, OBCs vs Others, and Rural vs Other. This index is calculated for each pairing listed by using a two-digit system of industrial classification by CSO. This is done primarily to capture the maximum variation among the groups.

It is quite evident that segregation index between female and male decreases from 2004–5 to 2011–12. The segregation between female and male is significantly higher in Tripura compared to the rest of India (see Figure 13.1). The index value decreases from 0.22

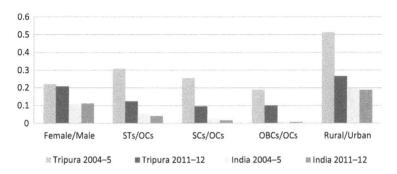

Figure 13.1 Hutchens' 'square root' segregation index by different groups

to 0.20, but at the same time the all-India level index value increases from 0.10 to 0.11. This index shows that between 2011–12, at least 20 percent of females had to shift their occupations to have identical occupational characteristics with the male workforce. In other words, around 20 percent of women are involved in different types of job compared to men in Tripura. As regards to social groups, between 2004–5, the highest dissimilarity is found by the STs group in comparison to other groups. The index value reduced significantly in the year 2011–12. The main reason of the decrease is the increase of other groups in farm-related activities and also because of under-representation in many categories.

In terms of rural vs urban, the index was high in 2004–5, but it decreased in 2011–12. The probable reason behind this is the increase of urban-type jobs in the rural area. For example, manufacturing increased from 25 percent to 47 percent during this period (Table 13.6). Another reason behind this was that urbanisation increased in different parts of rural Tripura. From Table 13.13, it is very much clear that urbanisation increased rapidly in Tripura. For example, the differences between Tripura and India in terms of urban population decreased from 10.72 to 4.98 during 2001 and 2011. The transformation from rural to urban is affecting the whole nature of the labour market. It is also evident from the index (Table 13.12) that the value changes from 0.51 to 0.26. One more important point to note is that the rise in urban population also indicates a rising trend in rural to urban migrations. From 82.94 percent, the rural population in Tripura went down to 73.82% in 2011. As mentioned earlier, the rural Tripura labour

Table 13.12 Hutchens' 'square root' segregation index by different groups

	2004–5		2011–12	
	Tripura	*All India*	*Tripura*	*All India*
Female vs male	0.221	0.108	0.207	0.112
STs vs others	0.308	0.053	0.123	0.041
SCs vs others	0.255	0.025	0.094	0.017
OBCs vs others	0.189	0.011	0.099	0.007
Rural vs urban	0.512	0.198	0.265	0.188

Source: IHDS (2004 and 2012)

Table 13.13 Percentage of urban population in India and Tripura, 1951–2011

Year	Percentage of urban population in India	Percentage of urban population in Tripura	Difference
1951	17.29	6.70	10.59
1961	17.97	9.02	8.95
1971	19.01	10.43	9.48
1981	23.34	11.00	12.34
1991	25.72	15.30	10.42
2001	27.78	17.06	10.72
2011	31.16	26.18	4.98

Source: Census, various rounds

market is dominated by agriculture, hunting, forestry and fishing sectors, and the urban market is controlled by wholesale, retail-related jobs and manufacturing sectors.

Conclusion

Modern growth theories suggest that the development of markets also means the expansion of job options. Despite the significant growth of Tripura's GDP (8.63 percent between 2005 and 2014 at constant price), expansion of its labour market has remained limited. There is a significant change in terms of composition of the labour market. Households are moving out from the farm sector, and their dependency on agriculture for employment is diminishing. Owing to the huge migration from rural to urban areas, the means of livelihood has changed from an agriculture base to a non-agricultural one. The formal salaried sector has seen no growth. Low-end jobs like daily wage jobs, particularly in the construction sectors, are in greater demand. The movement of labourers from one sector to another is not resulting in the improvement of the workers' socioeconomic conditions.

The Occupation Segregation Index still remains sizable in Tripura, significantly higher than the rest of India. The situation of marginalised groups like STs and SCs have improved during the period of study, but the degree of segregation is still high. The earning gap between males and females is considerable in Tripura. However, unlike in other parts of India, the gender gap in Tripura has diminished to some extent. It is clear from the analysis that the main problem in Tripura is not as much of quantity of jobs but the quality of the job. There is virtually no upward mobility except specific work for women, for example, in professional, technical and clerical jobs. The rural and urban gap has also decreased due to increasing urbanisation and also by increasing new types of jobs in rural Tripura.

This chapter raises certain important questions related to the development of the labour market in the state. For a long time, both at the central and state government levels, different policies like the Tripura Rural Livelihood Mission (TRLM), State Urban Livelihood Mission, Tripura, The Mahatma Gandhi National Rural Employment Guarantee Act (MGNREGA), etc. have been adopted to improve conditions of the prevailing narrow labour market. This study suggests that the success of these policies has been limited. Its geographical location poses another challenge for the state. Workers in Tripura are not in a healthy situation. There is a need for more affirmative action towards the marginalised groups and females in the state to widen the labour market.

Notes

1 According to Lewis theory, the marginal productivity of labourers in the subsistence economy is very low. If a worker gets an alternative job in the non-agriculture sector, wages will improve, reduce the disguised unemployment and eventually minimise incidents of poverty in the developing country. Kuznet's hypothesis also argued the U-shaped relationship between inequality and development – there is an increase in inequality in the early stage and a decrease in the later stage.

2 The National Industrial Classification (NIC) is an essential statistical standard for developing and maintaining comparable data bases according to economic activities.

3 The hierarchy of occupation can be seen in terms of wages, social protection and social status.

4 Here, 'double burden' refers to a situation where women have to work for a longer time, as they have to fulfil their household responsibilities (cooking, cleaning and caring) along with their jobs outside their homes.

References

Aedo, C., J. Hentschel, M. Moreno, and J. Luque. 2013. 'From Occupations to Embedded Skills: A Cross-country Comparison', Background Paper for the World Development Report.

Aggarwal, Suresh Chand. 2016. 'Structural Change, Jobless Growth and "Informalization" of Labor: Challenges in Post Globalized India', www. researchgate.net/profile/Suresh_Aggarwal3/publication/316734934_ Structural_Change_Jobless_Growth_and_'Informalization'_of_Labor_ Challenges_in_Post_Globalized_India/links/590f67b045851597818 75407/Structural-Change-Jobless-Growth-and-Informalization-of-Labor-Challenges-in-Post-Globalized-India.pdf.

Barik, D., T. Agrawal and S. Desai. 2015. 'After the Dividend: Caring for a Greying India', *Economic and Political Weekly*, 50(24): 108.

Beneria, Lourdes and Gita Sen. 1981. 'Accumulation, Reproduction and "Women's Role in Economic Development": Boserup Revisited', *Signs*, 7(2): 279–298.

Bergmann, Barbara R. 1974. 'Occupational Segregation, Wages and Profits When Employers Discriminate by Race or Sex', *Eastern Economic Journal*, 1(2): 103–110.

Blau, Francine D., and Marianne A. Ferber.1987. 'Discrimination: Empirical Evidence from the United States', *The American Economic Review*, 77(2): 316–320.

Boulet, Jac André and Laval Lavallée. 1984. *The Changing Economic Status of Women*, Canada: Economic Council of Canada.

Deb, Mahendra S. 2000. 'Economic Liberalization and Employment in South Asia', Part l, *Economic and Political Weekly*, XXXV(35) (l&2): January: 8–14.

DFID, EC. 2002. *Linking Poverty Reduction and Environmental Management: Policy Challenges and Opportunities*, Washington, DC: UNDP and World Bank.

Effroni, L. 1980. *Promotion and Wages in Government Service in Israel – Are Women Discriminated Against?* Jerusalem: Hebrew University (Hebrew).

FICCI. 2015. *Labour in Indian Agriculture*, Retrieved from ficci.in/spdocument/ 20550/FICCI-agri-Report%2009-03-2015.pdf. Accessed in January 2018.

Ghosh, Jayati. 2009. *Never Done and Poorly Paid: Women's Work in Globalising India*, New Delhi: Women Unlimited.

Ghosh, Jayati. 2014. 'Women's Work in the India in the Early 21st Century', https://scholar.googleusercontent.com/scholar?q=cache:aFmV4q0bYxsJ:scholar.google.com/&hl=en&as_sdt=0,5.

Goldin, Claudia. 1990. *The Gender Gap: An Economic History of American Women*, New York: Cambridge University Press.

Hutchens, Robert. 2001. 'Numerical Measures of Segregation: Desirable Properties and Their Implications', *Mathematical Social Sciences*, 42(1): 13–29.

Hutchens, Robert. 2004. 'One Measure of Segregation', *International Economic Review*, 45(2): 555–578.

Kemp, Alice Abel and E. M. Beck. 1986. 'Equal Work, Unequal Pay Gender Discrimination within Work-Similar Occupations', *Work and Occupations*, 13(3): 324–347.

Kuznets, Simone. 1955. 'Economic Growth and Income Inequality', *The American Economic Review*, pp.1–28.

Lewis, Arthur W. 1954. 'Economic Development with Unlimited Supplies of Labour', *Manchester School of Economic and Social Studies*, XXII: 139–191.

Mamgain, Rajendra P. 2017. 'Occupational Diversification in India: Trends and Determinants', in K. P. Kannan, Rajendra P. Mamgain and Preet Rustagi (eds), *Labour and Development*, New Delhi: Academic Foundation.

Melkas, H., and Richard Anker. 1998. *Gender Equality and Occupational Segregation in Nordic Labour Markets*, Geneva: International Labour Office.

Misra, Sangita and Suresh, Anoop K. 2014. 'Estimating Employment Elasticity of Growth for the Indian Economy', RBI Working Paper Series No. 06, Available at https://rbi.org.in/Scripts/PublicationsView.aspx?id=15763, accessed in May 2017.

Singha, Rajdeep. 2008. 'Industrial Promotion Policy and Employment', in R. K. Mishra and Nanditha Sethi (eds), *Rethinking India's Growth Strategy – Services vs. Manufacturing*, New Delhi: Concept Publication.

Sorensen, Annemette and Sara McLanahan. 1987. 'Married Women's Economic Dependency, 1940–1980', *American Journal of Sociology*, 93(3): 659–687.

Toren, Nina and Vered Kraus. 1987. 'The Effects of Minority Size on Women's Position in Academia', *Social Forces*, 1090–1100.

Treiman, Donald J., and Heidi I. Hartmann. (Eds). 1981. *Women, Work, and Wages: Equal Pay for Jobs of Equal Value*. Washington, DC: National Academy Press.

Index